BRIEF REVIEW in

Chemistry

PATRICK KAVANAH
Monroe-Woodbury Central High School
Central Valley, New York

ORDER INFORMATION

Send orders to:

PRENTICE HALL SCHOOL DIVISION
CUSTOMER SERVICE CENTER
4350 Equity Drive
P.O. Box 2649
Columbus, OH 43216

or

CALL TOLL-FREE: 1-800-848-9500
(8:00 AM–4:30 PM)

- Orders processed with your call. Please include the ISBN number on the back cover when ordering.
- **Your price includes all shipping and handling.**

PRENTICE HALL Textbook Programs that help you meet the requirements of the Regents:

Biology: The Study of Life
Chemistry: The Study of Matter
Physics: Its Methods and Meanings
Earth Science: A Study of a Changing Planet

Prentice Hall

Needham, Massachusetts   Englewood Cliffs, New Jersey

ABOUT THIS BOOK

Brief Review in Chemistry is a concise text and review aid for the New York State Syllabus in Chemistry and a means of preparing for the Regents Examination in this subject. The following features of its content and organization will be of special interest to teachers and students.

1. Brief, simple explanations of all understandings and fundamental concepts included in the syllabus.

2. Organization by units and topics follows the sequence of the syllabus. This organization is particularly effective for Regents preparation because the questions on the examination in recent years have been topically grouped in the same order.

Note: Content marked "Additional Materials" in Units 5, 6, 8, and 9, and the content of Units 10, 11, and 12 are tested only on Part II of the Regents Examination.

3. Hundreds of practice questions of Regents type; conveniently divided into topical groupings for more effective reinforcement of learning.

4. Many sample problems illustrating all the types of calculations that the student may be required to perform.

5. A special section devoted to interpretation and use of the *Reference Tables for Chemistry*.

6. Several of the most recent Regents Examinations.

7. A glossary and an exceptionally complete index makes it easy for the student to locate any specific term or subject matter.

8. A College Board Review section that reviews topics usually given light coverage in chemistry courses and includes a practice College Board chemistry test.

Credits

Editorial   Julia A. Fellows, Ann L. Collins, Natania Mlawer
Marketing   Arthur C. Germano, Joel Gendler
Design   Alison Anholt-White, Betty Fiora
Production   David Graham, Jo-Ann Connolly, Leanne Cordischi, Virginia Shine
Manufacturing   Holly Schuster

Cover Design: Richard Hannus ·

PRENTICE HALL
A Division of Simon & Schuster
Needham Heights, Massachusetts 02194
Englewood Cliffs, New Jersey 07632

ISBN 138316783

Printed in the United States of America
1 2 3 4 5 6 7 8   99 98 97 96 95 94

June 22nd
8:15am.

CONTENTS

UNIT 1   MATTER AND ENERGY

MATTER

SUBSTANCES. The term **substance** is used to refer to any particular variety of matter that always has the same properties and composition, regardless of how and where a specimen of it is obtained. For example, water is a substance; under given conditions, any sample of water has the same properties and the same composition. These properties and composition can be used to identify water. On the other hand, wood is not a substance; its properties and composition can vary widely.

A sample of any substance is **homogeneous;** that is, the properties and composition are the same throughout the sample.

There are two major kinds of substances:

1. Elements. A substance that cannot be decomposed into two or more other substances by means of a chemical change is called an **element.** An element consists entirely of atoms with the same atomic number. One hundred and six different elements are known to exist. Most of the elements are metals; typical examples are aluminum, iron, copper, silver, and mercury. Some familiar nonmetallic elements are carbon, sulfur, iodine, oxygen, and neon.

2. Compounds. A substance that can be decomposed into other substances by a chemical change is called a **compound.** Every compound consists of two or more elements chemically combined in definite proportions by weight. For example, the compound water always consists of the two elements hydrogen and oxygen in a weight ratio of 1:8. That is, if 9 grams of water is decomposed, 1 gram of hydrogen and 8 grams of oxygen are always obtained. The properties of compounds are usually quite different from those of their component elements.

MIXTURES. Like compounds, **mixtures** are always composed of two or more substances, but mixtures *differ* from compounds in the following ways:

1. The components of a mixture can be either elements or compounds.

2. The weight ratios of components in a mixture are *not* fixed.

3. The properties of the mixture are always intermediate between those of its components.

4. Some mixtures, such as solutions of salt in water or mixtures of gases, are homogeneous, but others, such as concrete (a mixture of sand, water, and cement), are **heterogeneous** (that is, samples are not uniform in composition throughout).

QUESTIONS

1. Which may be heterogeneous? (1) a substance (2) an element (3) a compound (4) a mixture
2. Elements A and B combine chemically to form C. Substance C must be (1) a solution (2) a compound (3) an element (4) a mixture
3. A solution of sodium chloride is a (1) heterogeneous compound (2) homogeneous mixture   (3) heterogeneous mixture (4) homogeneous compound
4. Which is the formula of a compound? (1) C (2) Cl_2 (3) N_2 (4) HF

ENERGY

DEFINITION OF ENERGY. Energy is defined as the capacity to do work. In the scientific sense, work is done whenever a force causes an object to move or to change its existing motion. Energy can therefore be thought of as the capacity to change the motion of objects.

FORMS OF ENERGY. Energy is associated with nearly all physical phenomena. It is customary to give special names to the energy associated with different phenomena. For example:

Kinetic energy—the energy associated with the motion of bodies.

Light energy—the energy associated with light waves (or other forms of electromagnetic radiation).

Electrical energy—the energy associated with an electric current.

Chemical energy—the energy associated with chemical changes.

Heat energy—the energy associated with the temperature of a body or system of bodies.

Potential energy—the energy associated with the relative positions of bodies in a system.

Mechanical energy—the energy associated with the doing of work.

Atomic or nuclear energy—the energy associated with changes in the mass of atoms.

CONSERVATION OF ENERGY. Energy can be changed from one form to another, and can be transferred from one body or system to another, but its total amount remains the same. No energy is either created or destroyed during such changes or transfers. For example, when gasoline burns in an automobile engine, chemical energy is converted to heat energy in the gases produced; as the gases expand in the cylinders of the engine, their heat energy is converted to mechanical energy of the pistons and crankshaft; some of this mechanical energy is converted to kinetic energy of the moving car; some of it is used to drive an electric generator, in which the energy is converted to electrical energy; the electrical energy can be used to produce light energy in the headlights, or it can be converted to chemical energy in the car's storage battery. In many of these energy conversion steps, some of the original energy is also changed to heat energy, as the result of friction in the moving parts, resistance of the electrical conductors, etc. However, if all of the energy is accounted for, it is found that the total amount remains the same.

ENERGY AND CHEMICAL CHANGE. Because energy is absorbed in the breaking of chemical bonds and released in the formation of new bonds, any chemical reaction will result in the net absorption or release of energy, usually in the form of heat. On this basis, two types of reactions are recognized:

1. Exothermic Reactions. A reaction that *releases* heat to its surroundings is called an **exothermic** reaction. In such a reaction, the energy released in the forming of new bonds is *greater* than the energy absorbed by the breaking of the original bonds.

2. Endothermic Reactions. A reaction that *absorbs* heat from its surroundings is called an **endothermic** reaction. In such a reaction, the energy released in the forming of new bonds is *less* than the energy absorbed by the breaking of the original bonds.

ACTIVATION ENERGY. The minimum amount of energy needed to initiate a reaction is called the **activation energy.** For example, although the paper in this book is in contact with the air, it is not burning. In order to make it burn, energy must be added to it until its temperature is high enough for burning to occur.

QUESTIONS

1. In what type of reaction do the products of the reaction always possess more potential energy than the reactants? (1) endothermic (2) exothermic (3) spontaneous (4) redox
2. Any chemical change that releases energy as it progresses is (1) isothermic (2) exothermic (3) nonthermic (4) endothermic
3. Which is NOT a form of energy? (1) light (2) temperature (3) heat (4) motion
4. All chemical reactions (1) are exothermic (2) are endothermic (3) give off heat (4) require activation energy

THERMOMETRY. The **temperature** of a substance is a measure of the average kinetic energy of the particles in the substance. The particles of all substances at the same temperature have the same average kinetic energy. Temperature difference indicates the direction of heat flow between two bodies. Whenever two bodies have different temperatures, heat flows from the body with the higher temperature to the body with the lower temperature. The heat transfer occurs spontaneously, and the exchange continues until the two have the same temperature.

The temperature of a body is usually measured by a **thermometer.** The most common type of thermometer contains a liquid that expands and flows into a capillary tube when it is heated, and contracts when it is cooled. This material must remain liquid over the desired temperature range, and it must expand and contract at an even rate. Liquid mercury is commonly used.

A thermometer is calibrated by establishing two fixed reference points of temperature, and then dividing the distance between the two points into the desired number of units. For normal use, the **fixed points** selected are the freezing point and the boiling point of water. The freezing point of water is the ice-water (solid-liquid) equilibrium temperature at 1 atmosphere pressure. The boiling point of water is the water-steam (liquid-gas) equilibrium temperature at 1 atmosphere pressure. On the **Celsius** scale the distance between these two points is divided into 100 equal units, called **degrees** (°). The freezing point is given a value of 0° C and the boiling point, 100° C.

The **Kelvin,** or **Absolute,** temperature scale, another scale frequently used in science, also considers the freezing and boiling points of water as fixed points, with the degree being the same size as the Celsius unit. On the Kelvin scale, however, the freezing point of water is 273 and the boiling point is 373 . The Celsius and Kelvin scales are related by the following equation:

$$K = °C + 273$$

QUESTIONS

1. The temperature of a substance is a measure of the average (1) mass of its molecules (2) potential energy of its molecules (3) kinetic energy of its molecules (4) attractive forces between its molecules

2. The two fixed points on a thermometer are (1) 273 K and 373 K (2) 100 K and 273 K (3) 32 K and 212 K (4) 0 K and 100 K

3. When the Celsius temperature changes 100 Celsius degrees, the same change in Kelvin degrees would be (1) 100 K (2) 173 K (3) 273 K (4) 373 K

4. Which temperature is equal to −23° C? (1) −250 K (2) −23 K (3) 250 K (4) 296 K

5. Which temperature is equal to 20 K? (1) −253° C (2) −293° C (3) +253° C (4) +293° C

6. A liquid's freezing point is −38° C and its boiling point is 357° C. What is the number of Kelvin degrees between the boiling point and the freezing point of the liquid? (1) 319 (2) 395 (3) 592 (4) 668

MEASUREMENT OF ENERGY. The energy involved in chemical reactions is usually measured in units of heat called **calories.** One calorie is the amount of heat needed to raise the temperature of one gram of water by one Celsius degree. For convenience, a larger unit, the **kilocalorie** (kcal), is also used. One kilocalorie equals 1,000 calories.

Two factors are necessary in the calculation of the calorie exchange: the temperature change and the number of grams of water involved in the change. The formula used to calculate the calories of heat exchanged is:

No. of cal = grams of water × temperature change

The change in a quantity, such as temperature (t), is indicated by the Greek letter Δ (delta). Using this notation, the formula is

No. of cal = grams of water $\times$ Δ t

SAMPLE PROBLEM

How many calories are released when 50.g of water are cooled from 75° C to 30° C?

Solution: Use the formula

No. of cal = grams of water $\times$ Δ t

grams of water = 50.

Δ t = initial temp. − final temp. = 75° C − 30° C = 45° C

Substituting:
  No. of cal. = 50. × 45 = 2250 cal or **2.0 × 10³ cal**

CALORIMETRY. A device commonly used in the laboratory to measure heat is the **calorimeter.** In this device the heat produced by a reaction is found indirectly by measuring the temperature change in a known mass of water in contact with the reaction vessel. Measurement of the heat change of a reaction by this indirect means is called **calorimetry.**

SAMPLE PROBLEM

In a calorimeter, 40 g of water surrounds a sealed reaction vessel. Before the reaction occurs, the temperature of the water is 20° C. After the reaction, the water temperature rises to 50° C. Approximately how many calories were released by the reaction?

Solution: Use the formula

No. of cal = grams of water $\times$ Δ t

grams of water = 40

Δ t = 50° C − 20° C = 30° C

Substituting:
  No. of cal = 40 × 30 = **1200 cal**

Assuming that no heat escaped from the calorimeter, the heat gained by the water is equal to the heat released by the reaction.

QUESTIONS

1. Which is the equivalent of 750. calories?
   (1) 0.750 kcal   (2) 7.50 kcal   (3) 75.0 kcal   (4) 750. kcal
2. If 150. grams of water is heated from 20 °C to 30 °C, the number of calories of heat energy absorbed is approximately
   (1) 10   (2) 150   (3) 1,500   (4) 15,000
3. If a 2.0 gram sample of water at 5.0 °C absorbs 5.0 calories of heat energy, the temperature of the sample will be raised by
   (1) 0.40 C°   (2) 2.5 C°   (3) 3.0 C°   (4) 10. C°
4. The temperature of 50. grams of water was raised to 50. °C by the addition of 1,000. calories of heat energy. What was the initial temperature of the water?
   (1) 10. °C   (2) 20. °C   (3) 30. °C   (4) 60. °C
5. A sample of water is heated from 10. °C to 15 °C by the addition of 30. calories of heat. What is the mass of the water?   (1) 5.0 g   (2) 6.0 g   (3) 30. g   (4) 150 g

PHASES OF MATTER

Matter may exist in three **phases—solid, liquid,** and **gas.** The particular phase of a substance at any given time depends upon the conditions of temperature and pressure. As either or both of these conditions change, the substance may change phase.

Figure 1-1 shows how the temperature and the phase of a certain substance change when heat is added to it at a constant rate. At the start (time = 0), the substance is in the solid phase. As heat is added to it, its temperature increases uniformly until its melting point is reached. At this point, the temperature remains constant while the substance is changing from the solid to the liquid phase. The change of phase is thus accompanied by an absorption of heat, but without a change of temperature.

When all of the substance has changed to the liquid phase, the temperature again increases uniformly (although at a different rate) as heat is added. When the boiling point is reached, the temperature once again remains constant while the substance changes phase from liquid to gas. When this phase change is completed, the temperature again resumes its rise (at still another rate).

If this substance in the gas phase is allowed to cool (that is, to lose heat), the cooling curve of temperature vs. time will resemble the reverse of the heating curve. The flat portions will occur at the same temperatures, with heat being released as the substance changes from gas to liquid, and then from liquid to solid. The amount of heat released during cooling will be the same as the amount absorbed during heating, in each section of the curve.

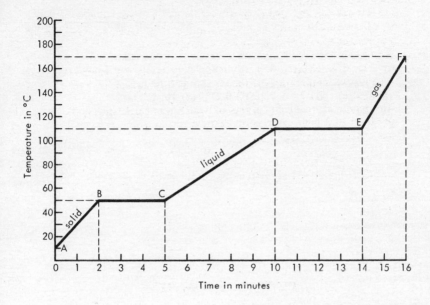

Figure 1-1. This graph is a heating curve for a fixed quantity of a hypothetical substance to which heat is being added at a constant rate and under constant pressure. At the start of the observations (Point A), the substance is in the solid phase at a temperature of 10° C. As heat is added to it, its temperature rises uniformly for 2 minutes. At a temperature of 50° C (Point B), the solid begins to melt. The temperature remains constant at 50° C until the phase change to liquid is complete (Point C). It has taken 3 minutes to add enough heat to melt the solid completely. From Point C to Point D, the substance is in the liquid phase and its temperature rises uniformly to 110° C. The temperature then remains constant while the liquid changes to the gas phase. This transition requires 4 minutes, indicating that the heat of vaporization is greater than the heat of fusion. At Point E, the substance is entirely in the gas phase, and its temperature again rises uniformly as heat is added to it.

The amount of heat absorbed by the substance during any portion of the graph may be read by multiplying the time period in question by the rate at which heat is being applied. For example, if heat is applied at the rate of 100 cal/min, and segment DE lasts for a period of 4 minutes, 4 min × 100 cal/min = 400 cal are absorbed during this time.

QUESTIONS

1-5. Base your answers to Questions 1-5 on Figure 1-1 (page 7), which represents the heating of a sample of a substance at a uniform rate of 100 cal/min.

1. The sample undergoes a phase change between points (1) *A* and *B*
   (2) *C* and *D*   (3) *D* and *E*   (4) *E* and *F*

2. The melting point temperature of the substance in °C is (1) 10 (2) 50
   (3) 80 (4) 110

3. The number of calories required to heat the sample from 10° C to its
   melting point is (1) 40   (2) 200   (3) 300   (4) 500

4. The number of calories required to melt the sample at its melting
   temperature is (1) 100   (2) 200   (3) 300   (4) 500

5. The average kinetic energy of the particles of the substance increases
   uniformly between points (1) *A* and *B*   (2) *A* and *F*   (3) *B* and *C*   (4) *B*
   and *E*

6. Which segment of the heating curve shown below represents an increase
   in the potential energy, but no change in the average kinetic energy of
   the molecules? (1) *AB*   (2) *BC*   (3) *CD*   (4) *EF*

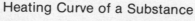

Heating Curve of a Substance

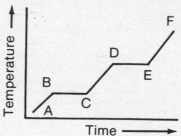

Time ⟶

7. When ice is melting, the temperature of the ice-water mixture remains
   constant because (1) heat is not being absorbed (2) the ice is colder
   than the water (3) heat energy is being converted to potential energy
   (4) heat energy is being converted to kinetic energy

8. When a given quantity of water is heated at a constant rate, the phase
   change from liquid to gas takes longer than the phase change from solid
   to liquid because (1) the heat of vaporization is greater than the heat of
   fusion (2) the heat of fusion is greater than the heat of vaporization
   (3) the average kinetic energy of the molecules is greater in steam than
   in water (4) ice absorbs energy more rapidly than water does

9. The temperature at which a substance in the liquid state freezes is the
   same as the temperature at which the substance (1) melts
   (2) sublimes (3) boils (4) condenses

GASES

GAS LAWS. Experience has shown that gases behave in accordance with the following laws:

1. Boyle's Law. If the temperature of a given mass of a gas remains constant, its volume varies inversely with its pressure. Letting V_1 and P_1 represent the initial volume and pressure of the gas, and V_2 and P_2 the new volume and pressure, we can express Boyle's Law mathematically as follows:

$$\frac{V_2}{V_1} = \frac{P_1}{P_2}$$

This can also be written:

$$P_2 V_2 = P_1 V_1$$

Thus we see that for a given mass of gas at constant temperature, the product of the pressure and the volume is always the same. We can therefore write:

$$PV = k$$

where k is a constant for that particular sample of gas.

(*See Sample Problem on next page.*)

QUESTIONS

1. A sample of hydrogen has a volume of 1.0 liter at a pressure of 760 torr. If the temperature is kept constant and the pressure is raised to 860 torr, the new volume, in liters, will be equal to

   (1) $\dfrac{760}{860}$ (2) $\dfrac{860}{760}$ (3) $860 - 760$ (4) $860 + 760$

2. A gas sample occupies 10 milliliters at 1.0 atmosphere of pressure. If the volume changes to 20 milliliters and the temperature remains the same, the pressure will be   (1) 1.0 atm   (2) 2.0 atm   (3) 0.25 atm   (4) 0.50 atm

3-4. Base your answers to Questions 3 and 4 on the graph at right, which represents the relationship between pressure and volume of a given mass at constant temperature.

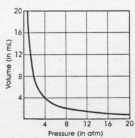

3. When the pressure equals 8 atm, what is the volume in milliliters?
   (1) 1   (2) 2   (3) 8   (4) 16

4. In this graph the product of the pressure and the volume equals a constant ($PV = K$). What is this constant?   (1) 16   (2) 12   (3) 8   (4) 4

SAMPLE PROBLEM

If 40 ml of a gas is stored at 760 torr pressure, what will the volume of the gas be if the pressure is increased to 800 torr?

Solution: Before doing any work, decide whether you expect the volume to increase or decrease, and whether the change will be relatively large or small. Since the pressure is increased, you will expect the volume to decrease. Since the pressure change is relatively small, the volume change should also be relatively small.

Method 1: Use the formula

$$\frac{V_2}{V_1} = \frac{P_1}{P_2}$$

The known values are P_1 = 760 torr P_2 = 800 torr V_1 = 40 mL
The unknown value is V_2

Substituting:

$$\frac{V_2}{40 \text{ mL}} = \frac{760 \text{ torr}}{800 \text{ torr}}$$

$$V_2 = \frac{760 \text{ torr}}{800 \text{ torr}} \times 40 \text{ mL} = 38 \text{ mL}$$

The result agrees with the prediction that the new volume will be a little smaller than the old. (If the result did not agree, we would check carefully for an error in the method or the calculations.)

Method 2: The formula can be restated to show that the unknown volume is always equal to the known volume multiplied by a "pressure fraction." This pressure fraction is less than 1 if the volume decreases and greater than 1 if it increases. We can therefore write the pressure fraction without using the formula. In this case, the volume should decrease; therefore, the pressure fraction must be $\frac{760}{800}$, that is, less than 1.

$$V_2 = V_1 \times \frac{760}{800} = 40 \times \frac{760}{800} = 38 \text{mL}$$

5. A 1.00-liter sample of a gas at a pressure of 1.00 atmosphere is compressed to 0.25 liter at constant temperature. What is the new pressure of the gas? **(1)** 0.50 atm **(2)** 2.0 atm **(3)** 0.25 atm **(4)** 4.0 atm

6. As the volume of a 1-mole sample of gas increases, with temperature remaining constant, the pressure of the gas **(1)** decreases **(2)** increases **(3)** remains the same

7. The pressure on 20 milliliters of a gas at constant temperature is changed from 4 atmospheres to 2 atmospheres. The new volume of the gas is   (1) 5 mL   (2) 10 mL   (3) 40 mL   (4) 80 mL

8. A sample of hydrogen gas has a volume of 32 mL at a pressure of 2 atm. If the temperature is kept constant and the volume is decreased to 16 mL the new pressure of the gas will be   (1) 1 atm   (2) 2 atm (3) 3 atm   (4) 4 atm

9. Which of the following will substantially change in volume when the pressure exerted on it is doubled?   (1) gas   (2) liquid   (3) solid   (4) all of these

2. Charles's Law. If the pressure of a given mass of a gas remains constant, its volume is directly proportional to its Kelvin temperature (T). This law can be expressed mathematically as:

$$\frac{V_2}{V_1} = \frac{T_2}{T_1}$$

It can be represented graphically by the straight-line curve in Figure 1-2.

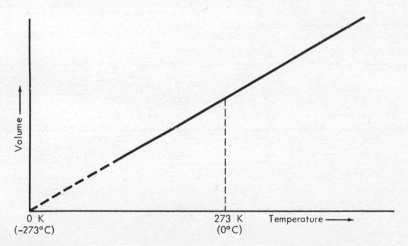

Figure 1-2. This graph represents the relationship between the volume of a fixed mass of a gas and its temperature, at constant pressure. Theoretically, the volume would be 0 at 0 K (−273° C), but all real gases change to the liquid phase at some temperature above 0 K as they are cooled. The temperature 0 K (absolute zero) has been approached very closely in the laboratory, but it can never be achieved.

Note that the volume of a given mass of gas, at constant pressure, changes by 1/273 of its volume at 0° C for each 1° C of temperature change. Theoretically its volume should become zero at 0 K (absolute zero), but all real gases change to liquids before that temperature is reached. Furthermore, a temperature of 0 K cannot be achieved in any real system, although it can be approached very closely.

SAMPLE PROBLEM

What will be the new volume of 50 mL of a gas that is raised from 27°C to 127°C at constant pressure?

Solution: Decide whether the volume will increase or decrease. Since the temperature is increased, the volume will also increase. Note that the temperature increase is not as great as the Celsius values might suggest. The temperatures must be converted to degrees Kelvin.

Method 1: Convert temperatures to Kelvin before doing anything else:

$$T_1 = 27° \text{ C} = 300 \text{ K} \quad (27 + 273)$$
$$T_2 = 127° \text{ C} = 400 \text{ K} \, (127 + 273)$$

Use the formula

$$\frac{V_2}{V_1} = \frac{T_2}{T_1}$$

$$V_1 = 50 \text{ mL} \qquad V_2 = ?$$

Substituting:

$$\frac{V_2}{50 \text{ mL}} = \frac{400 \text{ K}}{300 \text{ K}} \qquad V_2 = 50 \text{ mL} \times \frac{400}{300} = 66.7 \text{ mL}$$

Method 2. Multiply the known volume by a "temperature fraction," making the fraction greater than 1 to increase the volume, or less than 1 to decrease it. In this case, make the fraction greater than 1. Remember to convert to Kelvin temperatures.

$$V_2 = V_1 \times \frac{400}{300} = 50 \text{ mL} \times \frac{400}{300} = 66.7 \text{ mL}$$

QUESTIONS

1. **When 500 milliliters of hydrogen gas is heated from 30° C to 60° C at constant pressure, the volume of the gas at 60° C is equal to**

    (1) $500 \text{ mL} \times \dfrac{213}{243}$ (2) $500 \text{ mL} \times \dfrac{243}{213}$ (3) $500 \text{ mL} \times \dfrac{333}{303}$ (4) $500 \text{ mL} \times \dfrac{303}{333}$

2. At constant pressure, which curve best shows the relationship between the volume of an ideal gas and its absolute temperature? (1) A (2) B (3) C (4) D

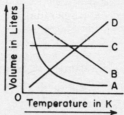

3. The temperature of a 180-mL sample of gas is decreased from 400 K to 200 K, pressure remaining constant. The new volume of the gas is (1) 90 mL   (2) 126 mL   (3) 273 mL   (4) 360 mL

4. The volume of a gas is 400 mL at $-20°C$. If the pressure of the gas is held constant and the temperature is changed to $40°C$, the final volume of the gas will be equal to 400 mL multiplied by
   (1) $\dfrac{293}{313}$ (2) $\dfrac{313}{293}$ (3) $\dfrac{253}{313}$ (4) $\dfrac{313}{253}$

5. At constant pressure, the volume of a mole of any ideal gas varies (1) directly with the radius of the gas molecules   (2) inversely with the radius of the gas molecules   (3) directly with the Kelvin (absolute) temperature   (4) inversely with the Kelvin (absolute) temperature

6. At constant pressure, the volume of a gas increases when its temperature is changed from $10°$ C to   (1) 263 K   (2) 273 K   (3) 283 K   (4) 293 K

7. The volume of a sample of a gas at $0°$ C is 100 liters. If the volume of the gas is increased to 200 liters at constant pressure, what is the new temperature of the gas in degrees Kelvin?   (1) 0 K   (2) 100 K   (3) 273 K   (4) 546 K

8. The volume of a gas is 250 liters at STP. If the pressure of the gas is held constant and the temperature is changed to $-25°$ C, the final volume of the gas, in liters, will be equal to
   (1) $250 \times \dfrac{248}{273}$ (2) $250 \times \dfrac{298}{273}$ (3) $250 \times \dfrac{273}{298}$ (4) $250 \times \dfrac{273}{248}$

9. The volume of 1 mole of an ideal gas at $25°$ C and 1 atmosphere of pressure is

   (1) 22.4 liters $\times \dfrac{1}{25}$ (3) 22.4 liters $\times \dfrac{298}{273}$

   (2) 22.4 liters $\times \dfrac{25}{1}$ (4) 22.4 liters $\times \dfrac{273}{298}$

STANDARD TEMPERATURE AND PRESSURE (STP). Because it is difficult to weigh quantities of a gas, the quantity of a gas is usually expressed in units of volume rather than weight (or mass).

However, since the volume of a gas varies considerably with its temperature and pressure, the quantity cannot be specified by volume alone. The temperature and pressure must also be known. In order to avoid the inconvenience of stating temperature and pressure every time a gas volume is given, certain **standard conditions of temperature and pressure (STP)** have been adopted. These standard conditions are **0° C** and **760 torr,** or **760 mm Hg,** or **1 atm.** Unless otherwise stated, the volume of a gas is assumed to be at **STP.** If the volume of a gas is measured under other conditions of temperature and pressure, its corresponding volume at **STP** can be calculated by applying the gas laws.

KINETIC THEORY OF GASES. A study of the gas laws and other behavior of gases has led to a **model** called the **kinetic theory of gases.** The assumptions of this theoretical model are:

1. All gases are composed of individual particles that are in continuous, random motion. The particles move in straight-line paths until they are deflected by some force.

2. Collisions that occur between gas particles may result in a transfer of energy from one particle to another, but the net amount of energy in a given system (an isolated sample of gas) remains the same. Although the kinetic energy of individual particles varies widely from moment to moment, the average kinetic energy is constant for a given temperature and is directly proportional to the Kelvin (Absolute) temperature of the gas. Figure 1-3 shows the distribution of energy among the particles of a gas for three different temperatures.

3. The volume of individual gas particles is negligible compared to the volume of space in which they move.

4. No forces of attraction are considered to exist between gas particles.

A gas that would behave exactly as predicted would be an "ideal" gas. Hydrogen and helium are the closest to ideal behavior. All *real* gases deviate in some degree from the gas laws because the assumptions above are only approximately true for real gases. Deviations are chiefly due to the following factors:

1. Real gas particles have a small but significant volume.

2. Gas particles do exert some attractive force on each other.

These factors become significant in gases at low temperatures, when the particles have relatively little kinetic energy, or under high pressures, when the particles are relatively close together.

QUESTIONS

1. Which statement best explains why a confined gas exerts pressure?
   (1) The molecules are in random motion.   (2) The molecules travel in straight lines.   (3) The molecules attract each other.   (4) The molecules collide with the container walls.

2. Which gas has properties that are most similar to those of an ideal gas at low temperature and high pressure?   (1) He   (2) O_2 (3) H_2S (4) CO_2

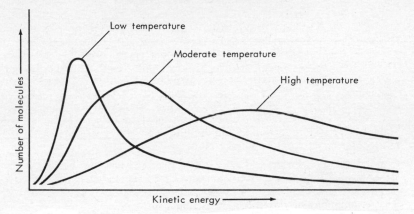

Figure 1-3. These curves show how the distribution of kinetic energy among the particles in a fixed mass of a gas changes as the temperature is changed. At low temperatures, most of the particles have small kinetic energies, and the average kinetic energy is small. As the temperature is increased, the average kinetic energy increases. However, at any temperature there are always some particles with small kinetic energies and some with large.

3. Which characteristic of real gas particles results in deviations from the gas laws? (1) The particles have volume. (2) The motions of the particles are random. (3) The particles are far apart. (4) The collisions of the particles cause pressure.

4. Under which conditions of temperature and pressure would a real gas be most likely to act as an ideal gas? (1) high temperature and high pressure (2) high temperature and low pressure (3) low temperature and high pressure (4) low temperature and low pressure

5. Standard temperature and pressure (STP) are (1) 0 K and 273 torr (2) 0 K and 760 torr (3) 273 K and 760 torr (4) 760 K and 273 torr

6. Which conditions generally cause the characteristics of a gas to deviate most from the ideal gas laws? (1) low temperature and low pressure (2) low temperature and high pressure (3) high temperature and low pressure (4) high temperature and high pressure.

AVOGADRO'S HYPOTHESIS. Avogadro's hypothesis was proposed to account for certain facts about the volumes of gases in chemical reactions. It states that under the same conditions of temperature and pressure, equal volumes of all gases contain the same number of particles. For example, 1 liter of oxygen gas contains the same number of particles as 1 liter of hydrogen gas, when both gases are at the same temperature and pressure, even though a particle of oxygen gas is 16 times heavier than a particle of hydrogen gas.

MOLES AND MOLAR VOLUME. In comparing quantities of different substances, the chemist uses a unit called the **mole.** The mole is defined as that quantity of a substance that contains 6.02×10^{23} particles, also called **Avogadro's number,** N_A. (The selection of this particular number is explained in Unit 5.) Since the mole contains a fixed number of particles, by Avogadro's Hypothesis 1 mole of any gas will occupy the same volume at a given temperature and pressure. At STP this volume is **22.4 liters,** and is called the **molar volume.**

QUESTIONS

1. At STP, 1 liter of O_2 would have the same number of molecules as (1) 1 liter of H_2 (2) 2 liters of CO (3) 3 liters of CO_2 (4) 0.5 liter of Ne

2. A sample of a gaseous substance contains 3.01×10^{23} molecules. The number of moles of the substance in this sample is (1) 1.00 (2) 2.00 (3) 0.25 (4) 0.50

3. How many moles of an ideal gas will occupy 44.8 liters at STP? (1) 1.0 (2) 2.0 (3) 22.4 (4) 44.8

LIQUIDS

NATURE OF LIQUIDS. The particles in liquids, like those in gases, have no regular arrangement and are in constant motion, but particles in liquids are relatively closer together and attractive forces are more effective. Thus liquids take the shape of the container, but they have definite volume.

VAPOR PRESSURE. Energy is assumed to be distributed among particles in liquids as it is among particles of gases. In any sample of liquid, some of the particles have sufficient energy to escape from the attractive forces of their neighbors, leave the body of the liquid, and become particles of **vapor.** (The term "vapor" is used to refer to the gas phase of a substance that is normally in the solid or liquid phase at room temperature.) The process of forming vapor is called **evaporation,** and it occurs at the surface of all substances at all temperatures. The rate of evaporation increases with increasing temperature, because as the temperature rises, more particles acquire sufficient kinetic energy to escape.

In a closed system (such as a liquid in a sealed container), the vapor produced by a liquid exerts a pressure, which is called the **vapor pressure** of the liquid. The vapor pressure increases as the temperature of the liquid is raised. It has a specific value for each substance at any given temperature.

BOILING POINT. As the temperature of a liquid rises, the vapor pressure of the liquid also rises until it becomes equal to the pressure upon the liquid. At this point, change of liquid to vapor can occur not only at the surface, but at any point within the liquid. This process is called **boiling,** and the temperature at which it occurs is called the **boiling point.** The **normal boiling point** of a liquid is the temperature at which its vapor pressure reaches standard atmospheric pressure (760 torr). For water this temperature is, by definition, 100°C. Where the actual air pressure is below 760 torr, as at elevations above sea level, a substance will boil at a temperature below its normal boiling point. If the pressure is greater than 760 torr, the boiling point will be higher than normal.

HEAT OF VAPORIZATION. The quantity of heat energy needed to convert a unit mass of a substance from its liquid phase to its vapor phase at constant temperature is called its **heat of vaporization.** (For example, the heat of vaporization of water at 100° C and 1 atm is 539.4 cal/g.) Heat added to a liquid at its boiling point overcomes the attractive forces between the particles of the liquid, separating them from each other and increasing the *potential energy* of the system. However, the process does not increase the average *kinetic energy* of either the liquid or the vapor particles. Therefore, the temperature remains constant during the phase change. Note that in condensing to the liquid phase (at constant temperature), each gram of vapor must release heat equal to its heat of vaporization.

QUESTIONS

1. Which is the most common property of all liquids? (1) definite shape (2) definite volume (3) high compressibility (4) high vapor pressure
2. The vapor pressure of 25 milliliters of water at 25°C will be the same as (1) 50 mL of water at 25 °C (2) 25 mL of water at 50° C (3) 50 mL of alcohol at 25° C (4) 25 mL of alcohol at 50° C
3. When the vapor pressure of a liquid is equal to the atmospheric pressure, the liquid will (1) freeze (2) boil (3) melt (4) condense
4. What is the normal boiling point of water? (1) 0 K (2) 100 K (3) 273 K (4) 373 K
5. A liquid in a container is boiling at a pressure of 790 torr. The normal boiling point of this liquid occurs at a pressure which is (1) below 760 torr (2) 760 torr (3) 790 torr (4) above 790 torr

SOLIDS

NATURE OF SOLIDS. Samples of substances in the solid phase have definite shape, definite volume, and crystalline structure.

CRYSTALS. A crystal consists of particles arranged in a regular, repeated geometrical pattern. Particles in a crystal possess kinetic energy due to vibration around their average positions in the crystal pattern, but these average positions do not change relative to those of the other particles in the crystal. Certain solids, such as glass and some plastics, do not have crystalline structure—they behave as if they were extremely viscous liquids—and are not considered true solids.

MELTING POINT. As energy is added to a solid, the kinetic energy of the particles is increased until they have sufficient energy to overcome the forces holding them in the crystal, and the substance begins to melt. The temperature at which this occurs is called the **melting point**. The melting point may also be defined as the temperature at which the solid and liquid phases exist in equilibrium.

HEAT OF FUSION. The amount of heat needed to convert a unit mass of a substance from solid to liquid at constant temperature is called its **heat of fusion**. For example, the heat of fusion of ice at 0° C and 1 atm is 79.72 cal/g. As in the case of boiling, heat added during melting does not increase the average kinetic energy of the particles, and the temperature remains constant until the phase change is complete. In freezing, each gram of the substance must release a quantity of heat equal to its heat of fusion.

SUBLIMATION. It is possible for a substance to pass directly from the solid phase to the gas phase, or from the gas phase to the solid phase, without passing through an observable liquid phase. This process is called **sublimation** and the substance is said to **sublime**. Solid carbon dioxide ("dry ice") and iodine vapor are two substances that sublime under normal room conditions.

QUESTIONS

1. **Which substance has a definite shape and a definite volume at STP?**
   (1) NaCl (aq) (2) $Cl_2(g)$ (3) $CCl_4(l)$ (4) $AlCl_3(s)$

2. **Which is an example of an exothermic phase change?** (1) liquid to solid   (2) liquid to gas   (3) solid to liquid   (4) solid to gas

3. **The energy required to change a unit mass of a solid to a liquid at constant temperature is called its heat of** (1) sublimation (2) condensation   (3) vaporization   (4) fusion

4. **Which change of phase is involved in determining the heat of fusion of a substance?** (1) melting of a solid   (2) sublimation of a solid   (3) boiling of a liquid   (4) condensation of a gas

5. **Which will sublime when heated at STP?** (1) $SO_2(aq)$ (2) $H_2O(l)$ (3) $N_2(g)$ (4) $I_2(s)$

6. **Which equation represents sublimation?** (1) $H_2O(l) \rightarrow H_2O(g)$ (2) $H_2O(s) \rightarrow H_2O(l)$ (3) $H_2O(s) \rightarrow H_2O(g)$ (4) $H_2O(g) \rightarrow H_2O(l)$

7. **Which substance will sublime at room temperature (25° C)?** (1) diamond (s) (2) aluminum (s) (3) carbon dioxide (s) (4) sodium chloride (s)

DEFINITION OF CHEMISTRY

Up to this point we have been considering some fundamental ideas relating to matter and energy, without regard to any specific chemical phenomena. Before we proceed to a study of chemical processes as such, it will be useful to present a definition of chemistry:

> **Chemistry is the study of the composition, structure, and properties of matter, the changes which matter undergoes, and the energy accompanying these changes.**

UNIT 2   ATOMIC STRUCTURE

ATOMS

FUNDAMENTAL PARTICLES. Such experiments as the "gold foil" experiment of Ernest Rutherford showed that all the positive charge and most of the mass of an atom is located in a small, dense, central zone called the **nucleus.**

ELECTRONS. The region surrounding the nucleus is occupied by **electrons,** which carry all the negative charge of the atom, but contain very little of the atom's mass. Each electron has one unit of negative charge and a mass of 1/1836 of that of a proton.

NUCLEONS. The nucleus of an atom consists of two types of particles, **protons** and **neutrons,** collectively known as **nucleons.** The exception is the simplest type of nucleus, the hydrogen nucleus, which consists of a single proton. The proton has a unit of positive charge; the neutron has zero charge. Each has a mass of approximately one atomic mass unit.

TABLE 2-1. SUMMARY OF PARTICLES IN THE ATOM

Particle	Symbol	Charge	Approx. Mass	Location
proton	$_1^1 H$	+1	1 a m u	nucleus
neutron	$_0^1 n$	0	1 a m u	nucleus
electron	$_{-1}^0 e$	−1	1/1836 a m u	outside nucleus

STRUCTURE OF ATOMS. Types of atoms differ from each other in the number of protons and neutrons in the nucleus and in the configuration of electrons surrounding the nucleus.

ATOMIC NUMBER. Henry Moseley's work with X-ray spectra showed that each element has a characteristic number of positive charges (protons) in the nucleus. The number of protons in the nucleus is called the **atomic number,** and determines what element an atom is. For example, all atoms in the universe that contain 11 protons are atoms of the element sodium. Atoms are normally electrically neutral because they contain equal numbers of protons and electrons, with the result that the unit positive charge of each proton is balanced by the unit negative charge of an electron.

ISOTOPES. The atoms of a given element may vary in the number of neutrons they contain. This variation does not change the chemical identity of the atom, but does affect its mass. Atoms that have the same number of protons but different numbers of neutrons are called **isotopes.**

MASS NUMBER. The sum of the protons and neutrons in the atom is called the **mass number**. Since both the number of protons and the number of neutrons are integers, it follows that the mass number of an atom is an integer. The mass number is *not* a mass; it is a pure number that is simply the sum of the number of protons and the number of neutrons in the atom. It is, however, *very nearly* the same as the mass of the atom in atomic mass units.

SYMBOLS OF ISOTOPES. A particular isotope of an element is represented by the symbol of the element with its atomic number as a subscript and its mass number as a superscript. For example, the isotope of sodium with mass number 23 is represented as follows:

$$\text{mass number} \rightarrow \quad _{11}^{23}\text{Na} \quad or \quad _{11}\text{Na}^{23}$$
$$\text{atomic number} \rightarrow$$

Note that the number of neutrons in an atom can be found by subtracting its atomic number from its mass number. For example, in an atom of sodium of mass number 23 ($_{11}^{23}\text{Na}$), there are 12 neutrons (23-11). There are three common isotopes of hydrogen, protium, $_1^1\text{H}$, deuterium, $_1^2\text{H}$, and tritium, $_1^3\text{H}$.

THE ATOMIC MASS UNIT (amu). The most common isotope of carbon, ^{12}C, has a mass number of 12. A unit of mass, called the **atomic mass unit (amu)** , has been defined as *exactly* 1/12 of the mass of the ^{12}C atom. Thus the mass of the ^{12}C atom is *exactly* 12 amu. The masses of all other atoms are *very nearly* whole numbers equal to their respective mass numbers.

ATOMIC MASS OF AN ELEMENT. If a table of atomic masses (or atomic weights) of the elements is examined, it is found that most of them are *not* close to being whole numbers. The reason for this is that a natural sample of an element usually consists of a mixture of isotopes. The atomic mass (atomic weight) of the element is an average of the masses of these isotopes, weighted in accordance with the proportions of the isotopes present. For example, natural chlorine consists of approximately 75% ^{35}Cl and 25% ^{37}Cl; the weighted average of these masses is approximately 35.5.

GRAM ATOMIC MASS. A **gram atomic mass** of an element is that quantity of the element whose mass in grams is equal numerically to its atomic mass (or atomic weight) in a.m.u. For example, 35.5 grams of chlorine is one gram atomic mass of chlorine. A gram atomic mass of any element contains *Avogadro's number* (6.02×10^{23}) of atoms (see Unit 5).

QUESTIONS

1. How many electrons are in a neutral atom of $_3^7\text{Li}$? (1) 7 (2) 10 (3) 3 (4) 4

2. The nucleus of a flourine atom has a charge of (1) 1+ (2) 9+ (3) 19+ (4) 0

3. The number of protons in the nucleus of carbon-13 is   (1) 19   (2) 13   (3) 7   (4) 6

4. The mass number of an atom is equal to the total number of its   (1) electrons, only   (2) protons, only   (3) electrons and protons   (4) protons and neutrons

5. Which pair of atoms are isotopes?   (1) $^{14}_6$C and $^{14}_7$N   (2) $^{40}_{19}$K and $^{40}_{18}$Ar   (3) $^{222}_{88}$Ra and $^{222}_{86}$Rn   (4) $^{40}_{19}$K and $^{42}_{19}$K

6. Which set of particles is arranged in order of increasing mass?   (1) H_2, H, H^+ (2) H^+, H, H_2 (3) H_2, H^+, H   (4) H, H^+, H_2

7. The existence of fractional atomic masses is best explained by the   (1) mass of electrons   (2) existence of isotopes   (3) inaccuracies in determining atomic masses   (4) varying number of protons in the nucleus of atoms

8. Isotopes of an element have a different   (1) number of electrons   (2) number of protons   (3) atomic number   (4) number of neutrons

9. Isotopes of the same element do not have the same   (1) number of electrons   (2) atomic number   (3) mass number   (4) electron configuration

10. Which pair of nuclei contain the same number of neutrons?   (1) $^7_3$Li and $^9_4$Be   (2) $^{40}_{19}$K and $^{40}_{20}$Ar   (3) $^{23}_{11}$Na and $^{22}_{11}$Na   (4) $^{23}_{11}$Na and $^{24}_{12}$Mg

11. Which atom has an equal number of protons and neutrons?   (1) $^1_1$H   (2) $^{12}_6$C   (3) $^{19}_9$F   (4) $^{39}_{19}$K

12. An atomic mass unit is equal to   (1) the mass of a hydrogen molecule   (2) $\frac{1}{1,836}$ the mass of a hydrogen atom   (3) the mass of a ^{12}C atom   (4) $\frac{1}{12}$ the mass of a ^{12}C atom

BOHR MODEL OF THE ATOM.

BOHR MODEL OF THE ATOM. Niels Bohr, the Danish physicist, proposed an atomic model that resembles our solar system; the electrons are thought of as revolving around the nucleus in concentric orbits. These orbits or **shells**, called **principal energy levels,** are the only regions in which electrons can be found within the atom.

PRINCIPAL ENERGY LEVELS. The principal energy levels are denoted by the letters K, L, M, N, O, P, Q, or by the numbers 1, 2, 3, 4, 5, 6, 7, respectively. Each level can contain only a specific number of electrons. For example, the K shell can hold 2 electrons, the L shell can hold 8 electrons, etc.

Electrons in shells closest to the nucleus possess smaller amounts of energy, while electrons farther from the nucleus have higher energies. If, in any given atom, the electrons are found in the lowest available energy levels, the atom is said to be in its **ground state.** When an atom absorbs energy, its electrons may move from an interior shell of low energy to higher energy levels in outer shells (leaving the shells closer to the nucleus partly or completely empty). When this occurs, the atom is said to be in an **excited state.** The excited state is an unstable one, and the electrons tend to return to lower energy levels.

QUANTUM THEORY OF ELECTRON ENERGIES. According to the Bohr theory, electrons can absorb only specific amounts of energy, called **quanta** (singular, **quantum**), corresponding to the differences in energy levels of the shells. When an electron falls back from an excited state to a shell of lower energy, it releases a quantum of energy equal to the difference in energy of the two levels. Fractions of a quantum are not possible; energy is always absorbed or released by atoms in definite amounts rather than in a continuous flow.

QUANTUM THEORY OF RADIATION. Radiant energy is also "quantized." Although radiation is transmitted as waves, its energy consists of quanta of a definite amount, which is directly proportional to the frequency of the radiation and inversely proportional to its wavelength. A quantum of radiation is called a **photon.**

SPECTRA. When an electron drops from one energy level to another, it emits a quantum of energy of a definite amount This energy appears as a photon of radiation of definite wavelength corresponding to the size of the quantum. If the atoms in a sample of an element are excited, as the atoms return to their ground state they emit a characteristic set of wavelengths of radiation, each wavelength corresponding to one of the possible "quantum jumps" that an electron in those atoms can make. Many of these wavelengths fall in the range that the eye detects as light, each wavelength producing a particular sensation of color. The **spectroscope** is an instrument that separates light into its various wavelengths and displays them as colored lines or bands against a dark background. The particular set of colored bands produced by a given element is called its **spectrum.** The spectrum is different for each element and can be used to detect and identify elements that are present in a sample of matter.

ORBITAL MODEL OF THE ATOM. The modern orbital model of the atom differs from the Bohr model in that it does not represent the paths of the electrons as planetary orbits, but specifies only the *probabilities* of finding electrons at various directions and distances from the nucleus. The regions in which there is high probability of finding electrons are called **orbitals** to distinguish them from the fixed orbits of the Bohr model. Orbitals vary in size, shape, and space orientation. The energy levels of electrons are given not by the shell letters (or numbers) of the Bohr model alone, but rather by a set of four **quantum numbers.**

PRINCIPAL QUANTUM NUMBER. The **principal quantum number, n,** defines the principal energy level of an electron in an atom. This number, which may be any positive integer, is the same as the shell designation of the Bohr model. For example, if an electron in the Bohr model were described as being in the third shell, then in the orbital model its principal quantum number is 3 ($n = 3$).

SUBLEVELS. Each principal energy level contains **sublevels** of energy. The total number of sublevels possible for each principal energy level is equal to the principal quantum number, n. For example, the number of sublevels in the first principal energy level is 1, since $n = 1$; the number of sublevels in the third principal energy level is 3, since $n = 3$.

The sublevel of lowest energy in each principal level is called the s sublevel. Every principal level has an s sublevel; it is identified by means of the principal shell number. For example, the 1s sublevel is in the first principal level ($n = 1$); the 3s sublevel is in the third principal level ($n = 3$).

If a principal level has a second sublevel, it is called a p sublevel; all principal levels of $n = 2$ or more have p sublevels. A third sublevel is called the d sublevel; all principal levels of $n = 3$ or more have a d sublevel. A fourth sublevel is called an f sublevel; this is found in levels of $n = 4$ or more. Although additional sublevels are present in principal levels beyond $n = 4$, they have not been named, because no atom in its ground state has electrons in these higher sublevels.

ORBITALS. An orbital can be thought of as a region inside the atom in which an electron may be found. Each sublevel has a characteristic number of orbitals. An s sublevel has 1; a p sublevel has 3; a d sublevel has 5; and an f sublevel has 7. Each orbital can hold a maximum of *two* electrons. The maximum number of electrons that can be present in any principal level can be easily calculated. For example, the first principal level ($n = 1$) has only one sublevel (the 1s sublevel), and this sublevel has only one orbital, which can hold 2 electrons. Therefore, the first principal level can hold only 2 electrons. The second principal level has an s sublevel with one orbital, and a p sublevel with three orbitals; this principal level can hold 8 electrons (2 in its s sublevel and 6 in its p sublevel). In general, each principal level can hold $2n^2$ electrons; for example, for $n = 3$, the maximum is 18; for $n = 4$, it is 32. (See Table 2-2.)

TABLE 2-2. ORBITALS AND ELECTRON CAPACITY OF THE FIRST FOUR PRINCIPAL LEVELS

Principal energy level (n)	Type of sublevel	Number of orbitals per type	Number of orbitals per level (n^2)	Maximum number of electrons ($2n^2$)
1	s	1	1	2
2	s	1	4	8
	p	3		
3	s	1	9	18
	p	3		
	d	5		
4	s	1	16	32
	p	3		
	d	5		
	f	7		

CHARACTERISTICS OF ORBITALS. Orbitals of any given sub-level differ from each other in terms of shape and spatial orientation. The s orbital is spherical, but since an orbital is a probability region, it should be pictured as a spherical cloud rather than as a sphere with definite edges.

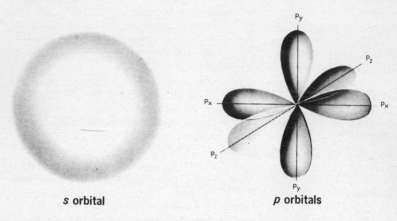

s orbital p orbitals

Figure 2-1. Visualization of s and p orbitals.

The p orbital has a dumbbell shape. As indicated above, there are three p orbitals in any p sublevel. These orbitals differ from each other by their arrangement in space. As shown, each of the p orbitals is at right angles to the others, permitting a set of xyz coordinates to be formed. These p orbitals are called p_x, p_y, and p_z. The d and f orbitals have more complex shapes. We shall be concerned only with the bonds formed by electrons in the s and p orbitals.

ELECTRON CONFIGURATIONS. The distribution of the electrons among the various orbitals of an atom is called the **electron configuration** of the atom. It is described by a written notation in which the number of electrons in each sublevel is indicated by a superscript. For example, the presence of 4 electrons in the $3p$ sublevel is indicated as follows:

$$\text{principal energy level} \rightarrow 3p^4 \leftarrow \text{number of electrons in sublevel}$$
$$\underset{\text{type of sublevel}}{\uparrow}$$

The complete configuration of an atom is shown by writing symbols for all the occupied sublevels in sequence. For example, the electron configuration of the oxygen atom is represented as follows:

$$1s^2 2s^2 2p^4$$

This means that there are 2 electrons in the $1s$ sublevel, 2 in the $2s$ sublevel, and 4 in the $2p$ sublevel, for a total of 8 (which agrees with the atomic number of oxygen). Note that the maximum superscript for

s is 2, for p is 6, for d is 10, and for f is 14.

This notation shows only the total number of electrons in each *sublevel*, but does not show how the electrons are distributed among the *orbitals* of each sublevel. This is usually done in one of two ways, as illustrated by Figure 2-2.

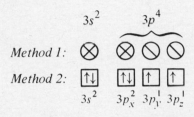

Figure 2-2. Showing electron occupancy of orbitals. In Method 1, a circle represents the orbital; the presence of one electron is indicated by a single diagonal line; the presence of two electrons (an "orbital pair" with opposite spins) is indicated by two lines forming a cross. In Method 2, a box represents the orbital, an arrow pointing up represents one electron, and an arrow pointing down represents a second electron of opposite spin. An orbital is filled when it has a pair of crossed lines (Method 1) or a pair of arrows (Method 2).

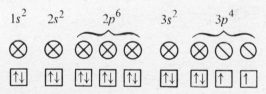

Figure 2-3. Various ways of indicating the electron configuration of the sulfur atom ($_{16}$S).

WRITING ELECTRON CONFIGURATIONS.

The electron configurations of all the elements can be built up in order of atomic number, starting with hydrogen, by adding one electron at a time according to the following rules:

1. Each added electron is placed in the sublevel of lowest energy available.
2. No more than two electrons can be placed in any orbital.
3. Before a second electron can be placed in any orbital, all the orbitals of that sublevel must contain at least one electron.
4. No more than four orbitals (one s and three p orbitals) can be occupied in the outermost principal energy level. The next electron must enter the next principal energy level.

Electron configurations for the first 18 elements are shown in Table 2-3 on the next page. Electron configurations of all the elements are included in the Periodic Table.

TABLE 2-3. ELECTRON CONFIGURATIONS OF THE FIRST 18 ELEMENTS

Element	At. No.	Sublevel Structure	Orbital Structure (1s, 2s, 2p, 3s, 3p)
H	1	$1s^1$	1s: ↑
He	2	$1s^2$	1s: ↑↓
Li	3	$1s^2 2s^1$	1s: ↑↓ 2s: ↑
Be	4	$1s^2 2s^2$	1s: ↑↓ 2s: ↑↓
B	5	$1s^2 2s^2 2p^1$	1s: ↑↓ 2s: ↑↓ 2p: ↑
C	6	$1s^2 2s^2 2p^2$	1s: ↑↓ 2s: ↑↓ 2p: ↑ ↑
N	7	$1s^2 2s^2 2p^3$	1s: ↑↓ 2s: ↑↓ 2p: ↑ ↑ ↑
O	8	$1s^2 2s^2 2p^4$	1s: ↑↓ 2s: ↑↓ 2p: ↑↓ ↑ ↑
F	9	$1s^2 2s^2 2p^5$	1s: ↑↓ 2s: ↑↓ 2p: ↑↓ ↑↓ ↑
Ne	10	$1s^2 2s^2 2p^6$	1s: ↑↓ 2s: ↑↓ 2p: ↑↓ ↑↓ ↑↓
Na	11	$1s^2 2s^2 2p^6 3s^1$	1s: ↑↓ 2s: ↑↓ 2p: ↑↓ ↑↓ ↑↓ 3s: ↑
Mg	12	$1s^2 2s^2 2p^6 3s^2$	1s: ↑↓ 2s: ↑↓ 2p: ↑↓ ↑↓ ↑↓ 3s: ↑↓
Al	13	$1s^2 2s^2 2p^6 3s^2 3p^1$	1s: ↑↓ 2s: ↑↓ 2p: ↑↓ ↑↓ ↑↓ 3s: ↑↓ 3p: ↑
Si	14	$1s^2 2s^2 2p^6 3s^2 3p^2$	1s: ↑↓ 2s: ↑↓ 2p: ↑↓ ↑↓ ↑↓ 3s: ↑↓ 3p: ↑ ↑
P	15	$1s^2 2s^2 2p^6 3s^2 3p^3$	1s: ↑↓ 2s: ↑↓ 2p: ↑↓ ↑↓ ↑↓ 3s: ↑↓ 3p: ↑ ↑ ↑
S	16	$1s^2 2s^2 2p^6 3s^2 3p^4$	1s: ↑↓ 2s: ↑↓ 2p: ↑↓ ↑↓ ↑↓ 3s: ↑↓ 3p: ↑↓ ↑ ↑
Cl	17	$1s^2 2s^2 2p^6 3s^2 3p^5$	1s: ↑↓ 2s: ↑↓ 2p: ↑↓ ↑↓ ↑↓ 3s: ↑↓ 3p: ↑↓ ↑↓ ↑
Ar	18	$1s^2 2s^2 2p^6 3s^2 3p^6$	1s: ↑↓ 2s: ↑↓ 2p: ↑↓ ↑↓ ↑↓ 3s: ↑↓ 3p: ↑↓ ↑↓ ↑↓

VALENCE ELECTRONS AND ELECTRON-DOT SYMBOLS. The chemical properties of atoms depend upon the electrons in the outermost principal energy level. These electrons are called **valence electrons.** Atoms with their valence electrons are often represented by **electron-dot diagrams,** in which the **kernel** of the atom is represented by the symbol of the element and the valence electrons by a pattern of dots. (The "kernel" of an atom consists of the nucleus and all but the valence electrons.) Electron-dot diagrams of atoms of atomic numbers 1 through 12 are shown in Figure 2-4.

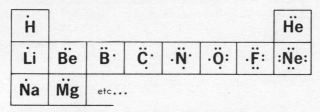

Figure 2-4. Electron-dot diagrams of the first 12 elements.

IONIZATION ENERGY. The energy that must be supplied to an atom in the gaseous phase to remove its most loosely bound electron from the attraction of the nucleus is called **ionization energy,** and is abbreviated I.E. This energy is greatest for low-energy electrons (those close to the nucleus), and least for high-energy electrons (those far from the nucleus). The quantity of energy needed to remove the second most loosely bound electron is called the **second ionization energy** of the atom. As might be expected, the second ionization energy is larger than the first, the third I.E. is larger than the second, etc. Ionization energies of representative elements are given in Reference Table K.

QUESTIONS

1. Which is the electron configuration of a $^3_1$ H atom in the ground state? (1) $1s^1$ (2) $1s^2$ (3) $1s^2 2s^1$ (4) $1s^2 2s^2$

2. Which is the electron configuration of a noble gas atom in the excited state? (1) $1s^1$ (2) $1s^1 2s^1$ (3) $1s^2 2s^2$ (4) $1s^2 2s^2 2p^2$

3. Which electron configuration represents an atom in an excited state? (1) $1s^2 2s^2$ (2) $1s^2 3p^1$ (3) $1s^2 2s^2 2p^5$ (4) $1s^2 2s^2 2p^6$

4. Which electron configuration represents a neutral atom of nitrogen in an excited state? (1) $1s^2 2s^2 2p^3$ (2) $1s^2 2s^2 2p^4$ (3) $1s^2 2s^1 2p^4$ (4) $1s^2 2s^1 2p^5$

5. The characteristic bright-line spectrum of an element is produced when electrons (1) **fall back to lower energy levels** (2) **are gained by a neutral atom** (3) **are emitted by the nucleus as beta particles** (4) **move to higher energy levels**

6. When an electron in an atom of hydrogen moves from the second to the first principal energy level, the result is the emission of (1) a beta particle (2) an alpha particle (3) quantized energy (4) gamma rays

7. What is the maximum number of electrons that can be contained in the 4th principal energy level?   (1) 8   (2) 18   (3) 32   (4) 50

8. What is the total number of electrons in the second principal energy level of a calcium atom in the ground state?   (1) 6   (2) 2   (3) 18 (4) 8

9. An atom with the electron configuration $1s^2 2s^2 2p^6 3s^2 3p^6 4s^2$ has an incomplete   (1) 3rd principal energy level   (2) 2s sublevel   (3) 2nd principal energy level   (4) 3s sublevel

10. What is the total number of electrons in the second principal energy level of a chlorine atom in the ground state?   (1) 5   (2) 7   (3) 8   (4) 17

11. Which sublevels are occupied in the outermost principal energy level of an argon atom in the ground state?   (1) 3s and 3d   (2) 3s and 3p (3) 2s and 3p   (4) 2p and 3d

12. An atom of which element in the ground state contains electrons with a principal quantum number (n) of 4?   (1) Kr   (2) Ar   (3) Ne   (4) He

13. How many sublevels are completely occupied in the second principal energy level of a sodium atom in the ground state?   (1) 1   (2) 2   (3) 3 (4) 4

14. How many occupied sublevels are in an atom of carbon in the ground state?   (1) 5   (2) 6   (3) 3   (4) 4

15. In which subshell would an electron have the highest energy?   (1) 3p (2) 2p   (3) 3s   (4) 4s

16. How many electrons occupy the 2p sublevel in an atom of boron in the ground state?   (1) 1   (2) 2   (3) 3   (4) 5

17. How many orbitals in a sulfur atom in the ground state contain only one electron?   (1) 1   (2) 2   (3) 3   (4) 4

18. Which is the correct electron-dot symbol for a boron atom in the ground state?   (1) $\dot{B}$ (2) $\overset{\cdot\cdot}{B}\cdot$ (3) $\overset{\cdot\cdot}{B}\cdot$ (4) $\cdot\dot{B}\cdot$

19. If the electron configuration of an atom of element X is $1s^2 2s^2 2p^4$, the electron-dot symbol for the element is

    (1) $X\!:$ (2) $\cdot\dot{X}\cdot$ (3) $\overset{\cdot\cdot}{\underset{\cdot\cdot}{:X:}}$ (4) $\cdot\underset{\cdot\cdot}{\dot{X}}\!:$

20. Which is the correct electron-dot symbol for the fluoride ion?

    (1) $:F:^{+}$ (2) $\overset{\cdot\cdot}{\underset{\cdot\cdot}{:F:}}^{+}$ (3) $F:^{-}$ (4) $\overset{\cdot\cdot}{:F:}^{-}$

21. Which orbital notation correctly represents the outermost principal energy level of oxygen in the ground state?

22. What is the name given to the amount of energy required to remove the most loosely bound electron from an atom in the gaseous phase? (1) ionization energy   (2) electron affinity   (3) electronegativity (4) valence energy

RADIOACTIVITY

NATURAL RADIOACTIVITY. The nuclei of certain atoms are not stable; they *decay* spontaneously, emitting electromagnetic radiation and several types of particles. The decay of, and emission of rays and particles from, such nuclei is called **radioactivity.** The nuclei of all isotopes with atomic numbers greater than 83 are unstable, and they undergo spontaneous decay. Many isotopes of the other elements are also unstable. When a change in the nucleus of an atom results in the transformation of the atom from one element to another, the change is called **transmutation.**

RADIOACTIVE EMISSIONS. Nuclear disintegration of naturally occurring radioactive atoms produces *alpha particles, beta particles,* and *gamma radiations.* These emissions differ from each other with respect to mass, charge, penetrating power, and ionizing power.

  1. Alpha decay. The emission of an alpha particle as a result of nuclear disintegration is called *alpha decay.* An atom that emits an alpha particle is called an *alpha emitter.* An alpha particle, composed of 2 protons and 2 neutrons, is actually the stable nucleus of helium. Alpha decay of an atom's nucleus reduces its atomic number by 2 units (by the loss of the 2 protons) and its mass number by 4 units (by the loss of the 2 protons plus the 2 neutrons). For example, alpha decay of a radium-226 nucleus reduces its atomic number from 88 to 86. It is then no longer an atom of radium; it has become an atom of radon (atomic number 86), with a mass number of 222, which is 4 units less than that of the original radium nucleus. Alpha decay of radium-226 is represented by the equation

$$^{226}_{88}\text{Ra} \quad \rightarrow \quad ^{222}_{86}\text{Rn} \quad + \quad ^{4}_{2}\text{He}$$

radium-226   radon-222   alpha particle
nucleus   nucleus   (helium nucleus)

  2. Beta decay. Nuclei that emit a beta particle as a result of nuclear disintegration are said to undergo *beta decay.* An atom that emits a beta particle is called a *beta emitter.* A beta particle is a high-speed electron. Beta decay of an atom's nucleus increases its atomic number by 1 unit, but its mass number remains unchanged. For example, the beta decay of lead-214 to bismuth-214 is represented by the equation

$$^{214}_{82}\text{Pb} \quad \rightarrow \quad ^{214}_{83}\text{Bi} \quad + \quad ^{0}_{-1}\text{e}$$

electron

  Remember that the atomic number is actually the positive charge of the nucleus. When a nucleus emits an electron, which has a charge of −1, the charge of the nucleus becomes 1 unit more positive. This is interpreted as the conversion of a neutron to a proton.

  Note that in all nuclear reactions, the sum of the mass numbers on the left side of the equation equals the sum of the mass numbers on the right side, and the sum of the atomic numbers (charges) on the left equals the sum of atomic numbers (charges) on the right.

3. Gamma radiation. Nearly all nuclear changes are accompanied by the emission of *gamma radiation*. This radiation is high-energy electromagnetic radiation of shorter wavelength than X rays. Gamma rays are not particles. Since gamma radiation has neither mass nor charge, its emission only reduces the energy content of a nucleus without changing either its mass or atomic number.

SEPARATING RADIOACTIVE EMISSIONS. Particles and rays emitted from radioactive atoms can be separated by passing them through magnetic or electric fields. Because alpha particles are helium nuclei, with a positive charge, they are deflected toward the negative electrode of an electric field. Beta particles, being electrons with a negative charge, are attracted to the positive electrode. (The deflections of these particles in a magnetic field are also due to their electric charge.) Gamma rays, on the other hand, have no charge and therefore are not deflected by either electric or magnetic fields.

HALF-LIFE. There is no way to predict when a single nucleus of a radioactive isotope will undergo decay. It may decay within the next second, or it may remain stable for a million years. However, it is possible to determine what *fraction* of the nuclei in a sample will decay within any given time. This *rate of decay* is constant for each isotope and different from any other. It can be expressed in terms of **half-life,** which is the time required for one-half the nuclei in a given sample to decay.

For example, the half-life of cobalt-60 is 5¼ years. This means that if we start with a specimen of cobalt-60 now, half of its atoms will decay during the next 5¼ years, leaving half of the original amount at the end of that time. During the next 5¼ years, half of the remaining atoms will decay, leaving one-fourth of the original amount. This continues indefinitely.

If the half-life of an isotope is represented by T, then the fraction of a sample that remains after time t is:

$$\text{Fraction remaining} = \left(\frac{1}{2}\right)^{t/T}$$

Note that t/T is simply the number of half-life periods that have elapsed. (See Sample Problem on page 31.) Reference Table H lists the half-life values for common radioisotopes.

QUESTIONS

1. **A radioactive atom will lose the greatest amount of mass when it emits**
   (1) a neutron (2) a proton (3) a beta particle (4) an alpha particle

2. **According to the equation $X \rightarrow \, ^{208}_{82}Pb + \, ^{4}_{2}He$, the nucleus correctly represented by X is (1) $^{204}_{80}Hg$ (2) $^{212}_{84}Po$ (3) $^{204}_{80}Bi$ (4) $^{212}_{84}Pb$**

3. **In the equation $^{226}_{88}Ra \rightarrow \, ^{222}_{86}Rn + X$, X represents (1) a neutron (2) a proton (3) a beta particle (4) an alpha particle**

4. **In the reaction $^{24}_{11}Na \rightarrow \, ^{24}_{12}Mg + X$, the particle represented by the letter X is (1) a proton (2) a neutron (3) an electron (4) a positron**

5. **When $^{234}_{90}Th$ emits a beta particle ($^{0}_{-1}e$), the element formed is (1) Ra (2) Th (3) Pa (4) U**

SAMPLE PROBLEMS

1. *What mass of iodine-131 (half-life 8 days) remains 32 days after a 100-gram sample of this isotope is obtained?*

Solution *(Method 1):* Reduce the mass by one-half for each successive half-life period until the total time is reached:

After 8 days, $1/2$ of 100 g, or 50 g, will remain.
After 16 days, $1/2$ of 50 g, or 25 g, will remain.
After 24 days, $1/2$ of 25 g, or 12.5 g, will remain.
After 32 days, $1/2$ of 12.5 g, or **6.25 g**, will remain.

Method 2: Divide the total time by the half-life to find the number of half-life periods. Then use the formula

$$\text{Fraction of isotope remaining} = \left(\frac{1}{2}\right)^n$$

where n = no. of half-life periods.

In this case, $n = \dfrac{32}{8} = 4$

Fraction remaining $= \left(\dfrac{1}{2}\right)^4 = \dfrac{1}{16}$

$\dfrac{1}{16} \times 100 \text{ g} = \mathbf{6.25 \text{ g}}$

2. *Analysis of charred wood at a prehistoric campsite reveals that it contains the equivalent of only one-fourth the quantity of carbon-14 that is found in living wood tissue. If the half-life of carbon-14 is 5,770 years, how old is the campsite?*

Solution: Since the carbon–14 content is reduced to $1/2$ after one half-life period, and to $1/4$ after two half life periods, two half-life periods must have elapsed. Therefore, the age of the campsite is $2 \times 5,770 = \mathbf{11,540 \text{ years}}$.

6. After 3 half-life periods, 12.5 grams of an original sample of a radio-isotope remains unchanged. What was the mass of the original sample? **(1)** 25.0 g **(2)** 50.0 g **(3)** 100. g **(4)** 200. g

7. As the pressure on a gaseous radioisotope increases, its half-life **(1)** decreases **(2)** increases **(3)** remains the same

8. A 40.0 milligram sample of ^{33}P decays to 10.0 milligrams in 50.0 days. What is the half-life of ^{33}P? **(1)** 12.5 days **(2)** 25.0 days **(3)** 37.5 days **(4)** 75.0 days

9. What total mass of a 16-gram sample of ^{60}Co will remain unchanged after 15.9 years? **(1)** 1.0 g **(2)** 2.0 g **(3)** 8.0 g **(4)** 4.0 g

10. The half-life of $^{14}_{6}C$ is 5,730 years. What fraction of a 1-gram sample of $^{14}_{6}C$ would remain after 17,190 years? **(1)** $1/2$ **(2)** $1/4$ **(3)** $1/8$ **(4)** $1/16$

UNIT 3   BONDING

THE NATURE OF CHEMICAL BONDS

ENERGY AND CHEMICAL BONDS. A **chemical bond** is formed when two atomic nuclei simultaneously attract the same electron or pair of electrons. Work must be done—that is, energy must be supplied —to break a chemical bond and separate the two atoms. It follows that when the same bond is formed, an equal amount of energy is released. The potential energy associated with changes in chemical bonds is called **chemical energy.**

THE STRENGTH OF CHEMICAL BONDS. When a chemical bond is formed, the resulting system is at a lower level of potential energy than before the bond formed, because energy is always released when a bond forms. If relatively little energy is released in the formation of the bond, the bond requires relatively little energy input to break it. Such a bond is said to be *weak*, and the system is relatively unstable. On the other hand, if a relatively large amount of energy is released in the formation of a bond, the bond is strong and the system is relatively stable.

BOND STRENGTH AND CHEMICAL CHANGE. Chemical changes tend to occur in a manner that leads to a condition of lower potential energy and hence greater stability. When such chemical changes occur, energy is given off. The potential energy (chemical energy) that can be released by a chemical change is considered to be stored in the bonds of the system before the change. Note that weaker bonds, or less stable systems, have more stored chemical energy than stable systems with strong bonds.

ELECTRONEGATIVITY. The electronegativity of an atom is a relative measure of its attraction for the electrons that form a chemical bond between it and another atom. Electronegativity values range from a low of 0.7 for cesium and francium to a high of 4.0 for fluorine. The lower the electronegativity value, the less the attraction of the atom for the bond electrons. Fluorine, with a value of 4.0, has the greatest attraction for the electrons of a chemical bond. Electronegativity values can be used to predict the type of bond that can be formed between two atoms. Typical electronegativity values are listed in Reference Table K.

TYPES OF BONDS BETWEEN ATOMS

Atoms form bonds in such a way as to become more like atoms of inert gas, that is, with a stable octet of 8 valence electrons. To reach this stable configuration, electrons may be transferred from one atom to another or may be shared, equally or unequally, by two atoms.

In most cases, these changes involve only the valence electrons of the atoms.

IONIC BONDS. An **ionic bond** is formed by the transfer of one or more electrons from one atom to another. The transfer of electrons results in the formation of charged particles, called **ions.**

The number of electrons transferred in ionic bonding is such that the atoms involved achieve an inert gas configuration. Because the electron configuration of the ion is different from that of its parent atom, its chemical properties are also different.

Electronegativity values can be used to tell whether a bond is likely to be ionic. When the difference between the electronegativity values of two atoms is 1.7 or greater, the bond formed between these two atoms is considered to be ionic. An important exception to this general rule is found in the combination of active metals, such as sodium, with hydrogen. Although the electronegativity difference between sodium and hydrogen is only 1.2, the bond is predominantly ionic. This is also true for the other compounds of this type. These compounds are known as the metal hydrides.

Figure 3-1 illustrates the formation of an ionic bond in the reaction between lithium and fluorine.

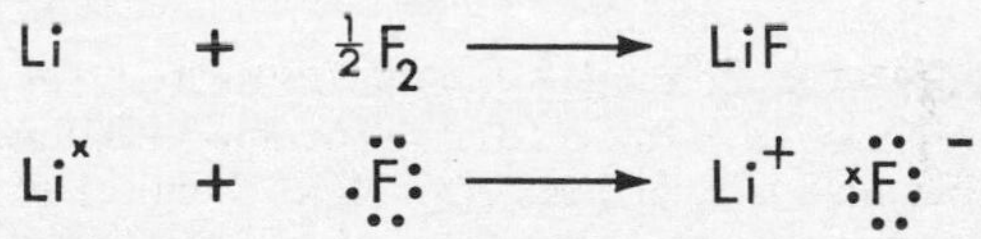

$$\text{Li} \quad + \quad \tfrac{1}{2}\text{F}_2 \longrightarrow \text{LiF}$$

$$\text{Li}^{\times} \quad + \quad \cdot\ddot{\text{F}}\text{:} \longrightarrow \text{Li}^{+} \quad {}_{\times}^{\cdot\cdot}\ddot{\text{F}}\text{:}^{-}$$

Figure 3-1. In this example of ionic bonding, the lithium atom transfers one electron to the fluorine atom, so that the fluorine atom has a full complement of 8 valence electrons. As a result of the electron transfer, the lithium atom becomes a positively charged ion, and the fluorine atom becomes a negatively charged ion.

IONIC SOLIDS. Substances in the solid phase that are formed by ionic bonding are called **ionic solids.** These solids have the following characteristics:

1. They have high melting points.

2. They do not conduct electricity.

3. They are crystalline in structure.

The ions in ionic solids are held in the relatively fixed positions of the crystal pattern by electrostatic forces. When the crystalline structure is destroyed by heating, the ions become free to move, either in the liquid or the vapor phase, and can then conduct an electric current. A similar change occurs when ionic solids are dissolved in water; the crystal lattice is destroyed, and the ions, linked to water molecules, become free to conduct electricity. Sodium chloride (NaCl) and magnesium oxide (MgO) are examples of ionic solids.

COVALENT BONDS. A **covalent bond** is formed when two nuclei share electrons, rather than transfer them from one atom to another. When the electronegativity difference between two atoms is less than 1.7, the bond is considered to be predominantly covalent.

1. Nonpolar Bonds. If both nuclei have the same electronegativity value, they attract electrons with equal force, and the electrons are shared equally between them. Such a bond is called a **nonpolar covalent bond.** A good example of this type of bonding is a molecule of chlorine (see Figure 3-2 on the next page). The atoms in the familiar diatomic molecules are held together by covalent bonds. A single covalent bond holds the atoms together in H_2, F_2, Cl_2, Br_2, and I_2. The oxygen atoms in the O_2 molecule are held together by two covalent bonds (a double bond), and the nitrogen atoms in the N_2 molecule are held together by three covalent bonds (a triple bond).

2. Polar Bonds. When the electronegativity values of the two atoms are different, the sharing of electrons in covalent bonding is unequal and the bond is said to be **polar covalent.** It is called polar because the element with the higher electronegativity value will attract the shared electrons more strongly, causing that portion of the molecule to appear to have a negative charge. The other portion will appear to have a positive charge. A molecule of hydrogen iodide (HI) exhibits this kind of bonding (see Figure 3-2).

3. Coordinate Covalent Bonds. In some cases, only one atom contributes both electrons in forming a covalent bond with another atom. In such cases, the bond is called a **coordinate covalent bond.** Polyatomic ions and radicals frequently exhibit this kind of bonding (see Figure 3-2). Coordinate covalent bonds are important in acid-base theory, and are discussed more fully in Unit 7.

MOLECULAR SUBSTANCES. A **molecule** can be defined as the smallest discrete particle of an element or compound formed by covalently bonded atoms. Stable molecules usually have structures such that each atom has an inert gas electron configuration when shared electrons of each bond are considered to belong to both bonding atoms. Molecular substances may exist as solids, liquids, or gases, depending on the strength of the forces of attraction between the molecules.

Molecular solids generally have the following characteristics:

1. They are soft.

2. They are poor conductors of heat and electricity.

3. They have relatively low melting points.

Examples of molecular substances are water (H_2O), carbon tetrachloride (CCl_4), ammonia (NH_3), sugar ($C_6H_{12}O_6$), and certain elements that occur as diatomic gases, such as oxygen (O_2) and hydrogen (H_2).

NETWORK SOLIDS. In certain solids, the covalently bonded atoms are linked into a giant network throughout the entire sample. Such substances are called **network solids** or **macromolecules.** In general, network solids possess the following characteristics:

1. They are hard.

2. They are poor conductors of heat and electricity.

3. They have high melting points (unlike other covalently bonded substances). Examples of such solids are asbestos, graphite, diamond, silicon carbide (SiC), and silicon dioxide (SiO_2).

Figure 3-2. Types of covalent bonding.

(a)

Cl_2 molecule

(a) Nonpolar covalent: In a chlorine molecule, the two chlorine atoms have the same electronegativity, so that the two electrons in the covalent bond are shared equally. As a result, the charge distribution in the molecule is symmetrical.

(b)

HI molecule

(b) Polar covalent: Iodine is more electronegative than hydrogen. Therefore, in the hydrogen iodide molecule, the iodine atom attracts the bonding electrons more strongly than the hydrogen atom. As a result, there is a nonsymmetrical charge distribution in the bond, and the iodine end has a negative charge, while the hydrogen end has a positive charge.

(c)

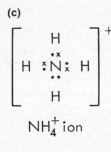

NH_4^+ ion

(c) Coordinate covalent: When both electrons in a covalent bond are contributed by one of the two atoms, the bond is called coordinate covalent. In the ammonia (NH_3) molecule, each of the three bonds consists of one electron from a hydrogen atom and one from the nitrogen atom. Since nitrogen has five valence electrons, this leaves two electrons free to form additional bonds. These two electrons can form a bond with a hydrogen ion ($H+$) to form the ammonium ion (NH_4^+) In this coordinate bond, both electrons are contributed by the nitrogen atom and none by the hydrogen ion.

METALLIC BONDING. Metallic atoms, which have few valence electrons and low ionization energies, cannot achieve the inert gas configuration by sharing electrons or donating them to other metallic atoms. Therefore, neither ionic nor covalent bonding is possible between metallic atoms. However, a relatively strong type of bonding, called **metallic bonding**, does occur in metals.

Metals consist of a crystalline lattice in which positive ions (or the kernels of the metallic atoms) are arranged in fixed patterns, and the valence electrons are free to move. These electrons do not belong to individual atoms, but rather to the crystal as a whole. The "sea of electrons" produces an attractive force that fixes the positions of the metallic ions. Because the electrons can move about freely, metals are good conductors of heat and electricity.

QUESTIONS

1. As a chemical bond forms between two hydrogen atoms, the potential energy of the atoms (1) decreases (2) increases (3) remains the same

2. The transfer of electrons from sodium atoms to chlorine atoms results in the formation of (1) coordinate covalent bonds (2) polar covalent bonds (3) nonpolar bonds (4) ionic bonds

3. What is a characteristic of ionic solids? (1) They conduct electricity. (2) They have high vapor pressures. (3) They have high melting points. (4) They are very malleable.

4. A certain solid, when it is in the liquid state or dissolved in water, will conduct electricity. In the solid state it will not conduct electricity. This solid must contain (1) ionic bonds (2) metallic bonds (3) covalent bonds (4) coordinate bonds

5. Which compound contains ionic bonds? (1) $NaH(s)$ (2) $C_6H_{12}O_6(s)$ (3) $CH_3OH(l)$ (4) $H_2O(l)$

6. A compound formed from potassium and chlorine will have (1) a molecular crystal structure (2) a high melting point (3) good heat conductivity in the solid state (4) poor electrical conductivity in solution

7. What type of bond exists in a molecule of iodine? (1) ionic (2) polar covalent (3) nonpolar covalent (4) metallic

8. A molecule of ammonia (NH_3) contains (1) ionic bonds, only (2) covalent bonds, only (3) both covalent and ionic bonds (4) neither covalent nor ionic bonds

9. Which sample of HCl most readily conducts electricity? (1) $HCl(s)$ (2) $HCl(l)$ (3) $HCl(g)$ (4) $HCl(aq)$

10. A proton (H^+) would be most likely to form a coordinate covalent bond with

(1)
$$H : \overset{\displaystyle H}{\underset{\displaystyle H}{\overset{\cdot\cdot}{\underset{\cdot\cdot}{C}}}} : H$$

(2)
$$H : \overset{\cdot\cdot}{\underset{\cdot\cdot}{O}} :$$
$$\qquad H$$

(3) $H : C :: C : H$

(4)
$$\left[H : \overset{\displaystyle H}{\underset{\displaystyle H}{\overset{\cdot\cdot}{\underset{\cdot\cdot}{N}}}} : H \right]^+$$

11. Which compound contains both ionic and covalent bonds?
    (1) HCl(*g*) (2) NaCl(*s*) (3) NH₄Cl(*s*) (4) CCl₄(*l*)

12. Which compound has the *lowest* melting point? (1) HCl (2) KCl
    (3) NaCl (4) LiCl

13. A solid substance is soft, has a low melting point, and is a poor
    conductor of electricity. The substance is most likely (1) an ionic
    solid (2) a network solid (3) a metallic solid (4) a molecular solid

14. The atoms in a molecule of hydrogen chloride are held together by
    (1) ionic bonds (2) polar covalent bonds (3) van der Waals forces
    (4) dipole-dipole attraction

15. The carbon atoms in a diamond are held together by (1) metallic
    bonds (2) hydrogen bonds (3) ionic bonds (4) covalent bonds

16. A certain substance is a poor conductor of heat and electricity and has
    a high melting point. The substance is most likely (1) Hg (2) He
    (3) CO₂ (4) SiO₂

17. Which compound is a network solid? (1) CH₄ (2) CO₂ (3) CaH₂
    (4) SiO₂

18. Which type of bond would be formed when a hydrogen ion (H⁺) reacts
    with an ammonia molecule (NH₃)? (1) a coordinate covalent bond
    (2) a nonpolar covalent bond (3) a metallic bond (4) an ionic bond

19. Which type of bonding involves positive ions immersed in a sea of
    mobile electrons? (1) ionic (2) nonpolar covalent (3) polar
    covalent (4) metallic

MOLECULAR ATTRACTION

The preceding sections described forces that bond *atoms* together.
The following sections will describe forces of attraction that exist between *molecules*. We shall see that a group of atoms covalently bonded
in a molecule may be attracted to similar molecules or to ions.

DIPOLES. When electrical charge is distributed asymmetrically in a
bond, a **polar bond** results, which is called a **dipole.** The uneven distribution of electric charge causes one end of the bond to have a positive
charge and the other end a negative charge.

A molecule composed of only two atoms is always a dipole if the
bond between the atoms is polar. Molecules containing *more* than two
atoms may have polar bonds, but still be nonpolar and therefore not
be dipoles. This occurs in the case of CO₂ and CCl₄. In both of these
instances the shape of the molecule is such that a symmetrical charge
distribution exists and the bond polarities counterbalance each other.
Water (H₂O), on the other hand, a polar molecule, is a dipole, in which
the hydrogen end is positive and the oxygen is negative (see Figure
3-3, page 38).

Dipoles, because of their polarity, are attracted to each other by
electrostatic forces.

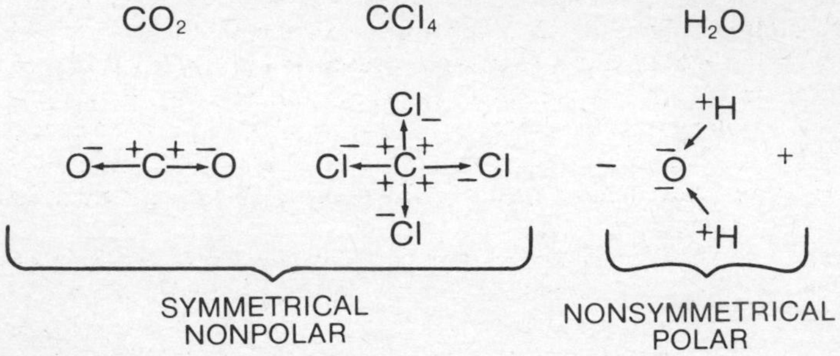

$$CO_2 \qquad CCl_4 \qquad H_2O$$

SYMMETRICAL
NONPOLAR

NONSYMMETRICAL
POLAR

Figure 3-3. Molecules with polar bonds. Molecules with polar bonds are not necessarily dipoles. In carbon dioxide and carbon tetrachloride, the polar bonds are symmetrically arranged, so that in each case the molecule as a whole is not a dipole. The water molecule is a dipole because of the nonsymmetrical arrangement of its polar bonds.

HYDROGEN BONDING. When hydrogen is covalently bonded to a highly electronegative atom of small atomic radius, it has only a small share of the electron pair that constitutes the bond. This results in a highly polar bond in which the hydrogen atom acts like a bare proton. The positive charge of the hydrogen atom allows it to be attracted to an atom of small radius and high electronegativity in a neighboring dipole. The resulting bond that is formed between the molecules is called a **hydrogen bond** (see Figure 3-4). Although a hydrogen bond is weak compared to the average covalent bond, it effectively increases the forces between the molecules and produces observable results, such as the high boiling point of water as compared with the lower boiling point of the chemically similar hydrogen sulfide (H_2S). Hydrogen bonding is important in compounds of hydrogen with fluorine, oxygen, or nitrogen.

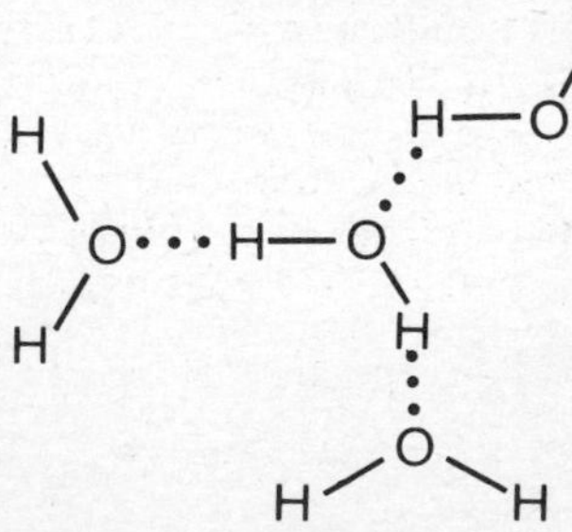

Figure 3-4. Hydrogen bonding. The oxygen atom of a water molecule can be attracted to a hydrogen atom in a neighboring molecule, forming a bond called a **hydrogen bond.** Hydrogen bonds (represented by broken lines in the diagram) are much weaker than covalent bonds, but do have significant effects on the physical properties of substances in which they occur.

VAN DER WAALS' FORCES. Even in nonpolar molecules, where dipoles and hydrogen bonding are absent, there are weak attractive forces between the molecules. Such forces are called **van der Waals' forces,** after the chemist who discovered them. These forces make it possible for small nonpolar molecules such as hydrogen (H_2), oxygen (O_2), and helium (He) to exist in liquid and solid phases under conditions of low temperature and high pressure (which bring the molecules relatively closer together).

Because van der Waals' forces are basically electrostatic, their effectiveness increases with a decrease in the distance between molecules and with an increase in the number of electrons in the molecules. For example, in a family of elements such as the inert gases, boiling points increase with increasing atomic number (and therefore with increasing molecular size and molecular mass), because more energy is needed to overcome the greater van der Waals' forces between atoms with larger numbers of electrons. A striking example of this is seen in the halogen family where, at room temperature, fluorine and chlorine (atomic numbers 9 and 17, respectively) are gases, bromine (atomic number 35) is a liquid, and iodine (atomic number 53) is a solid. The increase in van der Waals' forces with increasing molecular size also accounts for the higher boiling points of the heavier members of similar compounds, such as the alkane series of hydrocarbons.

Van der Waals' forces are due to momentary asymmetrical distributions of electrons, that is, to short-lived dipole attractions between molecules.

MOLECULE-ION ATTRACTION. When an ionic solid is placed in a solvent whose molecules are dipoles, such as water, liquid ammonia, or alcohol, there is an attraction between the positive and negative ions of the ionic compound and the oppositely charged poles of the solvent molecules. This molecule-ion attraction disrupts the crystal structure of the ionic compound, producing a solution of charged particles composed of ions linked to solvent molecules. For example, when salt (NaCl) is added to water, the negative ends of the water molecules are attracted to the sodium ions while the positive ends of the water molecules are attracted to the chlorine ions. With water as the dipole, this process is called **hydration,** and the positive and negative ions surrounded by water are called **hydrated ions.**

QUESTIONS

1. Which formula represents a nonpolar molecule?

(1) $H-\underset{\underset{\displaystyle H}{|}}{N}-H$ (2) $H-\!\!-\!\!-F$ (3) $F-\underset{\underset{\displaystyle F}{|}}{\overset{\overset{\displaystyle F}{|}}{C}}-F$ (4) $\underset{H}{\overset{O}{\diagup}}\underset{H}{\diagdown}$

2. The attraction between nonpolar molecules is called (1) van der Waals forces (2) hydrogen bonds (3) electrovalent forces (4) covalent bonds

3. Which is the formula of a nonpolar molecule containing nonpolar bonds?   (1) CO_2 (2) H_2 (3) NH_3 (4) H_2O

4. The forces of attraction which exist between hydrogen molecules in liquid hydrogen are due to   (1) ionic bonds   (2) hydrogen bonds (3) molecule-ion forces   (4) van der Waals forces

5. As the distance between two iodine molecules increases, the attraction of the van der Waals forces between them   (1) decreases (2) increases   (3) remains the same

6. In which noble gas are van der Waals forces the greatest?   (1) Ne (2) Xe   (3) Kr   (4) Ar

7. Which statement best explains why CCl_4 is a nonpolar molecule? (1) C and Cl are nonmetals.   (2) The C—Cl bonds are polar.   (3) CCl_4 is a liquid at STP.   (4) The CCl_4 molecule is symmetrical.

8. Hydrogen bonds are strongest between molecules of   (1) HF   (2) HCl (3) HBr   (4) HI

9. Dipole-dipole attractive forces are strongest between molecules of (1) H_2 (2) CH_4 (3) H_2O (4) CO_2

10. Which molecule is the most polar?   (1) H_2O (2) H_2S (3) H_2Se (4) H_2Te

11. Which atom will form the most polar bond with hydrogen?   (1) F (2) Cl   (3) Br   (4) I

12- 27. For questions 12-27, write the number of the bond or attractive force, chosen from the list below, that is most closely associated with that phrase.

(1) Ionic bond
(2) Network bonds
(3) Coordinate covalent bonds
(4) Hydrogen bonds
(5) Metallic bonds
(6) Van der Waals' forces
(7) Covalent bonds

12. Hold the iodine atoms together in a molecule of I_2

13. Hold the many molecules of I_2 together in a crystal of iodine

14. Account for the relatively high boiling and freezing points of pure water

15. Are illustrated by the compounds formed when fluorine reacts with active metals

16. Hold magnesium atoms in a crystal lattice

17. Mobile electrons in the crystal that permit electrical conductivity in the solid state

18. Responsible for the extremely high melting point of diamond (above 3 500° C)

19. Permit helium and hydrogen to exist in liquid or solid phases under conditions of low temperature and high pressure

20. Link a water molecule to a proton in the hydronium ion

21. Produce substances that are nonconductors in the solid phase and conductors in the liquid phase

22. Are weak enough to permit solid iodine to sublime readily upon heating

23. Cause the boiling point of hydrogen fluoride to be much higher than that of hydrogen chloride, hydrogen bromide, or hydrogen iodide
24. Link the atoms in a molecule of a diatomic gaseous element
25. Bond inert gas atoms in the liquid phase
26. Responsible for the formation of ice crystals
27. Account for the attraction between gas molecules in a non-ideal gas
28. The correct ranking of bonds in order of greatest to least bond strength is (1) covalent, van der Waals', hydrogen (2) van der Waals', hydrogen, covalent (3) covalent, hydrogen, van der Waals' (4) hydrogen, van der Waals', covalent
29. The attraction that exists between carbon dioxide molecules in solid carbon dioxide is due to (1) van der Waals forces (2) molecule-ion forces (3) ionic bonds (4) hydrogen bonds
30. Which of the following elements has the lowest normal boiling point? (1) Ne (2) He (3) Ar (4) Kr
31. Molecule-ion attractions are found in (1) Cu(s) (2) CO(g) (3) KBr(1) (4) NaCl(aq)
32. Which substance will conduct electricity in both the solid and liquid phases? (1) AgCl (2) Ag (3) H_2 (4) HCl

CHEMICAL FORMULAS

A **chemical formula** represents both quantitative and qualitative information regarding an element or compound. The expression H_2SO_4 tells us that one molecule of sulfuric acid contains 2 atoms of hydrogen, 1 atom of sulfur, and 4 atoms of oxygen, or that one mole contains atoms in those proportions. You can see, then, that a formula is a representation, in chemical symbols, of the composition of a substance.

MOLECULAR FORMULAS. In covalently bonded materials, the formula that represents the makeup of a molecule of the substance is called a **molecular formula.** This formula indicates the kind and number of atoms of each element needed to form the molecule.

EMPIRICAL FORMULAS. An empirical formula represents the simplest ratio in which atoms combine to form a compound. Such formulas are used to represent ionic compounds, which do not exist as molecules. For example, the formula $MgCl_2$ tells us that the atoms in magnesium chloride crystals are combined in the ratio of 1 magnesium ion to every 2 chlorine ions. There is no $MgCl_2$ molecule.

ORDER OF ELEMENTS IN FORMULAS. When writing formulas of ionic compounds, the symbol for the metallic ion or positive ion is generally written first. When writing formulas for compounds consisting of nonmetals, the symbol for the nonmetal with the lower electronegativity is written first. The name of the compound will end in -*ide*.

NOMENCLATURE

The chemical name of a compound usually indicates the chemical composition of the substance. The more common acids and bases are named in the table below.

TABLE 3–1. COMMON ACIDS AND BASES

Acids	Bases
HCl – hydrochloric	NaOH – sodium hydroxide
H_2SO_4 – sulfuric	NH_4OH – ammonium hydroxide
HNO_3 – nitric	$Ca(OH)_2$ – calcium hydroxide
H_3PO_4 – phosphoric	
H_2CO_3 – carbonic	
$HC_2H_3O_2$ (or CH_3COOH) – acetic	

The name of an acid can be converted to that of the corresponding salt by adding prefixes or suffixes. Table 3-2 (below) shows how the names of corresponding sodium salts are derived from the names of the acids of chlorine. The anion names of common salts are listed in Reference Table F.

TABLE 3–2. NAMES OF ACIDS AND THEIR CORRESPONDING SODIUM SALTS

Acid		Salt
HCl hydrochloric	drop *hydro;* change *ic* to *ide*	NaCl sodium chloride
HClO hypochlorous	change *ous* to *ite*	NaClO sodium hypochlorite
$HClO_2$ chlorous	change *ous* to *ite*	$NaClO_2$ sodium chlorite
$HClO_3$ chloric	change *ic* to *ate*	$NaClO_3$ sodium chlorate
$HClO_4$ perchloric	change *ic* to *ate*	$NaClO_4$ sodium perchlorate

MULTIPLE OXIDATION VALUES. In naming the salts of metals that have more than one oxidation number, the *Stock system* is used. In this system, Roman numerals indicate the oxidation number of the metal ion. For example, the iron oxide FeO is named iron (II) oxide to show that iron has an oxidation number of $+2$. Fe_2O_3 is named iron (III) oxide to show iron with a $+3$ oxidation number. In the same way, mercurous chloride, Hg_2Cl_2, is mercury (I) chloride, and mercuric chloride, $HgCl_2$, is mercury (II) chloride.

Nonmetal oxides and other such compounds are also named in accordance with the Stock system. For example, nitrous oxide, N_2O, is nitrogen (I) oxide; nitric oxide, NO, is nitrogen (II) oxide; nitrogen dioxide, NO_2, is nitrogen (IV) oxide.

QUESTIONS

1. The correct formula for aluminum sulfate is (1) Al_2S_3 (2) Al_3S_2 (3) $Al_2(SO_4)_3$ (4) $Al_3(SO_4)_2$

2. Which is an empirical formula? (1) N_2O_4 (2) P_4O_{10} (3) $C_6H_{12}O_6$ (4) Al_2O_3

3. The empirical formula of a compound is CH_2. The molecular formula of this compound could be (1) CH_1 (2) C_2H_2 (3) C_2H_4 (4) C_3H_3

4. Which compound has the same empirical and molecular formula? (1) H_2O_2 (2) NH_3 (3) C_2H_6 (4) Hg_2Cl_2

5. The correct formula for lead (IV) oxide is (1) PbO (2) Pb_2O (3) PbO_2 (4) Pb_2O_2

6. The correct formula for nickel (II) oxide is (1) NiO (2) Ni_2O (3) NiO_2 (4) Ni_3O_2

7. The correct formula for chlorous acid is (1) HClO (2) $HClO_2$ (3) $HClO_3$ (4) $HClO_4$

8. Using electronegativity values as a guide, which formula is correctly written? (1) F_6S (2) Cl_2O (3) Br_4C (4) I_3P

9. What is the correct formula for potassium hydride? (1) KH (2) KH_2 (3) KOH (4) $K(OH)_2$

10. What is the name of the calcium salt of sulfuric acid? (1) calcium thiosulfate (2) calcium sulfate (3) calcium sulfide (4) calcium sulfite

11. The correct name for the compound $NaClO_3$ is sodium (1) chloride (2) chlorate (3) perchlorate (4) chlorite

CHEMICAL EQUATIONS

A **chemical equation** represents changes in bonding and energy that occur during a chemical reaction. Qualitative and quantitative changes are recorded in a chemical equation.

A number, called a **coefficient,** is placed before formulas to indicate the ratios of moles (or molecules) involved in the reaction. The coefficient 1 is not written, but is understood. Equations are always balanced to conform to the laws of conservation of mass and charge. For example, the equation

$$2H_2 + O_2 \rightarrow 2H_2O + \text{heat}$$

gives the following information:

a. hydrogen + oxygen $\rightarrow$ water
b. 4 atoms + 2 atoms $\rightarrow$ 6 atoms
c. 2 molecules + 1 molecule $\rightarrow$ 2 molecules
d. 2 moles + 1 mole $\rightarrow$ 2 moles
e. energy is liberated (energy changes need not always be noted)

Notice that the law of conservation of mass is observed, as there are 6 atoms in both the reactants and in the product. It is not necessary, however, to have the same number of moles or molecules in reactants and products.

In a chemical equation it is often helpful to indicate the phase of the reactants and products, using the following symbols: (s) solid; (l) liquid; (g) gas; (aq) aqueous solution.

Using this notation, the equation above can be written

$$2H_2(g) + O_2(g) \rightarrow 2H_2O(l) + \text{heat}$$

QUESTIONS

1. **Given the unbalanced equation:**
$$Na + H_2O \rightarrow NaOH + H_2$$
What is the sum of the coefficients for the balanced equation? (1) 5 (2) 7 (3) 8 (4) 4

2. **When the equation** ____SiO_2 + ____C$\rightarrow$____SiC + ____CO **is correctly balanced using whole-number coefficients, the sum of all the coefficients is** (1) 6 (2) 7 (3) 8 (4) 9

3. **Which equation is correctly balanced?**
(1) $CaO + 2H_2O \rightarrow Ca(OH)_2$
(2) $NH_3 + 2O_2 \rightarrow HNO_3 + H_2O$
(3) $Ca(OH)_2 + 2H_3PO_4 \rightarrow Ca_3(PO_4)_2 + 3H_2O$
(4) $Cu + H_2SO_4 \rightarrow CuSO_4 + H_2O + SO_2$

4. **Given the unbalanced equation:**
$$(NH_4)_3PO_4 + Ba(NO_3)_2 \rightarrow Ba_3(PO_4)_2 + NH_4NO_3$$
What is the coefficient in front of the NH_4NO_3 when the equation is completely balanced with the smallest whole-number coefficients?
(1) 6 (2) 2 (3) 3 (4) 4

5. **In the balanced equation $2Na + 2H_2O \rightarrow H_2 + 2X$, the compound represented by X is** (1) Na_2O (2) Na_2O_2 (3) $NaOH$ (4) NaH

UNIT 4   THE PERIODIC TABLE

DEVELOPMENT OF THE PERIODIC TABLE

Since more than 100 elements are known, which vary greatly in their physical and chemical properties as well as in the characteristics of their compounds, the need for a method of classification of the elements is obvious.

The modern Periodic Table of the Elements, an outgrowth of many older arrangements, takes into account more recent discoveries about the elements and their properties. One of the earlier major insights was provided by the Russian chemist Mendeleev, who observed that similar chemical and physical properties appear at regular intervals when the elements are listed in order of increasing atomic weight. Today it is recognized, as a result of X-ray studies done by Moseley, an English physicist, that the regularity, or periodicity, of the properties of the elements is a function of the atomic number, not of the atomic weight. The modern Periodic Law states: *The properties of the elements are periodic functions of their atomic numbers.* The structure of the atom, which is related to atomic number, determines its properties.

PROPERTIES OF THE ELEMENTS IN THE PERIODIC TABLE

ARRANGEMENT OF THE TABLE. The Periodic Table is an arrangement of the elements, from left to right, in order of increasing atomic number.

The horizontal rows of the table are called **periods** or **rows.** The number of each period indicates the principal energy level in which the valence electrons of that period's elements are found. For example, the elements in Period 3 have their valence electrons in the third principal energy level ($n=3$). In each period, the number of valence electrons increases from left to right, and the properties of the elements change systematically through a period.

The vertical columns of the Periodic Table are called **groups** or **families.** The traditional designation for each group has been a combination of a Roman numeral and the letter A or B, such as IA or IIB. In this book, these designations are presented along with a new form which numbers the groups from 1 to 18. The elements in a group exhibit similar or related properties because the outermost shell of an atom of each element contains the same number and arrangement of s and p (valence) electrons.

Columns 1 and 2 (IA and IIA), designated as the s-block, contain elements in which the s orbitals are being filled with electrons.

Columns 3 through 11, designated as the d-block, contain elements in which the d-orbitals of the preceding principal energy level are being filled. These d-block elements include the transition elements. A transition element is an element whose atom has an incomplete d subshell or which gives rise to a cation or cations with incomplete d subshells.

Columns 13 through 18 (IIIA through VIIA and O), designated as the p-block, contain elements in which p orbitals are being filled.

At the bottom of the table are two series, the lanthanoid and actinoid series, which make up the f-block.

RADII OF ATOMS.   The **atomic radius** is generally considered to be one-half the distance between adjacent nuclei. Depending on the type of bonding, several conditions can be described. In all cases there are some factors that remain constant.

   1. **Trends in periods.** Atomic radii are periodic functions of the elements. Although radii can be measured in different ways, the trend within a period remains the same. The radius generally decreases from left to right within any period of the table. Within a period the number of kernel electrons remains constant while the number of protons increases from left to right. This increase in positive charge results in a greater attraction for the valence electrons and hence a smaller radius.

   2. **Trends in groups.** In any given group each successive member has more kernel electrons than the preceding member of the group. These electrons shield the nucleus from the valence electrons. In addition, the valence electrons are more energetic than those of the preceding period. Thus, the atomic radius increases as the atomic number increases.

TYPES OF ATOMIC RADII.   Three types of atomic radii are recognized.

   1. **Covalent radius.** The covalent radius is defined as the effective distance from the center of the nucleus to the outer valence shell of that atom in a covalent or coordinate covalent bond.

   2. **Van der Waals radius.** Atoms such as those of the noble gases do not normally form covalent bonds with other atoms. Van der Waals radii are a measure of the radii of atoms that do not form covalent bonds and the radii of other atoms when they are not bonded to a neighboring atom. The **van der Waals radius** is defined as half the closest distance between an atom and another atom with which it does not form a bond.

   3. **Atomic radius in metals.** The atomic radius of a metal is defined as half the distance between adjacent nuclei in a crystalline metal.

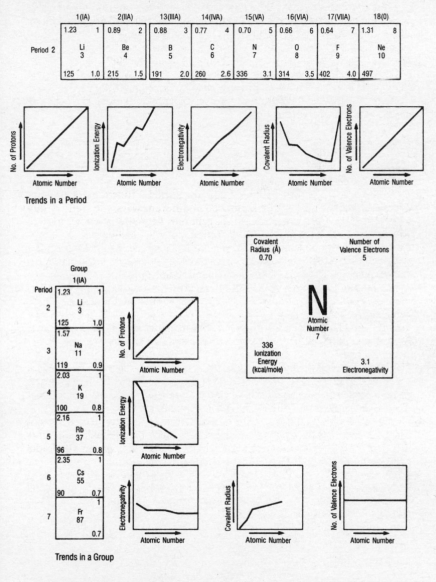

Figure 4-1. Trends of change in a period and in a group of the Periodic Table.

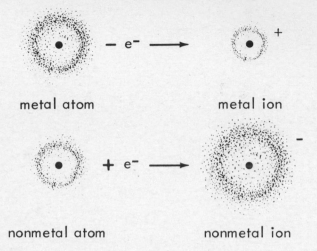

metal atom   metal ion

nonmetal atom   nonmetal ion

Figure 4-2. When a metallic atom loses an electron to become a positive ion, the particle decreases in size. When a nonmetallic atom gains an electron to become a negative ion, the particle increases in size.

IONIC RADIUS. Ions differ in size from their parent atoms. A loss or gain of electrons by an atom will cause a change in the size of the resulting ion.

Metals lose electrons in chemical reactions. The electron loss causes a reduction in the size of the resulting positive ion with respect to its parent atom. Hence, ionic radii of metals are smaller than their corresponding atomic radii.

With nonmetals, the opposite effect is observed. Nonmetallic atoms react chemically by gaining electrons. As more electrons are added, the size of the resulting negative particle increases. Thus, the ionic radii of nonmetals are larger than their corresponding atomic radii.

Atomic and ionic radii are usually measured in **Angstrom units** ($\overset{\circ}{A}$). ($1\overset{\circ}{A} = 10^{-8}$ cm.) Changes in atomic size due to ionization are shown in Figure 4-2.

METALS. Of the 106 known elements, roughly two-thirds of them are metals. Metals are located to the left of the dark diagonal line on the Periodic Table. The most metallic metals are found in the lower left corner of the table. In the atomic state metals are pictured as though their kernels form positive ions that are surrounded by the loosely held valence electrons. Metallic properties include the following:

   1. Have relatively low ionization energies.

   2. Have low electronegativity values.

   3. Tend to lose electrons to form positive ions with radii smaller than the atoms.

4. Are solids at room temperature, with the exception of mercury.

5. Are malleable and ductile.

6. Are good conductors of heat and electricity.

7. Have metallic luster.

NONMETALS. Nonmetals are found on the right side of the Periodic Table. Nonmetallic properties, most pronounced in those elements appearing in the upper right portion of the table, include the following:

1. Have relatively high ionization energies and high electron affinities.

2. Have high electronegativities.

3. Tend to gain electrons when they react with metals, and share electrons when they combine chemically with other nonmetals.

4. Are usually gases, molecular solids, or network solids at room temperature; bromine, an exception, is a volatile liquid at room temperature.

5. Are brittle in the solid phase.

6. Are poor conductors of heat and electricity.

7. Lack metallic luster.

SEMI-METALS (METALLOIDS). There is a natural change in the character of the elements as they are considered across any period of the Periodic Table. As the number of valence electrons changes from one to eight, the properties of the elements change from metallic to nonmetallic, ending with the stable octet of a noble gas. Between the metals and nonmetals are elements that have some properties of both metals and nonmetals. These elements are called **semi-metals**, or **metalloids**. In the Periodic Table used in this book, a darkened line divides the metals from the nonmetals. The semi-metals are found adjacent to this line. Boron, silicon, arsenic, and tellurium are examples of semi-metals.

QUESTIONS

1. The elements in the present Periodic Table are arranged according to their (1) atomic numbers (2) atomic masses (3) mass numbers (4) oxidation states

2. The majority of the elements in the Periodic Table are (1) metals (2) nonmetals (3) metalloids (4) noble gases

3. Elements in Period 3 are alike in that they all have the same number of (1) protons (2) neutrons (3) electrons in the valence shell (4) occupied principal energy levels

4. The diagram below represents two adjacent atoms of sulfur in an S_8 molecule. Distance X is closest to (1) 0.51 Å (2) 1.02 Å (3) 1.53 Å (4) 2.08 Å

5. Which electron configuration represents the atom in Period 2 with the largest covalent atomic radius? (1) $1s^22s^1$ (2) $1s^22s^2$ (3) $1s^22s^22p^1$ (4) $1s^22s^22p^2$

6. In general, the elements with *lowest* ionization energies would be classified as (1) halogens (2) noble gases (3) metals (4) nonmetals

7. The element in Period 3 that has the highest ionization energy is (1) a noble gas (2) a halogen (3) an alkali metal (4) an alkaline earth metal

8. The radius of a Na^+ *ion* would most likely be (1) 0.97 Å (2) 1.54 Å (3) 2.00 Å (4) 2.51 Å

9. A neutral oxygen atom (O) differs from an ion of oxygen (O^{2-}) in that the atom has (1) more electrons (2) fewer electrons (3) more protons (4) fewer protons

10. Magnesium has a smaller atomic radius than sodium because the magnesium atom has more (1) valence electrons (2) energy levels (3) protons (4) neutrons

11. When an atom loses an electron, its radius generally (1) decreases (2) increases (3) remains the same

12. When a fluorine atom becomes an ion, it will (1) gain an electron and decrease in size (2) gain an electron and increase in size (3) lose an electron and decrease in size (4) lose an electron and increase in size

13. Which electronegativity value is the most probable for a metalloid? (1) 1.0 (2) 2.0 (3) 3.0 (4) 4.0

14. An element that has both a high ionization energy and a high electronegativity is most likely a (1) metal (2) nonmetal (3) metalloid (4) noble gas

15. The atoms of the most active nonmetals have (1) small atomic radii and high ionization energies (2) small atomic radii and low ionization energies (3) large atomic radii and low ionization energies (4) large atomic radii and high ionization energies

16. Which is most characteristic of metals with very low ionization energies? (1) they are very reactive (2) they have small atomic radii (3) they form covalent bonds (4) they have high electronegativities

17. Which property would be generally associated with a very active metal? (1) large ionization energy (2) large atomic radius (3) tendency to form unstable compounds (4) tendency to form covalent compounds

18. A nonmetal which exists in the liquid phase at room temperature is (1) aluminum (2) mercury (3) hydrogen (4) bromine

19. As one proceeds from left to right across Period 3 of the Periodic Table, there is a decrease in (1) ionization energy (2) electronegativity (3) metallic characteristics (4) valence electrons

20. As one reads from left to right across Period 2, ionization energy generally (1) decreases, and atomic size decreases (2) decreases, and atomic size increases (3) increases, and atomic size increases (4) increases, and atomic size decreases

21. As one proceeds from left to right across Period 3, the number of electrons in the $2p$ subshell   (1) decreases   (2) increases   (3) remains the same

22. $1s^2 2s^2 2p^6 3s^2 3p^4$ is the electronic configuration of a neutral atom. This element belongs in Period   (1) 2   (2) 3   (3) 4   (4) 6

23. Which element is *not* a metalloid?   (1) antimony   (2) lead (3) tellurium   (4) arsenic

24. Which is an example of a metalloid?   (1) sodium   (2) strontium (3) silicon   (4) sulfur

25. Which element in Period 3 has both metallic and nonmetallic properties?   (1) Na   (2) Mg   (3) Si   (4) Ar

CHEMISTRY OF A GROUP

The elements in any group, or family, of the Periodic Table have related chemical properties. Inspection of a group shows that all of its members have the same number of valence electrons, and it is this similarity that accounts for the similarity in chemical properties.

Similarity in chemical properties may be illustrated by inspecting the types of compounds formed by the members of a group. The elements in Group 1(IA), for example, form chlorides that have the general formula MCl, where M represents any member of the group; that is, LiCl, NaCl, KCl, etc. By way of contrast, the elements in Group 2(IIA), form chlorides that have the general formula MCl_2 ($BeCl_2$, $MgCl_2$, $CaCl_2$, etc.).

As a general rule, the properties of the members of a group tend to change systematically as the atomic number of an element varies. In nontransition groups, the following changes occur as the atomic number increases:

1. The radius of an atom increases (see the discussion of atomic radii, pages 46-48).

2. The ionization energy generally decreases because of the larger distance between the nucleus and the valence electrons. This effect is enhanced by the fact that a larger kernel, containing more occupied energy levels, provides a shield that diminishes the attraction between the positive nucleus and the valence electrons.

It is important to keep in mind, however, that anomalies do occur in the properties of elements within a group. These exceptions to the rule frequently occur in Period 2 because of the small distance between the nucleus and the valence electrons, and because of the minimal shielding effect provided by the two electrons in the only filled principal energy level. For example, boron, the first member of Group 3(IIIA), does not form a $+3$ ion, so do the other members of that group.

GROUPS 1(IA) AND 2(IIA).   The elements of Group 1(IA), the **alkali metals**, and of Group 2(IIA), the **alkaline earth metals**, show typical metallic characteristics. Because of their high reactivity (the valence electrons are easily lost in a chemical change), these elements can be found in nature in compounds only. They usually can be reduced to their free states by the electrolysis of their compounds. The elements of both groups have relatively low ionization energies and low electronegativity values. They readily form ionic compounds, which are quite stable, and cannot achieve an inert gas configuration by covalent bonding.

In general, reactivity in both alkali and alkaline earth groups tends to increase with higher atomic numbers. In the same period, however, each Group 1(IA) member is more reactive than the adjacent Group 2(IIA) member; for example, in Period 3, Na is more reactive than its neighbor, Mg. This increased reactivity is due to the larger atomic sizes of elements in 1(IA) relative to Group 2(IIA), and the higher nuclear charges in Group 2(IIA).

GROUP 15(VA). The members of Group 15(VA), exhibit changes in properties from typical nonmetals (nitrogen and phosphorus), through metalloids (arsenic and antimony), to bismuth, which is metallic both in its properties and appearance. The progression is from nonmetal to metal with increasing atomic number. Generally, the reactivity of nonmetals in the same group decreases with increasing atomic number. This is not true with nitrogen and phosphorus, however. Nitrogen, a gas at room temperature, owes its relative stability to the fact that it is a **diatomic molecule,** with a **triple bond** between the two nitrogen atoms. The triple bond of diatomic nitrogen, $N \equiv N$, indicates that three pairs of electrons are being shared, and a large amount of energy is required to break a triple bond. Nitrogen forms important compounds, many of which, e.g., proteins, are essential to all living things. These compounds are relatively stable. The unstable compounds of nitrogen are used as explosives.

Phosphorus is also essential to life, and is found in DNA, RNA, bones, and teeth. At room temperature, phosphorus is in the solid state and is more reactive than nitrogen. Phorphorus exists as a **tetratomic molecule,** P_4, at room temperature. Because phosphorus has a larger atomic size, its bonding differs from that of nitrogen.

GROUP 16(VIA). The elements in Group 16(VIA) are similar to those in Group 15(VA) in that they show a progression from nonmetal to metal with increasing atomic number. Oxygen and sulfur, the first two members of 16(VIA), are typical nonmetals; selenium and tellurium are metalloids; and the last member, polonium, is a metal. Oxygen is the only element in this group that is a diatomic gas at room temperature; the others are in the solid state. Elemental oxygen is very active and readily forms compounds with most other elements. In combination with other elements, oxygen shows a negative oxidation state because of its high electronegativity. An exception occurs when oxygen combines with fluorine, the latter being more electronegative. Despite its high reactivity, oxygen is also found in the free state because it is continuously generated by plants during photosynthesis.

Since sulfur has a higher atomic number than oxygen, it is less reactive than oxygen, and exists abundantly in the free state. When combined with other elements, sulfur exhibits both negative and positive oxidation states, depending on the electronegativity of the element with which it combines.

Selenium and tellurium, both rare elements, usually show positive oxidation states in the compounds they form. With hydrogen, they exhibit a negative oxidation state. Polonium, a decay product of radioactive uranium, is extremely rare because of its radioactivity and short half-life. It is an alpha emitter, and gives rise to a stable isotope of lead (see discussion of radioactivity in Unit 2, pages 29-31).

GROUP 17(VIIA). Group 17(VIIA), the **halogen group**, contains elements that are typical nonmetals. Although all of the elements in this group are nonmetals, metallic character increases with higher atomic numbers.

All of the elements in 17(VIIA) have relatively high electronegativities, fluorine being the most electronegative. In compounds, fluorine can have only a negative oxidation state. The other elements of Group 17(VIIA) exhibit positive oxidation states when they form compounds with elements that are more electronegative than themselves. The ease with which the halogens form positive oxidation states increases with increasing atomic number. Such is the case because electronegativity values decrease as atomic numbers increase in Group 17(VIIA).

When the halogens exist in the free state, as diatomic molecules, their individual forms vary with atomic number. At room temperatures, fluorine and chlorine, having the lowest atomic numbers in the group, are gases; bromine is a liquid; and iodine and astatine, having the highest atomic numbers, are solids. These variations in physical form are the result of the increasing magnitude of the van der Waals' forces, which are stronger between larger molecules (see Unit 3, page 39, for a discussion of van der Waals' forces).

The halogens, because they are highly reactive, occur in nature in compounds only. The elements are usually prepared from their hydrogen **halides** (HF, HCl, HBr, HI, HAt) by removing an electron from the negative halide ion. With fluorine this is not possible, however. Because fluorine is the most electronegative element, there is no oxidizing agent available that can remove an electron from the fluorine ion. Diatomic fluorine can be prepared only by the electrolysis of its fused compounds. Chlorine, bromine, and iodine, on the other hand, can be prepared by chemical means.

GROUP 18(O). The elements in Group 18(O) all exist as **monatomic** gas molecules. The electron configuration of the atoms of these elements are very stable, because the outermost shell of each of them is complete.

The elements of Group 18(O) are variously referred to as the **rare gases**, **noble gases**, and **inert gases**. In a strict sense, the term "inert" is no longer applicable; in recent years, chemists have been able to synthesize compounds of krypton, xenon, and radon with the highly electronegative elements fluorine and oxygen. Compounds of the ligher noble gases — helium, neon, and argon — have not been prepared.

QUESTIONS

1. The most active metals are in Group   (1) 1(IA)   (2) 15(VA)
   (3) 13(IIIA)   (4) 17(VIIA)

2. The elements known as the alkali metals are found in Group
   (1) 1(IA)   (2) 2(IIA)   (3) 13(IIIA)   (4) 17(VIIA)

3. What is the total number of electrons found in the valence shell of an alkaline earth element in the ground state?   (1) 1   (2) 2   (3) 3 (4) 4

4. As the elements in Group 2(IIA) are considered from top to bottom on the Periodic Table, the number of electrons in the 2s subshell
   (1) decreases   (2) increases   (3) remains the same

5. Which group contains atoms that form +1 ions having an inert gas configuration?   (1) 1(IA)   (2) 11(IB)   (3) 17(VIIA)   (4) 7(VIIB)

6. Which of the Group 16(VIA) elements listed below has the greatest nuclear charge?   (1) F   (2) Cl   (3) Br   (4) I

7. Which element is most likely to form a compound with krypton?   (1) fluorine   (2) chlorine   (3) bromine   (4) iodine

8. Which group in the Periodic Table contains solid, liquid, and gaseous elements at room temperature?   (1) 18(O)   (2) 2(IIA)
   (3) 16(VIA)   (4) 17(VIIA)

9. Which represents the correct order of activity for the Group 17(VIIA) elements? (> means greater than.)
   (1) bromine > iodine > fluorine > chlorine
   (2) fluorine > chlorine > bromine > iodine
   (3) iodine > bromine > chlorine > fluorine
   (4) fluorine > bromine > chlorine > iodine

10. If the elements are considered from top to bottom in Group 16(VIA), the number of electrons in the outermost shell will
    (1) decrease   (2) increase   (3) remain the same

11. Which group contains an element that is a liquid at room temperature?   (1) 18(O)   (20) 2(IIA)   (3) 11(IB)   (4) 12(IIB)

12. Which element exists as a monatomic molecule at STP?
    (1) hydrogen   (2) nitrogen   (3) argon   (4) chlorine

13. All elements whose atoms in the ground state have a total of 5 electrons in their outermost p sublevel are called   (1) noble gases
    (2) metalloids   (3) halogens   (4) alkaline earth metals

14. In which Group do the elements usually form oxides which have the general formula M_2O_3?   (1) 1(IA)   (2) 2(IIA)   (3) 13(IIIA)
    (4) 14(IVA)

15. The oxide of metal X has the formula XO. Which group in the Periodic Table contains metal X?   (1) 1(IA)   (2) 2(IIA)   (3) 13(IIIA)   (4) 17(VIIA)

16. Which metal will form a compound with the general formula M_2CO_3 when it combines with a carbonate ion?   (1) beryllium   (2) aluminum   (3) calcium   (4) lithium

17. As the elements are considered from top to bottom in Group 15(VA) of the Periodic Table, the ionization energy   (1) decreases   (2) increases   (3) remains the same

18. Which group contains an element that has diatomic molecules with triple covalent bonds?   (1) 15(VA)   (2) 16(VIA)   (3) 7(VIIB)   (4) 18(O)

19. In which group do all the elements have the same number of electrons in the outermost principal energy level?   (1) 16(VIB)   (2) 9(VIII)   (3) 18(O)   (4) 14(IVA)

20. Which group contains two semi-metals (metalloids)?   (1) 2(IIA)   (2) 12(IIB)   (3) 13(IIIA)   (4) 17(VIIA)

21. Which element in Group 16(VIA) has the greatest tendency to gain electrons?   (1) Te   (2) Se   (3) S   (4) O

22. Which element forms a -2 ion with the largest radius?   (1) oxygen   (2) sulfur   (3) selenium   (4) tellurium

23. As the elements of Group 15(VA) are considered in order of increasing atomic radius, their tendency to lose electrons   (1) decreases   (2) increases   (3) remains the same

24. An atom in the ground state with eight valence electrons would most likely be classified as   (1) an active metal   (2) an inactive metal   (3) a noble gas   (4) a halogen

25. When atoms of the elements of Group 18(O) are compared in order from top to bottom, the attractions between the atoms of each successive element   (1) increase and the boiling point decreases   (2) decrease and the boiling point increases   (3) increases and the boiling point increases   (4) decrease and the boiling point decreases

26. Which element in Group 15(VA) is the most metallic?   (1) N   (2) P   (3) Bi   (4) As

CHEMISTRY OF A PERIOD.   As we study the elements of a period, from left to right, certain generalizations can be made about the properties of the elements.

1. The atomic number increases.

2. The atomic radius generally decreases.

3. The ionization energy generally increases.

4. There is generally a progression from very active metals, to less active metals, to semi-metals (metalloids), to moderately active nonmetals, to very active nonmetals, to an inert gas.

5. There is a transition from positive to negative oxidation states; elements near the center of the period may show both.

QUESTIONS

1. In the ground state, an atom of which element in Period 3 has the most loosely bound electron?   (1) Si   (2) Na   (3) S   (4) Ar

2. Which element in Period 2 would react with hydrogen to form an ionic hydride?   (1) carbon   (2) lithium   (3) nitrogen   (4) fluorine

3. Which period contains elements that are all gases at STP?   (1) 1   (2) 2   (3) 3   (4) 4

4. As one goes from lithium to fluorine in Period 2 of the Periodic Table, the atomic radius of the elements   (1) decreases   (2) increases   (3) remains the same

5. What is the total number of elements in Period 2 that are gases at room temperature and standard pressure?   (1) 1   (2) 2   (3) 3   (4) 4

6. Considered in succession, the elements in Period 2 of the Periodic Table show a decrease in atomic radius with increasing atomic number. This may best be explained by the fact that the   (1) nuclear charge increases   (2) number of principal energy levels increases   (3) number of neutrons decreases   (4) number of protons decreases

7. Which period contains more than one element that forms diatomic molecules of that element?   (1) 1   (2) 2   (3) 3   (4) 4

8. In a given period of the Periodic Table, the element with the lowest first ionization energy is always   (1) an alkaline earth metal   (2) an alkali metal   (3) a halogen   (4) an inert gas

9. All elements in Period 3 have   (1) an atomic number of 3   (2) 3 valence electrons   (3) 3 occupied principal energy levels   (4) an oxidation number of +3

10. Which element in Period 3 is the most active nonmetal?   (1) sodium   (2) magnesium   (3) chlorine   (4) argon

11. Which represents the electron configuration of a metalloid in the ground state?   (1) 2—3   (2) 2—5   (3) 2—8—5   (4) 2—8—6

12. Which element in Period 3 of the Periodic Table will only form chlorides with the general formula XCl_2?   (1) Mg   (2) Na   (3) Ar   (4) Si

13. The atomic number of a semi-metal (metalloid) in Period 4 is   (1) 19   (2) 26   (3) 33   (4) 36

14-18.   For questions 14 through 18, write the number of the word or expression that best completes the statement or answers the question. Base your answers on the partial Periodic Table shown below.

1	2	3	14	15	16	17	18
IA	IIA	IIIA	IVA	VA	VIA	VIIA	O

2	A				E			
3		J		D		M		R
4			L				G	

14. Which two elements would be least likely to react to form a compound? (1) A and G   (2) D and G   (3) J and M   (4) L and R

15. Which two elements would form the most highly ionic compound? (1) A and G   (2) D and M   (3) J and G   (4) L and M

16. What would be the probable formula for a compound formed from elements L and M?   (1) L_1M_1 (2) LM_2 (3) L_2M_3 (4) L_3M_2

17. Which element could form a compound that is normally called a hydride?   (1) A   (2) E   (3) M   (4) G

18. Which element has the lowest melting point?   (1) R   (2) J   (3) G   (4) D

TRANSITION ELEMENTS.   The transition elements are found in the center of periods 4, 5, and 6 of the Periodic Table. If Period 7 were complete, another series of transition elements would exist from atomic number 103 through atomic number 111. In the older form of the Periodic Table, the transition elements are shown as members of "B" families, while the new form shows them as occupying groups 3 to 11. The transition elements owe their position and name to their electron structure. Each transition series represents a series of elements in which the d orbitals of the next to the outermost principal energy level are being filled. In Period 4, scandium to copper make up a series of metals in which the $3d$ orbitals are being filled. The transition elements are typically hard solids with high melting points, with the notable exception of mercury, which is liquid at room temperature. Transition elements are characterized by:

1. **Multiple oxidation states.** When the transition elements react, they may use electrons from both s and d sublevels. The ionization energies of the d orbital electrons have values close to those of their s electrons, and different numbers of electrons can be removed, resulting in different oxidation states. In general, the transition elements are far less reactive than the preceding members of Columns 1 or 2 (IA or IIA).

2. **Colored ions.** The transition elements have several empty or half-filled d orbitals of close energy content. White light shining on these elements can excite electrons to slightly higher orbitals by the absorption of energy with the frequency of colors we can see when the electrons return to their ground state.

QUESTIONS

1. An element in which electrons from more than one energy level may be involved in bond formation is   (1) potassium   (2) calcium   (3) copper   (4) zinc

2. Which element can form more than one binary compound with chlorine?   (1) K   (2) Ca   (3) Fe   (4) Zn

3. A pure compound is blue in color. It is most likely a compound of   (1) sodium   (2) lithium   (3) calcium   (4) copper

4. Which solution contains colored ions?   (1) KCl (aq)   (2) HCl (aq)
   (3) NiCl$_2$(aq)   (4) LiCl(aq)

5. Which is the electron configuration of a transition element in the ground
   state?
   (1) $1s^2 2s^2 2p^6 3s^2 3p^6$
   (2) $1s^2 2s^2 2p^6 3s^2 3p^6 4s^2$
   (3) $1s^2 2s^2 2p^6 3s^2 3p^6 4s^2 3d^{10}$
   (4) $1s^2 2s^2 2p^6 3s^2 3p^6 4s^2 3d^{10} 4p^6$

6. The water solution of a compound is bright yellow. The compound could
   be   (1) KNO$_3$ (2) K$_2$CrO$_4$ (3) KOH   (4) K$_3$PO$_4$

7. Which represents a transition element?   (1) He   (2) Se   (3) Be   (4) Fe

UNIT 5 THE MATHEMATICS OF CHEMISTRY

CONCEPT OF THE MOLE

GRAM ATOMIC MASS. As explained on page 20, a **gram atomic mass** of an element is that quantity of an element whose mass in grams is numerically equal to its atomic mass. For example, the atomic mass of carbon (as given in the Periodic Table) is 12.01115. (This is the value for the mixture of isotopes found in a natural sample of carbon.) Therefore, 12.01115 grams of carbon is one gram atomic mass of carbon. A gram atomic mass of any element contains the same number of atoms. This number, 6.02×10^{23}, is called **Avogadro's number.**

THE MOLE. A **mole** is defined as Avogadro's number of particles. One mole is 6.02×10^{23} particles, which can be atoms, molecules, ions, electrons, or any other kind. The mole is a pure number, that is, without any associated units, and is designated by the symbol N. A mole of O_2 molecules (oxygen gas) is 6.02×10^{23} O_2 molecules, or N molecules. However, this quantity of oxygen gas contains 2 moles of oxygen *atoms*.

RELATIONSHIP BETWEEN ONE MOLE AND ONE GRAM ATOMIC MASS. We have stated that a gram atomic mass of an element contains N atoms. One mole of an element is also N atoms. Therefore one mole of an element is the same quantity as one gram atomic mass of that element. The mass of one mole in grams is numerically the same as the atomic mass of the element. Thus one mole of carbon has a mass of 12.01115 grams.

MOLECULAR (FORMULA) MASS. The **molecular (formula) mass** of a compound is the sum of the atomic masses of all the atoms in one molecule (or one formula unit) of the compound. The term **formula mass** is preferred for ionic compounds and network solids, which do not have discrete molecules.

SAMPLE PROBLEM

What is the molecular (formula) mass of Na_2CO_3?

Solution: Determine the atomic mass of each element in the formula by consulting the Periodic Table.

$$\text{atomic mass of Na} = 23 \text{ (amu)}$$
$$\text{atomic mass of C} = 12$$
$$\text{atomic mass of O} = 16$$

Find the total of the masses of all atoms in the formula.

Na:	2 X 23	=	46
C:	1 X 12	=	12
O:	3 X 16	=	48
Total:			**106** (amu)

GRAM MOLECULAR (GRAM FORMULA) MASS. A gram molecular (gram formula) mass of a compound is that quantity of the compound whose mass in grams equals its molecular (formula) mass. As in the case of the gram atomic mass, a gram molecular mass of a compound is equal to one mole.

SAMPLE PROBLEM

What is the mass in grams of one mole of water?

Solution: Calculate the molecular mass of water, H_2O.

H:	2 X 1	=	2
O:	1 X 16	=	16
Total:			**18** (amu)

The mass in grams of one mole of any substance is numerically equal to its molecular mass. Therefore, the mass of one mole of water is **18 grams.**

MOLE VOLUME OF A GAS. **Avogadro's law** states that equal volumes of gases at the same temperature and pressure contain equal numbers of molecules. The volume of a gas at STP that contains exactly one mole is called the **mole volume.** By Avogadro's law, the mole volume is the same for all gases. It has been determined experimentally that the mole volume of gases is 22.4 liters. Since one mole of any substance is a gram molecular mass, 22.4 liters of any gas at STP is one gram molecular mass. The mole volume is therefore also called the **gram molecular volume** of gases.

SAMPLE PROBLEM

What is the mass of 22.4 liters of CO_2 at S T P ?

Solution:

The molecular mass of CO_2 = $12 + (2 \times 16) = 44$ (amu)

The mass of one mole of CO_2 is therefore 44 grams.

Since 22.4 liters of any gas at STP is one mole of the gas, the mass of 22.4 liters of CO_2 is **44 grams.**

FINDING THE NUMBER OF MOLES IN A GIVEN QUANTITY.
In the case of a gas, the number of moles in a given volume at S T P can be found by dividing the volume in liters by 22.4. (If the volume is measured under other conditions, the volume is first corrected to S T P.) In the case of a liquid or solid, the number of moles in a given quantity can be found by dividing the mass of the sample in grams by its molecular mass.

SAMPLE PROBLEM

How many moles are present in 180 grams of NaOH?

Solution: Calculate the molecular mass of NaOH.

Na: 1×23 =   23
O: 1×16 =   16
H: 1×1 =   1
Total: **40** (amu)

One mole of NaOH therefore has a mass of 40 grams.

Number of moles in 180 grams $= \dfrac{180 \text{ grams}}{40 \text{ grams/mole}} = 4.5$ moles

---

QUESTIONS

1. **One mole of an ideal gas occupies a volume of 22.4 liters at   (1) 273 K and 760 torr   (2) 273 K and 0 torr   (3) 760° C and 273 torr   (4) 0° C and 273 torr**

2. **What is the volume, in liters, of 16.0 grams of O_2 at STP?   (1) 5.60 (2) 8.00   (3) 11.2   (4) 16.0**

3. What is the gram atomic mass of element chlorine?
   (1) 17g (2) 35g (3) 52g (4) 80g

4. How many moles of an ideal gas will occupy 44.8 liters at STP?
   (1) 1.0 (2) 2.0 (3) 22.4 (4) 44.8

5. Which sample of hydrogen gas at STP would occupy the largest
   volume? (1) 2 moles (2) 2 grams (3) 2 liters (4) 2×10^{23} molecules

6. The total number of moles represented by 20 grams of $CaCO_3$ is (1) 1
   (2) 2 (3) 0.1 (4) 0.2

7. A 38-gram sample of F_2 contains approximately the same number of
   molecules as (1) 14 g of N_2 (2) 2.0 g of H_2 (3) 36 g of H_2O (4) 40 g of
   Ne

8. The sample of oxygen at STP which represents the greatest mass is
   one (1) mole (2) gram (3) molecule (4) liter

9. The number of moles in 2.16 grams of silver is (1) 2.00×10^{-2}
   (2) 4.59×10^{-2} (3) 2.00×10^2 (4) 2.33×10^2

10. The mass of two moles of sulfuric acid expressed in grams, is equal to

    (1) $\dfrac{98}{2}$ (2) 2(98)   (3) $\dfrac{6.02 \times 10^{23}}{2}$ (4) $2(6.02 \times 10^{23})$

11. Gas A has twice as much mass as gas B. Compared to one mole of
    gas A, one mole of gas B contains (1) one-half as many molecules
    (2) the same number of molecules (3) twice as many molecules
    (4) 22.4 times as many molecules

12. What is the ratio by mass of hydrogen to oxygen in H_2O? (1) 1 : 2
    (2) 2 : 1 (3) 1 : 8 (4) 8 : 1

13. How many molecules are contained in 0.20 mole of N_2 at STP?
    (1) 1.2×10^{23} (2) 2.4×10^{23} (3) 3.0×10^{23} (4) 6.0×10^{23}

STOICHIOMETRY

Stoichiometry is the study of the **quantitative** relationships that are
implied by chemical formulas and chemical equations. Using stoichio-
metric methods, we can determine the proportions in which elements
combine to form substances. We will be concerned with two basic
kinds of chemical problems—those involving formulas and those involving equations. In solving these problems, the mole concept and
mole relationships are often useful.

PROBLEMS INVOLVING FORMULAS

1. Determining percentage composition. The **percentage composition**
of a compound is its composition in terms of the percentage of each
component present with respect to the whole.

SAMPLE PROBLEM

What is the percentage composition by mass of the elements in sodium sulfate, Na_2SO_4?

Solution: Calculate the formula mass of Na_2SO_4.

Na:	2×23	=	46
S:	1×32	=	32
O:	4×16	=	64
Total:			**142** (amu)

Calculate the percentage of the total mass corresponding to the mass of each element in the formula, as already determined.

$$\% \, Na = \frac{46}{142} \times 100 = 32.4\%$$

$$\% \, S = \frac{32}{142} \times 100 = 22.5\%$$

$$\% \, O = \frac{64}{142} \times 100 = 45.1\%$$

Total: **100.0%**

Note that the total of the individual percentages must equal 100, within the limits of precision of the calculation. (The total may be 99.9% or 100.1% because of rounding off.)

Ionic solids often include definite amounts of **water of hydration** as part of their crystal structures. Water will then appear as part of the empirical formula. Sometimes it is necessary to determine the percentage composition of either the compound or the water of hydration in the crystalline substance.

SAMPLE PROBLEM

What is the percentage of water by mass in sodium carbonate crystals, $Na_2CO_3 \cdot 10\,H_2O$?

Solution: Calculate the formula mass of the crystal. Since you are interested in the percent water and not in the separate elements of the water, treat the water molecule as a unit.

formula mass of $H_2O = (2 \times 1) + 16 = 18$

10 formula masses of $H_2O = 10 \times 18 = 180$

Calculate the formula mass of Na_2CO_3 and add the mass of water to find the total formula mass.

Na:	2×23	$=$	46
C:	1×12	$=$	12
O:	3×16	$=$	48
Na_2CO_3:			106
$10\,H_2O$:			180
Total:			286 (amu)

$$\%\,H_2O \;=\; \frac{180}{286} \times 100 = 63.0\%$$

2. Empirical formulas. An empirical formula represents the simplest ratio in which atoms combine to form a compound (page 41). The molecular formula of ethane is C_2H_6. The *simplest* ratio of carbon atoms to hydrogen atoms in this compound is 1:3. Therefore, the empirical formula of ethane is CH_3. Note that the molecular formula is always a simple multiple of the empirical formula.

If you know the mass ratio of elements in a compound, you can determine its empirical formula. For example, suppose you know that in a compound composed of carbon and hydrogen, the mass ratio of carbon to hydrogen is approximately 4:1. Recall that 1 gram-atom of carbon has a mass of approximately 12.0 g, while 1 gram-atom of hydrogen is about 1.0 g. This means that in our carbon compound, for every 1 gram-atom of carbon (12.0 g) there are 3 gram-atoms of hydrogen (3×1.0 g). Thus, the empirical formula of our compound is CH_3.

On the other hand, if you know the empirical formula of a compound, you can determine the mass ratio of its elements. The empirical formula CH_3, for example, tells you that there is 1 gram-atom of carbon for every 3 gram-atoms of hydrogen. Thus, the mass ratio of carbon to hydrogen in this compound is approximately 12:3, or 4:1.

QUESTIONS

1. **The percent by mass of oxygen in MgO (formula mass = 40) is closest to   (1) 16%   (2) 24%   (3) 40%   (4) 60%**

2. **What is the approximate percent composition by mass of $CaBr_2$ (formula mass = 200)?**
   (1) 20% Ca and 80% Br   (2) 25% Ca and 75% Br
   (3) 30% Ca and 70% Br   (4) 35% Ca and 65% Br

3. **Which compound contains the greatest percentage of oxygen by mass?   (1) BaO   (2) CaO   (3) MgO   (4) SrO**

4. **The percent by mass of nitrogen in $Mg(CN)_2$ is equal to**
   (1) $\dfrac{14}{16} \times 100$ (2) $\dfrac{14}{50} \times 100$
   (3) $\dfrac{28}{76} \times 100$ (4) $\dfrac{28}{50} \times 100$

5. A compound has the empirical formula CH_2 and a molecular mass of 42. Its molecular formula is (1) CH_2 (2) C_2H_4 (3) C_3H_6 (4) C_4H_8
6. What is the molecular formula of a compound that has a molecular mass of 92 and an empirical formula of NO_2? (1) NO_2 (2) N_2O_4 (3) N_3O_6 (4) N_4O_8
7. A compound contains 0.50 mole of carbon for each 1.0 mole of hydrogen. The empirical formula of this compound is (1) CH (2) CH_2 (3) C_2H (4) C_2H_2
8. The empirical formula of a compound is C_2H_3 and the molecular mass of the compound is 54. What is the molecular formula of the compound? (1) C_2H_4 (2) C_4H_6 (3) C_4H_8 (4) C_6H_{10}

3. Determining formula from percentage composition. The **empirical formula** of a compound can be determined if the percentage composition of the compound and the atomic masses of the elements in the compound are known. The **molecular formula** of a molecular compound likewise can be determined if the molecular mass is known.

SAMPLE PROBLEM

What is the empirical formula of a compound that consists of 58.80% barium, 13.75% sulfur, and 27.45% oxygen by mass?

Solution: If 100 grams of the compound were analyzed, it would consist of 58.80 grams of barium (58.80% × 100 grams), 13.75 grams of sulfur, and 27.45 grams of oxygen. Convert each of these masses to its equivalent in moles of the element, using the relationship:

$$\text{no. of moles} = \frac{\text{mass in grams}}{\text{atomic mass}}$$

$$\text{no. of moles of Ba} = \frac{58.80}{137} = 0.43$$

$$\text{no. of moles of S} = \frac{13.75}{32} = 0.43$$

$$\text{no. of moles of O} = \frac{27.45}{16} = 1.71$$

The numbers of atoms in the formula must be in the same ratios as the moles of the elements in any sample of the compound. Find the smallest whole numbers that are in the ratios 0.43 : 0.43 : 1.71. This can usually be done by dividing by the smallest factor.

$$\text{atoms of Ba} = \frac{0.43}{0.43} = 1$$

$$\text{atoms of S} = \frac{0.43}{0.43} = 1$$

$$\text{atoms of O} = \frac{1.71}{0.43} = 4$$

The empirical formula is therefore **$BaSO_4$**.

(If the results of the last step are not all whole numbers, multiply by the smallest factor that will produce whole numbers. For example, if the atomic ratios in a compound of aluminum and oxygen are found to be 1 Al to 1.5 O, multiply by 2 to obtain the whole-number ratio 2 Al to 3 O, or Al_2O_3.)

SAMPLE PROBLEM

By chemical analysis, a molecular compound was found to consist of 80% carbon and 20% hydrogen by mass. By measuring the volume of a known mass of the compound in the gaseous phase, its molecular mass was found to be 30. Find the empirical and the molecular formulas of the compound.

Solution: Determine the empirical formula by the method already described.

$$\text{Relative number of C atoms} = \frac{\% \text{ C}}{\text{atomic mass}} = \frac{80}{12} = 6.7$$

$$\text{Relative number of H atoms} = \frac{\% \text{ H}}{\text{atomic mass}} = \frac{20}{1} = 20$$

Convert to a whole-number ratio by dividing by the smaller number:

$$\text{atoms of C} = \frac{6.7}{6.7} = 1$$

$$\text{atoms of H} = \frac{20}{6.7} = 3$$

The empirical formula is therefore CH_3.

The formula mass of CH_3 is $12 + (3 \times 1) = 15$.

The actual molecular mass of the compound is 30.

Therefore, the molecule contains $\frac{30}{15} = 2$ formula units.

The actual molecular formula is therefore $2(CH_3) = \mathbf{C_2H_6}$.

QUESTIONS

1. A compound contains 50% sulfur and 50% oxygen by mass. The empirical formula of this compound is (1) SO (2) SO_2 (3) SO_3 (4) SO_4

2. A compound was found by analysis to consist of 85.6% carbon and 14.4% hydrogen. What is its empirical formula? (1) CH (2) CH_2 (3) C_2H (4) C_2H_2

3. A compound which contains 75% carbon and 25% hydrogen by mass has the formula (1) CH_4 (2) C_2H_2 (3) C_2H_6 (4) C_3H_8

4. A compound consists of 14.6% carbon and 85.4% chlorine by mass. What is the empirical formula? (1) CCl (2) CCl_2 (3) CCl_3 (4) CCl_4

PROBLEMS INVOLVING EQUATIONS. In the following types of problems, it is important to remember that the **coefficients** used in balancing chemical equations represent moles. In stoichiometry the following is assumed:

1. The reaction is a single reaction (no side reactions).

2. The reaction goes to completion.

3. The reactants are completely used (none remains after the reaction).

1. Mole ratio in chemical equations. In problems involving chemical reactions, the most essential factor for consideration is the balanced equation (Unit 3, pages 43-44). The most important feature to remember is that the coefficient ratio is both the *molecular* ratio and the *mole* ratio.

Consider the equation for the combination of ethane, C_2H_6:

$$2C_2H_6 + 7O_2 \rightarrow 4CO_2 + 6H_2O$$

In terms of the coefficient ratio, this equation states:

Two moles of ethane combine with 7 moles of oxygen to produce 4 moles of carbon dioxide and 6 moles of water. These mole ratios will exist regardless of the amounts of the substances involved.

SAMPLE PROBLEM

How many moles of water will be produced from the complete combustion of 3 moles of ethane?

Solution: The balanced equation shows the mole ratio between water and ethane to be 6:2. The following proportion can thus be set up and solved:

$$\frac{6 \text{ moles } H_2O}{2 \text{ moles } C_2H_6} = \frac{x \text{ moles } H_2O}{3 \text{ moles } C_2H_6}$$

$$x = \textbf{9 moles } H_2O$$

---

2. Mass-mass problems. A balanced equation shows the mole proportions of reactants and products. Knowing the mass of one substance—**reactant** or **product**—it is possible to calculate the mass of any of the other substances in the reaction.

SAMPLE PROBLEM

How many grams of sodium hydroxide are needed to neutralize 49 grams of sulfuric acid according to the equation:

$$H_2SO_4 + 2NaOH \rightarrow Na_2SO_4 + 2H_2O$$

Solution: The basic principle that applies is that the coefficients in the balanced equation represent moles of reactants and products. (Remember that the coefficient "1" is not written, but is understood.) This equation therefore states that 2 moles of NaOH react with 1 mole of H_2SO_4. Write this information under the corresponding formulas in the equation.

$$H_2SO_4 + 2\,NaOH \rightarrow Na_2SO_4 + 2\,H_2O$$
1 mole   2 moles

Convert the given mass (49 grams of H_2SO_4) to moles. First find the mole mass of H_2SO_4.

$$(2 \times 1) + 32 + (4 \times 16) = 98 \text{ grams/mole of } H_2SO_4$$

Convert 49 grams to moles.

$$\frac{49 \text{ grams}}{98 \text{ grams/mole}} = 0.5 \text{ mole of } H_2SO_4$$

Write this value above the formula in the equation, and write "x moles" for the unknown quantity of NaOH.

0.5 mole   x moles
$$H_2SO_4 + 2\,NaOH \rightarrow Na_2SO_4 + 2\,H_2O$$
1 mole   2 moles

We now write the proportion exactly as presented in the equation:

$$\frac{0.5}{1.0} = \frac{x}{2} \qquad\qquad x = \frac{0.5}{1.0} \times 2 \qquad\qquad x = 1 \text{ mole}$$

The mole mass of NaOH is 23 + 16 + 1 = 40 grams/mole.

The desired mass is therefore 1 mole $\times$ 40 grams/mole = **40 grams.**

3. Mass-volume problems. Mass-volume problems are recognized when the problem to be solved presents one of the substances in mass units (usually grams) and one of the substances in volume units (usually liters). Remember again that the mole unit serves to relate the quantities of products and reactants.

SAMPLE PROBLEM

How many liters of carbon dioxide at S T P are produced by the combustion of 342 grams of octane (C_8H_{18}) according to the equation

$$2 C_8H_{18} + 25 O_2 \rightarrow 16 CO_2 + 18 H_2O$$

Solution: Convert 342 grams of octane to moles.

mole mass of C_8H_{18} = $(8 \times 12) + (18 \times 1)$ = 114 grams

$$\frac{342 \text{ grams}}{114 \text{ grams/mole}} = 3 \text{ moles}$$

Write the known and unknown numbers of moles in the equation.

$$\overset{3 \text{ moles}}{\underset{2 \text{ moles}}{2 C_8H_{18}}} + 25 O_2 \rightarrow \overset{x \text{ moles}}{\underset{16 \text{ moles}}{16 CO_2}} + 18 H_2O$$

$$\frac{3}{2} = \frac{x}{16} \qquad x = 24 \text{ moles of } CO_2$$

Since 1 mole of any gas at STP   has a volume of 22.4 liters, the volume of 24 moles of CO_2 is

24 moles $\times$ 22.4 liters/mole = **537.6** liters

4. Volume-volume problems. At the same pressure and temperature, one mole of any gas occupies the same volume as one mole of any other gas. Therefore, the volumes of gases involved in a chemical reaction are proportional to the number of moles involved, which is indicated by the coefficients of the chemical equation.

SAMPLE PROBLEM

How many liters of ethane (C_2H_6) can be completely oxidized by reaction with 63 liters of oxygen?

Solution: Write a balanced equation for the reaction;

$$\underset{2 \text{ moles}}{\overset{x \text{ liters}}{2\,C_2H_6}} + \underset{7 \text{ moles}}{\overset{63 \text{ liters}}{7\,O_2}} \rightarrow 4\,CO_2 + 6\,H_2O$$

Write the given and unknown volumes over the appropriate formulas.

The coefficients in the equation are mole ratios. Since the volumes of gases are in the same ratio as the number of moles they contain, the mole ratios are the same as volume ratios for gases. Therefore we can write the proportion

$$\frac{x \text{ liters}}{2 \text{ moles}} = \frac{63 \text{ liters}}{7 \text{ moles}}$$

$$x = 18 \text{ liters}$$

QUESTIONS

1. Given the reaction: $C_3H_8(g) + 5\,O_2(g) \rightarrow 4H_2O(g) + 3CO_2(g)$
   What is the total number of liters of CO_2 produced when 150 liters of O_2 reacts completely with C_3H_8?   (1) 90   (2) 150   (3) 3.0   (4) 250

2. Given the balanced equation:
   $CH_4(g) + 2O_2(g) \rightarrow CO_2(g) + 2H_2O(g)$
   What is the total number of liters of O_2 needed to react completely with 10 liters of CH_4?   (1) 8.0   (2) 10   (3) 16   (4) 20

3. Given the reaction $N_2(g) + 3H_2(g) \rightarrow 2NH_3(g)$. How many liters of ammonia, measured at STP, are produced when 28.0 grams of nitrogen is completely consumed?   (1) 5.60   (2) 11.2   (3) 22.4   (4) 44.8

4. Given the reaction: $2C_8H_{18}(g) + 25O_2(g) \rightarrow 16CO_2(g) + 18H_2O(g)$
   What is the total number of liters of O_2 required for the complete combusion of 4.00 liters of C_8H_{18}?   (1) 25.0   (2) 50.0   (3) 100   (4) 200

5-6. **Base your answers to Questions 5-6 on the following equation:**
$C_8H_{16}(g) + 12O_2(g) \rightarrow 8CO_2(g) + 8H_2O(g)$

5. When 10 liters of C_8H_{16} is burned, how many liters of water vapor are produced? (1) 10 (2) 22.4 (3) 80 (4) 179.2

6. How many liters of CO_2 at STP are produced to burn completely 112 grams of C_8H_{16}? (1) 10 (2) 22.4 (3) 80 (4) 179.2

7. If 2 moles of the gas NO reacts completely with oxygen according to the equation $2NO + O_2 \rightarrow 2NO_2$, how many moles of O_2 will be consumed? (1) ½ (2) 1 (3) 2 (4) 4

8. If 3 moles of HCl are used in the reaction $6HCl + Fe_2O_3 \rightarrow 2FeCl_3 + 3H_2O$, then the number of moles of $FeCl_3$ produced is (1) 1 (2) 2 (3) 3 (4) 6

9-10. **Base your answers to Questions 9-10 on the following information:**
Oxygen and hydrogen gas are produced by the electrolysis of water according to the equation $2H_2O(l) \overset{elect}{\rightarrow} 2H_2(g) + O_2(g)$

9. How many moles of oxygen are produced in the electrolysis of 4.0 moles of water? (1) 8.0 (2) 2.0 (3) 6.0 (4) 4.0

10. How many liters of hydrogen gas at STP are produced in the electrolysis of 90 grams of water? (1) 10.0 (2) 22.4 (3) 56.0 (4) 112

11. Given the balanced equation: $C_2H_4 + 3O_2 \rightarrow 2CO_2 + 2H_2O$
How many liters of CO_2 at STP are produced when 15 liters of O_2 are consumed? (1) 10 (2) 15 (3) 30 (4) 45

12. Given the reaction: $CH_4(g) + 2O_2(g) \rightarrow CO_2(g) + 2H_2O(g)$
How many liters of $O_2(g)$ measured at STP are needed to completely burn 1.00 mole of methane? (1) 11.2 (2) 22.4 (3) 33.6 (4) 44.8

13. Given the balanced equation:
$3PbCl_2 + Al_2(SO_4)_3 \rightarrow 3PbSO_4 + 2AlCl_3$
How many moles of $PbSO_4$ will be formed when 0.050 mole of $Al_2(SO_4)_3$ is consumed? (1) 0.05 (2) 0.15 (3) 0.30 (4) 0.50

14. Given the reaction: $2H_2 + O_2 \rightarrow 2H_2O$
The total number of grams of O_2 needed to produce 54 grams of water is (1) 36 (2) 48 (3) 61 (4) 75

15. Given the reaction: $N_2 + 3H_2 \rightarrow 2NH_3$
How many grams of ammonia are produced when 1.0 mole of nitrogen reacts? (1) 8.5 (2) 17 (3) 34 (4) 68

16. According to the reaction $H_2 + Cl_2 \rightarrow 2HCl$, the production of 2.0 moles of HCl would require 70 grams of Cl_2 and (1) 1.0 g of H_2 (2) 2.0 g of H_2 (3) 3.0 g of H_2 (4) 4.0 g of H_2

17. Given the reaction: $S + O_2 \rightarrow SO_2$
What is the total number of grams of oxygen needed to react completely with 2.0 moles of sulfur? (1) 20 (2) 32 (3) 64 (4) 128

SOLUTIONS

A **solution** is a **homogeneous mixture** of two or more substances. The substance present in the larger amount is called the **solvent,** while the material present in the smaller quantity is called the **solute.** Solutions in which water is the solvent are called **aqueous solutions. Concentration**—the quantity of solute in a given measure (volume or mass) of solution—may be expressed in various ways.

MOLARITY. The **molarity,** M, of a solution is the number of moles of solute contained in one liter of solution. A 3 M solution contains 3 moles of solute per liter of solution, while a 0.5 M solution contains 0.5 mole of solute per liter of solution.

The concentration in moles per liter (the molarity) multiplied by the volume in liters is equal to the number of moles of solute in a solution.

moles of solute = molarity × volume

The mass in grams of solute is equal to the product of the number of moles of solute and the mole mass of that solute.

grams of solute = moles of solute × mole mass of solute

SAMPLE PROBLEM

What is the molarity of a solution that contains 4 moles of solute in 8 000 mL of solution?

Solution: Molarity is a measure of the number of moles of solute per liter of solution. Convert the volume to liters, and determine the ratio of moles to liters.

$$\frac{8\ 000\ mL}{1\ 000\ mL/liter} = 8\ liters$$

$$molarity = \frac{moles\ of\ solute}{liters\ of\ solution} = \frac{4}{8} = \textbf{0.5M}$$

SAMPLE PROBLEM

What is the molarity of a solution that contains 170 grams of sodium nitrate (NaNO₃) in 2 liters of solution?

Solution: Calculate the number of moles of solute.

mole mass of $NaNO_3$ = 23 + 14 + (3 × 16) = 85 grams

$$\text{moles of solute} = \frac{170 \text{ grams}}{85 \text{ grams/mole}} = 2 \text{ moles}$$

$$\text{molarity} = \frac{\text{moles of solute}}{\text{liters of solution}} = \frac{2}{2} = 1\,M$$

SAMPLE PROBLEM

How many grams of hydrogen chloride (HCl) are present in 5.0 liters of a 6 M solution of hydrochloric acid?

Solution: Since the molarity is 6 M, there are 6 moles of solute per liter of solution. The number of moles in 5.0 liters is

6 moles/liter × 5.0 liters = 30 moles

The mass of one mole of HCl = 1 + 35.5 = 36.5 grams.

The mass of 30 moles = 30 moles × 36.5 grams/mole = **1095 grams**

MOLALITY. The **molality,** m, of a solution is a measure of the number of moles of solute dissolved in 1 000 grams of solvent. This expression of concentration is used to determine the relationship between moles of solute and moles of solvent.

QUESTIONS

1. **What is the molarity of a solution that contains 4 grams of NaOH in 500 milliliters of solution? (Formula mass of NaOH = 40)   (1) 0.1 M (2) 2 M   (3) 0.2 M   (4) 0.5 M**

2. **What is the molarity of a solution that contains 28 grams of KOH (formula mass = 56) in 2.0 liters of solution?   (1) 1.0 M   (2) 2.0 M (3) 0.25 M   (4) 0.50 M**

3. **If 500 cubic centimeters of 2.0 M HCl is diluted with H_2O to a volume of 1 000 cubic centimeters, the molarity of the new solution will be (1) 1.0 M   (2) 2.0 M   (3) 0.25 M   (4) 0.50 M**

4. **How many moles of KNO_3 are required to make 0.50 liter of a 2.0 M solution of KNO_3?   (1) 1.0   (2) 2.0   (3) 0.50   (4) 4.0**

EFFECT OF SOLUTE ON SOLVENT. Dissolved particles affect some of the properties of a solvent. Boiling point, freezing point (melting point), vapor pressure, and osmotic pressure are among the properties of a solution that are affected. Such properties are called **colligative properties.** Colligative properties depend on the relative number of particles (molality) rather than on the nature of the particles in solution.

The presence of a solute raises the boiling point of the solvent in which it is found. The amount by which the boiling point is elevated is proportional to the concentration of dissolved solute particles. For example, one mole of a **nonelectrolyte** in 1 000 grams of water (a 1 molal solution) raises the boiling point of water by $0.52°C$.

The presence of a solute lowers the freezing point of the solvent in which it is found by an amount that is proportional to the concentration of dissolved solute particles. A 1 molal solution of a nonelectrolyte lowers the freezing point of water by $1.86°C$.

BEHAVIOR OF ELECTROLYTES. An **electrolyte,** such as NaCl, causes a change of larger magnitude in the properties of a solvent than does a nonelectrolyte. The reason for this is that a solution of one mole of a nonelectrolyte such as sugar contains one mole of dissolved particles (molecules). One mole of sodium chloride, on the other hand, dissociates to yield 2 moles of dissolved particles (ions). The abnormal behavior of electrolytes in solution provides evidence for the existence of ionic particles.

QUESTIONS

1. What is the freezing point of a solution that contains 1.00 mole of a nonelectrolyte dissolved in 1 000 grams of water?   (1) $0.00°$ C (2) $0.520°$ C   (3) $-1.86°$ C   (4) $-3.72°$ C

2. Which water solution will have the lowest freezing point?   (1) 1 molal $CaCl_2$ (2) 1 molal NaCl   (3) 1 molal $C_{12}H_{22}O_{11}$ (4) 2 molal $C_6H_{12}O_6$

3. Which 1 molal solution will have the highest boiling point?   (1) KNO_3 (2) $Mg(NO_3)_2$ (3) $Al(NO_3)_3$ (4) NH_4NO_3

4. NaOH is added to one beaker of distilled water, and C_2H_5OH is added to another beaker of distilled water. Both of the solutions that are formed will   (1) be strong electrolytes   (2) turn litmus paper blue   (3) have a lower boiling point than pure water   (4) have a lower freezing point than pure water

5. At standard pressure, a molal solution of sugar has a boiling point (1) greater than $100°C$ and a freezing point greater than $0°C$ (2) greater than $100°C$ and a freezing point less than $0°C$ (3) less than $100°C$ and a freezing point greater than $0°C$ (4) less than $100°C$ and a freezing point less than $0°C$

6. According to Reference Table L, which 0.1 molal solution will have the lowest freezing point?
   (1) HF   (2) HNO_2 (3) HNO_3 (4) CH_3COOH

7. A 1 kilogram sample of water will have the highest freezing point when it contains
   (1) 1×10^{17} dissolved particles   (2) 1×10^{19} dissolved particles
   (3) 1×10^{21} dissolved particles   (4) 1×10^{23} dissolved particles

RELATIONSHIP BETWEEN DENSITY AND MOLECULAR MASS.
We know that the mass in grams of 22.4 liters of any gas at STP is numerically equal to its molecular mass. If we determine the **density** of a gas in grams per liter, we can find the molecular mass by multiplying by 22.4.

**molecular mass (in grams per mole) =
    density (in grams per liter) × 22.4 (liters per mole)**

SAMPLE PROBLEM

The density of a gas is 1.96 grams/liter at S T P. What is its molecular mass?

Solution: Find the mass of 22.4 liters (one mole) by multiplying the mass of one liter by 22.4

1.96 grams/liter × 22.4 liters/mole = 43.9 grams/mole

The molecular mass is **43.9.**

If the molecular mass of a gas is known, its density can be calculated from the same relationship:

density (in grams per liter) = $\dfrac{\text{molecular mass}}{22.4}$

SAMPLE PROBLEM

What is the density of carbon dioxide, CO_2, at S T P ?

Solution: Find the mass of one mole of CO_2.

mole mass of CO_2 = 12 + (2 × 16) = 44 grams

One mole of CO_2 has a volume of 22.4 liters at S T P

Therefore its density is

$$\frac{\text{mass}}{\text{volume}} = \frac{44 \text{ grams}}{22.4 \text{ liters}} = \textbf{1.96 grams/liter}$$

QUESTIONS

1. A 9.6-gram sample of a gas has a volume of 3.0 liters at STP. What is its density, in grams per liter, at STP?   (1) 29   (2) 9.6   (3) 3.2   (4) 0.31

2. Eleven grams of a gas occupies 5.6 liters at STP. What is the molecular mass of this gas?   (1) 11   (2) 22   (3) 44   (4) 88

3. What is the molecular mass of a gas whose density is 1.25 grams per liter at STP?   (1) 14.0   (2) 17.9   (3) 20.0   (4) 28.0

4. What is the mass of 1.00 mole of a gas if 28.0 grams of this gas occupies 22.4 liters at STP?   (1) 1.00 gram   (2) 1.25 grams   (3) 22.4 grams   (4) 28.0 grams

5. What is the molecular mass of a gas whose density is 1.4 grams per liter at STP?   (1) 16   (2) 22   (3) 31   (4) 38

6. A 22.0-gram sample of a gas occupies 11.2 liters at STP. What is the gram molecular mass of the gas?   (1) 11.2 g   (2) 22.4 g   (3) 22.0 g   (4) 44.0 g

7. The gram molecular mass of a gas is 56 grams. Its density at STP in grams per liter is   (1) 1.0   (2) 5.6   (3) 2.5   (4) 0.40

HEAT OF VAPORIZATION. The quantity of heat needed to vaporize 1 gram of a given substance in the liquid phase at its normal boiling point is called the heat of vaporization of that substance (Unit 1, page 17). The amount of heat absorbed by a substance while it is being converted from a liquid to a gas is equal to the mass of the substance times its heat of vaporization.

SAMPLE PROBLEM

How many calories are absorbed when 50. grams of water at 100° C are vaporized?

Solution: The heat of vaporization of water is 539.4 cal/g. The amount of heat needed to vaporize 50. g of water at its boiling point will be equal to:

$$50. \, \cancel{g} \times 539.4 \, \frac{cal}{\cancel{g}} = \mathbf{2.7 \times 10^4 \, cal}$$

If 50. g of steam were converted to liquid water (condensation), the same number of calories would be involved, but this energy would be released rather than absorbed. Vaporization is an endothermic process; condensation is exothermic.

HEAT OF FUSION. The amount of heat needed to change 1 gram of a substance from a solid at its melting point to liquid at the same temperature is called the heat of fusion of that substance (Unit 1, page 18). The amount of heat absorbed by a given quantity of a substance while it changes from a solid to a liquid can be calculated by multiplying the mass of the substance times its heat of fusion.

SAMPLE PROBLEM

How many calories will be absorbed when 45 grams of ice, $H_2O(s)$, at 0° C melts to form liquid water at the same temperature?

Solution: The heat of fusion for water is 79.72 cal/g. The amount of heat absorbed when 45 grams of ice melt will be equal to:

$$45 \text{ g} \times 79.72\frac{\text{cal}}{\text{g}} = 3600 \text{ cal}$$

If 45 grams of liquid water at the freezing point were to solidify, the same number of calories would be released. Melting (fusion) is an endothermic process; freezing (crystallization) is an exothermic process.

COMBINED GAS LAWS. Both Boyle's Law and Charles's Law were discussed in Unit 1, on pages 9-12. Boyle's Law states the relationship between pressure and volume of a fixed mass of a gas at constant temperature. Charles's Law states the relationship between temperature and volume of a fixed mass of a gas at constant pressure. However, when either pressure or temperature varies, the other factor almost always changes also. To deal with problems in which pressure and temperature change simultaneously, the equations of Boyle's and Charles's Laws are combined into a "Combined Gas Law" equation. This equation is written:

$$\frac{P_1V_1}{T_1} = \frac{P_2V_2}{T_2}$$

When solving problems involving this relationship, it is important to remember that both pressure values must be expressed in the same units, and temperatures must be expressed in degrees Kelvin (°C + 273).

GRAHAM'S LAW. Unlike solids and liquids, gases have no definite volume. Gases spread out, or diffuse, to occupy all the space available to them. This spreading out of a gas is called **diffusion.** Different gases diffuse at different rates. At a given temperature, the rate of diffusion of a gas depends on the velocity of its molecules which, in turn, depends on their mass.

Since the temperature of a substance is a measure of the average kinetic energy of its particles, the molecules of two different gases at the same temperature will have the same average kinetic energy. Since KE $= \frac{1}{2}mv^2$, for the molecules of two gases (A and B) at the same temperature, the value of $\frac{1}{2}mv^2$ will be the same. If the molecules of gas A are lighter (less massive) than those of gas B, it follows that the velocity of these lighter molecules must be greater than that of the heavier molecules of gas B. The lighter gas, whose molecules have the greater velocity, will diffuse faster than the heavier gas.

Graham's Law is a statement of the relationship between mass and rate of diffusion. This law states: Under the same conditions of temperature and pressure, the relative rates of diffusion of two gases vary inversely as the square roots of their molecular masses.

UNIT 6   KINETICS AND EQUILIBRIUM

KINETICS

The branch of chemistry known as chemical kinetics is concerned with the *rates* of chemical reactions and the *mechanisms* by which they occur.

The **rate** of a chemical reaction is measured in terms of the number of moles of reactant consumed (or the number of moles of product formed) in a unit of time.

The **mechanism** of a chemical reaction attempts to describe the sequence of events by which the overall reaction takes place. For most reactions, however, only the net reaction, which represents the summation of the sequential reactions that have occurred, is observable. The net reaction is indicated by a chemical equation.

ENERGY AND REACTION RATES

ACTIVATION ENERGY. Energy is required to initiate a chemical reaction. **Activation energy** is defined as the minimum energy that is required to make a reaction occur. Activation energies vary with the nature of the reactants involved.

HEAT OF REACTION. The **heat of reaction** represents the difference in heat content between the products and the reactants of a chemical reaction. It is also the difference in **potential energy** between the products and reactants. Heat of reaction is denoted by ΔH (delta H), and it is a measure of the heat energy absorbed or released by a reaction system in the formation of its products.

$$\Delta H = H_{products} - H_{reactants}$$

If the products of a reaction have less potential energy than the reactants from which they are formed, the reaction is said to be **exothermic.** The algebraic sign of ΔH is *negative* for exothermic reactions. Consider the formation of water from hydrogen and oxygen:

$$H_2(g) + \tfrac{1}{2}O_2(g) \rightarrow H_2O(l) + 68.3 \text{ kcal}$$

This reaction is exothermic, and the heat of reaction has a negative value, namely, -68.3 kcal/mole H_2O.

An **endothermic reaction** is one in which the products have more potential energy than the reactants. In this case, the heat of reaction has a *positive* value. The decomposition of water, an endothermic reaction, is shown below. The heat of reaction is +68.3 kcal.

$$H_2O(l) + 68.3 \text{ kcal} \rightarrow H_2(g) + \tfrac{1}{2}O_2(g)$$

It is important to remember that a negative heat of reaction value indicates that the internal energy of the system is decreasing because energy is flowing out of it. A positive heat of reaction value tells us that the system's energy is increasing because energy is flowing into it. The heats of reaction for some common reactions are listed in Reference Table I, and additional values for the heats of reaction for the formation of some common substances are listed in Reference Table G.

POTENTIAL ENERGY DIAGRAM. The relationship between activation energy and heat of reaction for a given chemical reaction may be visualized by a graph in which potential energy of the system, shown on the vertical axis, is plotted against the reaction coordinate, which represents the progress of the reaction, on the horizontal axis.

In order for any reaction to occur, an **activated complex** must be formed. This intermediate product may be considered to be a temporary association of atoms or molecules from which the products of the reaction are derived. The energy that must be supplied to a system in order for the reactants to form an activated complex is the activation energy.

The highest point on the curve of a potential energy diagram represents the potential energy of the intermediate product, or the activated complex. The difference beween this point and the potential energy of the reactants is equal to the activation energy.

Once the formation of an activated complex has been achieved, the reaction can proceed to produce the products. The potential energy of the products will be lower than the peak energy of the activated complex. However, it may be higher than the potential energy of the reactants, in which case the reaction as a whole is endothermic. Or the potential energy of the products may be lower than of the reactants, in which case the reaction is exothermic.

It is important to understand that the heat of reaction is the difference between the potential energy of the reactants and that of the products. It is the same for a given reaction regardless of the amount of activation energy involved. If a catalyst is present, the activation energy is reduced, but the net heat of reaction is unchanged.

FACTORS THAT AFFECT REACTION RATES

Chemical reactions depend on collisions between reacting *species*—atoms, molecules, ions, or other particles. A reaction occurs only when the reactants have sufficient energy to form an activated complex. In general, any factor that causes more collisions to take place, or results in more effective collisions, will increase the rate of reaction.

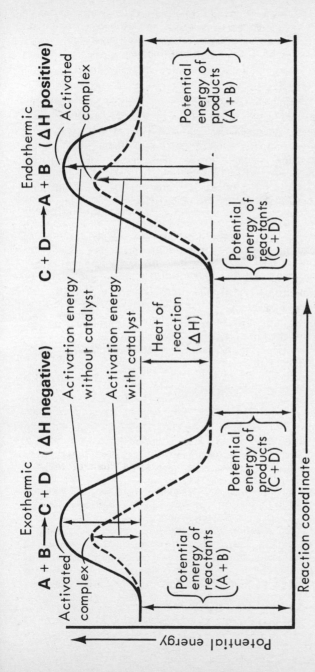

Figure 6-1. Potential energy diagram for a reversible reaction. The following points should be noted: (1) The activation energy is the difference between the potential energy of the activated complex (the highest point on the curve) and the potential energy of the reactants. (2) The heat of reaction is the difference between the potential energy of the reactants and the products; it is independent of the activation energy. (3) For a reversible reaction, the heat of reaction is numerically the same in both directions. (4) A catalyst reduces the activation energy; the reaction occurs more quickly, but the heat of reaction remains the same.

NATURE OF THE REACTANTS. The nature of the reactants, in terms of the kinds of bonds that must be broken and made, is a contributing factor in determining the rate of a chemical reaction. Those reactions that involve the least amount of bond rearrangement are usually rapid. For example, ionic substances react quickly in water, even at room temperature. Reactions that involve the breaking of bonds and the making of new ones, such as the reaction of oxygen and hydrogen to form water, take place at slow rates at room temperature.

CONCENTRATION. Whenever the concentration of one or more of the reactants is increased, the rate of the reaction increases. An increase in concentration, usually measured in moles per liter, increases the frequency of collisions.

Compressing a gas has the effect of increasing the concentration. Increased pressure on a gas raises the reaction rate accordingly.

TEMPERATURE. An increase in temperature will cause an increase in the rate of reaction for two reasons. Elevated temperatures cause particles to move faster and to have corresponding higher kinetic energy values (see Unit 1, page 15). Thus, not only is the number of collisions per unit time increased, but there is also a higher percentage of effective collisions.

REACTION MECHANISM. Most reactions do not occur in a single step, but rather by a series of steps, called the **reaction mechanism.** Each step is usually a two-particle collision. The number of steps and their complexity affects the rate of the overall reaction. The more steps required, the slower the reaction.

The reaction mechanism is not indicated by the net equation for a reaction. For example, in the reaction

$$N_2(g) + 3H_2(g) \rightarrow 2NH_3(g)$$

it is very unlikely that one nitrogen molecule and three hydrogen molecules will collide simultaneously. It is much more likely that the reaction occurs as a series of two-particle collisions, each representing the formation of a different activated complex.

CATALYSTS. Fast reactions have low activation energies, whereas slow reactions have high activation energies. The addition of a catalyst to a system changes its activation energy, and thereby changes its rate of reaction. A catalyzed reaction requires less activation energy. However, the overall reaction is not changed. In Figure 6-1, the activated complexes of the exothermic and endothermic reactions have comparatively less potential energy when catalyzed than the respective activated complexes formed without the aid of a catalyst. However, the potential energies of the products as well as the heats of reaction are the same, whether the reactions are catalyzed or not.

QUESTIONS

1. Heat of reaction, $\triangle H$, is equal to

   (1) $H_{products} + H_{reactants}$ (3) $H_{products} \times H_{reactants}$
   (2) $H_{products} - H_{reactants}$ (4) $H_{products} \div H_{reactants}$

2. The difference between the potential energy of the reactants and the potential energy of the products is   (1) $\triangle G$ (2) $\triangle H$ (3) $\triangle S$ (4) $\triangle T$

3. The difference between the heat content of the products and the heat content of the reactants is   (1) entropy of reaction   (2) heat of reaction   (3) free energy   (4) activation energy

4. For the reaction $A + B \rightarrow C$ + heat, the potential energy of the products, compared to the potential energy of the reactants, is   (1) less and the reaction is exothermic   (2) less and the reaction is endothermic   (3) greater and the reaction is exothermic   (4) greater and the reaction is endothermic

5. Given the reaction: $H_2(g) + \frac{1}{2}O_2(g) \rightarrow H_2O(g) + 57.8$ kcal
   If the activation energy for the forward reaction is 40.0 kilocalories per mole, the activation energy for the reverse reaction, in kilocalories per mole, will be   (1) 17.8   (2) 30.0   (3) 60.0   (4) 97.8

6. Given the reaction: $N_2(g) + O_2(g) + 43.2$ kcal$\rightarrow 2NO(g)$
   What is the heat of formation of nitrogen (II) oxide in kcal/mole?
   (1) $\triangle H = -43.2$ (2) $\triangle H = -21.6$ (3) $\triangle H = 21.6$ (4) $\triangle H = 43.2$

7. Given the reaction $A + B \rightarrow AB + 50$ kcal. If an activation energy of 5 kcal is required, the activation energy of the reverse reaction is   (1) 5 kcal   (2) 45 kcal   (3) 50 kcal   (4) 55 kcal

8. Nitrogen reacts with oxygen according to the equation,
   $N_2 + 2O_2 + 16.2$ kcal $\rightleftarrows 2NO_2$
   The heat of formation for NO_2 is   (1) -8.1 kcal/mole   (2) -16.2 kcal/mole   (3) 8.1 kcal/mole   (4) 16.2 kcal/mole

9. When one mole of a certain compound is formed from its elements under standard conditions, it absorbs 85 kilocalories of heat. A correct conclusion from this statement is that the reaction has a
   (1) $\triangle H^0_f$ equal to -85 kcal/mole   (2) $\triangle H^0_f$ equal to $+85$ kcal/mole
   (3) $\triangle G^0_f$ equal to -85 kcal/mole   (4) $\triangle G^0_f$ equal to $+85$ kcal/mole

10-18. Base your answers to Questions 10-18 on the potential energy diagram and the reaction below.

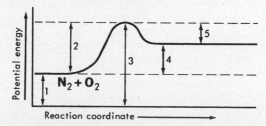

$$N_2(g) + O_2(g) = 2NO(g) \qquad \triangle H = +43.2 \text{ kcal}$$

10. The potential energy of the reactants, $N_2(g) + O_2(g)$, is represented by
(1) 1   (2) 2   (3) 3   (4) 5

11. The energy of activation for the forward reaction is represented by
(1) 1   (2) 2   (3) 3   (4) 4

12. Compared to the potential energy of the product, the potential energy of the reactants is   (1) less   (2) the same   (3) greater   (4) impossible to determine

13. The potential energy of the activated complex is represented by   (1) 1   (2) 5   (3) 3   (4) 4

14. The heat of formation of $NO(g)$, in kilcalories per mole, is   (1) -21.6 (2) 21.6   (3) -43.2 (4) 43.2

15. The heat of reaction is represented by   (1) 5   (2) 2   (3) 3   (4) 4

16. If a catalyst were introduced into the reaction, which interval would not be changed?   (1) 2   (2) 3   (3) 4   (4) 5

17. The effect on the rate of the reaction of raising the temperature of the system would be to   (1) decrease only the rate of the forward reaction   (2) decrease only the rate of the reverse reaction   (3) increase only the rate of the forward reaction   (4) increase the rate of both forward and reverse reactions

18. On the graph, the activation energy for the reverse reaction is given by interval   (1) 2   (2) 3   (3) 4   (4) 5

19. As the concentration of a reactant in a chemical reaction increases, the rate of the reaction generally   (1) decreases   (2) increases   (3) remains the same

20. The addition of a catalyst to a chemical reaction would result in a change in the   (1) activation energy   (2) heat of reaction   (3) potential energy of the reactants   (4) potential energy of the products

21. An increase in temperature increases the rate of all chemical reactions because the increase in temperature causes an increase in the   (1) activation energy of the reaction   (2) $\triangle H$ of the reaction   (3) free energy of the reaction   (4) effectiveness of collisions between particles

22. When a catalyst is added to a system at equilibrium, there is a decrease in the activation energy of   (1) the forward reaction, only   (2) the reverse reaction, only   (3) both the forward and reverse reactions   (4) neither the forward nor the reverse reaction

23-27. Base your answers to Questions 23-27 on the information below.

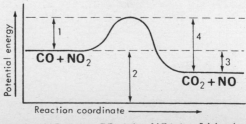

$CO(g) + NO_2(g) = CO_2(g) + NO(g) + 54$ kcal

23. The heat of reaction ($\triangle H$) is represented by   (1) 1   (2) 2   (3) 3   (4) 4

24. The energy of activation for the forward reaction is represented by (1) 1   (2) 2   (3) 3   (4) 4

25. If a catalyst were introduced into the reaction, it would change   (1) 1 and 2   (2) 1 and 3   (3) 1 and 4   (4) 3 and 4

26. The energy of activation for the reverse reaction is   (1) 1   (2) 2   (3) 3 (4) 4

27. The energy liberated when 2 moles of NO_2 is consumed is approximately   (1) 13.5 kcal   (2) 27 kcal   (3) 54 kcal   (4) 108 kcal

EQUILIBRIUM

When water is placed in an uncovered beaker, it evaporates over a period of time. Even if the beaker is covered, evaporation takes place, but because the vapor molecules cannot leave the system, some of them return to the liquid phase, a process called **condensation.** When water evaporates at the same rate at which condensation occurs, no net change in the system is seen, even though both processes are going on. When any reaction takes place under fixed conditions so that both forward and reverse reactions occur at the same rate, a condition of **equilibrium** exists.

Equilibrium is a state of balance between two opposite reactions, physical or chemical, which are taking place at the same rate. Rather than describing the activities of individual particles within a system, equilibrium describes the overall characteristics of the system. Equilibrium is a dynamic process, that is, it implies motion, in which the interactions of reactant particles are balanced by the interactions of product particles. Equilibrium is an important concept because most chemical reactions are **reversible,** that is, they are able to proceed in both directions.

It must be emphasized that the quantities of reactants and products are not necessarily equal during equilibrium. It is the *rate* of the two reactions, forward and reverse, that are equal. For equilibrium to exist, a closed system is usually necessary, so that neither reactants nor products escape.* Furthermore, any change in condition, for example, a temperature change, pressure change, or concentration change, may alter the conditions of equilibrium of a system.

---

*In some systems equilibrium is maintained by supplying fresh reactants while withdrawing products at the same rate. The Haber process is an example.

TYPES OF EQUILIBRIA

PHASE EQUILIBRIUM. Phase equilibrium can exist between solid and liquid phases and between liquid and gas phases. At a state of equilibrium, the rate at which the solid is becoming a liquid is equal to the rate at which the liquid is solidifying. The same kind of relationship exists for liquid-gas equilibrium, where the rate of evaporation is equal to the rate of condensation.

In general, if a solid or liquid is confined to a closed container, there will be, at some point in time, enough particles in the vapor phase so that the rate of return is equal to the rate of escape. When the rates are equal, a condition of dynamic equilibrium exists. At such a point, an **equilibrium vapor pressure** exists, which is characteristic of the solid or liquid at the existing temperature.

SOLUTION EQUILIBRIUM. The solubility of a solute is defined as the mass of solute (solid or gas) that dissolves in a given volume of solvent at equilibrium under stated conditions.

1. Solids in liquids. A solution equilibrium exists when the opposing processes—dissolving and crystallizing—occur at equal rates. At first there is no recrystallization of sugar as it dissolves in water. When the concentration of sugar molecules in solution increases sufficiently, solid sugar begins to recrystallize. At some concentration, the rate at which sugar crystallizes is equal to the rate at which sugar dissolves. A solution that exhibits a condition of equilibrium between the dissolved and crystallized solute is a **saturated solution.** Therefore, **solubility** may be redefined as the concentration of solute in a saturated solution.

2. Gases in liquids. Equilibrium may be attained in a closed system between a gas dissolved in a liquid and the undissolved gas above the liquid. Equilibrium is disturbed by a change in temperature or pressure. An increase in temperature decreases the solubility of gas, while an increase in pressure increases its solubility.

CHEMICAL EQUILIBRIUM. Chemical equilibrium is a state in which the concentrations of the reactants and products of a reaction remain constant. When equilibrium is reached, all observable properties of the system, such as color, pressure, and temperature, remain constant. As stated before, equilibrium means that the forward and reverse reactions are taking place at the same rate, and that there is no net change in the system.

LE CHATELIER'S PRINCIPLE

If a chemical system at equilibrium is disturbed in some way, it undergoes a change that tends to reduce the effects of the applied stress. The result is that equilibrium is re-established at a different point, that is, with altered concentrations of reactants and products. Stresses that can be applied to a chemical system include a change in the concentrations of reactants and/or products, a change in temperature, and a change in pressure.

THE HABER PROCESS. The Haber process for the manufacture of ammonia illustrates many of the aspects of a chemical equilibrium and the operation of Le Chatelier's principle. In this process, nitrogen and hydrogen are fed continuously into a reaction chamber, where the following reversible reaction occurs:

$$N_2 + 3H_2 \rightleftharpoons 2NH_3{}^*$$

The ammonia is withdrawn continuously by liquefying it, dissolving it in water, or other method that does not withdraw nitrogen or hydrogen. Although the reaction chamber is not a closed system, an equilibrium condition exists within it, and the concentrations of nitrogen, hydrogen, and ammonia remain constant while the process is in operation.

EFFECT OF CONCENTRATION. In a chemical equilibrium, if the concentration of one substance *increases*, the reaction that *reduces* the amount of that substance is favored. If the concentration of a substance *decreases*, the reaction that *produces* that substance is favored. A new equilibrium point results in either case. For example, in the Haber process, if more nitrogen is fed into the system, thus increasing its concentration, the rate of the reaction to the right will increase, reducing the nitrogen concentration and increasing that of ammonia. However, as the concentration of ammonia increases, the rate of the reverse reaction will also increase. Eventually, a new equilibrium will be reached, but with different concentrations of the three substances involved.

REACTIONS THAT "GO TO AN END." If one of the products of a reaction is withdrawn from the reaction system as fast as it is produced, and no fresh reactants are added, the reverse reaction cannot establish itself, and equilibrium is never reached. The reaction continues until one or more of the reactants are used up. The reaction is then said to *go to an end* (or *go to completion*). Products may be removed from a reaction system, either partially or entirely, if they are (1) gases formed in a liquid system, such as aqueous solution, (2) insoluble products, called **precipitates,** or (3) in ionic reactions, essentially un-ionized compounds, such as water.

EFFECT OF PRESSURE. An increase in pressure displaces the point of equilibrium in a direction that favors the formation of a smaller volume. Pressure changes are not effective if volume changes are not involved in the reaction. In the Haber process, 4 moles of reactants (1 mole of nitrogen and 3 moles of hydrogen) form 2 moles of product. Since molar volumes of gases at the same temperature and pressure are equal, the forward reaction of the Haber process results in a reduced volume. Therefore, an increase in pressure leads to the production of more ammonia.

---

*An equal sign ($=$) is sometimes used instead of a double arrow ($\rightleftharpoons$) to indicate a reversible reaction at equilibrium.

In the preparation of hydrogen chloride

$$H_2(g) + Cl_2(g) \rightleftharpoons 2HCl(g)$$

there is no change in volume as a result of the reaction. Therefore, a change in pressure does not affect the equilibrium.

A pressure change affects the equilibrium of a reaction only if gases are involved, because pressure changes have no appreciable effect on the volumes of solids and liquids.

EFFECT OF TEMPERATURE. An increase in temperature of a system at equilibrium favors a shift in equilibrium so that heat is absorbed, that is, an endothermic reaction is favored. A decrease in temperature, on the other hand, favors an exothermic reaction.

Of course, any chemical system in equilibrium undergoes simultaneous endothermic and exothermic reactions. It is important to note that when the temperature is elevated, the rates of both the endothermic and exothermic reactions increase, but that the endothermic reaction increases to a larger extent. For example, in the Haber process, raising the temperature favors the decomposition of ammonia, the endothermic reaction. Nevertheless, high temperatures are used in practice in order to increase the over-all rate of reaction.

EFFECT OF CATALYSTS. The addition of a catalyst changes the rates of both the forward and backward reactions equally, but produces no change in the equilibrium concentrations of the materials involved. A catalyst is likely to cause equilibrium to be established more quickly, but does not produce a net change in the reactants and products. Catalysts are used in the Haber process to increase the rate of reaction.

QUESTIONS

1. A solution in which equilibrium exists between dissolved and undissolved solute must be   (1) dilute   (2) saturated   (3) concentrated   (4) unsaturated

2. Equilibrium is reached in all reversible chemical reactions when the   (1) forward reaction stops   (2) reverse reaction stops   (3) concentrations of the reactants and the products become equal   (4) rates of the opposing reactions become equal

3. A gas is most soluble in a liquid under conditions of   (1) high temperature and high pressure   (2) high temperature and low pressure   (3) low temperature and high pressure   (4) low temperature and low pressure

4. As the pressure of a gas increases and the temperature remains constant, the solubility of the gas in water   (1) increases   (2) decreases   (3) remains the same

5. When chemical equilibrium is reached, the rate of the reverse reaction, compared to the rate of the forward reaction, is   (1) less   (2) greater   (3) the same

6. Which system at equilibrium will shift to the right when the pressure is increased?   (1) $NaCl(s) \rightleftarrows Na^+(aq) + Cl^-(aq)$ (2) $C_2H_5OH(l) \rightleftarrows C_2H_5OH(aq)$ (3) $NH_3(g) \rightleftarrows NH_3(aq)$ (4) $C_6H_{12}O_6(s) \rightleftarrows C_6H_{12}O_6(aq)$

7-8. Base the answers to questions 7-8 on the following equilibrium reaction.
$$3A(g) + B(g) + 2C(g) \rightleftarrows D(g) + 2E(g)$$

7. Which change will shift the equilibrium to the right?   (1) increasing the pressure on the system   (2) decreasing the pressure on the system   (3) increasing the concentration of D (4) decreasing the concentration of B

8. Which change will occur if the concentration of B is doubled at constant temperature?   (1) The concentration of C will increase   (2) The concentration of D will increase   (3) The value of the equilibrium constant will decrease   (4) The value of the equilibrium constant will increase

9-12. Base your answers to Questions 9-12 on the following information. Sulfur dioxide, oxygen, and sulfur trioxide are placed in a closed system and allowed to reach equilibrium at a certain temperature according to the reaction $2SO_2(g) + O_2(g) \rightleftarrows 2SO_3(g) + 45.0$ kcal

9. The $\triangle H$ for the formation of 1 mole of SO_0 is   (1) -22.5 kcal   (2) 22.5 kcal   (3) -45.0 kcal   (4) 45.0 kcal

10. The pressure is increased and the temperature is kept constant. Compared to the original number of moles of SO_2, the number of moles of SO_2 present after the new equilibrium is reached is   (1) greater   (2) less   (3) unchanged

11. The temperature is decreased and the pressure is kept constant. Compared to the original number of moles of O_2, the number of moles of O_2 present after the new equilibrum is reached is   (1) greater   (2) less   (3) unchanged

12. Additional SO_2 is added to the system, and the pressure and temperature are kept constant. Compared to the original number of moles of SO_3, the number of moles of SO_3 present after the new equilibrium is reached is   (1) greater   (2) less   (3) unchanged

13. When at equilibrium, which reaction will shift to the right if pressure is increased and the temperature is kept constant?   (1) $2H_2(g) + O_2(g) \rightleftarrows 2H_2O(g)$ (2) $2SO_3(g) \rightleftarrows 2SO_2(g) + O_2(g)$ (3) $2NO(g) \rightleftarrows N_2(g) + O_2(g)$ (4) $2CO_2(g) \rightleftarrows 2CO(g) + O_2(g)$

14. Given the reaction at equilibrium:
$$2SO_2(g) + O_2(g) \rightleftarrows 2SO_3(g) + 47 \text{ kcal}$$
The amount of $SO_3(g)$ will increase if there is   (1) an increase in temperature   (2) a decrease in pressure   (3) an increase in concentration of $SO_2(g)$ (4) a decrease in concentration of $O_2(g)$

15. The system $2SO_2(g) + O_2(g) \rightleftarrows 2SO_3(g) + 44$ kcal is at equilibrium at 25°C. What changes in conditions would result in the largest increase in concentration of SO_3? (1) increased pressure, increased temperature (2) increased pressure, decreased temperature (3) decreased pressure, decreased temperature (4) decreased pressure, increased temperature

16. Given the equilibrium system $H_2(g) + I_2(g) \rightleftarrows 2$ HI(g), as pressure increases and temperature remains constant, the number of moles of HI (1) increases (2) decreases (3) remains the same

17. In which reaction would an increase in pressure produce an increase in the amount of product? (Temperature remains constant.) (1) $CaCO_3(s) \rightarrow CaO(s) + CO_2(g)$ (2) $2HgO(s) \rightarrow 2Hg(s) + O_2(g)$ (3) $N_2(g) + 3H_2(g) \rightarrow 2NH_3(g)$ (4) $H_2(g) + Cl_2(g) \rightarrow 2HCl(g)$

18. Given the reaction at equilibrium: $N_2(g) + 3H_2(g) \rightleftarrows 2NH_3(g)$ If the volume of the reaction vessel is decreased at constant temperature, there will be an increase in the number of moles of (1) N_2, only (2) H_2, only (3) NH_3, only (4) N_2, H_2, and NH_3

19. Given the reaction at equilibrium: $2AB(g) + \text{heat} \rightleftarrows A_2(g) + B_2(g)$ The equilibrium will shift to the right when the (1) temperature increases (2) temperature decreases (3) pressure increases (4) pressure decreases

20. For a given system at equilibrium, lowering the temperature will always (1) increase the rate of reaction (2) increase the concentration of products (3) favor the exothermic reaction (4) favor the endothermic reaction

21. For the equilibrium system $2NO(g) + O_2(g) \rightleftarrows 2NO_2(g) + 27$ kcal, as the temperature of the system is increased, the amount of $O_2(g)$ (1) increases (2) decreases (3) remains the same

22. For a chemical system at equilibrium, a rise in temperature will (1) favor the endothermic reaction (2) favor the exothermic reaction (3) decrease the rates of the reaction (4) have no effect upon the equilibrium

23. Given the reaction at equilibrium:
$$2SO_2(g) + O_2(g) \rightleftarrows 2SO_3(g)$$
If the temperature remains constant, an increase in pressure will (1) have no effect on the equilibrium (2) shift the equilibrium to the right (3) shift the equilibrium to the left (4) change the value of the equilibrium constant

24. Given the reversible reaction $A(g) + B(g) \rightleftarrows C(g)$ at equilibrium. If the concentration of A is increased at constant temperature and pressure, which will also increase? (1) the rate of the forward reaction (2) the value of the equilibrium constant (3) the activation energy (4) the concentration of B

25. Given the reaction at equilibrium:
$$SO_2(g) + NO_2(g) \rightleftarrows SO_3(g) + NO(g)$$
The amount of $SO_3(g)$ will increase if the concentration of (1) NO(g) increases (2) $SO_2(g)$ increases (3) $NO_2(g)$ decreases (4) $SO_2(g)$ decreases

26. A catalyst is added to a system which is at equilibrium.
    If the temperature remains constant, there will be a change in the
    (1) point of equilibrium   (2) heat content of the products   (3) heat
    content of the reactants   (4) required activation energy

27. The purpose of a catalyst in a reaction is to   (1) change the activation
    energy required of the reaction   (2) provide the energy necessary to
    start the reaction   (3) increase the amount of product formed
    (4) decrease the amount of reactants used

28. When a catalyst is added to a system in equilibrium, the equilibrium
    concentration of the products   (1) increases   (2) decreases
    (3) remains the same

29. Which change may occur in a reaction system when a catalyst is
    added?   (1) The equilibrium point is reached more rapidly.   (2) The
    potential energy of the reactants increases.   (3) The potential energy
    of the products decreases.   (4) The heat of reaction becomes smaller.

30. The net effect of a catalyst is to change the   (1) potential energy of
    the reactants   (2) potential energy of the products   (3) heat of
    reaction   (4) rates of both the forward and reverse reactions

LAW OF CHEMICAL EQUILIBRIUM

When a reversible reaction reaches equilibrium, there is a mathematical relationship between the reactants and products: the product
of the molar concentrations on the right side of the equation (the
products) divided by the molar concentrations on the left side of the
equation (the reactants) is equal to a constant, K_{eq}, called the **equilibrium constant.** The concentration of each substance, in terms of its
molar concentration, is raised to the power of its coefficient in the balanced equation. To write the equilibrium expression for the reaction

$$N_2 + 3H_2 \leftrightarrows 2NH_3:$$

1. Make sure that the equation is balanced properly.

2. Place the products of the reaction in the numerator and the reactants in the denominator.

3. Place a square bracket around each substance involved. The
brackets are used to indicate concentration of the substance in moles
per liter.

4. Write the coefficient of each substance as a power of its concentration.

5. Set the expression equal to K_{eq}, which is the equilibrium constant
for a given reaction at a constant temperature.

reactants   product

$$N_2 + 3H_2 \rightleftharpoons 2NH_3$$

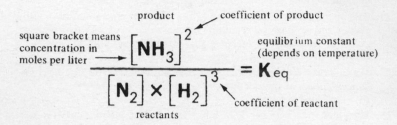

Figure 6-2. Writing an equilibrium expression. The multiplication sign is usually omitted.

SIGNIFICANCE OF THE EQUILIBRIUM CONSTANT. The equilibrium constant has a specific numerical value for any given chemical reaction at a particular temperature. Even though the concentrations of the substances involved may change, the value remains constant. For example, an increase in the concentration of NH_3 causes the reaction to go to the left, thus increasing the concentrations of N_2 and H_2. The value of K, however, remains constant.

Chemists use the value of K to predict the extent of a chemical reaction. When the value of K is *large*, the *products* of the reaction are favored. The system at equilibrium has a greater concentration of products than reactants. A *small* K value indicates that the *reverse reaction*, the formation of reactants, is favored, and there is relatively little product at equilibrium.

The equilibrium constant for any given chemical system changes only when the temperature of the system changes. This occurs because temperature changes have unequal effects in the forward and backward reactions of a reversible reaction. Some typical equilibria systems and the values of their expressions are listed in Reference Table M.

IONIZATION CONSTANT. Substances having ionic bonds dissociate in water to form positive and negative ions. Such a system attains a state of equilibrium between the ions and the un-ionized compound. The equilibrium constant for the system is called the **ionization constant** or the **dissociation constant, K_{ion}.**
For the reaction

$$MB(aq) \rightleftharpoons M^+(aq) + B^-(aq)$$

the equilibrium expression, at constant temperature, is

$$K_{ion} = \frac{[M^+][B^-]}{[MB]}$$

The higher the value of the ionization constant, the greater the degree of ionization in a reaction. (Ionization and K_{ion} are discussed more fully in Unit 7.)

QUESTIONS

1. Given the equilibrium expression:

$$K = \frac{[A]\ [B]}{[C]\ [D]}$$

Which pair represents the reactants of the forward reaction? (1) A and B (2) B and D (3) C and D (4) A and C

2. The equilibrium constant for a given system changes when (1) the temperature of the system is changed (2) the pressure of the system is changed (3) the concentration of one or more of the reactants is changed (4) a catalyst is added

3. Which is the correct equilibrium expression for the reaction
$4NH_3(g) + 5O_2(g) \rightleftarrows 4NO(g) + 6H_2O(g)$?

(1) $K = \dfrac{[4NH_3][5O_2]}{[4NO][6H_2O]}$

(3) $K = \dfrac{[4NO][6H_2O]}{[4NH_3][5O_2]}$

(2) $K = \dfrac{[NH_3]^4[O_2]^5}{[4NO][6H_2O]}$

(4) $K = \dfrac{[NO]^4[H_2O]^6}{[NH_3]^4[O_2]^5}$

4. Which equilibrium system contains the largest concentration of products at 25°C?

(1) $AgI(s) \rightleftarrows Ag^+(aq) + I^-(aq)$
$(K(eq) = 8.5 \times 10^{-17})$

(2) $CH_3COOH(aq) \rightleftarrows H^+(aq) + CH_3COO^-(aq)$
$(K(eq) = 1.8 \times 10^{-5})$

(3) $Pb^+(aq) + 2Cl^-(aq) \rightleftarrows PbCl_2(s)$
$(K(eq) = 6.3 \times 10^4)$

(4) $Cu(s) + 2Ag^+(aq) \rightleftarrows Cu^{+2}(aq) + 2Ag(s)$
$(K(eq) = 2.0 \times 10^{15})$

5. For the general equilibrium system $2A(g) + 3B(g) \rightleftarrows 3C(g) + 2D(g)$ at a constant temperature, K equals

(1) $\dfrac{[3C]\ [2D]}{[2A]\ [3B]}$ (2) $\dfrac{[C]^3[D]^2}{[A]^2[B]^3}$ (3) $\dfrac{[3C]^3[2D]^2}{[2A]^2[3B]^3}$ (4) $\dfrac{[2A]^2[3B]^3}{[3C]^3[2D]^2}$

6. For the general equilibrium system $A + B \rightleftarrows C$, which equilibrium constant results in the highest concentration of C? (1) 3×10^{-6} (2) 7×10^{-6} (3) 7×10^{-10} (4) 3×10^{-3}

7. What is the equilibrium expression for the reaction
$H_2(g) + I_2(g) \rightleftarrows 2HI(g)$?

(1) $K = \dfrac{2[HI]}{[H_2][I_2]}$

(3) $K = \dfrac{[H_2][I_2]}{[HI]^2}$

(2) $K = \dfrac{[H_2][I_2]}{2[HI]}$

(4) $K = \dfrac{[HI]^2}{[H_2][I_2]}$

8. Which would be the equilibrium constant of a chemical reaction that goes most nearly to completion? (1) 2×10^{-15} (2) 2×10^{-1} (3) 2×10^1 (4) 2×10^{15}

9. Which equation would have the equilibrium expression

$K = \dfrac{[C]^2}{[A][B]^2}$?

(1) $A + 2B \rightleftarrows 2C$ (3) $2C \rightleftarrows A + 2B$

(2) $A + B_2 \rightleftarrows C_2$ (4) $2A + B \rightleftarrows 2C$

10. In the general reaction $A + B \rightleftarrows AB$, which equilibrium constant most favors the production of $A + B$? (1) 9.1×10^{-10} (2) 4.3×10^{-7} (3) 4.7×10^{-12} (4) 3.5×10^{-3}

11. As a catalyst is added to a system at equilibrium, the value of the equilibrium constant
(1) decreases   (2) increases   (3) remains the same

12. Given the reaction: $A(g) + B(g) + heat = AB(g)$. As the pressure increases at a constant temperature, the value of the equilibrium constant (1) decreases   (2) increases   (3) remains the same

SOLUBILITY PRODUCT CONSTANT. In a saturated solution of an ionic solid, an equilibrium exists between the ions of the saturated solution and the excess solid.

$$AB(s) = A^+(aq) + B^-(aq)$$

When the temperature of the system is constant,

$$K = \dfrac{[A^+][B^-]}{[AB]}$$

Note that the concentration of a solid is a constant, regardless of the amount that is present. A change in the amount of solid has no effect on the concentrations of dissolved ions. The equilibrium expression can therefore be simplified as follows:

$$K_{eq} \times [AB] = [A^+][B^-]$$

Since [AB] is a constant, $K_{eq} \times$ [AB] is also a constant. This constant is called the **solubility product constant** and is represented by K_{sp}:

$$K_{eq} \times [AB] = K_{sp} = [A^+] [B^-]$$

The smaller the value of K_{sp} is for a substance, the less soluble it is. So-called "insoluble" substances have very small values of K_{sp}. For example,

$$K_{sp} \ CaSO_4 = 2.4 \times 10^{-5}$$

$$K_{sp} \ BaSO_4 = 1.6 \times 10^{-9}$$

Although both of these salts are only very slightly soluble, calcium sulfate is still about 100 times more soluble than barium sulfate. This means that in a very dilute solution containing both salts, the barium sulfate could be precipitated out before the calcium sulfate. Values of K_{sp} for slightly soluble salts are useful in analyzing the composition of unknown mixtures (qualitative and quantitative analysis). Values for several solubility product constants are listed in Reference Table M.

QUESTIONS

1. Which expression represents the solubility product constant, K_{sp}, of AgCl(s)?
   (1) $K_{sp} = [Ag^+][Cl^-]$ (3) $K_{sp} = \dfrac{[Ag^+]}{[Cl^-]}$

   (2) $K_{sp} = [Ag^+] + [Cl^-]$ (4) $K_{sp} = \dfrac{[Cl^-]}{[Ag^+]}$

2. Consider the reaction
   $$Al(OH)_3(s) \rightleftarrows Al^{3+}(aq) + 3OH^-(aq)$$
   at equilibrium. Which equilibrium expression is correct for this equation? (1) $K_{sp} = [Al^{3+}] [3OH^-]$ (2) $K_{sp} = [Al^{3+}] + [3OH^-]^3$
   (3) $K_{sp} = [Al^{3+}] [OH^-]$ (4) $K_{sp} = [Al^{3+}] [OH^-]^3$

3. The K_{sp} of barium sulfate is 8.7×10^{-11} at $18°$ C and 1.1×10^{-10} at $25°$ C. This indicates that as the temperature increases from $18°$ C to $25°$ C, the solubility of barium sulfate   (1) decreases   (2) increases   (3) remains the same

4. Which saturated solution would have the highest S^{2-} ion concentration?
   (1) CdS (K_{sp} at $18°$ C = 3.6×10^{-29})
   (2) CoS (K_{sp} at $18°$ C = 3.0×10^{-26})
   (3) PbS (K_{sp} at $18°$ C = 3.4×10^{-28})
   (4) FeS (K_{sp} at $18°$ C = 3.7×10^{-19})

5. Some compounds and their solubility product constants are shown below. Which compound is least soluble?   (1) AB, $K_{sp} = 8 \times 10^{-5}$
   (2) AC, $K_{sp} = 7 \times 10^{-6}$ (3) XY, $K_{sp} = 6 \times 10^{-7}$ (4) XZ, $K_{sp} = 5 \times 10^{-8}$

COMMON ION EFFECT. Consider the equilibrium system and the K_{sp} for the system:

$$AgCl(s) = Ag^+(aq) + Cl^-(aq)$$

$$K_{sp} = [Ag^+][Cl^-]$$

According to Le Chatelier's principle, the system can be shifted to the left by the addition of silver ion or chloride ion. When additional chloride ion is added, the concentration of the silver ion will be reduced and the amount of silver chloride will increase. This addition of an ion from a different salt (NaCl, KCl, etc.) reduces the solubility of the silver salt, and is called the *common ion effect.*

QUESTIONS

1. If a soluble salt yielding Cl^- is stirred into a flask containing a saturated ammonium chloride solution, the concentration of the $NH_4^+(aq)$ ions will   (1) decrease   (2) increase   (3) remain the same

2. Given the system at equilibrium:
$H_3PO_4 + 3H_2O \rightleftarrows 3H_3O^+ + PO_4^{3-}$
If $Na_3PO_4(s)$ is added, there will be a decrease in the concentration of
(1) Na^+ (2) PO_4^{3-} (3) H_3O^+ (4) H_2O

3. Given the equation $AgCl(s) \rightleftarrows Ag^+(aq) + Cl^-(aq)$. As NaCl(s) dissolves in the solution, temperature remaining constant, the $Ag^+(aq)$ concentration will   (1) decrease as the amount of AgCl(s) decreases   (2) decrease as the amount of AgCl(s) increases   (3) increase as the amount of AgCl(s) decreases   (4) increase as the amount of AgCl(s) increases

SPONTANEOUS REACTIONS

Spontaneous changes are changes that are observed to occur under given conditions. For example, if the external temperature is above $0°C$, ice is observed to melt to liquid water, whereas the reverse change from liquid water to ice is not observed. At temperatures below $0°C$, the opposite is observed: liquid water changes to ice, but ice does not change to water. Chemical reactions are also observed to go in one direction under one set of conditions, in the opposite direction under other conditions, or to remain in equilibrium under still another set of conditions.

FACTORS THAT DETERMINE THE DIRECTION OF SPONTANEOUS CHANGE. There are two fundamental tendencies in nature which together determine the direction of a spontaneous change. They are:

1. *The tendency to change to a condition of less energy.*
2. *The tendency to change to a condition of greater randomness.*

THE TENDENCY TOWARD LOWER ENERGY. A study of potential energy diagrams for reversible chemical reactions shows that the activation energy for the exothermic direction is less than that for the endothermic direction. Therefore, at any given temperature, the particles in a system are more likely to collide with enough energy to react in the exothermic direction than in the endothermic direction. On the basis of energy change alone, we expect spontaneous reactions to go in the exothermic direction. At ordinary temperatures, this is in fact what we usually observe. Most spontaneous chemical changes that we observe are exothermic.

THE TENDENCY TOWARD RANDOMNESS. Randomness is the disorder or lack of regularity in a system. It is measured by a quantity called **entropy.** The greater the disorder, the higher the entropy. It is usually necessary for particles to collide in a special way in order to form a more highly organized or regular arrangement. On the other hand, there are many ways in which they can collide to produce more disorder. Therefore it is to be expected that systems will tend to go from conditions of greater order (lower entropy) to conditions of greater disorder (higher entropy). On the basis of entropy change alone, we expect spontaneous reactions to go in the direction of greater entropy.

Examples of entropy change are changes from the solid, crystalline phase (great order, low entropy), to the liquid phase (more randomness, higher entropy), to the gaseous phase (maximum randomness, highest entropy). Compounds represent a state of greater order and lower entropy than the free elements of which they are composed.

IMPORTANCE OF TEMPERATURE. At low temperatures, the energy factor is dominant, and is more likely to influence the direction of a spontaneous change. At high temperatures, all the particles have more kinetic energy on the average, and activation energy is of less importance in limiting a reaction. Therefore entropy change tends to control the direction of spontaneous change at high temperatures. When the energy change favors one direction and the entropy change favors the reverse, the direction in which the change actually goes depends on the temperature.

FREE ENERGY CHANGE. The net effect of energy change and entropy change is called the **free energy change**. It is represented by the following mathematical expression:

$$\Delta G = \Delta H - T\Delta S$$

where ΔG is the free energy change of a given reaction; ΔH is the heat of reaction; ΔS is the entropy change of the reaction; and T is the absolute temperature in K.

In order for a reaction to be spontaneous, ΔG must be negative. Note that a negative value of ΔH tends to make ΔG negative and tends to make the reaction spontaneous. Note also that a positive value of ΔS (an increase in entropy) also tends to make ΔG negative and thus tends to make the reaction spontaneous.

When these two terms in the free energy expression oppose each other, that is, when one tends to make ΔG positive and the other tends to make it negative, the temperature determines which factor will be dominant. At low temperatures, ΔH is dominant; at high temperatures, ΔS is dominant. When the sum of the two terms is zero, that is, when ΔG is zero, the system is in equilibrium; neither direction is favored.

The decomposition of potassium chlorate illustrates the effect of temperature on making a reaction spontaneous. The equation of reaction is:

$$2KClO_3 \rightarrow 2KCl + 3O_2$$

The heat of reaction is positive; that is, it is an endothermic reaction, and energy change alone tends to *prevent* its occurrence. That is why potassium chlorate is stable at room temperatures. However, the reaction results in products that have more entropy—a gas and a solid that are simpler in organization. The entropy factor thus tends to make ΔG negative, but it is only at high temperatures that the factor $T\Delta S$ becomes large enough to overcome the energy factor and make the reaction spontaneous. When heated in a test tube to a sufficiently high temperature, potassium chlorate becomes unstable and decomposes.

QUESTIONS

1. As the reactants are converted to product in the reaction $A(g) + B(g) \rightarrow C(s)$, the entropy of the system (1) decreases (2) increases (3) remains the same

2. Which change represents an increase in the entropy of a system?

   (1) $C_6H_{12}O_6(s) \xrightarrow{\ H_2O\ } C_6H_{12}O_6(aq)$ (2) $H_2O(l) \rightarrow H_2O(s)$

   (3) $CO_2(g) \rightarrow CO_2(s)$ (4) $C_2H_5OH(g) \rightarrow C_2H_5OH(l)$

3. As 1 gram of $H_2O(s)$ changes to 1 gram of $H_2O(l)$, the entropy of the system (1) decreases (2) increases (3) remains the same

4. As a system becomes less random, its entropy (1) decreases (2) increases (3) remains the same

5. Which phrase best describes the reaction below?
$C(s) + \frac{1}{2}O_2(g) \rightarrow CO(g) + 26.4$ kcal (1) exothermic with an increase in entropy (2) exothermic with a decrease in entropy (3) endothermic with an increase in entropy (4) endothermic with a decrease in entropy

6. Given the reaction at 1 atm and 298 K:
$$NaOH(s) \xrightarrow{H_2O} Na^+(aq) + OH^-(aq) + 10.6 \text{ kcal}$$
The heat of reaction, $\triangle H$, is (1) negative and the reaction is spontaneous (2) negative and the reaction is not spontaneous (3) positive and the reaction is spontaneous (3) positive and the reaction is not spontaneous

7. A chemical reaction is most likely to occur spontaneously if the (1) free energy change ($\triangle G$) is negative (2) entropy change ($\triangle S$) is negative (3) activation energy (E) is positive (4) heat of reaction ($\triangle H$) is positive

8. For a given chemical reaction, $\triangle G$ will always be negative if $\triangle H$ is (1) negative and $T\triangle S$ is negative (2) negative and $T\triangle S$ is positive (3) positive and $T\triangle S$ is negative (4) positive and $T\triangle S$ is positive

9. Which statement is true if the free energy ($\triangle G$) of a reaction is zero?
(1) The rate of the forward reaction is zero
(2) The rate of the reverse reaction is zero
(3) The reaction is approaching equilibrium
(4) The reaction is at equilibrium

10. Which change of phase results in a decrease in entropy?
(1) $H_2O(l) \rightarrow H_2O(g)$ (2) $H_2O(l) \rightarrow H_2O(s)$
(3) $H_2O(s) \rightarrow H_2O(g)$ (4) $H_2O(s) \rightarrow H_2O(l)$

11. A 1 gram sample of a substance has the greatest entropy when it is in the
(1) solid state   (2) crystalline state
(3) liquid state   (4) gaseous state

12. The change in free energy of a chemical reaction is represented by
(1) ΔT (2) ΔS (3) ΔH (4) ΔG

UNIT 7   ACID-BASE THEORIES

ELECTROLYTES

An **electrolyte** is a substance that, when dissolved in water, forms a solution capable of conducting an electric current. The ability of a solution to conduct a current is due to the presence of ions. Electrolytes include all ionic compounds and many polar covalent compounds, such as acids, which react with water to form ions.

The abnormal effect of electrolytes on the boiling and freezing points of a solvent is best explained by the presence of ions in solution (see Unit 5, page 74). The elevation of the boiling point and depression of the freezing point depend on the number of particles in solution rather than on their nature.

ACIDS AND BASES

OPERATIONAL DEFINITIONS. Substances can be classified on the basis of observable properties. When a class of substances is defined in this way, the definition is called an **operational definition.** For example, acids in aqueous solution cause blue litmus to turn red. This statement is part of the **operational definition** of an acid.

CONCEPTUAL DEFINITIONS. Definitions can also be stated in terms of *inferences* or *interpretations* of observed facts. For example, an acid can be defined as a substance that produces an excess of hydrogen ions in aqueous solution. Since hydrogen ions cannot be observed, the preceding sentence is part of a **conceptual definition** of acids. Operational definitions tend to be used in the early stages of a scientific approach to a problem. As additional information and understanding accumulate in regard to the problem, the original operational definitions are usually replaced by much broader conceptual definitions. This has happened in the case of acids and bases.

OPERATIONAL DEFINITIONS OF ACIDS AND BASES

ACIDS. Acids can be defined operationally in terms of certain observable properties.

1. Aqueous solutions of acids conduct electricity. If the solution is a relatively good conductor, the acid is considered **strong.** If the solution is a relatively poor conductor, the acid is considered **weak.** (Conceptually, the strength of an acid is related to the degree to which it ionizes in aqueous solution. See "Conceptual Definitions of Acids and Bases" on page 101.)

2. **Acids react with certain metals to generate hydrogen gas.** The metals they react with are those found below hydrogen in a table of **standard reduction potentials** (Reference Table N). This property is difficult to observe in acids that are strong oxidizing agents, such as nitric acid and concentrated sulfuric acid. Only in very dilute solutions do nitric acid and sulfuric acid liberate hydrogen on reaction with metals.

3. **Acids cause acid-base indicators to change color.** Indicators are substances that show different colors in acidic and basic solutions. For example, litmus is red in an acidic solution and blue in a basic one. (Conceptually, an indicator changes color at a specific concentration of hydrogen ion.)

4. **Acids react with bases (hydroxides) to form water and a salt.** Such reactions are called **neutralization** reactions. (Conceptually, water is always one of the products because the hydrogen ion of the acid reacts with the hydroxide ion of the base: $H^+ + OH^- \rightarrow H_2O$.)

5. **Dilute aqueous solutions of acids have a sour taste.**

BASES. Like acids, **bases** may be defined operationally by their characteristic properties.

1. **Aqueous solutions of bases conduct electricity.** (Conceptually, stronger bases ionize more completely than weaker bases, and are therefore better conductors.)

2. **Bases cause color changes in acid-base indicators.** In addition to litmus, the indicator phenolphthalein is used, which is pink in a basic solution and colorless in an acid solution.

3. **Bases react with acids to form water and a salt.**

4. **Bases are caustic substances and have a slippery or soapy feeling.**

CONCEPTUAL DEFINITIONS OF ACIDS AND BASES

ARRHENIUS THEORY. Svante Arrhenius, a Swedish chemist, investigated the nature of electrolytes and of acids and bases. He defined acids conceptually as substances whose water solutions contained hydrogen ions as the only kind of positive ion. He defined bases as substances that yield hydroxide ions as the only negative ion in aqueous solution. He added further that the characteristic properties of acids in aqueous solution are due to an excess of hydrogen ions, while the characteristic properties of bases are due to an excess of hydroxide ions.

BRONSTED-LOWRY THEORY. In the Bronsted-Lowry theory of acids and bases, it is assumed that a hydrogen ion (which would be a bare proton, with no surrounding electrons) could not exist free in any chemical system. It must always be bonded to another species. In aqueous solutions, the "hydrogen ion" or proton bonds to a water molecule, forming the **hydronium ion,** H_3O^+. The Bronsted-Lowry theory then goes on to define an acid as any species, either a molecule or an ion, that can transfer, or *donate*, a proton to another species. An acid is thus defined as a **proton donor**. The definition does not mention ionization or dissociation in aqueous solution, and therefore extends the theory of acids and bases beyond reactions that involve aqueous solution, although these reactions are still covered by the theory.

BRONSTED-LOWRY ACIDS. In the reaction

$$NH_3 + H_2O \rightleftarrows NH_4^+ + OH^-$$

the water molecule, H_2O, is a Bronsted-Lowry acid, because it donates a proton to the ammonia molecule, NH_3 (thereby producing the ammonium ion, NH_4^+).

BRONSTED-LOWRY BASES. The Bronsted-Lowry theory defines a base as any species that can combine with, or *accept*, a proton. A base is thus defined as a **proton acceptor**. All bases must have at least one pair of unshared electrons. In the ammonia-water reaction above, the ammonia molecule is a base, because it accepts a proton from the water molecule.

In the reverse reaction

$$NH_4^+ + OH^- \rightleftarrows H_2O + NH_3$$

the OH^- ion is a base. It accepts a proton from the NH_4^+ ion, which is an acid in this reaction.

In the reaction between hydrogen chloride and water,

$$HCl + H_2O \rightleftarrows H_3O^+ + Cl^-$$

hydrogen chloride is an acid, which donates a proton to the water molecule to form the H_3O^+ ion. Water, in this reaction, acts as a base. In the reverse reaction, the hydronium ion is an acid and the chloride ion is a base.

AMPHOTERIC SUBSTANCES. In the Bronsted-Lowry sense, water sometimes behaves like an acid by *donating* a proton:

$$\underset{\text{acid}}{H_2O} + NH_3 \rightleftarrows NH_4^+ + OH^-$$

and sometimes acts like a base by *accepting* a proton:

$$\underset{\text{base}}{H_2O} + HNO_3 \rightleftarrows H_3O^+ + NO_3^-$$

Substances that can act either as an acid or a base, depending on the chemical environment, are called **amphoteric,** or **amphiprotic,** substances. The hydroxides of aluminum, zinc, lead, and chromium are amphoteric according to both acid-base theories discussed. In the presence of a strong base, these compounds behave like acids, while in the presence of a strong acid, they act like bases. According to the Bronsted-Lowry definition, species such as H_2O and HSO_4^- are also amphoteric, because they can either give or receive protons.

ACID-BASE REACTIONS

NEUTRALIZATION REACTIONS. A **neutralization reaction** occurs when equivalent quantities of an acid and a base are mixed. All neutralization reactions involve the combination of a hydrogen ion and a hydroxide ion to form water. For example, one mole of hydrogen ions reacts with one mole of hydroxide ions to form one mole of water:

$$H^+ + OH^- \rightleftarrows H_2O$$

ACID-BASE TITRATION. The process of adding measured volumes of an acid or base of known molarity to an acid or base of unknown molarity until neutralization occurs is called **titration.** The acid or base of known molarity is called the **standard solution.** The **end point** of the titration may be determined by using appropriate indicators, by noting specific temperature changes, or by measuring electrode potential changes.

The unknown molarity can be calculated from the volumes used and the known molarity of the standard solution. The procedure is as follows:

1. Write the balanced equation for the reaction. From the coefficients determine the ratio of reacting moles of acid and base. (In most cases the ratio will be 1:1, 1:2, or 2:1.)

2. Use the fact that the number of moles of solute is equal to the product of the volume in liters and the molarity:

> **moles of acid = liters of acid × molarity of acid**
> **moles of base = liters of base × molarity of base**

3. Set the ratio of moles equal to the ratio indicated by the equation. If the ratio is 1:1, then

$$\frac{\text{moles of acid}}{\text{moles of base}} = \frac{\text{liters of acid} \times \text{molarity of acid}}{\text{liters of base} \times \text{molarity of base}} = 1$$

Or,

liters of acid × molarity of acid = liters of base × molarity of base

The unknown molarity can be calculated from this relationship.

SAMPLE PROBLEM

How many milliliters of 0.2 M KOH are needed to neutralize 20 mL of 0.1 M HCl?

Solution: Write the balanced equation for the reaction.

$$KOH + HCl \rightarrow H_2O + KCl$$

Find the number of moles in the given solution (20 mL of 0.1 M HCl).

no. of moles = molarity × volume in liters
Convert 20 mL to liters: 20 mL = 0.020 liters
no. of moles of HCl = 0.1 × 0.020 = 0.002 mole

We see from the equation that the mole ratio of KOH to HCl is 1:1. Therefore, we need 0.002 mole of KOH. Calculate the number of liters of 0.2 M KOH that contains 0.002 mole.

$$\text{volume in liters} = \frac{\text{no. of moles}}{\text{molarity}}$$

$$= \frac{0.002}{0.2} = 0.01 \text{ liter, or } \mathbf{10 \text{ mL}}$$

NORMALITY OF SOLUTIONS. Acid-base titrations become simpler if concentrations are expressed in terms of **normality** rather than molarity. An acid solution has a normality of 1 (1 N) if it contains one mole of replaceable hydrogen ion per liter of solution. It can be seen that when the formula of an acid contains only one H atom, a 1 M solution is also a 1 N solution:

$$HCl \rightarrow H^+ + Cl^-$$

One mole of HCl produces one mole of H^+. The normality of a solution of HCl is always the same as its molarity.

In the case of H_2SO_4, one mole of acid produces two moles of H^+:

$$H_2SO_4 \rightarrow 2H^+ + SO_4^{--}$$

Therefore, a 1 M solution of H_2SO_4 is 2 N, and the normality is always twice the molarity for H_2SO_4.

The normality of a base is defined in a similar way, but in terms of moles of OH^- per liter. Thus, a 1 M solution of NaOH is 1 N, while a 1 M solution of $Ca(OH)_2$ is 2 N.

It can be seen that one liter of a 1 N solution of any acid will exactly neutralize one liter of a 1 N solution of any base, regardless of their formulas and the mole ratios of the reaction. This is true because the 1 N solution of acid has 1 mole of H^+ per liter and the 1 N solution of the base has 1 mole of OH^- per liter. In general, volumes of reacting acids and bases will be inversely proportional to their normalities:

$$\frac{\text{volume of acid}}{\text{volume of base}} = \frac{\text{normality of base}}{\text{normality of acid}}$$

or,

volume of acid × normality of acid =
    volume of base × normality of base

*This topic is not required by the New York State syllabus.

SAMPLE PROBLEM

How many mL of 0.2 M H_2SO_4 will neutralize 10 mL of 1 M NaOH?

Solution:

Change molarities to normalities.

$$0.2 \text{ M } H_2SO_4 = 2 \times 0.2 = 0.4 \text{ N}$$

$$1 \text{ M NaOH} = 1 \text{ N}$$

Use the relationship

volume of acid × normality of acid =
volume of base × normality of base

$$x \text{ mL} \times 0.4 = 10 \text{ mL} \times 1$$

$$x = \frac{10}{0.4} = 25 \text{ mL of } H_2SO_4$$

CONJUGATE ACID-BASE PAIRS. According to the Bronsted-Lowry theory, acid-base reactions involve a transfer of protons from the acid, the proton donor, to the base, the proton acceptor. In order to accept a proton, a base must have at least one pair of unshared electrons. This pair of electrons can form a covalent bond with the proton from the acid in the reaction. The bond formed is called a **coordinate covalent bond.** As explained on page 34, the electrons in a coordinate covalent bond are provided by only one member of the bonding partners.

All acid-base reactions are reversible. An acid transfers a proton, and thereby becomes a base, capable of accepting a proton. A base accepts a proton to become an acid. Each such pair, made up of an acid and a base related by the transfer of a proton, is called a **conjugate acid-base pair.** In the following equation,

$$\text{Acid}_1 + \text{Base}_2 \rightleftarrows \text{Acid}_2 + \text{Base}_1$$

Acid_1 and Base_1 are a conjugate pair. Base_1 is the conjugate of Acid_1, and Acid_1 is the conjugate acid of Base_1. Acid_2 and Base_2 are a second conjugate pair. For example,

Conjugate pair (HCl ↔ Cl^-)

Conjugate pair (H_2O ↔ H_3O^+)

$$\underset{\text{Acid}_1}{HCl} + \underset{\text{Base}_2}{H_2O} \rightleftarrows \underset{\text{Acid}_2}{H_3O^+} + \underset{\text{Base}_1}{Cl^-}$$

HCl and Cl^- are a conjugate acid-base pair. HCl is the acid, which changes to the base Cl^- by donating a proton. Cl^- changes to HCl by accepting a proton. Similarly, H_3O^+ and H_2O are a conjugate acid-base pair. Reference Table L lists sample conjugate acid-base pairs and the values of the equilibrium constants (called K_a for acid reactions) for these systems. Examination of this table will also reveal several substances that are listed as both acids and bases, that is, they are amphiprotic.

STRENGTH OF ACIDS AND BASES. As pointed out before, the *strength* of an acid or a base refers to the degree to which it ionizes in solution. Strong acids have weak conjugate bases, and strong bases have weak conjugate acids.

QUESTIONS

1. If 6 milliliters of 1 M HCl is exactly neutralized by 3 milliliters of KOH, the molarity of the KOH is   (1) 1 M   (2) 2 M   (3) 3 M   (4) 9 M

2. As 0.1 mole of $Ba(OH)_2(s)$ dissolves in 1 liter of 0.1 M H_2SO_4, the conductivity of the solution   (1) decreases   (2) increases   (3) remains the same

3. A 30 milliliter sample of HCl is completely neutralized by 10 milliliters of a 1.5 M NaOH solution. What is the molarity of the HCl solution?
   (1) 0.25   (2) 0.50   (3) 1.5   (4) 4.5

4. How many milliliters of 2.0 M NaOH are needed to exactly neutralize 50 milliliters of 2.0 M HCl?   (1) 25   (2) 50   (3) 100   (4) 200

5. How many moles of OH^- ions would be needed to exactly neutralize 1 liter of 2 M HCl?   (1) 1   (2) 2   (3) 3   (4) 0.5

6. Which Brönsted acid has a conjugate base that has amphoteric properties?   (1) HCl   (2) HNO_3 (3) H_3O^+ (4) HSO_4^-

7. Which reaction illustrates amphoterism?
   (1) $H_2O + H_2O \rightarrow H_3O^+ + OH^-$ (2) $HCl + H_2O \rightarrow H_3O + Cl^-$
   (3) $NaCl \rightarrow Na^+ + Cl^-$ (4) $NaOH \rightarrow Na^+ + OH^-$

8. What are the Brönsted-Lowry bases in the reaction
   $H_2S + H_2O \rightleftarrows H_3O^+ + HS^-$?   (1) H_2S and H_2O (2) H_2S and H_3O^+
   (3) HS^- and H_2O (4) HS^- and H_3O^+

9. In the reaction $NH_3 + H_2O \rightleftarrows NH_4^+ + OH^-$, the two Brönsted acids are   (1) NH_3 and H_2O (2) NH_3 and OH^- (3) NH_4^+ and H_2O
   (4) NH_4^+ and OH^-

10. How many liters of 2.5 M HCl are required to exactly neutralize 1.5 liters of 5.0 M NaOH?   (1) 1.0   (2) 2.0   (3) 3.0   (4) 4.0

11. A 2.0 milliliter sample of NaOH solution is exactly neutralized by 4.0 milliliters of a 3.0 M HCl solution. What is the concentration of the NaOH solution?   (1) 1.5 M   (2) 4.5 M   (3) 3.0 M   (4) 6.0 M

12. Which solution will be exactly neutralized by 1.0 liter of 1.0 M NaOH?   (1) 1.0 liter of 0.50 M HCl   (2) 1.0 liter of 2.0 M HCl
    (3) 0.50 liter of 0.50 M HCl   (4) 0.50 liter of 2.0 M HCl

13. In the reaction of $H_2O + H_2O \rightleftarrows H_3O^+ + OH^-$, water is acting as   (1) a Brönsted acid, only   (2) a Brönsted base, only   (3) neither a Brönsted acid nor base   (4) both a Brönsted acid and base

14. Which is the conjugate base of the HSO_4^- ion? (1) H_2SO_4 (2) H_3O^+
    (3) SO_4^{2-} (4) OH^-

15. In the reaction $NH_2^- + HOH \rightleftarrows NH_3 + OH^-$, the two
    Brönsted-Lowry acids are (1) HOH and NH_2^- (2) HOH and NH_3
    (3) OH^- and HOH (4) OH^- and NH_3

16. Which is a Brönsted acid-base conjugate pair? (1) SO_3^{2-} and SO_2
    (2) CO_3^{2-} and CO (3) H_3O^+ and H_2 (4) NH_4^+ and NH_3

17. What is the conjugate base of $H_2PO_4^-$? (1) H^+ (2) PO_4^{3-}
    (3) HPO_4^{2-} (4) H_3PO_4

18. In the reaction $HSO_4^- + H_2O \rightleftarrows H_3O^+ + SO_4^{2-}$, the HSO_4^- ion is (1) a
    proton donor (2) amphiprotic (3) a proton acceptor (4) a base

19. A 0.1 M solution of acetic acid and a 0.1 M solution of ammonium
    hydroxide, both at 25° C, *differ* in that the acetic acid solution has a
    larger (1) ionization constant (2) pH (3) H_3O^+ concentration
    (4) OH^- concentration

IONIZATION CONSTANT

The ionization constant for acids, K_a, is used to determine the relative strengths of acids (see Unit 6, page 92). For example, an acid with a $K_a = 1.8 \times 10^{-5}$ is stronger than an acid with a $K_a = 5.8 \times 10^{-10}$, although both of these acids are considered weak when compared, for example, to sulfuric acid or hydrochloric acid.

For the reaction $HB = H^+ + B^-$,

$$K_a = \frac{[H^+] \, [B^-]}{[HB]}$$

Ionization constants can be determined for all acids that do not ionize completely. For those acids that do ionize completely, there is no equilibrium established. Referring to the expression above, you can see that for fully dissociated acids the denominator is zero, and thus the K_a value is infinite.

IONIZATION CONSTANT OF WATER. Water is a very weak electrolyte, ionizing according to the equation

$$H_2O = H^+ + OH^- \quad (or \ 2H_2O = H_3O^+ + OH^-)$$

At a given temperature, the ionization constant is

$$K_a = \frac{[H^+] \, [OH^-]}{[H_2O]}$$

Since the concentration of water is almost a constant for all reactions in aqueous solution, its value can be incorporated with that of the ionization constant, K_a, to give the constant K_W.

$$K_a \times [H_2O] = [H^+] \, [OH^-]$$
$$K_W = [H^+] \, [OH^-]$$

The last expression states that the product of the hydrogen ion concentration and the hydroxide ion concentration of water or of an aqueous solution is a constant, K_W, at a constant temperature.

Since the hydronium ion, H_3O^+, is simply a hydrogen ion attached to a water molecule, the hydronium ion concentration is the same as the hydrogen ion concentration. The value of K_W is the same for hydronium ion concentration as for hydrogen ion concentration.

$$K_W = [H_3O^+] \ [OH^-]$$

The numerical value of the ionization constant of pure water at 25°C is 1.0×10^{-14}. Thus, at 25°C,

$$[H^+] \ [OH^-] = 1.0 \times 10^{-14}$$

and

$$[H^+] = [OH^-] = 1.0 \times 10^{-7}$$

In pure water, the hydrogen ion and hydroxide ion concentrations are equal (1.0×10^{-7} moles per liter). In an acid solution, the hydrogen ion concentration is greater than the hydroxide ion concentration. In a basic solution, the hydroxide ion concentration is greater. However, K_W is a constant. Therefore, the product of the concentrations of H^+ and OH^- must always be 1.0×10^{-14} (at 25°C). If we know one of the concentrations, we can calculate the other.

pH (HYDROGEN ION CONCENTRATION). For convenience in calculations, the hydrogen ion concentration can be expressed by a **pH value.** For convenience in calculations, the hydrogen ion concentration can be expressed by a pH value. The pH is defined as the negative logarithm of the hydrogen ion concentration. An example will make the concept more clear:

In pure water, the $[H+]$ is 1×10^{-7}. The log of 10^{-7} is -7. Since the pH of a solution is defined as the negative log of the hydrogen ion concentration, the pH of pure water is 7.

In an acid solution, $[H^+]$ will be larger than 10^{-7}. For example, it may be 10^{-3}. The pH of such a solution would be 3.

Solutions with pH values smaller than 7 are acid; solutions with pH values greater than 7 are basic. The practical range of pH values is from about zero (for concentrated strong acids) to about 14 (for concentrated strong bases).

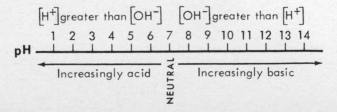

SAMPLE PROBLEM

What is the concentration of the hydroxide ion in a solution in which the pH is 3?

Solution: Find the hydrogen ion concentration by using the relationship

$$[H^+] \; = \; 10^{-pH}$$

Therefore, $[H^+] \; = \; 10^{-3}$

In an aqueous solution, the product of the hydrogen and hydroxide ion concentrations is always 10^{-14}.

$$[H^+] \; [OH^-] \; = \; 1.0 \times 10^{-14}$$

$$[OH^-] \; = \; \frac{1.0 \times 10^{-14}}{[H^+]} \; = \; \frac{1.0 \times 10^{-14}}{1.0 \times 10^{-3}}$$

$$[OH^-] \; = \; 1.0 \times 10^{-11} \text{ moles per liter}$$

SALTS. A salt, one of the products of a neutralization reaction, is an ionic compound containing at least one positive ion (other than hydrogen) and at least one negative ion (other than hydroxide). All salts are strong electrolytes, and are considered to be completely ionized in aqueous solution.

Some salts react with water to form solutions that are acidic or basic. This process is called **hydrolysis,** which is essentially the reverse of a neutralization reaction.

Salts formed from the reaction of a strong acid and a weak base give aqueous solutions that are acidic. For example, ammonium chloride is a salt derived from hydrochloric acid, a strong acid, and ammonium hydroxide, a weak base. An aqueous solution of ammonium chloride yields the original acid and the original base.

$$NH_4Cl + H_2O \rightleftarrows HCl + NH_4OH$$

Since the acid is relatively stronger than the base, there are more hydrogen ions than hydroxide ions in solution. Thus, the solution is acidic.

Salts derived from a strong base and a weak acid give aqueous solutions that are basic, because there are more hydroxide ions than hydrogen ions in solution. An example of this is the hydrolysis of sodium carbonate.

$$Na_2CO_3 + 2H_2O \rightleftarrows H_2CO_3 + 2NaOH$$

Carbonic acid is a weak acid, and sodium hydroxide is a strong base. Salts such a sodium chloride, formed from a strong acid (hydrochloric acid) and a strong base (sodium hydroxide), do *not* hydrolyze in solution.

$$NaCl + H_2O \rightleftarrows NaOH + HCl$$

Since there is an excess of neither hydrogen ions nor hydroxide ions, aqueous sodium chloride is neutral.

SUMMARY OF HYDROLYSIS

1. The salt of a strong acid and a weak base hydrolyzes to give an acidic solution.

2. The salt of a strong base and a weak acid hydrolyzes to give a basic solution.

3. The salt of a strong acid and a strong base does not hydrolyze.

QUESTIONS

1. If the pH of a solution is 6, the H_3O^+ ion concentration, in moles per liter, is   (1) 1×10^{-6} (2) 1×10^6 (3) 1×10^{-8} (4) 1×10^8

2. What is the H_3O^+ ion concentration, in moles per liter, of a solution with a pH of 4?   (1) 1×10^{-4} (2) 4×10^{-1} (3) 1×10^4 (4) 4×10^4

3. Which hydrogen ion concentration indicates the most acidic solution?   (1) 1×10^{-11} M   (2) 1×10^{-9} M   (3) 1×10^{-7} M   (4) 1×10^{-5} M

4. A water solution of K_2CO_3 has a pH greater than 7. The solution has   (1) an equal number of hydronium ions and hydroxide ions   (2) more hydronium ions than hydroxide ions   (3) fewer hydronium ions than hydroxide ions   (4) neither hydronium ions nor hydroxide ions

5. What is the K_w of water at 25° C?   (1) 1×10^{-14} (2) 1×10^{-7} (3) 1×10^{-2} (4) 1×10^7

6. Equal volumes of 0.1 M solutions of KOH and HNO_3 are mixed. The pH of the resulting solution is closest to   (1) 1   (2) 7   (3) 3   (4) 11

7. If the $[OH^-] = 1 \times 10^{-4}$ at 298 K for a given solution, the H^+ of the solution is equal to   (1) 1×10^{-14} (2) 1×10^{-10} (3) 1×10^{-6} (4) 1×10^{-4}

8. Which could be the pH of a solution whose H_3O^+ ion concentration is less than the OH^- ion concentration?   (1) 9   (2) 2   (3) 3   (4) 4

9. Red litmus will turn blue when placed in an aqueous solution of   (1) HCl   (2) CH_3COOH (3) CH_3OH (4) KOH

10. What is the pH of a 0.10 M solution of NaOH?   (1) 1   (2) 2   (3) 13   (4) 14

11. The pH of a 0.001 M solution of HCl (aq) is approximately   (1) 1   (2) 2   (3) 3   (4) 13

12. Which saturated solution at 25° C has the highest pH?
    (1) $Ba(OH)_2$ ($K_{sp} = 5.0 \times 10^{-3}$)
    (2) $Ca(OH)_2$ ($K_{sp} = 1.3 \times 10^{-6}$)
    (3) $Mg(OH)_2$ ($K_{sp} = 4.2 \times 10^{-15}$)
    (4) $Pb(OH)_2$ ($K_{sp} = 8.9 \times 10^{-12}$)

13. Phenolphthalein will be pink in a solution whose H_3O^+ ion concentration in moles per liter is (1) 1×10^{-1} (2) 1×10^{-3} (3) 1×10^{-6} (4) 1×10^{-9}

14. When additional solid NaCl dissolves in a solution of NaCl in water, the pH of the solution (1) decreases (2) increases (3) remains the same

15. A solution at 25° C with a pH of 7 contains (1) more H_3O^+ ions than OH^- ions (2) fewer H_3O^+ ions than OH^- ions (3) an equal number of H_3O^+ ions and OH^- ions (4) no H_3O^+ ions or OH^- ions

16. Which pH indicates the highest concentration of H_3O^+ ions? (1) 1 (2) 7 (3) 10 (4) 14

17. A 0.1 M acid solution at 298 K would conduct electricity best if the acid had a K_a value of (1) 1×10^{-7} (2) 1.8×10^{-5} (3) 1×10^{-2} (4) 6.7×10^{-4}

18. The K_w value for a sample of water at 1 atmosphere and 298 K will be most likely to change when there is an increase in the (1) concentration of H^+ ions (2) concentration of OH^- ions (3) pressure (4) temperature

19. Which compound is correctly classified as a salt? (1) KNO_3 (2) HNO_3 (3) CH_3COOH (4) C_2H_5OH

20. A water solution of NaCl and a water solution of HCl are similar in that both solutions (1) contain H_3O^+ ions (2) have a pH more than 7 (3) turn blue litmus paper red (4) are strongly acidic

21. When K_2CO_3 is dissolved in water, the resulting solution turns litmus paper (1) red and is acidic (2) blue and is acidic (3) red and is basic (4) blue and is basic

22. When hydrochloric acid is neutralized by sodium hydroxide, the salt formed is sodium (1) hydrochlorate (2) chlorate (3) chloride (4) perchloride

23. A solution of K_2CO_3 would have a pH closest to (1) 1 (2) 5 (3) 3 (4) 8

24. For each of the following reactions, the base is precisely titrated to the endpoint by the acid. In which reaction would the resulting mixture of products have a pH of less than 7?
    (1) $3HCl + Al(OH)_3 \rightarrow AlCl_3 + 3H_2O$
    (2) $HCl + KOH \rightarrow KCl + H_2O$
    (3) $HNO_3 + NaOH \rightarrow NaNO_3 + H_2O$
    (4) $HC_2H_3O_2 + NaOH \rightarrow NaC_2H_3O_2 + H_2O$

25. Which of the following acids ionizes to the least extent at 298 K? (1) HF (2) HNO_2 (3) H_2S (4) H_2O

UNIT 8   REDOX AND ELECTROCHEMISTRY

OXIDATION AND REDUCTION

OXIDATION. In the simplest terms, **oxidation** is the combination of an element with oxygen. If we examine the reaction between a metal and oxygen, we find that the metal in undergoing oxidation loses electrons to the oxygen.

$$Ca + \tfrac{1}{2}O_2 \longrightarrow CaO$$

$$\overset{xx}{Ca} + .\overset{\bullet}{\underset{\bullet\bullet}{O}}: \longrightarrow Ca^{2+} + \overset{\bullet\bullet}{\underset{x\bullet}{^xO}}:^{2-}$$

Calcium may undergo a similar reaction with other electronegative elements. For example:

$$Ca + Cl_2 \longrightarrow CaCl_2$$

$$\overset{xx}{Ca} + 2.\overset{\bullet\bullet}{\underset{\bullet\bullet}{Cl}}: \longrightarrow Ca^{2+} + 2 \overset{\bullet\bullet}{\underset{\bullet\bullet}{^xCl}}:^{-}$$

In both reactions calcium undergoes the same change; it loses electrons to another atom and acquires a positive charge. Because of the similarity in these reactions, we may extend the definition of oxidation to include any reaction in which an element *loses* electrons.

REDUCTION. In both of the reactions considered in the preceding section, the atoms which reacted with the calcium gained electrons. The *gain* of electrons is defined as *reduction*, and the atoms that acquire the electrons are said to be *reduced*. Oxygen and chlorine are reduced when they react with calcium.

The positive ions formed in the oxidation of calcium can change back to metallic calcium by accepting electrons. This would be reduction. Most metals occur naturally in the combined, or oxidized, condition. In order to obtain the metal in atomic form, it must be "reduced" from its ores.

REDOX. Whenever electrons are lost by one atom, they must be gained by another. Therefore, oxidation and reduction can never occur alone. Whenever one occurs, the other must occur also. Reactions involving oxidation and reduction are commonly called **redox** reactions.

OXIDATION NUMBER. It is often difficult to determine which atoms have gained or lost electrons in a reaction. The concept of **oxidation number,** or **oxidation state,** is convenient for keeping track of the number, as well as the transfer, of electrons in a chemical reaction. The oxidation number of an atom is a positive, negative, or zero charge assigned to the atom in a chemical formula in accordance with certain arbitrary rules. The oxidation number is not an ionic charge, although in many cases it is the same as the ionic charge. The rules for assigning oxidation numbers are as follows:

1. Each atom of a free element (that is, an element not in chemical combination with another element) has an oxidation number of zero. Thus, metallic sodium, Na, has an oxidation number of zero; so does each hydrogen atom in hydrogen gas, H_2, and each chlorine atom in chlorine gas, Cl_2.

2. In ionic compounds consisting of monatomic ions, each atom has an oxidation number equal to its ionic charge. Thus, in $CaCl_2$, the oxidation number of Ca is $+2$, and that of each Cl is -1. In $FeCl_2$, Fe has an oxidation number of $+2$; in $FeCl_3$, it is $+3$.

3. The metals of Group 1(IA) always have an oxidation number of $+1$, the charge on their ions in their compounds.

4. The metals of Group 2(IIA) always have an oxidation number of $+2$, the charge on their ions in their compounds.

5. Fluorine always has an oxidation number of -1 in its compounds.

6. Oxygen always has a negative oxidation number in its compounds, except in those containing fluorine. The oxidation number of oxygen is usually -2. In the peroxides (such as H_2O_2), its oxidation number is -1. In combination with fluorine in OF_2, the oxidation number of oxygen is $+2$.

7. Hydrogen has an oxidation number of $+1$ in all its compounds except the metal hydrides (such as LiH and CaH_2); its oxidation number in the metal hydrides is -1.

OXIDATION NUMBERS IN COMPOUNDS. The total of the oxidation numbers in a compound must be zero. After oxidation numbers have been assigned to the atoms in a formula in accordance with the rules given above, there will often be one element remaining for which there is no rule. In such cases, that atom is given an oxidation number that will make the total for the compound equal zero. In adding oxidation numbers, be sure to multiply the oxidation number of each atom by its subscript number, to find the total contributed by that element in the compound.

For example, in the compound Na_2S, by Rule 3 we give Na an oxidation number of $+1$. Since there are two atoms of Na, the total contributed by Na is $+2$. To make the sum zero for the formula as a whole, the oxidation number of S must be -2.

In H_2SO_4, we give an oxidation number of $+1$ to H (by Rule 7), and -2 to O (by Rule 6). The total contributed by H and O is therefore $+2 + (-8) = -6$. Therefore, the oxidation number of S must be $+6$.

$$+2 + (+6) + (-8) = 0$$

Be sure to take into account the subscript numbers when assigning the last oxidation number. For example, in $K_2Cr_2O_7$, we have a net amount of -12 to be balanced by 2 Cr atoms. Therefore, we assign an oxidation number of $+6$ to Cr in this compound. We then have:

$$[2 \times (+1)] + [2 \times (+6)] + [7 \times (-2)] = 0$$

OXIDATION NUMBERS IN IONS. The oxidation numbers of all the atoms in an ion must add up to the charge on the ion. In the SO_3^{2-} ion, the 3 O's contribute a total of -6; therefore, the oxidation number of S must be $+4$, to leave a net charge of -2.

QUESTIONS

1. **As a sodium atom is oxidized, the number of protons in its nucleus**
   (1) decreases (2) increases (3) remains the same

2. **When a neutral atom undergoes reduction, its oxidation number**
   (1) decreases (2) increases (3) remains the same

3. **What is the oxidation number of nitrogen in HNO_2?** (1) -1 (2) -2
   (3) $+3$ (4) $+4$

4. **The element hydrogen will have a negative oxidation number when it forms a binary compound with** (1) sulfur (2) selenium (3) oxygen
   (4) potassium

5. **In the reaction $2H_2S + 3O_2 \rightarrow 2SO_2 + 2H_2O$, the oxidation number of oxygen changes from**
   (1) -4 to 0 (2) -2 to 0 (3) 0 to -4 (4) 0 to -2

6. **In the reaction $3Cu + 8HNO_3 \rightarrow 3Cu(NO_3)_2 + 2NO + 4H_2O$, what change in oxidation state does nitrogen undergo?**
   (1) $+5$ to -2 (2) $+5$ to $+2$ (3) -2 to -5 (4) -2 to $+5$

7. **If element X forms oxides XO and X_2O_3, the oxidation numbers of element X are** (1) $+1$ and $+2$ (2) $+2$ and $+3$ (3) $+1$ and $+3$
   (4) $+2$ and $+4$

8. **Oxygen has an oxidation number of -1 in** (1) H_3O^+ (2) OH^-
   (3) H_2O (4) H_2O_2

9. **What is the algebraic sum of the oxidation numbers of all the atoms in the compound $K_2Cr_2O_7$?** (1) -14 (2) -5 (3) 0 (4) $+9$

10. **What is the oxidation number of oxygen in OF_2?** (1) $+1$ (2) $+2$
    (3) -1 (4) -2

11. **Which element can only have oxidation states of $+1$, 0, or -1?**
    (1) Cs (2) F (3) H (4) He

CHANGES IN OXIDATION NUMBER. A redox reaction can be recognized by the fact that the oxidation numbers of some of the atoms change as a result of the reaction. In a simple case, for example

$$Ca + \tfrac{1}{2}O_2 \rightarrow CaO$$

the oxidation number of calcium changes from 0 to +2, and that of oxygen from 0 to −2. This is therefore an oxidation-reduction (redox) reaction in which Ca is oxidized and O is reduced.

The following reaction is a somewhat more complex example:

$$\overset{+4}{MnO_2} + \overset{-1}{4HCl} \rightarrow \overset{+2}{MnCl_2} + 2H_2O + \overset{0}{Cl_2}$$

Some of the chlorine is oxidized from −1 in HCl to 0 in Cl_2. The manganese is reduced from +4 in MnO_2 to +2 in $MnCl_2$.

EXTENDED DEFINITION OF OXIDATION AND REDUCTION. On the basis of reactions like those above, **oxidation** is more completely defined as any chemical change in which an oxidation number *increases*, that is, becomes more positive or less negative. For example, a change in oxidation number from −3 to −1, from −1 to +2, or from +2 to +7 are oxidations.

Reduction is likewise defined as any chemical change in which an oxidation number *decreases*, that is, becomes less positive or more negative. A change in oxidation number from −1 to −3, from +2 to −1, or from +7 to +2 are examples of reduction.

This extended meaning of oxidation and reduction is visualized in Figure 8-1.

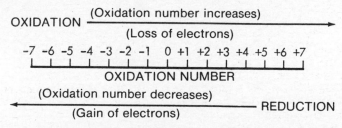

Figure 8-1. The extended meaning of oxidation and reduction.

OXIDIZING AND REDUCING AGENTS. In every redox reaction, the substance (atom or ion) being oxidized loses electrons to the substance being reduced. In the reaction between calcium and oxygen, the calcium loses electrons to the oxygen. Calcium may be considered to cause or assist the reduction of oxygen by giving electrons to it. Calcium is therefore called a **reducing agent** in this reaction. Similarly, oxygen may be considered to cause or assist the oxidation of the calcium by accepting electrons from it. Oxygen is therefore called an **oxidizing agent.**

In every redox reaction, the substance being oxidized acts as a reducing agent on the substance being reduced. The substance being reduced acts as an oxidizing agent on the substance being oxidized.

Substances with a strong tendency to accept electrons and become reduced are called strong oxidizing agents. Oxygen and the elements of Group 17(VIIA) (the halogens) are strong oxidizing agents.

Substances with a strong tendency to lose electrons and become oxidized are strong reducing agents. The elements of Group 1(IA) are strong reducing agents.

QUESTIONS

1. **A reducing agent is a substance that** (1) gains protons (2) loses protons (3) gains electrons (4) loses electrons

2. **Which change in oxidation number represents reduction?** (1) -1 to $+1$ (2) -1 to -2 (3) -1 to $+2$ (4) -1 to 0

3. **In the half-reaction $Pb^0 \rightarrow Pb^{2+} + 2e^-$, the Pb^0** (1) gains protons (2) loses protons (3) is oxidized (4) is reduced

4. **In the half-cell reaction $Ba^0 \rightarrow Ba^{2+} + 2e^-$, which is true of the barium atom?** (1) It gains protons. (2) It loses protons. (3) It gains electrons. (4) It loses electrons.

5. **In the reaction $Cl_2 + H_2O \rightarrow HClO + HCl$, the Cl_2 is** (1) oxidized, only (2) reduced, only (3) both oxidized and reduced (4) neither oxidized nor reduced

6. **In the reaction $Ca + NiCl_2 \rightarrow CaCl_2 + Ni$, the oxidation number of the chlorine** (1) decreases (2) increases (3) remains the same

7. **Which half-cell reaction correctly represents reduction?**
   (1) $Sn^0 \rightarrow Sn^{2+} + 2e^-$ (3) $Sn^0 + 2e^- \rightarrow Sn^{2+}$
   (2) $Sn^{2+} \rightarrow Sn^0 + 2e^-$ (4) $Sn^{2+} + 2e^- \rightarrow Sn^0$

8. **Which half-reaction correctly represents oxidation?**
   (1) $F_2 \rightarrow 2F^- + 2e^-$ (3) $H_2 \rightarrow 2H^+ + 2e^-$
   (2) $F_2 + 2e^- \rightarrow 2F^-$ (4) $H_2 + 2e^- \rightarrow 2H^+$

9. **In the reaction $Mg + ZnCl_2 \rightarrow MgCl_2 + Zn$, which is true of the magnesium?** (1) It is oxidized by losing electrons. (2) It is oxidized by gaining electrons. (3) It is reduced by losing electrons. (4) It is reduced by gaining electrons.

10. **In the reaction $Sn^{2+}(aq) + 2Ag^+(aq) \rightarrow Sn^{4+}(aq) + 2Ag(s)$, the oxidizing agent is** (1) Sn^{2+} (2) Ag^+ (3) Sn^{4+} (4) Ag

11. Which is the oxidizing agent in the reaction below?
$$2Al + 3CuSO_4 \rightarrow Al_2(SO_4)_3 + 3Cu$$
(1) Al^{3+} (2) Cu^{2+} (3) S^{6+} (4) O^{2-}

12. In all oxidation-reduction reactions there is a conservation of
(1) charge but not mass (2) mass but not charge (3) neither mass nor charge (4) both mass and charge

13. In the half-reaction $Mg \rightarrow Mg^{2+} + 2e^-$, the magnesium (1) gains electrons and is oxidized (2) gains electrons and is reduced (3) loses electrons and is oxidized (4) loses electrons and is reduced

14. Which is the oxidizing agent in the following reaction?
$$Cl_2(aq) + 2KBr(aq) \rightarrow 2KCl(aq) + Br_2(aq)$$
(1) Cl_2 (2) KCl (3) KBr (4) Br_2

15. In the reaction $Sn^{2+} + 2Fe^{3+} \rightarrow Sn^{4+} + 2Fe^{2+}$, the reducing agent is
(1) Fe^{2+} (2) Fe^{3+} (3) Sn^{2+} (4) Sn^{4+}

16. Which equation correctly represents reduction?
(1) $Na^+ + 1e^- \rightarrow Na^0$ (3) $Na^+ \rightarrow Na^0 + 1e^-$
(2) $Cl^- + 1e^- \rightarrow Cl^0$ (4) $Cl^- \rightarrow Cl^0 + 1e^-$

17. In the reaction $Zn + Cu^{2+} \rightarrow Zn^{2+} + Cu$, the oxidizing agent is (1) Zn (2) Cu (3) Zn^{2+} (4) Cu^{2+}

18. How many moles of electrons are needed to reduce 1 mole of Fe^{3+} to Fe^{2+}? (1) 1 (2) 2 (3) 3 (4) 5

19. How many moles of electrons would be required to completely reduce 0.50 mole of Cu^{2+} ions to Cu? (1) 1.0 (2) 2.0 (3) 0.25 (4) 0.50

20. Which is a redox reaction?
(1) $Ba^{2+} + SO_4^{2-} \rightarrow BaSO_4$
(2) $H^+ + OH^- \rightarrow H_2O$
(3) $Sn^0 + Sn^{4+} \rightarrow 2Sn^{2+}$
(4) $H^+ + NH_3 \rightarrow NH_4^+$

21. Which is an oxidation-reduction reaction?
(1) $Ca(s) + H_2SO_4(aq) \rightarrow CaSO_4(s) + H_2(g)$
(2) $Ca^{2+}(aq) + SO_4^{2-}(aq) \rightarrow CaSO_4(s)$
(3) $CaO(s) + H_2SO_4(aq) \rightarrow CaSO_4(s) + H_2O(l)$
(4) $Ca(OH)_2(aq) + H_2SO_4(aq) \rightarrow CaSO_4(s) + 2H_2O(l)$

22. Which is an example of an oxidation-reduction reaction?
(1) $HCl + NaOH \rightarrow NaCl + H_2O$
(2) $C(s) + H_2O \rightarrow H_2 + CO$
(3) $CaCO_3 \rightarrow CaO + CO_2$
(4) $BaCl_2 + Na_2SO_4 \rightarrow BaSO_4 + 2NaCl$

23. Which is a redox reaction?
(1) $Cu(NO_3)_2 + H_2S \rightarrow CuS + 2HNO_3$
(2) $CuCl_2 + 2AgNO_3 \rightarrow Cu(NO_3)_2 + 2AgCl$
(3) $Cu(OH)_2 + 2HNO_3 \rightarrow Cu(NO_3)_2 + 2H_2O$
(4) $Cu + 2AgNO_3 \rightarrow Cu(NO_3)_2 + 2Ag$

ELECTROCHEMISTRY

HALF-REACTIONS. Every redox reaction consists of two parts—the oxidation process and the reduction process. Each of these parts is called a **half-reaction,** and separate electronic equations can be written for each. Consider, for example, the redox reaction

$$Mg + Cl_2 \rightarrow MgCl_2$$

The half-reactions may be expressed as follows:

Oxidation: $Mg^0 \rightarrow Mg^{2+} + 2e^-$

Reduction: $Cl_2^0 + 2e^- \rightarrow 2Cl^-$

Note that both the mass and the charge are balanced in each equation. In the oxidation half-reaction, the indicated charge is zero on both sides. In the reduction half-reaction, the charge is -2 on both sides. Note also that if the two half-reactions are combined, the complete reaction is obtained, and the electrons cancel out (as they must, since electrons cannot be created or destroyed by the reaction):

$$Mg^0 + Cl_2^0 \rightarrow Mg^{2+} + 2Cl^-$$

HALF-CELLS. In a redox reaction there is a transfer of electrons from the substance being oxidized to the substance being reduced. It is possible to separate the oxidation and reduction half-reactions, and have them occur in separate vessels, if an arrangement like that in Figure 8-2 is used. The two solutions are connected by a **salt bridge,** which allows ions to move from one solution to the other. The substance being oxidized is connected to the substance being reduced by an electrical conductor (usually a metallic wire). Electrons are transferred through the wire. This flow of electrons constitutes an electric current. The flow of charge is made continuous by the migration of ions through the salt bridge.

The complete system is called an **electrochemical cell,** or simply a **chemical cell.** Each of the vessels in which one half-reaction is taking place is called a **half-cell** (See Figure 8-2).

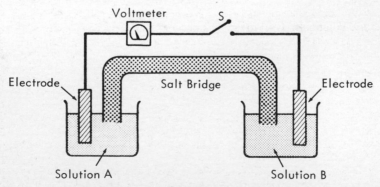

Figure 8-2. A chemical cell.

ELECTRIC POTENTIAL. Electrons flow through the external circuit of the chemical cell because there is a **difference of electric potential** between the two electrodes. This potential difference is a measure of the free energy of the redox reaction. It is usually expressed in units called **volts,** and it can be measured by a voltmeter. The flow of current carries electrical energy, which can be used to do work. A chemical cell is thus a device that converts chemical energy directly to electrical energy.

ELECTRODE POTENTIAL. It is assumed that any half-reaction develops a certain electric potential, which measures the tendency of the reaction to occur. However, it is not possible to measure the potential of a single half-reaction. It is possible to measure only the *difference* in potential between one half-reaction and another when they are paired in a chemical cell.

The hydrogen half-reaction $[2H^+ + 2e^- = H_2(g)]$ has been selected as a reference half-reaction with which to compare the electrode potentials of other half-reactions. The voltage developed between any given half-reaction and the hydrogen half-reaction is called the **standard electrode potential** (E^0) of that half-reaction. The measurement must be made under specified standard conditions, which are usually 1 molar concentrations at 25°C.

OXIDATION AND REDUCTION POTENTIALS. Every half-reaction is reversible. In one direction it is an oxidation half-reaction. In the reverse direction it is a reduction half-reaction. For example:

Oxidation: $2F^- \rightarrow F_2(g) + 2e^-$
Reduction: $F_2(g) + 2e^- \rightarrow 2F^-$

Tables of standard electrode potentials for various half-reactions will be found in many chemistry textbooks and other reference books. One such table is given in the *Reference Tables for Chemistry* that you will use when taking the Chemistry Regents Examination. In this table (Reference Table N) the half-reactions are shown in the reduction direction. This is therefore a table of standard *reduction* potentials. In other books the tables may list the half-reactions as oxidations. These are tables of standard *oxidation* potentials. The oxidation and reduction potentials of the same half-reaction have the same numerical value, but opposite signs. For example:

Oxidation: $2F^- \rightarrow F_2(g) + 2e^-$ $E^0 = -2.87$
Reduction: $F_2(g) + 2e \rightarrow 2F^-$ $E^0 = +2.87$

It does not matter whether a table of standard electrode potentials lists the half-reactions as oxidations or as reductions. The potential of the reverse reaction can always be found by taking the value given in the table and changing its sign.

When paired with a hydrogen half-cell, a half-reaction proceeds in the direction (either oxidation or reduction) that has a positive value of $E^°$. Electrons are driven through the external circuit with the voltage indicated.

NET POTENTIAL OF A REDOX REACTION. Any oxidation half-reaction may be paired with any reduction half-reaction to produce a complete redox reaction. The net potential difference of the combined reactions can be calculated by adding the half-cell potentials, being sure to use the correct algebraic sign for each half-reaction. For example, in the reaction $Mg + Cl_2 \rightarrow MgCl_2$, magnesium is oxidized and chlorine is reduced. Consulting the table, we can write:

Oxidation: $\quad Mg \qquad\qquad\qquad \rightarrow \quad Mg^{2+} \quad + \quad 2e^- \quad E^0 \;= +2.37$

Reduction: $\quad \underline{Cl_2 \quad + \quad 2e^- \quad \rightarrow \quad 2Cl^- \qquad\qquad\qquad\quad E^0 \;= +1.36}$

$\qquad\qquad\quad Mg \quad + \quad Cl_2 \quad \rightarrow \quad Mg^{2+} \quad + \quad 2Cl^- \;\; E^0 \;= +3.73$

In combining half-reactions, the electrons transferred must balance. For the reaction $2Na + Cl_2 \rightarrow 2\,NaCl$, the half-reactions are:

Oxidation: $\quad 2(Na \qquad\qquad\qquad \rightarrow \quad Na^+ \quad + \quad e^-) \quad E^0 \;= +2.71$

Reduction: $\quad \underline{Cl_2 \quad + \quad 2e^- \quad \rightarrow \quad 2Cl^- \qquad\qquad\qquad\quad E^0 \;= +1.36}$

$\qquad\qquad\quad 2\,Na \; + \quad Cl_2 \quad \rightarrow \quad 2\,Na^+ \quad + \quad 2Cl^- \;\; E^0 \;= +4.07$

Note that the oxidation potentials are *not* multiplied by a coefficient.

POTENTIAL OF A CHEMICAL CELL. The maximum voltage of a chemical cell, at standard concentrations and temperature, can be calculated by combining the oxidation and reduction potentials of the separate half-reactions as explained in the preceding section. It should be understood, however, that as the reactions proceed, the concentrations in the half-cells will change. As a result, the voltage will change also.

While a chemical cell is delivering current, energy is being given off and the system is not at equilibrium. Eventually, the overall chemical system will reach equilibrium. This means that no further net change in the system can occur. At equilibrium, the voltage of the cell becomes zero and current flow ceases in the external conductor.

USE OF STANDARD ELECTRODE POTENTIALS. The tendency of a redox reaction to occur can be determined by means of standard electrode potentials. For example, consider the possible redox reaction

$$Zn + Pb(NO_3)_2 \rightarrow Pb + Zn(NO_3)_2$$

If this reaction occurs, zinc is oxidized and lead is reduced as follows:

Oxidation: $\quad Zn \qquad\qquad\qquad \rightarrow \quad Zn^{2+} \quad + \quad 2e^- \quad E^0 \;= +0.76$

Reduction: $\quad Pb^{+2} \; + \quad 2e^- \quad \rightarrow \quad Pb \qquad\qquad\qquad\quad E^0 \;= -0.13$

We can now find the potential of the overall reaction by adding the potentials of the two half-reactions. In this case, the sum is $+0.76 - 0.13 = +0.63$. A positive value for the sum of the E^0 values means that the reaction *as written* is spontaneous. In other words, zinc will replace lead from a solution of a lead salt.

The reverse reaction is not spontaneous. The signs of both E^0 values would be reversed, and their sum would be -0.63.

The table of standard electrode potentials in the *Reference Tables for Chemistry* lists reduction half-reactions. In this table, metals with negative reduction potentials are found below hydrogen. These metals have positive oxidation potentials, and in a table that lists oxidation half-reactions they are usually found above hydrogen. These are the metals that can replace hydrogen from an acid. When, for example, magnesium is added to an aqueous acid, the net reaction is

$$Mg \; + \quad 2H^+ \qquad \rightarrow \quad Mg^{2+} \; + \quad H_2$$

Oxidation:	Mg		$\rightarrow$	Mg^{2+} +	$2e^-$	E^0	= +2.37
Reduction:	$2H$ +	$2e^-$	$\rightarrow$	H_2		E^0	= 0.00
	Mg +	$2H^+$	$\rightarrow$	Mg^{2+} +	H_2	E^0	= +2.37

Since the overall E^0 is positive (+2.37), magnesium replaces hydrogen from an acid, and the reaction occurs spontaneously.

If the potential of the overall redox reaction is negative, no reaction takes place. Metals with negative oxidation potentials (positive reduction potentials) do not replace hydrogen from acid.

$$Cu \; + \quad 2H^+ \quad \rightarrow \quad \text{No reaction}$$

Oxidation:	Cu		$\rightarrow$	Cu^{2+} +	$2e^-$	E^0	= -0.34
Reduction:	$2H^+$ +	$2e^-$	$\rightarrow$	H_2		E^0	= 0.00
	Cu +	$2H^+$	$\rightarrow$	Cu^{2+} +	H_2	E^0	= -0.34

E^0 is negative (-0.34); therefore, the reaction does not occur spontaneously.

ELECTROCHEMICAL CELLS. A sample electrochemical cell is shown in Figure 8-3. The two half-reactions are:

reduction: Cu^{2+} + $2e^-$ $\rightarrow$ Cu^0 +0.34 v
oxidation: Zn^0 $\rightarrow$ $2e^-$ + Zn^{2+} +0.76 v

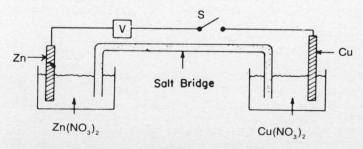

Figure 8-3. When the switch is closed, electrons will flow from the anode (Zn) through the wire to the cathode (Cu). Positive ions will flow through the salt bridge toward the cathode.

The E^0 value for the reduction reaction ($+0.34$ v) is written as it appears in Reference Table N. The oxidation value ($+0.76$ v) is written with a sign opposite to that shown in the table. The sum of the two is the maximum potential for the cell ($+1.10$v). When the calculated voltage has a positive value, the reaction is spontaneous. This voltage represents the maximum voltage that can be obtained at 25°C with a 1 molal solution. As the cell operates, the concentrations of the ions change, and so does the voltage. As the ion concentrations change, the reverse reactions tend to take place. At some concentration, the rates of the forward and reverse reactions become equal. When this equilibrium is established, the voltage will be 0.00 v.

ELECTROLYTIC CELLS. Many combinations of redox half-reactions will not occur spontaneously. This can be predicted by adding the half-cell potentials. When the sum of these potentials is a negative value, the reactions will not occur spontaneously. Although such combinations cannot be used to produce an electric current, a current from an external source can be used to make the reactions occur. This type of reaction is called **electrolysis.**

In the electrolysis of water, an electric current causes the water molecules to split into hydrogen and oxygen molecules:

$$2H_2O \xrightarrow{\text{elec}} 2H_2 + O_2$$

The half-reactions are:

oxidation: $2H_2O \rightarrow 4e^- + 4H^+ + O_2(g)$ (-1.23 v)
reduction: $4H^+ + 4e^- \rightarrow 2H_2$ (0.00 v)

ELECTRODES. In both electrochemical and electrolytic cells, the electrode at which oxidation takes place is called the **anode**. The electrode at which reduction takes place is called the **cathode**. A simple memory device to associate the process with the correct electrode is:

RED CAT: *RED*uction occurs at the *CAT*hode
AN OX: The *AN*ode is the site of *OX*idation.

In an electrochemical cell, the cathode is considered to be the positive electrode and the anode to be the negative electrode. In an electrolytic cell, the polarities are reversed—the anode is positive and the cathode negative.

ELECTROPLATING. One practical use of the electrolytic cell is the process of **electroplating.** This process makes it possible to add an even layer, or ''plate,'' of a desired metal to another surface, usually another metal. The layer of chromium found on automobile bumpers is added to steel by this process.

In an electrolytic cell, the object to be plated is made the cathode. The solution in which the object is submerged contains ions of the metal to be plated, and the anode is a piece of the same metallic element. At the cathode, reduction causes the metallic ions to come out of solution onto the surface to be plated. As these ions are removed from solution at the cathode, they are replaced at the anode by oxidation of the same element.

QUESTIONS

1. Given the chemical cell:
   Zn, Zn^{2+}(1M) and Cu^{2+}(1M), Cu
   As the reaction in this cell takes place, the mass of the copper electrode   (1) decreases   (2) increases   (3) remains the same

2. Given the cell reaction:
$$Zn(s) + Cu^{2+}(aq) \rightarrow Zn^{2+}(aq) + Cu(s)$$
   The negative electrode in this cell is   (1) Zn(s)   (2) Cu^{2+}(aq)
   (3) Zn^{2+}(aq)   (4) Cu(s)

3. Which molecule-ion pair will react spontaneously at 298 K?
   (1) Cl_2 + F^- (2) I_2 + Br^- (3) F_2 + I^- (4) Br_2 + Cl^-

4. Which reaction occurs when bromine is added to an aqueous solution of iodide ions?
   (1) $2I^- + Br_2 \rightarrow I_2 + 2Br^-$
   (2) $I_2 + 2Br^- \rightarrow Br_2 + 2I^-$
   (3) $2I^- + 2Br^- \rightarrow I_2 + Br_2$
   (4) $I_2 + Br_2 \rightarrow 2I^- + 2Br^-$

5. Which metal will react spontaneously with Cu^{2+}(aq) at 25°C?   (1) Ag
   (2) Au   (3) Mg   (4) Hg

6. What is the maximum E^o voltage for the cell with the equation Ni + $Cu^{2+} \rightarrow Ni^{2+}$ + Cu?   (1) 0.11   (2) 0.23   (3) 0.34   (4) 0.59

7. Given the reaction: Mg + $2Ag^+ \rightarrow 2Ag^0 + Mg^{2+}$
   The potential difference (E^0) of this cell is   (1) 0.77 V   (2) 1.57 V
   (3) 3.17 V   (4) 3.97 V

8. The potential (E^0) for the standard hydrogen half-cell reaction is
   (1) -0.41 volt   (2) -0.83 volt   (3) 0.00 volts   (4) 0.78 volt

9. Given the reaction: $2Cr + 3Cu^{2+} \rightarrow 3Cu + 2Cr^{3+}$
   What is the net potential (E^0) for the overall reaction?   (1) $+0.40$ volt
   (2) $+0.46$ volt   (3) $+1.08$ volts   (4) $+2.50$ volts

10. Which half-reaction occurs at the negative electrode in an electrolytic cell in which an object is being plated with silver?
    (1) $Ag^0 + 1e^- \rightarrow Ag^+$ (3) $Ag^+ + 1e^- \rightarrow Ag^0$
    (2) $Ag^0 \rightarrow Ag^+ + 1e^-$ (4) $Ag^+ \rightarrow Ag^0 + 1e^-$

11. Which ion can be most easily reduced?   (1) Cu^{2+} (2) Zn^{2+} (3) Ni^{2+}
    (4) Ca^{2+}

12. Which element is most likely to be found uncombined in nature?
    (1) Na   (2) Ca   (3) Mg   (4) Ag

13. Which oxidation is most likely to occur?
    (1) $Cu \rightarrow Cu^{2+} + 2e^-$ (3) $Ag \rightarrow Ag^{1+} + 1e^-$
    (2) $Mg \rightarrow Mg^{2+} + 2e^-$ (4) $Au \rightarrow Au^{3+} + 3e^-$

14. As the reaction in a chemical cell approaches equilibrium, the potential of the cell   (1) decreases   (2) increases   (3) remains the same

15. Oxygen and copper are produced during the electrolysis of a $CuSO_4$ solution. Which reaction occurs at the negative electrode?   (1) The copper atom is oxidized.   (2) The copper ion is reduced.   (3) The oxygen atom is oxidized.   (4) The oxygen ion is reduced.

BALANCING REDOX REACTIONS

It is usually difficult to balance redox reactions by inspection or trial-and-error. This is especially true when only some of the particles of a species undergo oxidation or reduction. For example, consider the following unbalanced equation for the preparation of Cl_2 by reacting HCl with $KMnO_4$:

___$KMnO_4$ + ___HCl → ___KCl + ___$MnCl_2$ + ___H_2O + ___Cl_2

Some of the Cl in HCl is oxidized as follows:

$$2Cl^- \rightarrow Cl_2 + 2e^-$$

But some of the Cl remains unchanged in oxidation number. There is no clue as to how the Cl's divide among the products, and no way to begin the balancing by inspection. However, if we write electron transfer equations for the oxidation and reduction, and balance the electrons that are transferred, we obtain coefficients for starting the balancing procedure. The method is as follows:

1. Assign oxidation numbers to all atoms in the equation:

$$\overset{+1\ +7\ -2}{KMnO_4} + \overset{+1\ -1}{HCl} \rightarrow \overset{+1\ -1}{KCl} + \overset{+2\ -1}{MnCl_2} + \overset{+1\ -2}{H_2O} + \overset{0}{Cl_2}$$

2. Write equations for the electron gains and losses:

Oxidation: $2Cl^- \rightarrow Cl_2{}^0 + 2e^-$
Reduction: $Mn^{7+} + 5e^- \rightarrow Mn^{2+}$

3. Multiply the oxidation and reduction expressions by coefficients that will equalize the numbers of electrons gained and lost:

$5(2Cl^- \rightarrow Cl_2{}^0 + 2e^-)$: $10Cl^- \rightarrow 5Cl_2{}^0 + 10e^-$
$2(Mn^{7+} + 5e^- \rightarrow Mn^{2+})$: $2Mn^{7+} + 10e^- \rightarrow 2Mn^{2+}$

4. Step 3 tells us that for every 2 atoms of Mn that are reduced, 10 atoms of Cl are oxidized and 5 molecules of Cl_2 are produced. This is the clue we need. We enter 2 as the coefficient of the compound containing Mn on the left and 5 as the coefficient of the Cl_2 produced. We know this is the correct ratio, because all the Mn is reduced. We can also enter the coefficient 2 for the $MnCl_2$ produced.

_2_ $KMnO_4$ + ___HCl → ___KCl + _2_ $MnCl_2$ + ___H_2O + _5_ Cl_2

5. The rest of the balancing procedure is simple. We balance the K by entering the coefficient 2 for the KCl produced:

_2_ $KMnO_4$ + ___HCl → _2_ KCl + _2_ $MnCl_2$ + ___H_2O + _5_ Cl_2

6. We can now add all the Cl atoms on the right (16) and balance them with the coefficient 16 for HCl:

$\underline{2}$ KMnO$_4$ + $\underline{16}$ HCl → $\underline{2}$ KCl + $\underline{2}$ MnCl$_2$ + ___H$_2$O + $\underline{5}$ Cl$_2$

7. Finally, we balance the H with the coefficient 8 for H$_2$O:

$\underline{2}$ KMnO$_4$ + $\underline{16}$ HCl → $\underline{2}$ KCl + $\underline{2}$ MnCl$_2$ + $\underline{8}$ H$_2$O + $\underline{5}$ Cl$_2$

8. A check of the oxygen shows that it, too, is in balance.

A second method is to write the oxidation and reduction half-reactions (see Table of Standard Oxidation Potentials):

Oxidation: $\quad$ 2Cl$^-$ $\qquad\qquad\qquad\qquad$ → $\quad$ Cl$_2$ $\quad$ + $\quad$ 2e$^-$
Reduction: $\quad$ MnO$_4^-$ $\quad$ + $\quad$ 8H$^+$ $\quad$ + $\quad$ 5e$^-$ $\quad$ → $\quad$ Mn^{2+} $\quad$ + $\quad$ 4H$_2$O

Again we balance the electrons:

10Cl$^-$ $\qquad\qquad\qquad\qquad$ → $\quad$ 5Cl$_2$ $\quad$ + $\quad$ 10e$^-$
2MnO$_4^-$ $\quad$ + $\quad$ 16H$^+$ $\quad$ + $\quad$ 10e$^-$ → $\quad$ 2Mn^{2+} $\quad$ + $\quad$ 8H$_2$O

From these half-reactions, we obtain the necessary coefficients as before. The added advantage of this method is that it also gives us the coefficients directly for the HCl and the H$_2$O, thus saving a few inspection steps.

Sometimes the half-reactions are added to produce an equation that shows only the particles involved in the oxidation and reduction:

2MnO$_4^-$ $\quad$ + $\quad$ 16H$^+$ $\quad$ + $\quad$ 10Cl$^-$ → $\quad$ 2Mn^{2+} $\quad$ + $\quad$ 8H$_2$O $\quad$ + $\quad$ 5 Cl$_2$

The K$^+$ ions and those Cl$^-$ ions that are not affected are omitted from the equation. These omitted ions are called **spectator ions.** They need not be shown because they do not participate in the reaction but pass through unchanged.

QUESTIONS

1. What is the coefficient of H$_2$O when the equation below is completely balanced?
$$\_NH_3 + 5O_2 \rightarrow \_NO + \_H_2O$$
(1) 12 $\quad$ (2) 6 $\quad$ (3) 5 $\quad$ (4) 4

2. When the equation
$$\_Cu + \_HNO_3 \rightarrow \_Cu(NO_3)_2 + 2NO + \_H_2O$$
is completely balanced using whole numbers, the coefficient of the HNO$_3$ will be $\quad$ (1) 8 $\quad$ (2) 2 $\quad$ (3) 6 $\quad$ (4) 4

3. What is the coefficient of Fe^{2+} when the redox equation below is correctly balanced?
$$\_Fe^{2+} + \_NO_3^- + \_H^+ \rightarrow \_Fe^{3+} + \_NO + 2H_2O$$
(1) 1 $\quad$ (2) 2 $\quad$ (3) 3 $\quad$ (4) 4

UNIT 9   ORGANIC CHEMISTRY

Organic chemistry is the study of carbon and carbon compounds. Organic compounds are found extensively in nature, and they are the predominant constituents of all living organisms.

The number of organic compounds—natural and synthetic—is vast. Since carbon is able to form four covalent bonds with other carbon atoms as well as with atoms of many elements, the number and variety of organic compounds is many times greater than the number of inorganic compounds.

Major sources of raw materials from which organic compounds are obtained include petroleum, coal, wood and other plant products, and animals.

CHARACTERISTICS OF ORGANIC COMPOUNDS

Organic compounds, being nonpolar generally, are insoluble in water and in other polar solvents. They are soluble, however, in nonpolar solvents, such as benzene and carbon tetrachloride. Those organic compounds that are somewhat polar—some alcohols and organic acids—are soluble in water. An example is acetic acid, which is water soluble.

Because they are not composed of ions and have a nonpolar nature, organic compounds are nonelectrolytes. (Organic acids are weak electrolytes.) Lack of polarity limits the attraction between molecules, and the relatively weak intermolecular forces between organic molecules result in the low melting points of these compounds—generally below 300°C.

The covalent bonds between atoms within organic molecules are strong, however. Thus, high-energy complexes (intermediates) do not form readily (see Unit 6, page 81), and an organic reaction is generally slower than a similar inorganic reaction. As a rule, high activation energies are often necessary for reactions involving organic reactants.

To summarize, organic compounds usually show the following characteristics:

1. They are nonpolar.
2. They are insoluble in water.
3. They are nonelectrolytes.
4. They have low melting points.
5. They react slower than do inorganic compounds.
6. They often require high activation energies.

BONDING. The carbon atom has four valence electrons and can therefore form four covalent bonds. The four bonds are directed in

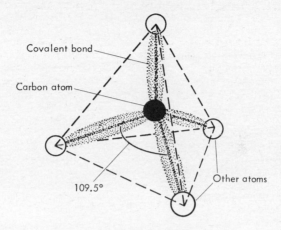

Figure 9-1. Representation of the theoretical spatial arrangement of the four carbon bonds.

space toward the corners of a regular tetrahedron. Two carbon atoms can form a covalent bond by sharing a pair of electrons (one electron is donated by each carbon atom). The result is a single carbon-to-carbon bond, represented as

$$-\overset{\displaystyle |}{\underset{\displaystyle |}{C}}-\overset{\displaystyle |}{\underset{\displaystyle |}{C}}-$$

Carbon atoms may also share two pairs of electrons to form a double carbon-to-carbon bond.

$$\overset{\diagdown}{\diagup}C=C\overset{\diagup}{\diagdown}$$

Lastly, carbon atoms may form a triple bond, by sharing three pairs of electrons.

$$-C\equiv C-$$

The covalent bonding of carbon compounds results in the formation of substances that are molecular in structure.

STRUCTURAL FORMULAS. Structural formulas attempt to show the bonding patterns and approximate shapes of molecules. But it is important to remember that structural formulas are two-dimensional representations of three-dimensional molecules. Each carbon atom can be pictured as the center of a tetrahedron, and each of its covalent bonds—a pair of electrons—may be represented by a short line.

ISOMERS. Isomers are compounds that have the same molecular formula, but different structural formulas. For example, propanal and acetone have the molecular formula C_3H_6O, but have different structural arrangements. Thus, propanal and acetone are isomers.

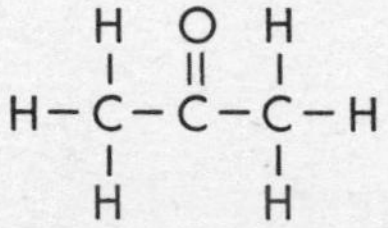

$$\underset{\text{Acetone}}{H-\overset{\displaystyle H}{\underset{\displaystyle H}{C}}-\overset{\displaystyle O}{\overset{\displaystyle \|}{C}}-\overset{\displaystyle H}{\underset{\displaystyle H}{C}}-H} \qquad \underset{\text{Propanal}}{H-\overset{\displaystyle H}{\underset{\displaystyle H}{C}}-\overset{\displaystyle H}{\underset{\displaystyle H}{C}}-\overset{\displaystyle O}{\overset{\displaystyle \|}{C}}-H}$$

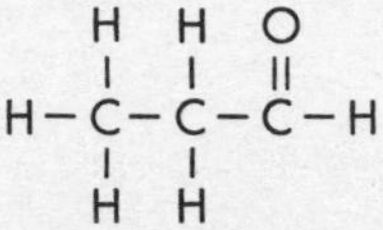

Likewise, n-butane and isobutane are isomers having the molecular formula C_4H_{10} (see page 131). Isomers are distinguishable from each other because they have different physical and chemical properties.

As the number of atoms in a molecule increases, the number of possible spatial arrangements, and thus the number of possible isomers, increases.

SATURATED AND UNSATURATED COMPOUNDS. Organic compounds in which the carbon atoms are bonded entirely by single bonds are called **saturated** compounds. Methane, CH_4, is a saturated compound.

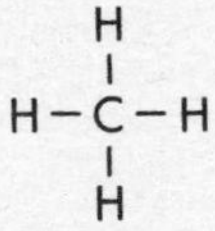

$$H-\overset{\displaystyle H}{\underset{\displaystyle H}{C}}-H$$

Methane

Unsaturated compounds, on the other hand, are organic compounds that consist of at least two adjacent carbon atoms that bond by sharing more than one pair of electrons. The bond formed may be double, as in ethylene (C_2H_4):

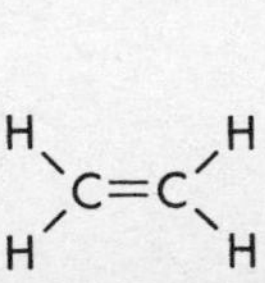

$$\overset{\displaystyle H}{\underset{\displaystyle H}{>}}C=C\overset{\displaystyle H}{\underset{\displaystyle H}{<}}$$

Ethylene
(ethene)

or triple, as in acetylene (C_2H_2):

$$H-C\equiv C-H$$

Acetylene
(ethyne)

Ethylene and acetylene are unsaturated compounds.

HOMOLOGOUS SERIES OF HYDROCARBONS

A **homologous series** of compounds is a group of related compounds in which each member differs from the one before it by the same additional unit. Homologous series actually simplify the study of organic chemistry, because compounds can be classified into groups having related structures and properties. Thus, when the boiling point of a compound is known, we can predict the boiling points of compounds in the same homologous series. In general, as the members of a homologous series increase in molecular mass, their boiling points and melting (freezing) points increase. This is due to the fact that van der Waals' forces increase with increasing molecular mass.

HYDROCARBONS. **Hydrocarbons** are organic compounds that contain only atoms of carbon and hydrogen. These compounds are the parent compounds from which most other organic compounds are named. Several homologous series of hydrocarbons—the alkanes, alkenes, and alkynes—are described next.

ALKANES. The **alkanes** comprise a homologous series of saturated hydrocarbons. The alkane family is also known by the name of its first member, methane, or by one of its high molecular weight members, **paraffin.** The general formula of the alkane series is C_nH_{2n+2}, so that each succeeding member differs from the compound before it by a CH_2 unit. Using the general alkane formula, you can find the molecular formula of any saturated hydrocarbon. For example, a saturated hydrocarbon having 20 carbon atoms has the molecular formula $C_{20}H_{42}$.

The first five members of the alkane series are shown in Table 9-1 (page 130). They, as well as other organic compounds, are usually named according to the **IUPAC** (International Union of Pure and Applied Chemistry) **system of nomenclature.** The alkane series shows isomerism beginning with the fourth member of the series, butane. Isomers of butane (C_4H_{10}) and pentane (C_5H_{12}) are shown on page 131.

ALKENES. The **alkene** group is a series of unsaturated hydrocarbons having one double bond ($C=C$). The general formula of this series is C_nH_{2n}. The alkene family is also called the **ethylene** series* or the **olefin** series. The first four members are shown in Table 9-2 (page 131). Note that the alkenes are named from the corresponding alkane by changing the alkane ending "**-ane**" to "**-ene.**" There is no alkene that corresponds to methane, because alkenes, by definition, have one carbon-to-carbon double bond. Therefore, the first member of the alkene series contains two atoms of carbon.

There are other hydrocarbon series comprising compounds that contain more than one double bond. The **dienes,** for example, are unsaturated hydrocarbons that have two double bonds. Such compounds, however, are not alkenes.

---

*Ethylene is the common name of C_2H_4. Ethene is the IUPAC name of the same compound.

TABLE 9-1. FIRST FIVE MEMBERS OF THE ALKANE SERIES

General formula: C_nH_{2n+2}

Hydrocarbon	Molecular formula	Structural formula
Methane	CH_4	H – C – H with H above and H below the C
Ethane	C_2H_6	H – C – C – H with H above and below each C
Propane	C_3H_8	H – C – C – C – H with H above and below each C
Butane	C_4H_{10}	H – C – C – C – C – H with H above and below each C
Pentane	C_5H_{12}	H – C – C – C – C – C – H with H above and below each C

ALKYNES. The **alkyne** group is a series of unsaturated hydrocarbons that contain one triple bond, and have the general formula C_nH_{2n-2}. This series is also called the **acetylene** series.* The alkynes are named, according to the IUPAC system, from the corresponding alkane by changing the suffix "**-ane**" to "**-yne.**" (See Table 9-3, page 132.)

*Acetylene is the common name of C_2H_2, and ethyne is the IUPAC name.

```
    H   H   H   H                  H   H   H   H   H                        H
    |   |   |   |                  |   |   |   |   |                        |
H − C − C − C − C − H        H − C − C − C − C − C − H                  H − C − H
    |   |   |   |                  |   |   |   |   |                        |
    H   H   H   H                  H   H   H   H   H                  H     |     H
                                                                      |     |     |
Normal or n-butane                   n-pentane                    H − C − C − C − H
                                                                      |     |     |
          H                                H                         H     |     H
          |                                |                               |
      H − C − H                        H − C − H                      H − C − H
                                                                          |
      H       H                        H       H   H                      H
      |       |                        |       |   |
  H − C − C − C − H              H − C − C − C − C − H              2, 2-dimethyl
      |   |   |                      |   |   |   |                    propane
      H   H   H                      H   H   H   H

   2-methyl propane                 2-methyl butane
```

TABLE 9-2. SAMPLE MEMBERS OF THE ALKENE SERIES

General formula: C_nH_{2n}

Hydrocarbon	Molecular formula	Structural formula
Ethene	C_2H_4	$\begin{array}{c} H \qquad\qquad H \\ \diagdown \qquad \diagup \\ C = C \\ \diagup \qquad \diagdown \\ H \qquad\qquad H \end{array}$
Propene	C_3H_6	H − C = C − C − H, with H above each C, and H below the third C
2-Butene	C_4H_8	H − C − C = C − C − H, with H above each C, and H below first and fourth C
2-Pentene	C_5H_{10}	H − C − C = C − C − C − H, with H above each C, and H below first, fourth, and fifth C

TABLE 9-3. SAMPLE MEMBERS OF THE ALKYNE SERIES

General formula: C_nH_{2n-2}

Hydrocarbon	Molecular formula	Structural formula
Ethyne	C_2H_2	H – C ≡ C – H
Propyne	C_3H_4	H – C ≡ C – C – H (with H above and below the final C)
2-Butyne	C_4H_6	H – C – C ≡ C – C – H (with H above and below the first and last C)
2-Pentyne	C_5H_8	H – C – C ≡ C – C – C – H (with H above and below the first C, and above and below the last two C)

BENZENE. The alkanes, alkenes, and alkynes are hydrocarbon series that consist of *open chains* of carbon atoms. The hydrocarbon chain ends when a carbon atom is bonded to three hydrogen atoms in addition to an adjacent carbon atom.

There are other hydrocarbons however, that form closed chains, and they are known as **cyclic hydrocarbons.** The **benzene** family is a series of cyclic unsaturated hydrocarbons having the general formula C_nH_{2n-6}. Benzene, C_6H_6, is the simplest member of the series, and toluene, C_7H_8 (or $C_6H_5CH_3$), is the second member.

Benzene   Toluene

For simplicity, the chemist often uses one of the following short-hand representations of a benzene or a toluene ring.

Benzene   Toluene

The presence of the ring implies that there is a carbon atom at each bend in the ring with one hydrogen atom attached to it.

The structure of benzene is often considered as the **"superposition"** or "average" of single and double bonds—actually a hybrid of the two structures represented below.

or simply,

Even though it is an unsaturated compound, benzene behaves more like a saturated hydrocarbon in many reactions. Specifically, it is less reactive than other unsaturated compounds.

QUESTIONS

1. All carbon-carbon bonds in a saturated hydrocarbon molecule are
   (1) single covalent   (2) double covalent   (3) triple covalent
   (4) coordinate covalent

2. Ethane, ethene, and ethyne are all similar in that they are
   (1) hydrocarbons (2) unsaturated compounds (3) saturated
   compounds (4) cyclic compounds

3. Compared with inorganic compounds, organic compounds usually
   have (1) greater solubility in water (2) a tendency to form ions more
   readily   (3) more rapid reaction rates (4) lower melting points

4. A toluene molecule *differs* from a benzene molecule in that the toluene
   molecule contains one additional carbon atom and (1) one additional
   hydrogen atom (2) two additional hydrogen atoms (3) three
   additional hydrogen atoms (4) four additional hydrogen atoms

5. Each member of a homologous series of hydrocarbons differs from each adjacent member of that series by a carbon atom and (1) one hydrogen atom (2) two hydrogen atoms (3) three hydrogen atoms (4) four hydrogen atoms

6. Which formula represents a saturated hydrocarbon? (1) CH_4 (2) C_2H_4 (3) C_3H_6 (4) C_4H_8

7. Which is characteristic of most organic compounds? (1) they have very strong intermolecular forces (2) they are primarily ionic in character (3) they generally have low melting points and low boiling points (4) they are all highly soluble in water

8. As the molecular mass of the compounds of the alkane series increases, their boiling point (1) decreases (2) increases (3) remains the same

9. What is the total number of bonds between adjacent carbon atoms in an ethyne molecule? (1) 1 (2) 2 (3) 3 (4) 5

10. The general formula for the alkyne series is (1) C_nH_n (2) C_nH_{n-2} (3) C_nH_{2n} (4) C_nH_{2n-2}

11. A molecule of ethene is similar to a molecule of methane in that they both have the same (1) structural formula (2) molecular formula (3) number of carbon atoms (4) number of hydrogen atoms

12. What compound is a member of the homologous series with the general formula C_nH_{2n}? (1) acetylene (2) benzene (3) propene (4) toluene

13. Which is the formula of a saturated hydrocarbon? (1) C_2H_2 (2) C_2H_4 (3) C_5H_8 (4) C_5H_{12}

14. The total number of covalent bonds in a molecule of C_3H_8 is (1) 11 (2) 10 (3) 3 (4) 8

15. The benzene series has the general formula (1) C_nH_{2n} (2) C_nH_{2n-2} (3) C_nH_{2n+2} (4) C_nH_{2n-6}

16. Which compound is a member of the alkane series? (1) C_2H_6 (2) C_3H_6 (3) C_4H_6 (4) C_6H_6

17. Which is the third member of the alkene series? (1) propane (2) propene (3) butane (4) butene

18. Which molecular formula represents pentene? (1) C_4H_8 (2) C_4H_{10} (3) C_5H_{10} (4) C_5H_{12}

19. Which structural formula represents propene?

$$(1) \quad H-\overset{\overset{\displaystyle H}{|}}{C}=\overset{\overset{\displaystyle H}{|}}{C}-\overset{\overset{\displaystyle H}{|}}{\underset{\underset{\displaystyle H}{|}}{C}}-H$$

$$(3) \quad H-\overset{\overset{\displaystyle H}{|}}{C}=C=\overset{\overset{\displaystyle H}{|}}{C}-H$$

$$(2) \quad H-C\equiv C-\overset{\overset{\displaystyle H}{|}}{\underset{\underset{\displaystyle H}{|}}{C}}-H$$

$$(4) \quad H-\overset{\overset{\displaystyle H}{|}}{\underset{\underset{\displaystyle H}{|}}{C}}-\overset{\overset{\displaystyle H}{|}}{\underset{\underset{\displaystyle H}{|}}{C}}-\overset{\overset{\displaystyle H}{|}}{\underset{\underset{\displaystyle H}{|}}{C}}-H$$

20. Which molecule contains a triple covalent bond? (1) C_2H_2 (2) C_2H_4 (3) C_3H_6 (4) C_3H_8

21. Which is the first member of the alkyne series? (1) CH_2 (2) CH_4 (3) C_2H_2 (4) C_2H_4

22. What is the empirical formula for members of the alkene series of hydrocarbons? (1) CH (2) CH_2 (3) CH_3 (4) CH_4

23. What is the total number of covalent bonds in a molecule of ethane? (1) 6 (2) 2 (3) 7 (4) 4

OTHER ORGANIC COMPOUNDS

There are other series of organic compounds in which one or more hydrogen atoms of a hydrocarbon, saturated or unsaturated, is replaced by other elements. Although such a compound is not necessarily prepared directly from its hydrocarbon parent, the nonhydrocarbon usually derives its name from the corresponding hydrocarbon.

FUNCTIONAL GROUPS. There are specific groupings of atoms that give characteristic properties to an organic molecule to which they are attached. These arrangements of atoms are called **functional groups**. They include the groups we are concerned with here, $-OH$ (the alcohols), $-COOH$ (the organic acids), $-CHO$ (the aldehydes), and

$$-\overset{\overset{\displaystyle O}{\|}}{C}-$$ (the ketones), as well as others.

In general, an organic compound other than a hydrocarbon can be thought of as containing one or more functional groups that are attached to a hydrocarbon radical, which we may represent as **R**.

ALCOHOLS. Alcohols are organic compounds in which one or more hydrogen atoms of a hydrocarbon are replaced by an $-OH$ group. The $-OH$ group is called a **hydroxyl group**. No more than one hydroxyl group may be attached to any one carbon atom.

Although compounds containing the $-OH$ group resemble the Arrhenius bases of inorganic chemistry, alcohols do not have the properties of bases. The $-OH$ group of an alcohol does not form the hydroxide ion in aqueous solution.

MONOHYDROXY ALCOHOLS. Monohydroxy (monohydric) alcohols have only one $-OH$ group. These alcohols may be classified according to the number of carbon chains attached to the carbon atom having the $-OH$ group.

Primary alcohols are alcohols in which the carbon attached to the $-OH$ group is attached to only one other carbon atom of a hydrocarbon chain. Thus, the carbon attached to the $-OH$ group is at the end of the hydrocarbon chain. A typical primary alcohol can be represented as R-OH, where R represents the hydrocarbon molecule aside from the hydroxyl group. The end group of a primary alcohol has the structural formula

$$- \underset{\underset{\displaystyle H}{|}}{\overset{\overset{\displaystyle H}{|}}{C}} - OH$$

which is frequently written as $-CH_2OH$.

According to the IUPAC system of nomenclature, primary alcohols are named from the corresponding hydrocarbon by replacing the final -e with the suffix -ol. The common names of alcohols were formerly derived from the name of the corresponding hydrocarbon by changing -ane to -yl, and adding the word *alcohol*. Although the common names are still in use, IUPAC names are preferred. The table below gives the names of the first four primary alcohols.

TABLE 9-4. SEVERAL PRIMARY ALCOHOLS

Molecular formula	IUC name	Common name
CH_3OH	Methanol	Methyl alcohol
C_2H_5OH	Ethanol	Ethyl alcohol
C_3H_7OH	Propanol	Propyl alcohol
C_4H_9OH	Butanol	Butyl alcohol

Secondary alcohols are alcohols in which the carbon attached to the $-OH$ group is attached to two other carbon atoms. Secondary alcohols can be represented as

$$R - \underset{\underset{\displaystyle R'}{|}}{\overset{\overset{\displaystyle H}{|}}{C}} - OH$$

where R and R' represent hydrocarbon radicals which may be the same or different.

Tertiary alcohols are alcohols in which the carbon attached to the $-OH$ group is attached to three other carbon atoms. Tertiary alcohols can be represented as

$$R - \underset{\underset{\displaystyle R''}{|}}{\overset{\overset{\displaystyle R'}{|}}{C}} - OH$$

where the hydrocarbon radicals may be the same or different.

DIHYDROXY ALCOHOLS. Compounds containing two $-OH$ groups are called **dihydroxy (dihydric) alcohols,** or **glycols.** The most important glycol is 1, 2 ethanediol, commonly called ethylene glycol. It has the structural formula

$$
\begin{array}{ccc}
 & H & H \\
 & | & | \\
H- & C- & C-H \\
 & | & | \\
 & OH & OH
\end{array}
$$

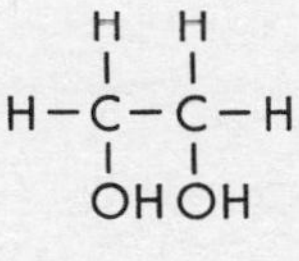

Ethylene glycol (1, 2-ethanediol)

Ethylene glycol is commonly used as an antifreeze.

TRIHYDROXY ALCOHOLS. Compounds with three $-OH$ groups are known as **trihydroxy (trihydric) alcohols.** Glycerol (or glycerine), produced from the hydrolysis of fats, is an important trihydroxy alcohol. It has the structural formula

$$
\begin{array}{cccc}
 & H & H & H \\
 & | & | & | \\
H- & C- & C- & C-H \\
 & | & | & | \\
 & OH & OH & OH
\end{array}
$$

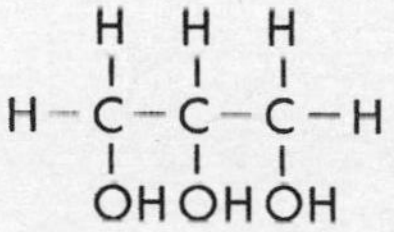

Glycerol (1, 2, 3-propanetriol)

ORGANIC ACIDS. Organic acids constitute a family of organic compounds containing the functional group $-COOH$. Organic acids are named by dropping the final *-e* of the corresponding alkane and replacing it with the suffix *-oic* followed by the word *acid*. Thus, the first member of the organic acid series, containing one carbon atom, is methanoic acid, $HCOOH$, which is commonly known as formic acid. The second member of the series, CH_3COOH, ethanoic acid, is usually called by its common name, acetic acid. In general, organic acids are weak acids.

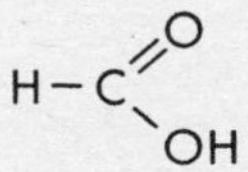

$$
H-C\overset{\displaystyle O}{\underset{\displaystyle OH}{<}}
$$

Formic acid
(methanoic acid)

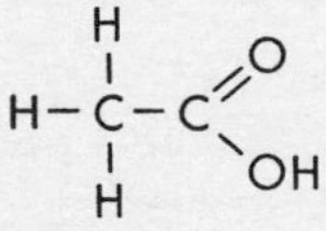

$$
\begin{array}{c}
H \\
| \\
H-C-C\overset{\displaystyle O}{\underset{\displaystyle OH}{<}} \\
| \\
H
\end{array}
$$

Acetic acid
(ethanoic acid)

Other functional groups include aldehydes $(-CHO)$, esters $(-COOR)$, and amines $(-NH_2)$. Amino acids, the building blocks of all proteins, contain two functional groups, $-COOH$ and $-NH_2$.

ALDEHYDES. When primary alcohols are treated with an oxidizing agent in an acid solution, they are oxidized to form a class of compounds called **aldehydes.** The functional group of the aldehydes is

$$
\begin{array}{c}
\text{H} \\
| \\
-\text{C} = \text{O}
\end{array}
$$

The first member of the aldehyde family is

$$
\begin{array}{c}
\text{H} \\
| \\
\text{H} - \text{C} = \text{O}
\end{array}
$$

The common name for this compound is **formaldehyde.** Its IUPAC name is obtained by adding the suffix **"-al"** to the stem **"methan-"** to give **methanal.** In aldehydes, the functional group always includes a terminal (end) carbon atom. The general formula for members of this family is

$$
\begin{array}{c}
\text{H} \\
| \\
\text{R} - \text{C} = \text{O}
\end{array}
$$

In abbreviated form, this formula is RCHO.

KETONES. The oxidation of secondary alcohols is similar to that of the primary alcohols except that the functional group is produced on a non-terminal, or secondary carbon atom. This family of organic compounds is called the **ketones,** and has the structure R-CO-R'. R and R' represent hydrocarbon radicals which may be the same or different. The simplest member of the ketone family is

$$
\begin{array}{ccccc}
\text{H} & & \text{O} & & \text{H} \\
| & & || & & | \\
\text{H} - \text{C} & - & \text{C} & - & \text{C} - \text{H} \\
| & & & & | \\
\text{H} & & & & \text{H}
\end{array}
$$

The common name for this compound is **acetone.** Its IUPAC name is obtained by adding the suffix **"-one"** to the stem **"propan-"** to give propanone. Propanone (acetone) is an important industrial solvent.

ETHERS. When two primary alcohols are treated with a dehydrating agent, water is removed from the molecules and the two alcohol chains are joined by an oxygen "bridge": R-OH + R'-OH→R-O-R' + H_2O. The class of compounds formed in this way is called the **ethers**, and has the structure R-O-R'. The best known member of this family is

diethyl ether, which is used as a general anaesthetic. The formula for
diethyl ether is

$$
\begin{array}{ccccccc}
& H & H & & H & H & \\
& | & | & & | & | & \\
H - & C - & C - & O - & C - & C - & H \\
& | & | & & | & | & \\
& H & H & & H & H &
\end{array}
$$

ORGANIC REACTIONS

Organic reactions frequently involve only the functional groups of
the reacting species. In many cases this means that the greater part
of the reactant molecule is left unchanged during a chemical reaction.
Two reactions that often involve parts of a molecule other than its
functional groups (if any) are substitution and addition.

SUBSTITUTION. A **substitution reaction** is the replacement of one
kind of atom or group by another kind of atom or group.

When saturated hydrocarbons are involved in a substitution reaction,
one or more hydrogen atoms must be removed so that replacement
with other atoms or groups can occur.* Hydrogen atoms of saturated
hydrocarbons can be replaced by halogen atoms. The general term
for halogen substitution is **halogenation,** and the products of the reaction are called **halogen derivatives.**

When ethane reacts with chlorine, the products of the reaction are
ethyl chloride and hydrogen chloride. One atom of the chlorine molecule reacts with one of ethane's hydrogen atoms (to form hydrogen
chloride) and the other chlorine atom replaces the hydrogen (to form
ethyl chloride).

$$
\begin{array}{ccccc}
H\ H & & H\ H & & \\
| \ \ | & & | \ \ | & & \\
H-C-C-H & + \ \ Cl_2 \longrightarrow & H-C-C-Cl & + & HCl \\
| \ \ | & & | \ \ | & & \\
H\ H & & H\ H & & \text{Hydrogen} \\
\text{Ethane} & \text{Chlorine} & \text{Ethyl chloride} & & \text{chloride}
\end{array}
$$

ADDITION. Addition reactions usually involve adding one or more
atoms or groups at a double bond, which results in the saturation of
the bond. Thus, addition is characteristic of unsaturated compounds.

---

*Reactions involving saturated hydrocarbons, excepting combustion and
thermal decomposition reactions, always involve the removal and replacement of hydrogen.

In the case of a reaction between ethene and chlorine, the double bond of the ethene molecule is broken and a chlorine atom is added to each of the available bonding sites. The product of the reaction is the halogen derivative dichloroethane (or ethyl dichloride).

$$
\underset{\text{Ethene}}{\begin{array}{c} H \\ \diagdown \\ H \diagup \end{array} C = C \begin{array}{c} \diagup H \\ \diagdown H \end{array}}
\quad + \quad
\underset{\text{Chlorine}}{Cl_2}
\quad \longrightarrow \quad
\underset{\text{1, 2-Dichloroethane}}{H - \overset{\displaystyle H}{\underset{\displaystyle Cl}{C}} - \overset{\displaystyle H}{\underset{\displaystyle Cl}{C}} - H}
$$

Hydrogen may also be added to an unsaturated compound in the same way chlorine is added. This process is called **hydrogenation,** and it usually requires the presence of a catalyst and an elevated temperature.

Unsaturated compounds tend to be more reactive than saturated compounds. Therefore, addition reactions take place more readily than do substitutions. Although organic reactions are generally slower than inorganic reactions, some additions are approximately as rapid as reactions between ions.

ESTERIFICATION. Organic acids can react with alcohols to produce an organic product called an **ester,** plus water. This kind of reaction, which is reversible and proceeds slowly, is called **esterification.** The reaction is similar to a neutralization reaction in inorganic chemistry in which an acid and a base react to form a salt and water. Esterification, however, is not an ionic reaction, and esters are covalent, not ionic, compounds. An example of esterification is the reaction between acetic acid and ethanol in the presence of concentrated sulfuric acid, a dehydrating agent, to form the ester ethyl acetate and water.

$$
\underset{\text{Acetic acid}}{CH_3C \begin{array}{c} \diagup O \\ \diagdown OH \end{array}}
\quad + \quad
\underset{\text{Ethanol}}{HOC_2H_5}
\quad \rightleftharpoons \quad
\underset{\text{Ethyl acetate}}{CH_3\overset{\displaystyle O}{\overset{\|}{C}} - O - C_2H_5}
\quad + \quad
\underset{\text{Water}}{H_2O}
$$

Fats are esters that are derived from glycerol, a trihydroxy alcohol, and long-chain organic acids (fatty acids).

SAPONIFICATION. The breaking apart of an ester to produce an acid and an alcohol is called **hydrolysis.** This is the reverse of esterification. When the hydrolysis of an ester is carried out in the presence of a base, the process is called **saponification.** In making soap, fat, a glycerol ester, is saponified by hot alkali (base). The products of the reaction are soap, which is salt of an organic acid, and glycerol.

FERMENTATION. Fermentation is a chemical process whereby molecules are broken down. Enzymes, secreted by living organisms, act as catalysts in fermentation. Yeasts, for example, secrete enzymes that convert glucose into ethanol and carbon dioxide. The enzymes secreted by yeasts in the fermentation of sugar are collectively known as zymase.

$$C_6H_{12}O_6 \xrightarrow{\text{zymase}} 2\,C_2H_5OH + 2\,CO_2$$

Glucose   Ethanol   Carbon dioxide

OXIDATION. Perhaps the most familiar reaction of organic compounds is that of **oxidation.** We derive most of our energy from the combustion of hydrocarbons. Natural gas consists of almost pure methane, which burns readily to produce carbon dioxide and water. The gasoline that fuels our automobile engines is a little more difficult to burn. If there is sufficient time and oxygen, the combustion will be complete, and the products will be carbon dioxide and water. However, when the supply of oxygen is limited or when there is not sufficient time for complete burning, different products are formed. In addition to water, which is always a product of oxidation of organic compounds, the other products of partial burning are carbon or carbon dioxide. The amounts of each of these depend on the amount of oxygen available.

POLYMERIZATION. Polymers are organic compounds made up of chains of smaller units bonded together. The formation of these molecules is called **polymerization,** and each individual unit of a polymer is called a **monomer.** While plastics, such as nylon, rayon, and polyethylene, are the best known of the polymers, there are many naturally occurring polymers, such as proteins, starches, and cellulose. There are two methods by which polymerization occurs — **condensation** and **addition.**

Condensation polymerization results from the bonding of monomers by a dehydration reaction similar to that found in the formation of ethers (page 138). In the case of an ether, the −OH groups of adjacent primary alcohols react. A dehydrating agent removes a water molecule from between the alcohols, leaving an oxygen "bridge" as a link between the alcohol radicals. Once these two reacting sites are used, no more dehydration can occur.

The difference between this process and the formation of a condensation polymer is that, in the latter, the monomers have at least **two** functional groups. Thus, when dehydration occurs between two molecules, there are still sites remaining where further dehydration can occur. The ends of such a chain will always have an −OH group available, and more molecules can be added to the chain. Some examples of condensation polymers include silicones, polyesters, phenolic plastics, nylon, and the naturally occurring polymers (protein, starches, and cellulose).

ADDITIONAL MATERIALS . . .

Addition polymerization involves the joining of monomers of unsaturated compounds by "opening" a multiple bond in the carbon chain. One of the most common plastics, polyethylene, is formed in this manner. When ethene (ethylene) is in the presence of a suitable catalyst, the double bond between the two carbon atoms is opened. This makes it possible for the "free radical" to join a second unit, thus making a *dimer*, or two-unit chain. This chain is still free to continue adding more and more units at the end, until it has an extremely high molecular mass, when it is called polyethylene.

$$nC_2H_4 \rightarrow (C_2H_4)n$$

Ethene   Polyethylene

QUESTIONS

1. A reaction between an acid and alcohol produces an ester and (1) carbon dioxide (2) water (3) glycerol (4) ethanol

2. The reaction $C_3H_6 + H_2 \rightarrow C_3H_8$ is an example of (1) substitution (2) addition (3) polymerization (4) esterification

3. If $C_2H_4Br_2$ is the only product of a reaction between ethene and bromine, the reaction is (1) an addition reaction (2) a substitution reaction (3) an esterification reaction (4) a hydrogenation reaction

4. The product of a reaction between a hydrocarbon and chlorine was 1, 2-dichloropropane. The hydrocarbon must have been (1) C_5H_{10} (2) C_2H_4 (3) C_3H_6 (4) C_4H_8

5. The reaction $C_3H_5(C_{17}H_{35}COO)_3 + 3NaOH \rightarrow 3C_{17}H_{35}COONa + C_3H_5(OH)_3$ is an example of (1) polymerization (2) fermentation (3) esterification (4) saponification

6. The fermentation of $C_6H_{12}O_6$ will produce carbon dioxide and (1) a polymer (2) a soap (3) an ester (4) an alcohol

7. The reaction $C_4H_{10} + Br_2 \rightarrow C_4H_9Br + HBr$ is an example of (1) substitution (2) addition (3) fermentation (4) polymerization

8. Which reaction produces ethyl alcohol as one of the principal products? (1) an esterification reaction (2) a neutralization reaction (3) a saponification reaction (4) a fermentation reaction

9. Which compound will react with CH_3COOH to form the ester methyl ethanoate? (1) CH_3OCH_3 (2) CH_3COCH_3 (3) CH_3OH (4) CH_3COOH

10. Compounds which have the same molecular formula but different molecular structures are called (1) isomers (2) isotopes (3) allotropes (4) homologs

11. The compound C_4H_9OH is an isomer of (1) $C_3H_7COCH_3$ (2) $C_2H_5OC_2H_5$ (3) $CH_3COOC_2H_3$ (4) CH_3COOH

12. Which compound is an isomer of CH_3COOH? (1) $HCOOCH_3$ (2) CH_3CH_2OH (3) CH_3CH_2COOH (4) CH_3COOCH_3

13. What is the IUPAC name for the compound below?

$$
\begin{array}{c}
\text{H} \quad \text{H} \\
| \qquad | \\
\text{H—C—C—H} \\
| \qquad | \\
\text{Br} \quad \text{Br}
\end{array}
$$

   (1) dibromoethyne   (3) 1, 2-dibromoethyne
   (2) dibromoethane   (4) 1, 2-dibromoethane

14. Which compound contains three hydroxyl groups per molecule?
   (1) butanol   (2) glycerol   (3) ethanol   (4) methanol

15. What is the total number of carbon atoms in a molecule of 2, 2-dimethylpropane? (1) 5 (2) 2 (3) 3 (4) 4

16. The structural formulas

$$
\begin{array}{c}
\text{H} \quad \text{H} \quad \text{H} \quad \text{H} \\
| \quad\ | \quad\ | \quad\ | \\
\text{H—C}=\text{C—C}=\text{C—H}
\end{array}
\text{ and }
\begin{array}{c}
\text{H} \quad \text{H} \\
| \quad\ | \\
\text{H—C}\equiv\text{C—C—C—H} \\
| \quad\ | \\
\text{H} \quad \text{H}
\end{array}
$$

represent molecules which are both   (1) halogen addition products
(2) unsaturated hydrocarbons   (3) members of the alkynes
(4) isomers of butane

17. Which structural formula represents an alcohol?

$$
(1)\
\begin{array}{c}
\text{H} \quad \text{O} \\
| \qquad || \\
\text{H—C—C—H} \\
| \\
\text{H}
\end{array}
\qquad
(3)\
\begin{array}{c}
\text{H} \quad\ \ \text{H} \\
| \qquad | \\
\text{H—C—O—C—H} \\
| \qquad\ | \\
\text{H} \quad\ \ \text{H}
\end{array}
$$

$$
(2)\
\begin{array}{c}
\text{H} \quad \text{H} \quad \text{H} \\
| \quad\ | \quad\ | \\
\text{H—C—C—C—H} \\
| \quad\ | \quad\ | \\
\text{H} \quad \text{H} \quad \text{OH}
\end{array}
\qquad
(4)\
\begin{array}{c}
\text{H} \quad \text{O} \\
| \qquad || \\
\text{H—C—C—O—H} \\
| \\
\text{H}
\end{array}
$$

18. Which is an isomer of the compound propanoic acid, CH_3CH_2COOH? (1) CH_2=CHCOOH (2) $CH_3CH_2CH_2COOH$
(3) $CH_3CH(OH)CH_2OH$ (4) $HCOOCH_2CH_3$

19. What is the total number of carbon atoms contained in an ethyl group? (1) 1 (2) 2 (3) 3 (4) 4

20. What is the formula for pentanol? (1) C_5H_{12} (2) $C_5H_{11}OH$ (3) C_4H_{10} (4) C_4H_9OH

21. The formula of methanoic acid is (1) HCHO (2) HCOOH (3) CH_3OH (4) $HCOOCH_3$

22. A solution of methanol *differs* from a solution of acetic acid in that the solution of acetic acid (1) contains molecules only (2) has a pH of 7 (3) turns red litmus to blue (4) conducts electricity

23. Which compound represents a member of the benzene series? (1) acetylene (2) ethylene (3) toluene (4) propene

24. An example of an organic acid is
    (1) $CH_3CH_2CH_2COOH$ (3) CH_3CH_2OH
    (2) CH_3COCH_3 (4) HCHO

25. Which compound is a hydrocarbon?

(1) ⬡—CH_3 (2) ⬡—OH   (3) ⬡—COOH   (4) ⬡—Cl

26. Which type of compound would have the following structural formula?

$$\begin{array}{ccc} H & H & H \\ | & | & | \\ H-C-C-C-H \\ | & | & | \\ OH & OH & OH \end{array}$$

    (1) an ester   (3) a hydrocarbon
    (2) an acid   (4) an alcohol

27. Which formula correctly represents an ester?
    (1) $CH_3CH_2CH_2OH$ (3) CH_3COOCH_3
    (2) CH_3COCH_3 (4) CH_3CH_2COOH

28. A molecule of which alcohol contains more than one hydroxyl group? (1) propanol (2) butanol (3) pentanol (4) glycerol

29. The compound CH_3COOCH_3 is classified as (1) an acid (2) an alcohol (3) an ester (4) a hydrocarbon

30. Which is the formula for ethanoic acid?
    (1) CH_3COOH (3) CH_3CH_2COOH
    (2) CH_3CH_2OH (4) $CH_3CH_2CH_2OH$

31. Which organic reaction involves the bonding of monomers by a dehydration process? (1) substitution (2) oxidation (3) addition polymerization (4) condensation polymerization

32. The reaction represented by the equation $nC_2H_4 \rightarrow (-C_2H_4-)_n$ is called (1) saponification (2) esterification (3) fermentation (4) polymerization

UNIT 10   APPLICATIONS OF CHEMICAL PRINCIPLES

Scientific research can be arbitrarily divided into two types—pure and applied. **Pure research** is study undertaken without consideration of any immediate practical or commercial applications. **Applied research** is undertaken with some practical goal in mind. Such goals may include the solution of a particular problem, the development of a marketable product, or the improvement of a product already on the market.

INDUSTRIAL APPLICATIONS

HABER PROCESS. In its uncombined form, nitrogen makes up about 78% of the earth's atmosphere. Although nitrogen is quite unreactive, its compounds are of immense commercial importance. These compounds are used in the production of fertilizers, plastics, and explosives. The **Haber Process** is a method by which molecular nitrogen (N_2) can be combined with hydrogen to form ammonia. The ammonia produced by this process can either be used directly or as the starting material for many other industrial applications.

In 1906, Fritz Haber, a German chemist, conceived the process for the production of ammonia. The basic reaction is

$$N_2 + 3H_2 \rightleftarrows 2NH_3 + 22 \text{ kcal}$$

At equilibrium, all three substances involved form a mixture of gases in the reaction chamber. To make this a commercial process, the ammonia must be separated and drawn off as it is formed and fresh supplies of nitrogen and hydrogen introduced continuously. Under ordinary conditions, the reaction is slow to reach equilibrium and the concentration of ammonia at equilibrium is too small to be useful. However, because the system is in equilibrium, it is possible to use Le Chatelier's Principle to increase the rate of yield of ammonia. The effects of the different factors are discussed in the following paragraphs.

1. Concentration. An increase in the concentration of either nitrogen or hydrogen will shift the equilibrium to the right and increase the yield of ammonia. Lower concentrations of ammonia also favor the reaction to the right. Lower concentrations of ammonia are achieved by removing the ammonia continuously during the process.

2. Pressure. Increased pressure will favor the reaction toward the side having the smaller number of gas molecules. Increased pressure therefore favors the production of ammonia.

3. **Temperature:** The reaction to the right is exothermic. Therefore, lowering the temperature would favor the reaction to the right and shift the equilibrium toward a greater concentration of ammonia. However, lowering the temperature would slow the rate of reaction, so that it would take longer to reach equilibrium. In practice, fairly high temperatures (about 500°C) are used to produce a satisfactory *rate* of reaction, and very high pressures (about 1000 atmospheres) are used to produce a satisfactory *concentration,* or output, of the desired product.

4. **Catalyst:** Although the presence of a catalyst does not cause the equilibrium to shift, it does increase the rates of reactions. In combination with other factors, a catalyst allows the reaction to proceed at a reasonable rate. Metallic catalysts, such as platinum or iron, are used. When iron is used, some aluminum oxide or silicon oxide enhance its effect.

The final combination of conditions must be selected to obtain the maximum output of ammonia at reasonable conditions with minimum cost.

CONTACT PROCESS. Sulfuric acid, H_2SO_4, is probably the most extensively used compound in industry. It is used in the manufacture of fertilizers, the production of steel, and the processing of petroleum, to list just a few of its varied uses. Millions of tons of sulfuric acid are produced yearly, much of it by the **contact process.**

Elemental sulfur, the raw material for the process, is obtained either from underground deposits or during the refining of petroleum. This elemental sulfur can be easily burned in oxygen to produce sulfur dioxide:

$$S + O_2 \rightarrow SO_2 + \text{Heat}$$

The sulfur dioxide can be further reacted with oxygen to produce sulfur trioxide:

$$2\ SO_2 + O_2 \rightleftarrows 2\ SO_3 + \text{Heat}$$

Under normal conditions, this reaction is quite slow. In order to speed up the rate of the reaction, the sulfur dioxide and oxygen are passed over a solid catalyst, such as platinum or vanadium pentoxide. At a temperature of 450°C, the reaction yields about 95% product. It can be seen that, like the Haber reaction, high pressure favors the formation of the product SO_3, while the high temperatures favor the reverse (endothermic) reaction.

The sulfur trioxide thus produced could be reacted directly with water to produce sulfuric acid:

$$SO_3 + H_2O \rightarrow H_2SO_4$$

However, this reaction proceeds very slowly. To speed up the entire process, the sulfur trioxide is dissolved in sulfuric acid to produce pyrosulfuric acid:

$$SO_3 + H_2SO_4 \rightarrow H_2S_2O_7$$

The pyrosulfuric acid reacts rapidly with water to produce two molecules of sulfuric acid:

$$H_2S_2O_7 + H_2O \rightarrow 2\ H_2SO_4 + Heat$$

The sulfuric acid produced by this process is almost twice as dense as water, having a density of 1.84 g/L. It is noticeably viscous and is sometimes called *oil of vitriol*. Its concentration is 18M. Large amounts of heat are released when the acid is mixed with water. In order to prevent this heat from being concentrated between the layers of acid and water, the denser acid must be poured into the water, thus allowing full mixing and distribution of heat throughout the solution.

QUESTIONS

1-4. Base your answers to Questions 1-4 on the following information: In the Haber process, nitrogen, hydrogen, and ammonia are at equilibrium in a closed system under conditions of high temperature and pressure. The equation representing the system is:

$$N_2 + 3H_2 \rightleftharpoons 2NH_3 + 22\ kcal$$

1. The temperature is increased and the pressure is kept constant. Compared to its original concentration, the new equilibrium concentration of (1) NH_3 is less (2) NH_3 is more (3) N_2 is less (4) H_2 is the same

2. Which of the following will cause an increase in the production of ammonia? (1) removal of nitrogen gas (2) a decrease in pressure (3) an increase in the temperature (4) removal of ammonia

3. The presence of a catalyst in the system (1) increases the concentration of the products (2) causes a decrease in the pressure (3) increases the rates of all reactions (4) retards the reverse reaction

4. The pressure on the system is increased while the temperature is kept constant. At the new equilibrium the number of moles of (1) NH_3 increases (2) H_2 increases (3) N_2 increases (4) N_2 is unchanged

5. Which equation represents a reaction that occurs during the contact process?
   (1) $ZnO + C \rightarrow Zn + CO$
   (2) $2Al + Cr_2O_3 \rightarrow Al_2O_3 + 2Cr$
   (3) $S + O_2 \rightarrow SO_2$
   (4) $N_2 + 3H_2 \rightarrow 2NH_3$

6. The Haber process is used to produce
   (1) sulfur dioxide   (2) ammonia
   (3) sulfuric acid   (4) sodium chloride

7. In the haber process, the gases used as the reactants are a mixture of (1) oxygen and ammonia (2) oxygen and hydrogen (3) nitrogen and hydrogen (4) nitrogen and oxygen

8. **In the contact process, sulfur trioxide is produced in the following system:**

$$2SO_2(g) + O_2(g) \rightleftharpoons 2SO_3(g) + 44 \text{ kcal}$$

Which change in conditions would result in the largest increase in concentration of SO_3?   (1) increased pressure and increased temperature   (2) increased pressure and decreased temperature   (3) decreased pressure and increased temperature   (4) decreased pressure and decreased temperature

9. **Given the contact process at equilibrium:**
$$2SO_2 + O_2 \rightarrow 2SO_3 + \text{heat}$$
An increase in pressure and a decrease in temperature will favor the formation of additional

(1) SO_2 only   **(2) SO_3 only**

(3) SO_2 and SO_3   **(4) SO_2 and O_2**

10. **Which reaction is used during the contact process?   (1) $2SO_2 + O_2 \rightarrow 2SO_3$ (2) $N_2 + 3H_2 \rightarrow 2NH_3$ (3) $Al + Cr_2O_3 \rightarrow Al_2O_3 + 2Cr$ (4) $2NaCl \rightarrow 2Na + Cl_2$**

REFINING OF METALLIC ELEMENTS. In Reference Table N, the table of standard electrode potentials has been partially reproduced to show the relative activity of the metals. Since this is a table of reduction potentials, the metals near the top of the table are the least chemically reactive. That is, they have the least tendency to be oxidized or form ions. Those at the bottom of the table are the most reactive. Since potassium, lithium, and sodium are extremely reactive, they are never found in nature in their atomic or uncombined state. The ions of these metals can be reduced to the atomic state only with considerable difficulty. On the other hand, the metals near the top of the table, such as silver and gold, are relatively unreactive. These metals can be found in nature in the elemental state or in compounds from which they can easily be reduced. In between these extremes are elements such as iron, copper, and zinc. These elements are easy to separate from their compounds, yet can be maintained in their atomic state without difficulty.

Zinc and copper are often found in nature in the form of sulfides. The metals in these sulfides can be isolated by a process called "roasting," in which the ore is reacted with oxygen, causing the metal to be reduced to its elemental form:

$$CuS + O_2 \rightarrow Cu + SO_2$$

The oxidation state of the copper has been changed from $+2$ to 0. Thus the copper has been reduced.

In a similar manner, zinc sulfide (sphalerite or zincblende) can be converted to an oxide by reaction with oxygen:

$$ZnS + 3/2\ O_2 \rightarrow ZnO + SO_2$$

After the conversion of the sulfide to an oxide, the elemental metal can be obtained by reduction with carbon. The carbon is generally obtained by heating coal in the absence of air to produce coke.

$$2\,ZnO + C \rightarrow 2\,Zn + CO_2$$

$$Fe_2O_3 + 3\,C \rightarrow 2\,Fe + 3\,CO$$

Carbon monoxide is also a reducing agent and may be used to reduce the iron oxide:

$$Fe_2O_3 + 3\,CO \rightarrow 2\,Fe + 3\,CO_2$$

Other metals may be too reactive to be reduced by carbon. These metals require different reducing agents. These reducing agents include H_2 and metals which are more reactive than the desired product:

$$WO_3 + 3H_2 \rightarrow W + 3H_2O$$

$$Cr_2O_3 + 2Al \rightarrow 2\,Cr + Al_2O_3$$

ELECTROLYSIS. Many metals are too reactive to be reduced economically by reaction with reducing agents. The most common method of reducing these metals is **electrolysis.** Figure 10-1 shows the arrangement of a typical electrolytic cell.

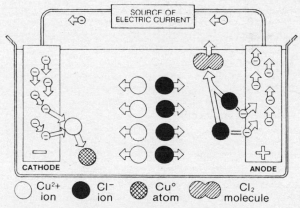

Figure 10-1. Electrolysis of copper chloride, $CuCl_2$.

In the process of electrolysis, electrons are forced by a battery or other source of electrons through a wire to the electrode at which reduction is to occur. This electrode becomes the cathode. Reduction occurs at the cathode as electrons flow from the electrode to combine with the metallic ion.

$$Cu^{2+} + 2e^- \rightarrow Cu^0$$

While there is an excess of electrons at the cathode, the other electrode, the anode, has a deficiency of electrons. Negative ions are attracted to this electrode and are oxidized as they yield their electrons:

$$2\,Cl^- \rightarrow Cl_2 + 2e^-$$

The active metals of Column 1(IA) (the alkali metals) and Column 2(IIA) (the alkaline earth metals) of the periodic table are all obtained by the electrolysis of their fused (melted) salts.

Perhaps the most common type of electrolysis involves the reduction of aluminum metal from aluminum oxide. The Al_2O_3 is found in the mineral bauxite, which must be purified and then dissolved in molten cryolite, Na_3AlF_6, to produce a solution that is an electrolyte. The overall reaction for the process is:

$$Al_2O_3 \rightarrow 2\ Al + 3/2\ O_2$$

CORROSION. In order to obtain most metals in their elemental form, it is necessary to reduce them from their compounds. This fact suggests that these metals are chemically active. In fact, most metals will react with common oxidizing agents and return to the ionic condition. The process by which metals combine with elements such as oxygen is called **corrosion.** It often requires the presence of water as a catalyst in order to proceed at an appreciable rate.

Since aluminum is a more reactive metal than iron, it might be predicted that aluminum would corrode faster than iron. While it is true that aluminum reacts rapidly and easily with oxygen to produce aluminum oxide, the newly formed oxide layer adheres tightly to the metallic aluminum and seals it from further corrosion. Zinc undergoes a similar process, thus reducing its deterioration.

Of the metals in common use, iron is one of the most vulnerable to corrosion. As iron oxide forms, it flakes off, exposing more unoxidized surface area. A great deal of time and money are spent in efforts to prevent, or at least minimize, the corrosion of iron. Three methods commonly used to combat corrosion are:

1. *Coating:* Iron can be covered with paint, oil, porcelain, or some corrosion-resistant metal, such as aluminum or zinc.

2. *Alloying:* Although pure iron corrodes rapidly, the process can be essentially halted by alloying the iron with nickel or chromium to produce "stainless steels."

3. *Cathodic Protection:* When iron is placed in contact with a metal more easily oxidized than itself, such as zinc or magnesium, the more active metal will be oxidized. As the more active metal is oxidized, the electrons flow from the "sacrificial" metal to the iron and prevent oxidation. In this type of protection, the more active metal acts as the anode, and is oxidized. The iron, as the less active metal, is the cathode.

BATTERIES. A **chemical cell** is a device which separates the oxidation half from the reduction half of a redox reaction. Electron transfer takes place through a wire that connects the electrodes of the two "half-cells."

The movement of electrons through the wire constitutes an electric current. Thus, in a chemical cell, chemical energy is transformed into electrical energy.

Batteries are combinations of chemical cells, and are available in a variety of electrode combinations. The common flashlight "battery" is really a single chemical cell (see Figure 10-2). It has an anode of zinc and a cathode of manganese dioxide. Between the two electrodes there is a moist paste of ammonium chloride and zinc chloride. The paste allows

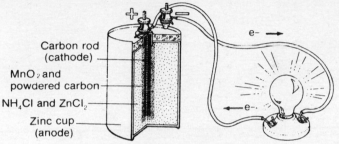

Carbon rod (cathode)

MnO_2 and powdered carbon

NH_4Cl and $ZnCl_2$

Zinc cup (anode)

e-

e-

Figure 10-2. A typical dry cell. The presence of the MnO_2 around the carbon rod prevents the formation of hydrogen gas at the anode.

the flow of electrons between the two electrodes. The maximum voltage that can be obtained from this type of cell is 1.5 volts. Such "dry cells," as they are called, are usually placed end-to-end in a flashlight to form a battery with a total voltage equal to the number of dry cells multiplied by 1.5.

The type of battery used in most cars is called a **lead storage battery.** The electrodes are made of lead and lead dioxide submerged in a solution of sulfuric acid. When electrons are drawn from the cell the reactions are:

anode: $Pb + HSO_4^- + H_2O \rightarrow PbSO_4 + 2e^- + H_3O^+$

cathode: $PbO_2 + HSO_4^- + 3H_3O^+ + 2e^- \rightarrow PbSO_4 + 5H_2O$

Overall:

$$Pb + 2HSO_4^- + 2H_3O^+ + PbO_2 \rightarrow 2PbSO_4 + 4 H_2O$$

As electrons are drawn from the cell, the amount of acid (H_3O^+) decreases. The solid $PbSO_4$ accumulates on the electrodes. When the battery is being charged, the reactions are reversed. The lead sulfate is converted into Pb and PbO_2.   This cell can be charged and discharged over and over , until there is a final "fatigue" of one of the electrodes.

Since the concentration of sulfuric acid changes from a maximum in a fully charged cell to a minimum in a discharged cell, the density of the acid can be used to indicate the relative charge on the battery. A fully charged battery has a density of 1.260 g/mL. As the cell is discharged and the amount of acid present in solution decreases, the density decreases.

Nickel and cadmium may also be used to generate an electric current.

In the NiCad (nickel-cadmium) battery, the cadmium serves as the negative anode and nickel hydroxide as the positive cathode. The probable reaction for this type of cell is:

$$2 \ Ni(OH)_3 + Cd \rightarrow 2Ni(OH)_2 + Cd(OH)_2$$

During discharge the nickel is reduced from an oxidation state of $+3$ to $+2$, while the cadmium is oxidized from 0 to $+2$. In this type of cell, the concentration of electrolyte remains constant. Since there are no gaseous products, the battery may be sealed and does not require the periodic addition of water as does the lead storage battery. A second advantage over the lead battery is associated with the uniform concentration of the electrolyte. As the lead battery discharges, the concentration of the electrolyte decreases and the maximum voltage which can be obtained decreases. In the NiCad battery, the electrolyte concentration remains constant and the voltage also remains constant.

QUESTIONS

1. In order to obtain metals from their sulfide ores, the ores are usually first converted into (1) sulfates (2) sulfites (3) oxides (4) carbonates

2. Which metallurgical process is illustrated by the following equation?
$$Fe_2O_3 + 3CO + Heat \rightarrow 2 \ Fe + 3 \ CO_2$$
   (1) roasting (2) reduction (3) corrosion (4) electrolysis

3. Which of the following occurs during the electrolysis of fused $CaCl_2$?
   (1) calcium ions are reduced (2) calcium atoms are reduced
   (3) chloride ions are reduced (4) chlorine atoms are reduced

4. Which metal can reduce the chromium III ion? (1) Pb (2) Fe (3) Ni
   (4) Al

5. During the electrolysis of fused NaCl, which reaction occurs at the positive electrode? (1) chloride ions are oxidized (2) chloride ions are reduced (3) sodium ions are oxidized (4) sodium ions are reduced

6. Which group includes three metals that are generally obtained from their compounds by electrolysis? (1) aluminum, magnesium, sodium (2) gold, silver, magnesium (3) mercury, aluminum, iron (4) mercury, tin, lead

7. Which metal is commonly obtained from its compounds by reduction with carbon? (1) lithium (2) iron (3) aluminum (4) calcium

8. Which reaction occurs at the negative electrode during the electrolysis of fused calcium fluoride?
   (1) $CaF_2 \rightarrow Ca^{2+} + F_2$
   (2) $2F^- \rightarrow F_2 + 2e^-$
   (3) $Ca^{2+} + 2e^- \rightarrow Ca^0$
   (4) $Ca^0 \rightarrow Ca^{2+} + 2e^-$

9. Which property would be associated with a very active metal? (1) a tendency to form unstable compounds (2) reduction to the atomic state by carbon (3) only found in nature in the combined form (4) high ionization energy

10. An electrolytic cell differs from an electrochemical cell in that an electrolytic cell (1) produces an electric current by means of a chemical reaction (2) produces a chemical reaction by means of an electric current (3) has oxidation and reduction occurring at the electrodes (4) has ions migrating between the electrodes

11. Which ion can be most easily reduced? (1) Cu^{2+} (2) Zn^{2+} (3) Ni^{2+} (4) Ca^{2+}

12. Group 1(IA) metals are obtained commercially from their fused salts by (1) transmutation (2) fractional distillation (3) electrolysis (4) polymerization

13. One of the metals that is usually alloyed with iron in the production of stainless steel is (1) calcium (2) aluminum (3) copper (4) chromium

14. Which metal may be connected to an iron pipe to prevent corrosion of the iron? (1) Co (2) Sn (3) Pb (4) Mg

15. Which metal must be combined with chromium to produce stainless steel? (1) radium (2) iron (3) copper (4) zinc

16. The self-protective coating that forms on aluminum metal is (1) an oxide (2) a sulfide (3) an oxalate (4) a chloride

17. Which type of chemical reaction is the corrosion of iron? (1) redox (2) substitution (3) polymerization (4) decomposition

18. Given the probable reaction for the nickel-cadmium battery:
$$2Ni(OH)_3 + Cd \rightarrow Ni(OH)_2 + Cd(OH)_2$$
Which species is oxidized during the discharge of the battery? (1) Ni^{3+} (2) Ni_{2+} (3) Cd^0 (4) Cd^{2+}

19. When fully charged, the electrodes of a lead-acid battery are (1) $PbSO_4$ and Pb (2) PbO_2 and Pb (3) Pb and Pb^{+2} (4) PbO_2 and $PbSO_4$

PETROLEUM

When petroleum is brought from the ground it is called **crude oil.** This mixture of organic hydrocarbons is not only a source of gasoline and other fuel oils, but it is also a raw material for the manufacture of plastics, textiles, rubber, and detergents.

FRACTIONAL DISTILLATION. Because petroleum is a mixture of different compounds, each compound retains its characteristic boiling point. The process of **fractional distillation** separates these different substances by taking advantage of these different boiling points. The mixture of crude oil is heated and all the components are injected into the bottom of a fractionating tower. The portion (fraction) with the highest boiling point cools to its condensation point and condenses. Those fractions with lower boiling points rise in the tower and continue to cool until they finally condense. The separate fractions are separated into these general groups:

gases	1-5 carbons
gasoline	5-12 carbons
kerosene, fuel oils	12-18 carbons
lubricants	16+ carbons
paraffins	20+ carbons
asphalt	36+ carbons

The percentages of these fractions in crude oil are fairly constant. There is not enough gasoline obtained from the distillation to satisfy modern-day technology. The yield of gasoline can be increased by a process called "cracking." In this process, fractions from the kerosene and lubricant series are heated to approximately 500°C in the presence of a catalyst (Al_2O_3). As a result, the long-chain molecules are broken into shorter chains of the gasoline series. A second process, reformation, reforms straight-chain compounds into branched compounds, which burn better.

Natural gas is a mixture that consists primarily of methane (CH_4) and ethane (C_2H_6). It is found in underground deposits and is an excellent fuel. In many parts of the country it is delivered to homes by means of pipelines. Bottled gas, also used as a fuel, is composed of propane or butane and is obtained from the lightest petroleum fractions.

QUESTIONS

1. **Which equation represents a simple example of cracking?**
   (1) $N_2 + 3H_2 \rightarrow 2NH_3$
   (2) $S + O_2 \rightarrow SO_2$
   (3) $C_3H_8 + 5O_2 \rightarrow 3CO_2 + 4H_2O$
   (4) $C_{14}H_{30} \rightarrow C_7H_{16} + C_7H_{14}$

2. **During the cracking process, large molecules of hydrocarbons are broken down into smaller molecules. This process generally requires an increase in temperature and catalysts such as**
   (1) oxides of aluminum and silicon
   (2) oxides of sulfur and nitrogen
   (3) sulfides of sodium and potassium
   (4) sulfides of hydrogen and magnesium

3. **Petroleum, a starting material for many chemical products, is a complex natural mixture of**
   (1) aldehydes   (2) ethers   (3) hydrocarbons   (4) ketones

4. **In crude petroleum, fractions can be separated according to their different boiling points by**
   (1) the contact process   (2) the Haber process
   (3) fractional distillation   (4) cracking

5. **A commercial process in which large molecules are broken down into smaller molecules to increase the yield of gasoline from petroleum is called**
   (1) polymerization   (2) hydrogenation
   (3) esterification   (4) cracking

UNIT 11   NUCLEAR CHEMISTRY

ARTIFICIAL RADIOACTIVITY

RADIOACTIVE ISOTOPES. None of the naturally occurring elements with atomic numbers greater than 82 have any stable isotopes. All of them eventually decay into a stable isotope of lead. In addition to these radioactive isotopes that are found naturally, there are numerous radioactive isotopes of the other elements that can be produced by bombarding stable nuclei with high-energy particles, such as protons, alpha particles, and neutrons. For example, if the normally stable nuclei of beryllium are bombarded by protons (hydrogen nuclei), some of the beryllium nuclei are changed to lithium nuclei, and helium nuclei (alpha particles) are given off. This reaction can be represented as follows:

$$_1^1H + {}_4^9Be \rightarrow {}_3^6Li + {}_2^4He$$

Note that this lithium nucleus is not the stable isotope found in nature ($_3^7Li$), but the unstable, or radioactive, isotope of mass number 6. Thus, a radioactive isotope of lithium has been produced from a stable isotope of beryllium.

PARTICLE ACCELERATORS. Since both a proton and a beryllium nucleus have positive charges, they repel each other. The proton must therefore have a high kinetic energy in order to overcome the repulsive forces and collide with, or interact with, the beryllium nucleus. This is true of all bombardments of nuclei with protons and alpha particles, which are positively charged. These particles are given sufficient energy by being injected into a particle accelerator. There are various types of accelerators, but they all use electric and magnetic forces to gradually increase the speed of the particles before directing them toward the target material.

Neutrons have no electric charge and therefore cannot be accelerated. On the other hand, they do not need as much energy to interact with nuclei because there is no repulsive force to overcome.

ARTIFICIAL TRANSMUTATION. Any change in the nucleus of an atom that converts it from one element to another is called **transmutation.** When the change is brought about by bombarding the nucleus with high-energy particles, the process is called **artificial transmutation.** The conversion of beryllium to lithium by bombardment with protons, mentioned above, is an example of artificial transmutation. Another example, in which a neutron is the bombarding particle, is the transmutation of aluminum to a radioactive isotope of sodium:

$$_0^1n + {}_{13}^{27}Al \rightarrow {}_{11}^{24}Na + {}_2^4He$$

155

NUCLEAR EQUATIONS. In nuclear equations, the symbols represent atomic nuclei. The superscript indicates the mass number and the subscript indicates the atomic number (number of protons). When writing nuclear equations, it is necessary that the sum of the mass numbers of the reactants be equal to the sum of the mass numbers of the products. The same is true of the atomic numbers. This is illustrated below, using the same nuclear reactions described earlier:

$$\text{mass number} = 1 + 9 = 10 \qquad 6 + 4 = 10$$
$$^{1}_{1}\text{H} + ^{9}_{4}\text{Be} \rightarrow ^{6}_{3}\text{Li} + ^{4}_{2}\text{He}$$
$$\text{atomic number} = 1 + 4 = 5 \qquad 3 + 2 = 5$$

$$\text{mass number} = 1 + 27 = 28 \qquad 24 + 4 = 28$$
$$^{1}_{0}\text{n} + ^{27}_{13}\text{Al} \rightarrow ^{24}_{11}\text{Na} + ^{4}_{2}\text{He}$$
$$\text{atomic number} = 0 + 13 = 13 \qquad 11 + 2 = 13$$

In a nuclear reaction, if all but one of the elements of the reaction are known, the unknown element can be predicted using mass numbers and atomic numbers. Consider the following example: Find the unknown product formed when an alpha particle collides with a nucleus of Al-27 to form P-30. From the information given, a partial equation can be constructed:

$$^{27}_{13}\text{Al} + ^{4}_{2}\text{He} \rightarrow ^{30}_{15}\text{P} + ?$$

The sum of the mass numbers of the reactants is 31. Thus, the sum of the mass numbers of the products must be 31. The mass number of the unknown must be 1. The sum of the atomic numbers of the reactants is 15, and the same must be true for the products. Thus, the atomic number of the unknown must be 0. The particle with a mass of 1 and an atomic number of 0 is the neutron. The completed equation is:

$$^{27}_{13}\text{Al} + ^{4}_{2}\text{He} \rightarrow ^{30}_{15}\text{P} + ^{1}_{0}\text{n}$$

NUCLEAR ENERGY

MASS DEFECT AND BINDING ENERGY. The total atomic mass of a nucleus is always less than the sum of the masses of its protons and neutrons as free particles (uncombined in a nucleus). For example, consider the following information: The atomic mass of a free proton = 1.00728; that of a free neutron = 1.00867. A helium nucleus contains 2 protons and 2 neutrons. The expected mass of the $^{4}_{2}\text{He}$ nucleus is:

$$(2 \times 1.00728) + (2 \times 1.00867) = 2.01456 + 2.01734 = 4.03190.$$

However, the actual atomic mass of a $^{4}_{2}\text{He}$ nucleus is 4.00150. Thus, there is a *decrease* in mass of 0.03040 when 1 $^{4}_{2}\text{He}$ nucleus is formed from 2 protons and 2 neutrons. This difference between the total mass of the free nucleons and their mass when combined in a $^{4}_{2}\text{He}$ nucleus is known as the **mass defect** of helium. Similar calculations can be made for other nuclei.

Mass defect is explained by the fact that, in the nucleus, nucleons are bound together by strong forces of attraction. To separate these nucleons requires energy. Conversely, when these particles come together to form the nucleus, energy is released. The mass defect is equivalent to the amount of energy released.

Mass defect may be used as a measure of the stability of a nucleus. The greater the mass defect, the greater amount of energy released as a result of its formation from the nucleons and, therefore, the more stable the nucleus. The amount of energy necessary to reverse the process—break down a nucleus into free nucleons—is known as the **binding energy** of the nucleus. The binding energy of a nucleus is equal to the energy of its mass defect. It is usually expressed as binding energy per nucleon (see Figure 11-1).

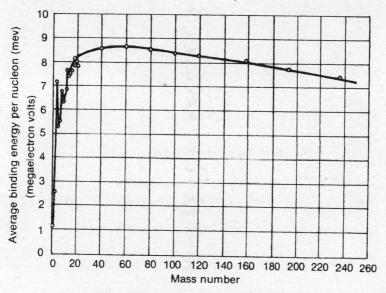

Figure 11-1. Binding energy per nucleon.

NUCLEAR REACTIONS. In nuclear reactions, mass is converted to energy. There are two basic types of nuclear reaction—fission and fusion. **Fission reactions** involve the "splitting" of a heavy nucleus to produce lighter nuclei. **Fusion reactions** involve the combining of light nuclei to produce a heavier nucleus. In both types of reaction, the total nuclear mass of the product(s) is *less* than the total nuclear mass of the reactant(s). In other words, nuclear reactions involve some "loss" of mass. In reality, this mass is not lost; it is converted to energy.

Nuclear reactions involve energies much greater than those found in ordinary chemical reactions. The quantity of energy (E) produced by the conversion of mass can be calculated using Einstein's equation: $E = mc^2$, where m = mass and c = the velocity of light. If m is measured in kilograms and c is measured in meters per second, the energy E is expressed in joules. The value of c is 3.00×10^8 meters per second. The square of this quantity is 9.00×10^{16}. Thus, the energy equivalent to 1 kilogram of mass is 9.00×10^{16} joules—an enormous amount. The conversion of even a few milligrams of mass produces a very large amount of energy.

FISSION REACTION. A fission reaction begins with the capture of a slow-moving neutron by a nucleus of a heavy element, such as uranium or plutonium. The resulting nucleus is very unstable, and immediately "splits," or undergoes fission. The products of this fission are two middle-weight nuclei, one or more neutrons, and a great amount of energy (see Figure 11-2).

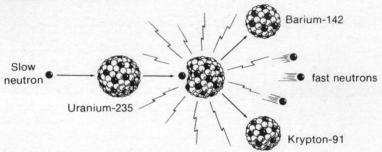

Figure 11-2. Nuclear Fission.

There is a small loss of mass during a fission reaction, which accounts for the large amount of energy released. The equation for the reaction illustrated above is:

$$^1_0n + {}^{235}_{92}U \rightarrow {}^{142}_{56}Ba + {}^{91}_{36}Kr + 3\ {}^1_0n + \text{energy}$$

An important feature of a fission reaction is the production of neutrons. These neutrons can become reactants to be captured by other U-235 nuclei, which will in turn undergo fission and release more neutrons. This is known as a **chain reaction,** in which one reaction is the cause for further similar reactions (Figure 11-3). When such a reaction is uncontrolled, the energy is released in a single, explosive burst. This is

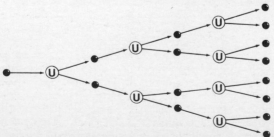

Figure 11-3. An uncontrolled fission reaction. (Efficiency is greater than 1.)

the principle used in a nuclear bomb. There are methods by which the rate of a chain reaction can be controlled by limiting the number of neutrons that are allowed to interact with U-235 nuclei (Figure 11-4).

(Excess neutrons absorbed by other materials.)

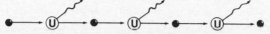

Figure 11-4. A controlled fission reaction. (Efficiency = 1.)

Such controlled reactions produce a constant release of energy. Controlled nuclear reactions are carried out in nuclear reactors.

FISSION PRODUCTS. The equation shown earlier for the fission of U-235 represents a typical fission of this isotope. The fission of U-235 is complicated by the fact that different U-235 nuclei split in different ways to produce different middle-weight elements. In fact, more than 200 isotopes of 35 different elements have been identified among the fission products of U-235. Many of these isotopes have unstable nuclei, and are thus radioactive. The radiation associated with these "by-products" of nuclear fission, and the handling and disposal of these unwanted radioactive substances, present special problems and are among the major disadvantages of the use of nuclear energy.

FUSION REACTIONS. The graph in Figure 11-1 (page 157) indicates that if two very light nuclei fuse to form a heavier nucleus, the binding energy per nucleon of the product is much greater than that of the two lighter nuclei. This means that the difference in energy will be given off in such a fusion reaction. The energy produced is the equivalent of a loss of mass. Figure 11-5 is another way of showing the same result. This graph shows

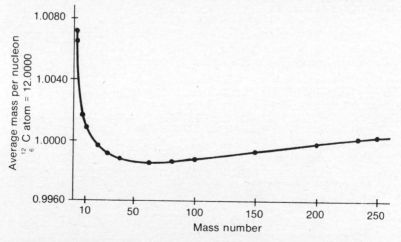

Figure 11-5. This graph shows the relationship between average mass per nucleon and mass number. The fusion of two light nuclei to form a heavier nucleus actually results in a decrease in average mass per nucleon.

the mass per nucleon in atomic nuclei of different masses. The fusion of two light nuclei results in a decrease of mass per nucleon. The decrease in mass appears as energy. As in the case of fission, the products formed in a fusion reaction are more stable than the reactants.

The tremendous amounts of energy produced in the sun and stars are the result of fusion reactions. The overall reaction can be represented as:

$$4 \, {}^{1}_{1}\text{H} \rightarrow {}^{4}_{2}\text{He} + 2 {}^{0}_{1}\text{e} + E$$

The hydrogen bomb (thermonuclear device) also releases energy by a fusion reaction. One reaction used is:

$${}^{2}_{1}\text{H} + {}^{2}_{1}\text{H} \rightarrow {}^{4}_{2}\text{He} + E$$

A fission bomb is used to provide the high temperatures and activation energy needed for this reaction to start.

QUESTIONS

1. **Which particle is electrically neutral?**
   (1) proton   (2) positron   (3) neutron   (4) electron
2. **What is the mass number of a deuterium atom?**
   (1) 1   (2) 2   (3) 3   (4) 4
3. **Which particle cannot be accelerated by the electric or magnetic fields in a particle accelerator?**
   (1) neutron   (2) proton   (3) alpha particle   (4) beta particle
4. **A device used to give charged particles sufficient kinetic energy to penetrate the nucleus of an atom is**
   (1) an accelerator   (2) an electroscope
   (3) a Geiger counter   (4) a scintillation counter
5. **Given the reaction:**
   $${}^{27}_{13}\text{Al} + {}^{4}_{2}\text{He} \rightarrow {}^{30}_{15}\text{P} + {}^{1}_{0}\text{n}$$
   This reaction is best described as   (1) beta decay   (2) artificial transmutation beta decay   (3) fission   (4) fusion
6. **Which equation represents artificial transmutation?**
   (1) $H_2O \rightarrow H^+ + OH^-$ **(2) $UF_6 + 6Na \rightarrow 6NaF + U$**
   (3) ${}^{238}_{92}U \rightarrow {}^{234}_{90}Th + {}^{4}_{2}He$ **(4) ${}^{27}_{13}Al + {}^{4}_{2}He \rightarrow {}^{30}_{15}P + {}^{1}_{0}n$**
7. **Given the equation:**
   $${}^{238}_{92}\text{U} + {}^{4}_{2}\text{He} \rightarrow {}^{241}_{94}\text{Pu} + {}^{1}_{0}\text{n}$$
   This reaction is an example of   (1) addition   (2) condensation   (3) substitution   (4) transmutation
8. **In the reaction:**
   $$X + {}^{1}_{1}\text{H} \rightarrow {}^{6}_{3}\text{Li} + {}^{4}_{2}\text{He}$$
   The nucleus represented by X is
   (1) ${}^{9}_{3}Li$ (2) ${}^{10}_{5}B$ (3) ${}^{9}_{4}Be$ (4) ${}^{10}_{6}C$
9. **In the reaction:**
   $${}^{6}_{3}\text{Li} + {}^{1}_{0}\text{n} \rightarrow {}^{4}_{2}\text{He} + X$$
   The species represented by X is
   (1) ${}^{2}_{1}H$ (2) ${}^{3}_{1}H$ (3) ${}^{3}_{2}He$ (4) ${}^{4}_{2}He$
10. **Which of the following nuclei would have the greatest binding energy per nucleon?   (1) hydrogen   (2) helium   (3) iron   (4) uranium**

11. Which atom can undergo nuclear fission when its nucleus captures a neutron? (1) $_1^1H$ (2) $_1^2H$ (3) $_{92}^{235}U$ (4) $_{92}^{238}U$

12. For a given mass, the energy released is greatest for a reaction involving (1) slow oxidation (2) rapid oxidation (3) fission (4) fusion

13. When a uranium nucleus breaks up into fragments, which type of nuclear reaction occurs?
    (1) fusion   (2) fission
    (3) replacement   (4) redox

14. The energy equivalent of the mass defect is known as (1) an alpha particle (2) binding energy (3) half-life (4) kinetic energy

15. The equation $_1^2H + _1^2H \rightarrow _2^4He$ represents (1) fusion (2) fission (3) alpha decay (4) k-capture

16. When neutrons and protons combine to form a stable nucleus, the actual mass of the nucleus, compared to the total mass of its parts, is (1) less (2) greater (3) the same

NUCLEAR REACTORS

TYPES OF REACTORS. A **nuclear reactor** is a device for controlling nuclear reactions so that the energy liberated by the reactions can be converted to a useful form at a constant rate. Some reactors (breeder reactors) are designed to produce new sources of nuclear fuel at the same time they produce energy. The two types of nuclear reactors presently in use are fission reactors and breeder reactors.

FISSION REACTORS. Fission reactors produce energy from the fission of U-235. While these reactors may differ in design, there are certain components common to all. These components include fuel, moderators, control rods, coolants, and shields. (See Figure 11-6.)

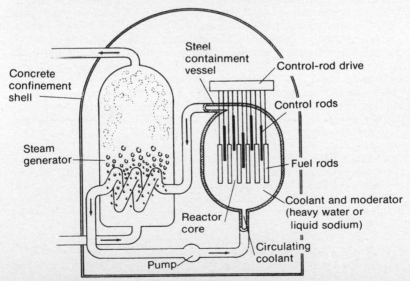

Figure 11-6. Schematic diagram of a nuclear reactor.

Fuel. Uranium-235 is the only naturally occurring isotope of uranium that will undergo fission. Unfortunately, the percentage of U-235 in pure uranium is only 0.7%. The remainder is almost all U-238, which is not fissionable. The very low concentration of U-235 in a natural sample of uranium is not sufficient to sustain a chain reaction for any period of time. By a complex process, U-235 can be separated from pure uranium and used to produce "enriched" uranium, which contains about 3.0% U-235. This mixture is used to produce uranium oxide for use as fuel in a reactor. Pellets of uranium oxide are packed in stainless steel tubes called *fuel rods* (Figure 11-6).

Moderators. Moderators are used to slow down the neutrons produced as a result of fission reactions. When produced, these neutrons are moving at relatively high velocities. It is necessary to slow them down so they can be captured by the U-235 nuclei. Some material, called a moderator, is placed in the reactor to absorb some of the energy of the fast-moving neutrons without absorbing the neutrons themselves. Some materials used as moderators include hydrogen, deuterium, beryllium, graphite, and molten metals, such as sodium.

Control rods. Control rods are used to control the rate of the fission reaction. This is accomplished by controlling the supply of neutrons that are available as reactants with U-235 nuclei. Substances such as cadmium or boron are very effective absorbers of neutrons. Control rods made from one of these substances are located side-by-side with the fuel rods in the reactor. By inserting and withdrawing these rods, the supply of neutrons can be regulated and, in cases of emergency, shut off completely.

Coolants. The fission reaction produces large amounts of heat. This heat, which can eventually be converted to other forms of energy, must be removed from the reactor core, where the fuel is stored. Otherwise, this core could melt. Water is the most common coolant, although some reactors use such materials as molten sodium, heavy water (deuterium oxide), air, helium, or carbon dioxide. When a material such as heavy water or liquid sodium is used, it can serve both as coolant and moderator.

Shields. The core of a reactor is surrounded by a containment vessel in which the coolant circulates. The walls of this vessel are lined with thick steel slabs to reduce the flow of radiation from the core. The containment vessel, in turn, is surrounded by thick concrete blocks designed to protect personnel from radiation exposure.

BREEDER REACTORS. Even when enriched, the uranium fuel used in a fission reactor still contains far more U-238 isotopes than U-235. Although this heavier isotope is not fissionable, it can undergo a transmutation when its nucleus is struck by a neutron. Thus, in a fission reactor, some of the neutrons produced will strike U-238 nuclei with the following result:

$$^{238}_{92}\text{U} + ^{1}_{0}\text{n} \rightarrow ^{239}_{94}\text{Pu} + 2^{0}_{-1}\text{e}$$

Plutonium-239 is a fissionable isotope. Thus, while the reactor is using up its nuclear fuel (U-235), it is producing Pu-239, which can itself be used as a fuel in a fission reactor:

$$^{239}_{94}Pu + ^{1}_{0}n \rightarrow ^{117}_{56}Ba + ^{90}_{38}Sr + 3\ ^{1}_{0}n$$

Nuclear reactors that are specifically designed to produce fissionable fuel are called **breeder reactors**. Although the idea of using breeder reactors seems attractive at first, there is a great deal of controversy about them. Plutonium is perhaps the most toxic of all known substances. Extremely small amounts have caused cancer in small animals. At present, research is being conducted towards producing U-233, a fissionable isotope, by neutron bombardment of thorium-232 in a breeder reactor.

FUSION REACTORS. The idea of harnessing the energy produced by nuclear fusion reactions is an attractive one for several reasons. Most important, perhaps, is the fact that the fuel, deuterium, is inexpensive and abundant in sea water. In addition, fusion is a "clean" process, in that the isotopes produced are stable, unlike the radioactive isotopes produced in fission reactions.

The major disadvantage of the fusion process as a source of energy is the extremely high activation energies required to produce the reactions. The reactants in a fusion reaction are both positively charged nuclei. In order for them to react, they must have sufficient energy to overcome the repulsive forces that exist between them. In order for a fusion reaction to occur, temperatures on the order of 10^9 degrees Celsius are required. No conventional materials can withstand such high temperatures for extended periods of time. In addition, the high-energy nuclei would quickly lose energy in collisions with the walls of their container, thus stopping the fusion process. The most promising efforts to date involve the use of "magnetic bottles" as confinement chambers. The reactant nuclei are confined in very strong magnetic fields. However, by present estimates, fusion reactors will not be in use before the turn of the century at the earliest.

RADIOACTIVE WASTES

Proper disposal of radioactive wastes presents one of the most serious problems faced by the nuclear industry. Nuclear power plants produce many unwanted radioactive fission products. Long-lived isotopes, such as $^{137}_{55}Cs$ and $^{90}_{38}Sr$, with half-lives of 30 and 29 years respectively, are examples of such products. The half-lives of these isotopes are short enough to present significant radiation releases and long enough to contaminate their surroundings for generations. Even after three half-lives, a period of 90 years, one-eighth of the original amounts of these isotopes remains.Radioactive substances having medium and long half-lives are often sealed in special containers and stored in underground chambers or in isolated areas. The radioactivity from these isotopes will remain a problem long after the nuclear reactors that produced them have ceased to serve their purpose.

Gaseous wastes, such as Rn-222, Kr-85, and N-16, are stored until they decay to safe levels. They are then released into the air. Still other isotopes with low-level radioactivity are released into the environment as they are produced, provided that they do not pose a health threat.

USES OF RADIOISOTOPES

TRACERS. Radioisotopes of an element have the same chemical properties as the stable, or non-radioactive, isotopes of that element. The fact that they can be detected or "traced" as they decay makes it possible to determine their locations at all times. When used to follow the path of a chemical process, a radioisotope is called a **tracer.** C-14 is one of the most useful tracer isotopes, and has been used to study photosynthesis and the pathway followed by carbon in many organic processes.

Isotopes with short half-lives can be used in medical diagnosis. I-131 is used to diagnose disorders of the thyroid, while technetium-99 can be used to locate brain tumors. Since these radioisotopes have short half-lives, they will be quickly eliminated without harm to the patient.

RADIATION. Some radioisotopes have the ability to kill living tissues, and are used in the treatment of some cancers. Both radium and cobalt-60 release intense radiation, which can be used to destroy cells in a tumor.

Radiation can also be used to treat foods and grains. Bacteria, yeasts, molds, and insect eggs present in the food sample can be destroyed by irradiation, thus making it possible for the foods to be stored for long periods of time without spoiling.

DATING. The half-life of a radioisotope is a constant factor, not affected by temperature and pressure. Thus, it can be reasoned that each radioactive substance is presently decaying at the same rate as when the substance was formed. For example, C-14 decays by beta decay:

$$^{14}_{6}C \rightarrow ^{14}_{7}N + ^{0}_{-1}e$$

It is assumed that the ratio of carbon-14 to carbon-12 in the atmosphere has remained fairly constant for many thousands of years. Since photosynthesis uses CO_2 from the atmosphere to produce sugar, plants that produce the sugar and the animals that eat the plant products will have C-14 and C-12 in their tissues. When the plant or animal dies, the C-14 continues to decay at the same rate. With the passage of time, there is less and less C-14. By comparing the amount of C-14 that remains to the amount of C-12 that is present, the amount of C-14 that has decayed can be calculated.

The half-life of C-14 is 5700 years. If a sample of wood shows that the C-14 to C-12 ratio is only one-half the expected ratio, it can be deduced that one-half of the original C-14 has decayed and the object is 5700 years old.

The U-238→Pb-206 decay series also provides a means of dating certain minerals. As time passes, the amount of U-238 in a mineral sample decreases and the amount of Pb-206 increases. The amount of Pb-206 present represents the amount of U-238 that has decayed. By comparing it to the U-238 that remains, the age of the rock can be calculated. Calculations based on this method indicate that the earth is at least 4.5 billion years old.

QUESTIONS

1. Which substance is used as a moderator in a nuclear reactor?
   (1) aluminum (2) graphite (3) plutonium (4) helium
2. The main purpose of the moderator in a fission reactor is to
   (1) remove heat   (2) produce heat
   (3) slow down neutrons   (4) speed up neutrons
3. In a nuclear reactor, the neutrons can be slowed by collisions with
   (1) uranium atoms (2) graphite (3) cadmium (4) boron
4. In a fission reaction, which of the following is needed to continue the chain reaction?
   (1) protons (2) neutrons (3) electrons (4) gamma radiation
5. Which of the following could be used as a fuel in a nuclear fission reactor? (1) U-235 (2) U-238 (3) protium (4) deuterium
6. In a nuclear reactor, the radioisotope U-235 serves as a
   (1) shield   (2) coolant
   (3) neutron absorber   (4) fissionable material
7. A requirement for a fusion reactor is (1) extremely high temperatures (2) heavy atomic nuclei as fuel (3) inexpensive equipment (4) operators with little training
8. In a nuclear reactor the amount of uranium present remains fairly constant. The rate of the reaction is controlled by the amount of
   (1) barium (2) alpha particles (3) beta particles (4) neutrons
9. A substance which can be used both as the moderator and the coolant in a nuclear reactor is (1) graphite (2) cadmium (3) liquid sodium (4) plutonium
10. A sample of wood was analyzed and found to have only ½ the ratio of C-14 to C-12 as in a living sample. (The half-life of C-14 = 5700 years.) The wood is probably about (1) 2800 years old (2) 5700 years old (3) 11,200 years old (4) 17,000 years old
11. A reactor in which more fuel is produced is called a (1) fusion reactor (2) breeder reactor (3) steam reactor (4) reversible reactor
12. The fuel produced in a breeder reactor is (1) uranium (2) plutonium (3) cadmium (4) helium
13. When radioisotopes are used in medical treatment or diagnosis and are ingested by the patient, it is important that they (1) be inexpensive (2) have long half-lives (3) have short half-lives (4) emit only alpha radiation
14. Which of the following radioisotopes is used in the diagnosis of the diseases of the thyroid? (1) I-131 (2) Co-60 (3) Tc-99 (4) U-235
15. A radioisotope that is sometimes used by doctors to pinpoint a brain tumor is (1) carbon-12 (2) lead-206 (3) technetium-99 (4) uranium-238

UNIT 12 LABORATORY ACTIVITIES

MEASUREMENT

SIGNIFICANT FIGURES. When making a measurement, all of the indicated markings on the scale of the measuring instrument are recorded, *plus* one more estimated figure. These recorded values are called **significant figures.** Figure 12-1 shows the measurement of an object using a metric rule. The scale of the rule is marked in centimeters and tenths of a centimeter (millimeters). When making a measurement, centimeters and tenths of a centimeter are read directly from the scale, and hundredths of a centimeter are estimated. In this case, the object being measured falls about halfway between 7.10 cm and 7.20 cm. Thus, the third figure in the measurement is estimated to be .05 cm, and the measurement should be recorded as 7.15 cm. In this measurement, the figures read directly from the scale are said to be *certain*. The last figure is *uncertain*.

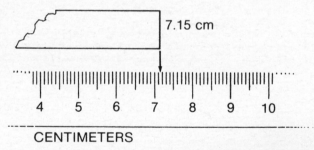

Figure 12-1. Significant figures in measurement. The length of the object is reported as 7.15 cm, which contains 3 significant figures.

In expressing scientific data, it is important to use only significant figures. If too many or too few figures are expressed, an incorrect impression about the precision of the measurements may be given. For example, if the above measurement were expressed as 7.1 cm, anyone reading this value would assume that only the 7 was certain and the .1 was estimated, or uncertain. On the other hand, if it were expressed as 7.155 cm, it would indicate a greater degree of precision than the instrument allows. Significant figures include *all* certain digits plus *one* uncertain digit—no more, no less.

SIGNIFICANT FIGURES IN COMPUTATIONS. In scientific work, it is frequently necessary to make mathematical computations using measured values. The basic rule in computing with measurements is: The answer should not be more precise than the least precise measurement in the group.

Addition and subtraction. When adding or subtracting measurements, the answer should be rounded off so that it is not more precise than the least precise measurement. Consider the following examples:

Addition

32.34 g	In the group of measurements being added, the
2.6 g	least precise measurement is 2.6 g. The tenths
+ 1.3412 g	place is uncertain. Therefore, the tenths place in
36.2812 g	the sum is also uncertain. All figures to the right of this place have no meaning. The result should be rounded off to one uncertain figure: **36.3 g.**

Subtraction

531.46 mL	The least precise measurement is 86.3 mL.[*] The
– 86.3 mL	tenths place is uncertain. The answer should be
445.16 mL	rounded off to this place. The answer should be **445.2 mL.**

Multiplication and division. When multiplying or dividing measurements, the answer should not contain more significant figures than are present in the measurement having the fewer significant figures.

Multiplication

24.24 cm	There are 4 significant figures in 24.24, only 3 in
× 43.9 cm	43.9. Therefore, round off the product to 3 significant figures: **1060**
21816	
7272	To help you understand this rule, all uncertain
9696	figures are printed in *italics*. Every figure that results
1064.*136* cm²	from multiplication by an uncertain figure is itself uncertain.

Note that a zero used only to locate the decimal point is *not* a significant figure. The result 1060 has only 3 significant figures. We would write it 1060. if the final zero were significant, indicating that the 6 was certain.

[*] **Note:** To avoid confusion between the small letter l and the figure 1, the capital letter L is used as the abbreviation for "liter" in this unit. Both forms of the abbreviation are considered acceptable and have the same meaning.

Division

$$\frac{5.1\ g}{213\ L} = 0.239\ g/L$$

The measurement 5.1 g has 2 significant figures. The result should be rounded off to 2 significant figures: **0.24 g/L**

The 0 is not a significant figure above. It serves only to locate the decimal point. Study the following examples to understand how to determine the number of significant figures in any quantity.

significant figures

2077	4
20.77	4
20770	4 (Final zero not significant)
20770.	5
.207	3
.2070	4 (Final zero is significant)
.00207	3 (First two zeros not significant)
.0020	2
4.0020	5
1,000,000	1 (probably)
2.00	3
200	1

LABORATORY SKILLS

IDENTIFICATION OF COMMON LAB EQUIPMENT. The pieces of equipment illustrated in Figure 12-2 are commonly used in the chemistry laboratory. You should be able to identify each piece and know how each is used.

USING THE LABORATORY BALANCE. The most common types of balances found in secondary school laboratories are the triple beam balance (Figure 12-3) and the "dial" type of balance. In each type, a beam or beams hold sliding masses that can be moved to predetermined positions on each beam. The masses must be placed precisely in the precut notches to provide valid readings. On the triple beam balance, the front beam is not notched. The rider on this beam is moved to a position that causes the balance to reach its balanced, or equilibrium, position. The reading is then made by adding the total masses on each of the beams. These balances have a sensitivity of 0.01 g, and should be read to this place.

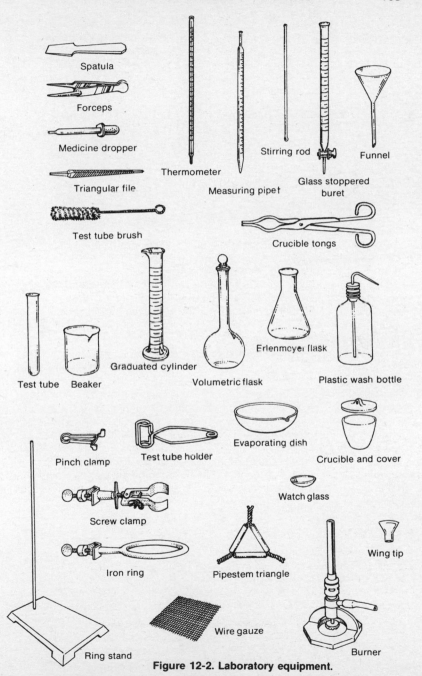

Spatula

Forceps

Medicine dropper

Triangular file

Thermometer

Measuring pipet

Stirring rod

Glass stoppered buret

Funnel

Test tube brush

Crucible tongs

Test tube   Beaker

Graduated cylinder

Volumetric flask

Erlenmeyer flask

Plastic wash bottle

Pinch clamp

Test tube holder

Evaporating dish

Crucible and cover

Screw clamp

Watch glass

Iron ring

Pipestem triangle

Wing tip

Ring stand

Wire gauze

Burner

Figure 12-2. Laboratory equipment.

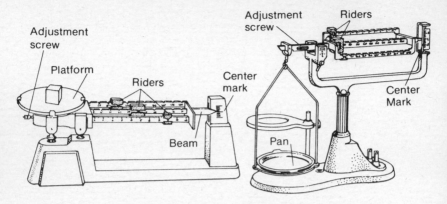

Figure 12-3. Two types of triple-beam balance.

On the "dial" type of balance, sliding masses are used on the beams measuring hundreds of grams and tens of grams. Ones, tenths, and hundredths of grams are dialed on the wheel.

One important point should be made concerning the use of laboratory balances: chemicals should *never* be placed directly on the pan of the balance. Paper should be placed on the pan, and the chemical to be weighed should be placed on the paper. The mass of the paper should be considered when measuring the mass of the chemical.

USING THE GAS BURNER. Figure 12-4 shows typical gas burners used in the laboratory. The gas jet is in the "off" position when the valve handle is at a right angle to the outlet. To use the burner, the handle must be turned to the "on" position (parallel to the gas outlet). The flow of gas to the burner can be controlled by turning the adjustment knob at the base of the burner. Not all types of burners have this knob. A properly adjusted flame will have two distinct cones. The point at the top of the inner cone is the hottest area of the flame. The gas-air mixture is controlled by the air adjustment device, which may be a "collar" on the barrel of the burner, or a handle at the base. If the air supply is too low,

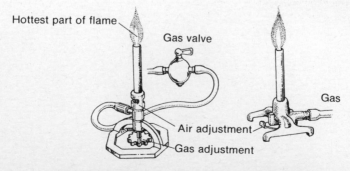

Figure 12-4. Two types of laboratory gas burners.

the flame will be tall and will have some traces of yellow color due to incomplete combustion. Adjustment of the air control device will reduce the height of the flame and produce the two distinct cones. When too much air is present there will be a noticeable "roaring" or "fluttering" noise to the burner.

WORKING WITH GLASS TUBING. The glass tubing used in laboratories is usually a "soft" type of glass, which can easily be cut and shaped. To cut a piece of tubing, place it on the lab table surface. Place a corner of a triangular file on the spot marking the length of tubing you desire. While holding the tubing securely with one hand, make one firm stroke away from you with the file, scratching the glass. Pick up the tubing and place your thumbs on the opposite side from the scratch (Figure 12-5A). Push firmly with your thumbs, causing the glass to snap at the scratch (Figure 12-5B).

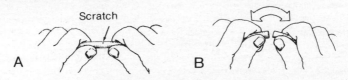

Figure 12-5. Cutting glass tubing.

After a piece of glass has been cut, the edges are quite sharp and should be polished. Place the cut end of the glass into a burner flame, positioning it in the hottest part of the flame. Rotate the glass as you heat it and continue heating until the flame becomes a bright yellow. If you look at the cut end you will notice that the sharp edge has become smooth. The tube should be removed from the flame before the opening starts to close. Place the glass on a nonflammable surface and *allow it to cool* before touching it. *Hot glass can cause painful burns.*

If you wish to bend a piece of tubing, first place a flame spreader, or "wing tip," on the burner. Hold the glass as illustrated in Figure 12-6 and rotate it in the flame. As the glass heats, the flame will become yellow and the glass will soften. Remove the glass from the flame and simply lift the ends with a smooth motion, causing the glass to bend.

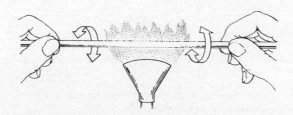

Figure 12-6. Heating glass tubing prior to bending.

FILTRATION. A piece of filter paper can be used to separate a solid from a solution. Fold the piece of filter paper as shown in Figure 12-7 and tear off a small section of one corner. Place the filter paper into a funnel and "tack" it into position by slightly wetting it with distilled water from a wash bottle. Press the filter paper gently to assure full contact with the glass.

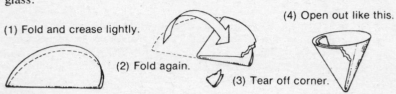

(1) Fold and crease lightly.

(2) Fold again.

(3) Tear off corner.

(4) Open out like this.

Figure 12-7. Folding a filter paper. Tearing off a corner (3) prevents air from leaking down the fold.

The beaker that is to receive the filtrate should be positioned so that the longer side of the funnel stem touches the wall of the beaker (Figure 12-8). Pour the mixture into the funnel along a glass rod, as shown, to prevent splashing. After all the liquid has been poured from the beaker, use a wash bottle to remove any solid which remains in the beaker. In order to insure that no solute remains with the precipitate in the funnel, wash the precipitate with small amounts of water from the wash bottle.

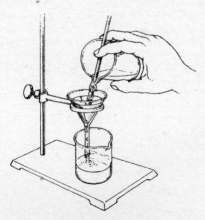

Figure 12-8. Proper filtration setup.

DILUTION OF ACIDS. It is often necessary to dilute an acid for a particular purpose. This operation must be performed with considerable care. When done improperly, a serious accident can result. Acids react exothermically with water, releasing large amounts of heat. For this reason, *the acid must be poured into the water*. Acids are more dense than water, and begin to sink and mix. This mixing action results in the released heat being spread throughout the solution. If water is poured into an acid, the water tends to stay on the top of the acid. All of the heat that is generated is concentrated in one area at the top of the mixture. If the reaction is vigorous enough, it may even cause the water to boil, splattering hot water and acid. To prevent this, *always add acid to water.*

TRANSFER OF SOLIDS. When chemicals are purchased, the label should contain information regarding the purity of the material. In the laboratory, care must be taken to insure that contamination of the chemical does not occur. To maintain the purity of a chemical, reagent that is removed from its container is never returned to the container. Whenever possible, chemicals are poured from the bottle in the manner indicated in Fig. 12-9.

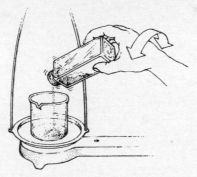

Figure 12-9. Pouring solid reagent.

By gently rotating the bottle back and forth, the reagent will come out in a controlled, steady flow. When it is necessary to use a spatula to remove chemicals, be sure that the spatula is clean. *Do not return excess reagent to the container.* When transferring a solid reagent to a test tube or other small-mouthed container, it is best to use a piece of paper. The reagent is first poured from its container to the paper. The paper is then used to pour the reagent into the test tube, as shown in Figure 12-10.

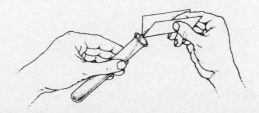

Figure 12-10. Using a creased paper to transfer a solid.

POURING OF LIQUIDS. When pouring liquids, it is important that none of the liquid is lost in the transfer. The use of a stirring rod will help prevent accidental losses. When two hands can be used in the transfer, use one hand to hold the stirring rod as close to the bottom of the receiving vessel as possible. Place the vessel containing the liquid against the stirring rod and pour carefully. The liquid will cling to the rod and no splattering will occur. When only one hand is free, follow the procedure shown in Figure 12-8. Since it is impossible to pour every drop of liquid from the vessel it will be necessary to rinse the vessel. Use a wash bottle and wash with two or three small rinsings.

When transferring liquids from a reagent bottle, remove the stopper by grasping it between the forefinger and middle finger as shown in Figure 12-11.

Figure 12-11. Removing the stopper from a liquid reagent bottle.

Do not set the stopper down. Pour from the side of the bottle opposite the label as shown. If pouring into a wide-mouthed container, use a stirring rod to prevent splashing. If pouring into a test tube, support the tube in a test tube rack or with a holder, as shown in Figure 12-12. As with solids, never return excess reagent to its container.

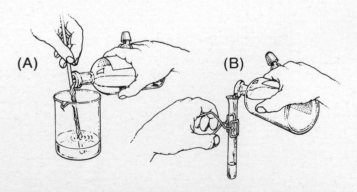

(A) **(B)**

Figure 12-12. Proper methods of pouring liquid reagents into a wide-mouthed container (A) and into a test tube (B).

HEATING MATERIALS. When materials are heated in the laboratory, common sense rules can help prevent accidents. The vessel containing the material being heated must be open. Do not heat stoppered test tubes or flasks. When heating, be sure that the opening of a test tube is not directed toward yourself or anyone else. When heating liquids, it is often a help to add boiling chips to prevent "bumping." When evaporating a solvent, use a fume hood if the solvent is a hazardous material. Flammable materials should only be heated with an electric mantle or heater. *Do not use open flames in the presence of flammable materials.*

READING LIQUID LEVELS. The most commonly used instruments for measuring liquids in the laboratory are graduated cylinders, burettes, and measuring pipets. In all of these, the surface of the liquid will be slightly curved. This curved surface is called a **meniscus.** The curvature is due to the combined effects of the pull of gravity and the attraction (or lack of attraction) of the liquid for the glass. Liquids that are attracted to the glass are said to "wet" the glass. Most liquids will "wet" the glass, and the shape of the meniscus is concave (curved downward). Liquids that do not wet the glass, such as mercury, form a convex meniscus.

When reading the scale of an instrument containing a liquid, you read to the *bottom* (or top) of the meniscus. When making such readings, it is vital that the eye be at the proper level. Errors caused by incorrect eye alignment are called *parallax errors.* Figure 12-13 shows the correct and incorrect lines of sight in viewing a meniscus.

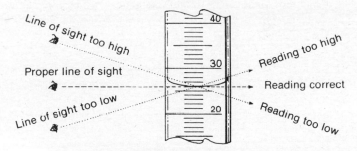

Figure 12-13. Reading a meniscus.

When measuring the volume of a liquid in a graduated container, the measurement should be recorded in significant figures—that is, the markings on the scale (certain) plus an estimated value (uncertain). In most cases, the larger the measuring device, the less precise the scale. For example, the scale on a 100-mL graduated cylinder is usually marked in 10-mL and 1-mL increments. Thus, volume is estimated to the nearest 0.1 mL. A 10-mL cylinder is marked in 1-mL and 0.1 mL increments. The volume of a liquid in this instrument is estimated to the nearest 0.01 mL.

Graduated cylinders are designed to measure the volume of the liquid they are holding. Thus, the 0-mL point is at the bottom of the scale. (Some graduated cylinders have double scales, one with 0 at the bottom, one with 0 at the top.) Burets and pipets are designed to *deliver* quantities of liquids. The scales on these instruments have the 0-mL marking at the top, and permit you to read the amount that has been delivered from the zero mark. Figure 12-14 illustrates measurements made with both types of scale.

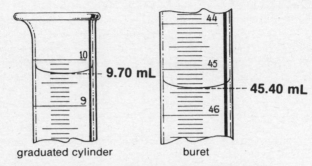

graduated cylinder   buret

Figure 12-14. Reading a graduated cylinder and a buret.

THERMOMETERS. The mercury thermometer commonly used in the laboratory has a range of $-20°C$ to $110°C$. Since the smallest graduation is a single degree, temperatures are read to the nearest degree, and then an estimate is made to tenths of a degree. Thermometers are designed to be either entirely immersed in a substance (total immersion), or to be immersed to a specific point. A 76-mm immersion thermometer has a line etched 76 mm from the tip of the bulb. The thermometer should be immersed in the material to the 76 mm mark, while the remainder of the thermometer is kept at room temperature.

QUESTIONS

1. **How many significant figures are present in 3.000?   (1) 1   (2) 2
   (3) 3   (4) 4**

2. **How many significant figures are present in 3,000?   (1) 1   (2) 2
   (3) 3   (4) 4**

3. **The number of significant figures present in 0.0040 is   (1) 1   (2) 2
   (3) 3   (4) 4**

4-8. **For the operation shown at the left in Questions 4-8, select the answer
   that has the correct number of significant figures.**

4. **Add: 1167.2 + 34.28 + 17.019   (1) 1218.5   (2) 1218.499   (3) 1218.50
   (4) 1218**

5. **Subtract: 39.48 − 3.384   (1) 36.1   (2) 36.09   (3) 36.10   (4) 36.094**

6. **Divide: 2476 by 16   (1) 150   (2) 154   (3) 154.5   (4) 155**

7. **Multiply: 47.8 × 3.2   (1) 150   (2) 152   (3) 153   (4) 152.96**

8. **Multiply: 8.924 × 3.1   (1) 28   (2) 27   (3) 27.7   (4) 27.6664**

9. **A laboratory balance has scales indicating hundreds of grams and tens
   of grams. The front arm has a scale indicating grams and tenths of a
   gram. To what fraction of a gram should masses be reported when
   using this balance?   (1) tens   (2) units   (3) tenths   (4) hundredths**

10. The diagram on the right represents a portion of a
    50-mL buret. Which of the following represents the
    volume of liquid delivered from the buret?
    (1) 35.3 mL   (2) 35.30 mL   (3) 34.7 mL
    (4) 34.70 mL

11. The diagram below represents a portion of a triple beam balance. If
    the beams are in balance, with the riders in the positions shown,
    what is the total mass in grams of the object being massed?

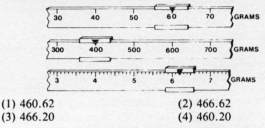

    (1) 460.62   (2) 466.62
    (3) 466.20   (4) 460.20

LABORATORY ACTIVITIES

WATER OF HYDRATION. Ionic solids often include definite amounts
of water of hydration as part of their crystal structures. Water will then
appear as part of the empirical formulas of these compounds. A common
experiment performed in the laboratory is designed to determine the
percentage of water, by mass, in the crystal, or to determine the number
of water molecules associated with each molecule of ionic substance
with which it is associated.

In this experiment, the mass of the hydrated crystal is measured. The
crystal is repeatedly heated and the mass remeasured until a constant
mass is obtained. The "lost" mass is assumed to be due to the water
driven out of the crystal. The percentage of water, by mass, in the crystal
is determined by the relationship:

$$\% \text{ water} = \frac{\text{mass of water driven off}}{\text{mass of hydrated crystal}} \times 100$$

After heating, the substance remaining is called an *anhydrous* salt.

If the empirical ratio between the ionic solid and the water molecules is
desired, the problem is treated as an empirical formula problem. The
mass, in grams, of each substance is converted to moles, and the molar
ratio is then converted to a whole-number ratio.

FLAME TESTS. It will be recalled from Unit 2 that when electrons
absorb energy, they can be raised to higher energy levels. When they
return from this "excited" state to the "ground" state, energy is emitted. When this amount of energy corresponds to the visible spectrum,
the energy is seen in the form of light. Every element gives off a spectrum of color that can be used to identify the element.

Large amounts of energy are required to raise the atoms of most elements to an excited state. However, certain metallic ions are easily

excited, even by the heat from a burner flame. This test for the presence of certain metallic elements is called a **flame test**. In conducting a flame test, a wire loop of either platinum or nichrome is first dipped into an HCl solution. The loop then placed into a burner flame to burn off any impurities. The wire loop is then dipped into the solution being tested and placed back into the flame. The color of the flame may be used to identify the metallic ion present in the sample.

SOLUBILITY CURVES. In a typical solubility experiment, a known mass of a solute is placed into a test tube and a measured volume of water is added. The solution is heated until all of the solute has dissolved, and then allowed to cool. When crystallization first occurs, the temperature is recorded. The procedure is repeated using different known quantities of solute and the same volume of water. The results are compared with standard solubility values for that solute.

Standard solubilities are usually expressed in grams of solute per 100 grams of water. Knowing that 1 mL of water has a mass of 1 gram, this relationship can be calculated as follows:

$$\frac{\text{mass of solute (g)}}{\text{mass of water (g)}} = \frac{x \text{ g solute}}{100 \text{ g water}}$$

Solubility curves are normally plotted with temperature along the X axis (abscissa) and grams of solute/100g of water along the Y axis (ordinate).

TITRATION. Titration is a method by which a solution of known concentration is reacted with a solution of unknown concentration in order to determine the concentration of the unknown solution. A common laboratory activity involves the reaction between an acid and a base in the process of neutralization. According to the Arrhenius concept, all acid-base neutralizations have the same net ionic equation:

$$H^+ + OH^- \rightarrow H_2O$$

One example of a titration experiment is the addition of a standard acid solution (concentration known) to a base solution of unknown concentration. The reaction is complete at the point when the mixture contains equimolar concentrations of H^+ and OH^- ions. An indicator is used to determine precisely when this neutralization point, or *endpoint*, is achieved. **Indicators** are substances that change color in response to changes in the concentrations of the two ions.

In this titration, a couple of drops of phenolphthalein is added to a known volume of the base solution. This indicator is red in a solution with excess OH^- ions (base). A buret is used to deliver standard acid solution to the base solution. As the H^+ ion concentration of the mixture increases, the red color fades to pink. At the point where the mixture becomes neutral (endpoint), it turns colorless.

When performing a titration, it is necessary to accurately measure the volumes of the solutions used. This is the reason why burets are used to deliver the solutions. It is also necessary to know the normality of one of the solutions (the standard solution). The concentration of the other solution can be determined using the relationship:

Normality × Volume = Normality × Volume
(Standard Solution)   (Unknown Solution)

SAMPLE PROBLEM

What is the normality of a hydrochloric acid solution if 42.24 mL of 0.125 N sodium hydroxide solution are required to neutralize 25.00 mL of the acid?

Solution: N × 25.00 mL = 0.125 N × 42.24 mL
(acid)

$$N \text{ (acid)} = \frac{42.24 \text{ mL} \times 0.125 \text{ N}}{25.00 \text{ mL}}$$

N (acid) = **.211**

USE OF THE CALORIMETER. The double-walled calorimeter is often used in the laboratory to determine the quantity of heat exchanged in a chemical reaction. Such a calorimeter is suitable for use when the heat is exchanged within the calorimeter. It cannot be used in cases where an external source of heat, such as a burner flame, is necessary to provide energy for the reaction.

The reaction of sodium hydroxide and water is one example of a reaction in which the heat exchanged can be measured in a calorimeter. To determine the heat exchanged in this reaction, start with a known volume of water in the calorimeter (a Styrofoam cup will suffice). Measure and record the temperature of the water. Add a measured quantity of sodium hydroxide pellets to the water. When the pellets are added and the mixture stirred, the temperature of the solution will rise. The energy responsible for this increase in temperature must come from the process of dissolving. Thus, the reaction is exothermic. When all visible reaction stops, the final temperature of the solution is measured and recorded. From the known quantities of water and sodium hydroxide and the calculated temperature change, the heat of reaction can be determined.

SAMPLE PROBLEM

When 2.2 g of sodium hydroxide pellets are dissolved in 200.0 g of water, the temperature increases from 22.2° C to 24.8° C. What is the heat of reaction?

Solution: Step 1. Find the number of calories represented by this temperature change.

Calories = mass × specific heat capacity × ΔT

= 200.0 g × 1 cal/g × 2.6 C°

= 520 calories

Step 2. Heat of reaction (solution) would be expressed in cal/mole. Convert grams of NaOH to moles of NaOH.

$$\frac{2.2 \text{ g}}{40 \text{ g/mole}} = 0.055 \text{ mole}$$

Step 3. Calculate the heat of reaction in cal/mole.

$$\frac{520 \text{ cal}}{.055 \text{ mole}} = \textbf{9450 cal/mole of NaOH}$$

HEAT OF COMBUSTION. In order to determine the heat of combustion of a given substance, the mass of the substance is measured before and after burning to determine the amount of material that actually undergoes combustion. The heat given off is absorbed by water in a calorimeter (Figure 12-15). The number of calories produced is determined by measuring the increase in temperature of the known quantity of water in the calorimeter.

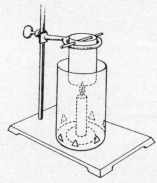

Figure 12-15. Apparatus setup for determining heat of combustion.

SAMPLE PROBLEM

A candle having a mass of 45.63 g is placed under a metal calorimeter containing 224 g of water at a temperature of 12.4° C. The candle is lighted and allowed to burn as shown in Figure 12-15 for several minutes before it is extinguished. The water temperature reaches a maximum reading of 44.6° C. The mass of the candle after burning is 44.77 g. Find the heat of combustion of the candle.

Solution: Step 1. Determine the mass of the candle that burned.

mass that burned = initial mass – final mass

= 45.63 g – 44.77 g

= 0.86 g

Step 2. Determine the number of calories of heat produced.

$$\text{calories} = \text{mass} \times \text{specific heat content} \times \Delta T$$
$$= 224 \text{ g} \times 1 \text{ cal/g} \times 32.2 \text{ C}°$$
$$= 7210 \text{ calories}$$

Step 3. Calculate the heat of combustion (cal/g).

$$\frac{7210 \text{ cal}}{0.86 \text{ g}} = \textbf{8390 cal/g}$$

MOLAR VOLUME OF A GAS. By reacting magnesium with excess HCl and collecting the hydrogen gas produced, it is possible to calculate the volume occupied by a mole of hydrogen gas at STP. The equation for this reaction is:

$$Mg + 2 \text{ HCl} \rightarrow MgCl_2 + H_2$$

According to the equation, each mole of magnesium reacted will yield one mole of hyrogen gas. If the mass of magnesium reacted and the volume of hydrogen collected are recorded in addition to temperature and pressure data, the calculations can be performed.

Typical lab results: mass of magnesium reacted   0.0471 g
                   volume of H_2 collected   45.9 mL
                   temperature   22.0 °C
                   pressure   755 torr

1. Convert grams of magnesium to moles of magnesium:

$$\text{moles Mg} = \frac{0.0471 \text{ g}}{24.3 \text{ g/mole}}$$
$$= 0.00194 \text{ moles}$$

2. Correct for the presence of water vapor. The hydrogen gas collected in this experiment is collected by water displacement. Some water evaporates and mixes with the hydrogen. Thus, the total pressure of the collected gas consists of the partial presence of hydrogen gas and water vapor.

$$P_{total} = P_{H_2} + P_{H_2O}$$

If the room pressure was measured at 755 torr and the temperature recorded at 22.0 °C, then the partial pressure of H_2O can be determined from the reference tables.

$$P_{H_2} = P_{total} - P_{H_2O}$$
$$= 755 \text{ torr} - 20. \text{ torr}$$
$$= 735 \text{ torr}$$

3. **Calculate the volume of H_2 gas at STP.** The hydrogen was collected at a pressure of 735 torr and a temperature of 22°C. The combined gas law is used to calculate the volume which this gas would occupy at STP:

$$Vol_{STP} = \frac{45.9 \text{ mL} \times 735 \text{ torr} \times 273 \text{ K}}{760 \text{ torr} \times 295 \text{ K}}$$

$$= 41.1 \text{ mL}$$

4. **Calculate the volume occupied by 1 mole.** The 41.1 mL of hydrogen was produced by 0.00194 mole of magnesium. According to the equation for the reaction, there is a 1:1 correspondence between moles of hydrogen and moles of magnesium used. Therefore 0.00194 mole of hydrogen was produced. To find the volume occupied by one mole of hydrogen gas solve the proportion:

$$\frac{41.1 \text{ ml}}{0.00194 \text{ mole}} = \frac{x \text{ mL}}{1.00 \text{ mole}}$$

$$x \text{ mL} = 21.200 \text{ mL}$$

PERCENT ERROR. The percent error of a given value is a comparison of that value with the number that is accepted as the "true" value. For example, the accepted volume occupied by a mole of any gas at STP is 22 400 mL. In the preceding experiment, the experimental volume of H_2 gas at STP was determined to be 21 200 mL. To find the percent error, the following relationship is used:

$$\% \text{ error} = \frac{\text{difference beween accepted and experimental}}{\text{accepted}} \times 100$$

$$= \frac{22\ 400 \text{ mL} - 21\ 200 \text{ mL}}{22\ 400 \text{ mL}} \times 100\%$$

$$= 5.36\%$$

INORGANIC AND ORGANIC SUBSTANCES

The differences between the bonding in organic substances and inorganic substances provide a basis for laboratory tests that can be used to differentiate between the two types of compounds. Ionic bonding is characteristic of inorganic compounds, while covalent bonding predominates in organic substances. The differences between the properties of these bonds provide general statements of difference between organic and inorganic compounds. Organic compounds tend to have low melting points, dissolve in nonpolar solvents, be nonelectrolytes, and decompose rather easily. Inorganic compounds generally have high melting points, dissolve in polar solvents such as water, are electrolytes, and are difficult to decompose by heat.

These differences are generalities and must be modified when necessary. For example, organic acids do ionize slightly and are weak electrolytes. Plastics have high melting points, even though they are organic.

LABORATORY REPORTS

The laboratory report is the method by which the experimenter conveys the essence of an experiment to a reader. All laboratory reports should begin with a suitable title and a purpose for the experiment. The procedure should be simply stated and it may contain references to a more detailed description of the experiment given in a particular laboratory manual.

The heart of the laboratory report is an orderly presentation of the observations made in the laboratory. These include both quantitative readings taken from burets, balances, etc., and qualitative visual observations, such as the appearances of solutions and precipitates. Whenever possible, data should be arranged into a table or graph. The conclusions are arrived at after the observed data is used in the necessary calculations.

QUESTIONS

1. How many calories are absorbed when the temperature of 225 mL of water is raised from 22.0°C to 36.0°C?   (1) 3150 cal   (2) 4950 cal   (3) 8100 cal   (4) 13050 cal

2. In a titration experiment, 15.0 mL of 0.200 M NaOH is used to exactly neutralize 25.0 mL of HCl. The concentration of the HCl is   (1) 0.120 M   (2) 1.20 M   (3) 0.1333 M   (4) 3.33 M

3. A sample of hydrogen gas is collected over water and equalized to a barometric pressure of 749 torr. The room temperature is 23.0°C. What is the pressure of the hydrogen gas?   (1) 726 torr   (2) 728 torr   (3) 760 torr   (4) 770 torr

4. Given the reaction $Mg + 2HCl \rightarrow MgCl_2 + H_2$. How many moles of hydrogen gas will be produced when 0.00184 moles of magnesium react with excess HCl?   (1) 0.00184   (2) 0.00092   (3) 0.00368   (4) 22.4

5. The accepted value for the heat of condensation of water is 539.4 cal/g. In a laboratory experiment, a student determines the value to be 565.0 cal/g. The percent error in the student's determination is   (1) 4.6%   (2) 1.04%   (3) 10.4%   (4) 46%

6. A student determined in the laboratory that one mole of $KMnO_4$ had a mass of 171.54 g. The mass of one mole of $KMnO_4$ in an accepted chemistry reference is 158.04 g. What is the percent error of the mass of one mole of $KMnO_4$ as determined by the student?
   (1) 0.787%   (2) 7.87%
   (3) 8.54%   (4) 13.5%

7-9. Base your answers to questions 7 through 10 on the data below,
      which represent the results of an experiment to determine the heat
      of combustion of a solid.

mass of empty container	200. g
mass of container with water	375 g
temp of water before reaction	24.0 °C
temp of water after reaction	30.0 °C

7. Calculate the temperature change of the water in degrees Celsius.
    (1) 175   (2) 54   (3) 14   (4) 6
8. The number of calories absorbed by the water was (1) 175   (2) 29
    (3) 1050   (4) 2250
9. If in the above experiment, .80 grams of solid had burned, the heat
    of combustion would be (1) 840   (2)1800   (3) 1300   (4) 2900 (all
    ans. in cal/g)
10. When 5 grams of a substance is burned in a calorimeter, 3 kilo-
    calories of energy is released. The energy released per gram of sub-
    stance is (1) 600 cal   (2) 1700 cal   (3) 5.000 cal   (4) 15.000 cal

11-16. Base your answers to questions 11-16 on the information and data
       provided below.

       A student performed a laboratory experiment to determine the
       molar volume of a gas. The data obtained during the experiment
       were as follows:
          barometric pressure: 755 torr
          temperature: 27 °C
          mass of 100. cm of Mg ribbon: 1.000 g
          length of Mg ribbon reacted: 4.25 cm
          volume of H_2 gas collected over water: 46.2 mL
          vapor pressure of water at 27 °C: 27 torr

11. The mass of the magnesium ribbon reacted was (1) 4.25 g
    (2) 0.425 g   (3) 0.0425 g   (4) 0.00425 g
12. The number of moles of Mg ribbon reacted was (1) 0.00132
    (2) 1.032   (3) 0.00175   (4) 1.75
13. The partial pressure due to hydrogen was (1) 755 torr   (2) 25 torr
    (3) 780 torr   (4) 728 torr
14. The volume of dry hydrogen gas at standard pressure was
    (1) 44.1 mL   (2) 46.2 mL   (3) 46.5 mL   (4) 47.2 mL
15. The volume of dry hydrogen at standard temperature and pressure
    was (1) 40.1 mL   (2) 42.0 mL   (3) 44.1 mL   (4) 48.7 mL
16. The volume occupied by one mole of the dry hydrogen gas at STP
    would be (1) 2,240 mL   (2) 22,400 mL   (3) 23,000 mL   (4) 24,500
    mL
17. Mg was reacted with an excess of dilute HCl and the H_2 gas produced
    collected in a eudiometer. The volume of H_2 in the eudiometer was
    corrected to conditions of STP. If 94.1 mL of H_2 was produced, how
    much Mg reacted in the experiment?
    (1) 0.01 g   (2) 0.10 g   (3) 0.05 g   (4) 0.50 g

GUIDE TO THE REFERENCE TABLES FOR CHEMISTRY

In answering questions in the Regents Examination in Chemistry, you will be expected to use the reference tables to find needed information. In some cases the question will refer you to the tables, but in other cases it will be left to your judgment as to whether to consult the tables. The purpose of this section of the book is to indicate the kinds of information you can get from the tables and the types of questions for which this information is useful.

TABLE A
Physical Constants and Conversion Factors

These constants are of basic importance in physics and chemistry. The molal freezing and boiling point constants are listed here. One mole of particles will elevate the boiling point $0.52 \ C°$ and depress the freezing point of water $1.86 \ C°$. When applying these values to particular substances, be sure to check the bonding of the molecules. One mole of NaCl, which is ionic, will produce two moles of particles in solution and thus depress the freezing point $3.72 \ C°$, while one mole of ethylene glycol, which is covalently bonded, will reduce the freezing point $1.86 \ C°$

QUESTIONS

A-1. Which of the following is equivalent to 254 cal?   **(1) 25.4 kcal**
    (2) 1060 J   (3) 60.8 J   (4) 254 000 kcal

A-2. Which of the following is equivalent to 736 kJ?   **(1) 736 000 kcal**
    (2) 176 kcal   (3) 3.08 kcal   (4) 3080 kcal

A-3. If 58.5 g of NaCl were dissolved in 1.00 L of water, the freezing point of the resulting solution would be   **(1) 1.86°C**
    (2) $-1.86°C$ (3) 3.72°C   (4) $-3.72°C$

A-4. Which of the following is equivalent to 1 kcal?   **(1) 4.18 J**
    (2) 4.18 kJ   (3) 0.239 kJ   (4) 0.239 J

A-5. What is the total number of kilocalories of heat needed to change 150. grams of ice to water at 0°C?   **(1) 12.0**   **(2) 1.88**   **(3) 70.**
    (4) 230.

TABLE B
Standard Units

For each property of matter that can be measured, there is a standard unit that is defined and against which measurements of that property are made. The basic unit of length is the kilogram, which was traditionally defined as the length of a standard metal bar kept at the International Bureau of Standards in Sevres, France. In 1983 the meter was redefined as the distance light travels in a vacuum during 1/299 792 458 of a second.

The basic unit of mass is the kilogram, which is defined as the mass of a standard metal cylinder also kept at the International Bureau of Standards. Other units of length and mass, such as the centimeter and the gram, are derived from the meter and the kilogram. The first part of Reference Table B presents a list of standard units and their symbols.

The second part of this table presents a list of selected prefixes that can be used with various units. The symbols for the prefixes are also given. A kilometer (km), for example, is 10^3 times the length of a meter, while a nanometer (nm) is 10^{-9} or 1 billionth of a meter.

B-1. According to Reference Table B, the symbol for a micromole would be (1) kmol (2) mol (3) nmol (4) μmol

B-2. According to Reference Table B, which of the following units would be used to report the pressure of a gas? (1) K (2) C (3) dPa (4) mV

B-3. Which of the following prefixes is used to express 1/1000? (1) kilo (2) milli (3) micro (4) nano

TABLE C
Density and Boiling Points of Some Common Gases

The table may be of some help in problems involving the molecular weights of gases, since 22.4 liters of a gas at S.T.P. contains the molecular weight of the gas in grams. Therefore, the molecular weight of a gas can be found by multiplying its density in grams per liter by 22.4, or its density can be found by dividing its molecular weight by 22.4. If, for example, the molecular weight of a compound of carbon and oxygen is found to be 28, then its density is

$$28/22.4 = 1.25 \text{ grams/liter}$$

and by consulting the table you can see that the gas must be carbon monoxide.

Note that the boiling points are given in Kelvin units, that is, degrees above absolute zero (which is $-273°C$). The boiling point information indicates which gases are least difficult to liquefy (for example, sulfur dioxide and ammonia). It also indicates the order in which gases can be separated from a mixture in the liquid state. For example, nitrogen will boil off from liquid air before oxygen.

QUESTIONS

C-1. At STP, which gas is least dense? (1) HCl (2) NO (3) NH_3 (4) H_2S

C-2. It is found by experiment that 22.4 liters of an oxide of sulfur at STP has a measured mass of 64.8 grams. Its formula is probably (1) SO_2 (2) SO_3 (3) S_2O_4 (4) SO

C-3. Which gas has a greater density at STP than air at STP?
(1) NH_3 (2) CO   (3) N_2 (4) O_2

C-4. The density of a gas is 2.0 grams per liter at STP. Its molecular mass is approximately   (1) 8.0   (2) 22   (3) 45   (4) 67

C-5. The gram molecular mass of a gas is 44.0 grams. What is the density of the gas at STP?   (1) 0.509 g/L   (2) 1.43 g/L   (3) 1.96 g/L   (4) 2.84 g/L

TABLE D
Solubility Curves

This table presents the solubility of eight different salts and three different gases in 100 mL of water at temperatures between 0°C and 100°C. All of the salts show the expected increase in solubility with increasing temperature. Each of the gases shows decreasing solubility with increasing temperature, a characteristic of all gases. If a different quantity of water than 100 mL is used, the amount of solute will vary proportionately.

QUESTIONS

D-1. A solution contains 90 grams of a salt dissolved in 100 grams of water at 40°C. The solution could be an unsaturated solution of   (1) KCl   (2) KNO_3 (3) NaCl   (4) $NaNO_3$

D-2. Based on Reference Table D, which of the following substances is most soluble at 60° C?   (1) NH_4Cl (2) KCl   (3) NaCl   (4) $NaNO_3$

D-3. A solution contains 52 grams of solute per 100 grams of water at 80°C. This solution could be a saturated solution of   (1) NaCl   (2) $NaNO_3$ (3) KCl   (4) $KClO_3$

D-4. Which two salts are equally soluble in 100 mL of H_2O at 76°C?   (1) NaCl and $KClO_3$ (2) NaCl and KCl   (3) $NaNO_3$ and KNO_3 (4) KCl and KNO_3

D-5. Given 100 mL of water at 10°C that contains 60 grams of $NaNO_3$. In order to form a saturated solution at 10°C, how many more grams of $NaNO_3$ must be added?   (1) 19   (2) 38   (3) 60   (4) 79

TABLE E
Table of Solubilities in Water

This table can be used to determine the name of the product expected to precipitate when two salt solutions are mixed. Look at the new combinations of cation and anion that result from a double replacement reaction. The designation of either nearly insoluble (i) or slightly soluble (ss) for either or both of the products shows the formation of a precipitate. It is also possible to determine some quantitative information about solubility from this table.

QUESTIONS

E-1. What is the name of the solid that forms when silver nitrate is mixed with sodium chloride? (1) silver nitrate (2) silver chloride (3) sodium chloride (4) sodium nitrate

E-2. According to Reference Table E, which of the following compounds would most likely have the smallest K_{sp}? (1) barium chloride (2) calcium sulfate (3) magnesium nitrate (4) silver acetate

E-3. Based on Reference Table E, which of the following compounds is the most soluble in water? (1) AgI (2) AgCl (3) $PbCl_2$ (4) $Pb(NO_3)_2$

TABLE F
Selected Polyatomic Ions

This table can be used to identify the names, formulas, and charges of some common polyatomic ions. The numbers given after the formulas represent the charges on the ions. A charge of $+1$ or $1-$ is shown by $+$ or $-$. Other charges are shown by including both the magnitude and the charge, such as $2+$ or $3-$. Oxidation numbers are written in the opposite order, such as $+1$ or $+2$. This table can be useful in determining the correct formulas of substances and in identifying ionic compounds.

QUESTIONS

F-1. What is the formula of sodium chromate? (1) Na_2CrO_4 (2) $Na_2Cr_2O_7$ (3) $NaCrO_4$ (4) $Na(CrO_4)_2$

F-2. What is the oxidation number of chromium in sodium chromate? (1) -2 (2) $+2$ (3) $+4$ (4) $+6$

F-3. Which formula correctly represents mercury (I) chloride? (1) Hg_2Cl (2) $HgCl_2$ (3) Hg_2Cl_2 (4) Hg_2Cl_4

F-4. Which of the following is an ionic compounds? (1) CF_4 (2) H_2O (3) Na_2SO_4 (4) $CHCl_3$

TABLE G
Standard Energies of Formation

In addition to providing information about the formulas of various compounds, there are two major uses of this table:

1. The column headed "Heat (Enthlapy) of Formation" can be used to identify exothermic and endothermic reactions and, more importantly, recognize the relative stability of compounds. The table shows that the heat of formation of aluminum oxide is -400.5 kcal/mol. The negative $(-)$ value means that, in an exothermic reaction, 400.5 kcal of heat were released when a mole of aluminum oxide was formed. Therefore, an identical amount of heat, 400.5 kcal, must be added to aluminum oxide to decompose it into its elements. Since only 64.8 kcal were released when a mole of HF was formed, only 64.8 kcal will be needed to break it apart. The more energy that is released when a substance is formed, the more stable it will be.

2. The values in the column headed "Free Energy of Formation" indicate whether or not a substance is formed spontaneously. Those compounds having a negative ΔG value will form spontaneously. The relationship

$$\Delta G - \Delta H \quad T\Delta S$$

is used to calculate this value, with ΔG as a measure of the free energy, ΔH the heat of reaction, T the kelvin temperature, and ΔS a measure of the entropy.

QUESTIONS

G-1. Based on Reference Table G, which of the following compounds is the most stable? (1) CO (2) CO_2 (3) NO (4) NO_2

G-2. Based on Reference Table G, how many kcal of heat are released when 0.500 mol of KCl is formed from its elements at 1 atm and 278 K?

G-3. Given the reaction: $A(g) + B(g) \longrightarrow AB(g)$ with $\Delta H_f^\circ = -10$ kilocalories per mole and $\Delta G_f^\circ = +2$ kilocalories per mole. This reaction is
(1) exothermic and will occur spontaneously
(2) exothermic and will not occur spontaneously
(3) endothermic and will occur spontaneously
(4) endothermic and will not occur spontaneously

G-4. A chemical reaction will always occur spontaneously if the reaction has a
(1) negative ΔG (2) positive ΔG
(3) negative ΔH (4) positive ΔII

G-5. The free energy change, ΔG, must be negative when
(1) ΔH is positive and ΔS is positive
(2) ΔH is positive and ΔS is negative
(3) ΔH is negative and ΔS is positive
(4) ΔH is negative and ΔS is negative

G-6. In a chemical reaction, the difference in potential energy between the products and the reactants is equal to
(1) ΔS (2) ΔG (3) ΔH (4) ΔT

G-7. According to Reference Table G, which compound is formed in a reaction in which the entropy increases?
(1) aluminum oxide (2) magnesium oxide
(3) potassium chloride (4) hydrogen fluoride

G-8. According to Reference Table G, which compound forms spontaneously from its elements?
(1) C_2H_4 (2) C_2H_2 (3) NO_2 (4) CO_2

TABLE H
Selected Radioisotopes

See page 30 for a discussion of the meaning of half-life. The symbol for each decay mode listed on this chart is given in Reference Table J. When projecting the amount of radioactive material present at a future date, reduce the mass of the sample for each half-life period. To calculate the amount of sample present at a prior point in time, double the amount of sample for each half-life period.

QUESTIONS

H-1. What is the number of hours required for potassium-42 to pass through three half-life periods?
(1) 6.2 hours   (2) 12.4 hours   (3) 24.8 hours   (4) 37.2 hours

H-2. What fraction of a sample of carbon-14 will remain after 17 190 years?   (1) 1/2   (2) 1/3   (3) 1/4   (4) 1/8

H-3. Approximately how many grams of a 40-gram sample of iodine-131 would remain unchanged after 16 days?   (1) 2.5 g   (2) 5 g   (3) 10 g   (4) 20 g

H-4. A sample of ^{131}I contains 10 grams. Approximately how many grams of iodine will remain after 24 days?   (1) 1.3   (2) 2.5   (3) 5.0   (4) 10

H-5. After one mole of ^{90}Sr has disintegrated for a period of 56 years, how many atoms of the original ^{90}Sr remain unchanged?
(1) 24×10^{23} (2) 1.5×10^{23} (3) 3.0×10^{23} (4) 6.0×10^{23}

TABLE I
Heats of Reaction

The heats of reaction listed in this table are the energy exchanges for 1 mole of reactant. The heat exchanged for a mole of product can be calculated using a simple proportion.

QUESTIONS

I-1. According to Reference Table I, the greatest amount of energy would be given up by the complete oxidation of   (1) $CH_4(g)$
(2) $C_3H_8(g)$ (3) CH_3OH (4) $C_6H_{12}O_6$

I-2. According to Reference Table I, the amount of heat liberated when 1 mole of water is produced by the complete combustion of 1 mole of methane is   (1) 13.8 kcal   (2) 106.4 kcal   (3) 212.8 kcal   (4) 319.2 kcal

TABLE J
Symbols Used in Nuclear Chemistry

This table is useful in identifying the particles involved in nuclear reactions and in completing the equations for such reactions. For example, if a given nucleus is bombarded with neutrons, we know that it is reacting with the particle $_0^1$n. The lower number (subscript) is the charge on the particle, and the upper number (superscript) is the mass number. Note that the electron is also called a beta particle.

SAMPLE QUESTION

A uranium isotope decays to thorium according to the reaction

$$_{92}^{238}U \rightarrow \ _{90}^{234}Th + X$$

What is X? (1) an electron (2) a proton (3) a neutron (4) an alpha particle

Solution: To balance the charges (subscripts) on both sides of the equation, the charge on X must be +2. To balance the mass numbers (superscripts), the mass number of X must be 4. Therefore X is $_2^4$He, an alpha particle.

QUESTIONS

J-1. Radioactive chlorine-38 can be produced by the reaction

$$_{17}^{37}Cl + X \rightarrow \ _{17}^{38}Cl$$

X is (1) a deuteron (2) an electron (3) a proton (4) a neutron

J-2. In the reaction $_{12}^{25}Mg$ + alpha particle $\rightarrow \ _{13}^{28}Al$ + X, X is (1) an electron (2) a proton (3) a neutron (4) a deuteron

TABLE K
Ionization Energies and Electronegativities

This table shows the ionization energies and electronegativity values for Groups 1 and 2 (the s-block) and Groups 13 through 18 (the p-block) elements of the Periodic Table.

The ionization energy is a measure of the difficulty of removing an electron from an atom of the given element. The smaller the value of the ionization energy, the more easily an electron can be removed, and the more metallic the properties of the element. The table reveals that ionization energy generally decreases from top to bottom within any group, that is, it decreases as the atomic number increases. It increases from left to right within any period. Thus, metallic character and ease of forming positive ions increases from top to bottom of the table, and decreases from left to right.

The electronegativity value measures the tendency of an atom to attract and hold the electron pair of a chemical bond. The greater the difference in electronegativity between two elements, the greater the ionic character of a bond between them. A difference of 1.7 units or more indicates a predominantly ionic bond. A difference less than 1.7 units indicates a predominantly covalent bond.

QUESTIONS

K-1. In a given horizontal row of the Periodic Table, the element having the lowest first ionization energy is in Group   (1) 1   (2) 2   (3) 15   (4) 17

K-2. Which pair of elements forms a compound possessing the strongest ionic character?   (1) Na and F   (2) Rb and F   (3) Li and I   (4) K and Cl

K-3. Nonmetallic atoms possess   (1) high ionization energies and low electronegativities   (2) high ionization energies and high electronegativities   (3) low ionization energies and low electronegativities   (4) low ionization energies and high electronegativities

K-4. In Group 16, as the atomic number increases, the tendency to give up electrons   (1) decreases   (2) increases   (3) remains the same

K-5. As one reads from left to right in Period 3 of the Periodic Table, the ionization energy generally tends to   (1) increase   (2) decrease   (3) remain the same

K-6. As one reads from left to right in Period 2, ionization energy generally   (1) decreases and atomic size decreases   (2) decreases and atomic size increases   (3) increases and atomic size decreases   (4) increases and atomic size increases

K-7. Which bond has the least ionic character? (1) P—Cl (2) H—Cl (3) Br—Cl (4) O—F

K-8. Which of the following electron configurations will have the smallest first ionization energy? (1) $1s^2 2s^2 2p^4$ (2) $1s^2 2s^2 2p^2$ (3) $1s^2 2s^2 2p^6 3s^1$ (4) $1s^2 2s^1$

K-9. As one proceeds from left to right across a given period of the Periodic Table, the electronegativities of the elements (1) increase (2) decrease (3) remain the same

K-10. Which type of bonding is usually exhibited when the electronegativity difference between two atoms is 1.2? (1) ionic (2) metallic (3) network (4) covalent

TABLE L
Relative Strengths of Acids in
Aqueous Solution at 1 atm and 298 K

Refer to pages 107-108 for a discussion of Bronsted acid-base theory. According to the theory, an acid is a substance that yields a proton (H^+) in solution, forming its conjugate base. The relative strength of an acid is the degree to which the reaction forming the base occurs at equilibrium, that is, the value of the ionization constant K_a. The larger the value of K_a, the stronger the acid and the weaker the conjugate base. In this table, the strongest acids are at the top of the list on the left. The strongest bases are at the bottom of the list on the right.

Note that the same substance may appear as an acid and as a base. HSO_4^- is an example. Such substances are called amphiprotic (or amphoteric). They act as acids in the presence of a strong base, and as bases in the presence of a strong acid. For example, in the presence of the strong acid HCl, HSO_4^- will react as a base, accepting a proton to form H_2SO_4. But in the presence of the strong base NH_3, it will act as an acid, donating a proton and forming NH_4^+ and SO_4^{2-}.

QUESTIONS

L-1. Which can behave as either an acid or a base? (1) NH_4^+ (2) NO_3^- (3) HCO_3^- (4) Cl^-

L-2. The conjugate base of the HSO_4^- ion is (1) H_2SO_4 (2) SO_4^{-2} (3) H_2O (4) SO_3

L-3. Which is the strongest acid? (1) HCl (2) NH_4^+ (3) SO_4^{-2} (4) HSO_4^-

L-4. Which Bronsted acid is strongest? (1) HS^- (2) CO_2 (3) NH_4^+ (4) HSO_4^-

L-5. As conjugate acid strength decreases, the strength of the conjugate base (1) increases (2) decreases (3) remains the same

L-6. Which of the following acids has the strongest conjugate base? (1) HCl (2) HNO_3 (3) HSO_4^- (4) H_2S

L-7. Which substance is amphiprotic (amphoteric)? (1) HCl (2) NO_3^- (3) Cl^- (4) HSO_3^-

TABLE M
Constants for Various Equilibria

This table presents the values for several chemical equilibria systems and solubility expressions. The first two values are variations of the same reaction. In the first equation, water is shown as ionizing into hydrogen ions (H^+) and hydroxide ions (OH^-), while the second equation shows this ionization producing hydronium ions (H_3O^+). The value of the equilibrium constant is called K_w to indicate that it is the ionization constant for water. Note that K_w has the same value (1×10^{-14}) in both cases. This fact can serve as a reminder that the product of $[H^+][OH^-]$ must equal 1×10^{-14} in all cases. The next four values indicate that the bases listed are weak and the species are mostly present as reactants since the values of their equilibrium constants are quite small. The large value for the ammonia (NH_3) equilibrium shows that in an equilibrium situation more ammonia is present than nitrogen or hydrogen.

The lower portion of the table shows the K_{sp} values for a variety of salts. The small values indicate that the salts are not very soluble. The smaller K_{sp} value, the less soluble the salt, with silver iodide (AgI) being the least soluble. The most soluble salt listed is lithium carbonate (Li_2CO_3).

QUESTIONS

M-1. Based on Reference Table M, which of the following compounds is the least soluble in water? (1) AgI (2) AgCl (3) $PbCl_2$ (4) PbI_2

M-2. Based on Reference Table M, a saturated solution of which salt would be most dilute? (1) AgCl (2) BaSO$_4$ (3) Li$_2$CO$_3$ (4) PbCrO$_4$

M-3. Based on Reference Table M, in a saturated solution of BaSO$_4$ at 1 atmosphere and 298 K, the product of [Ba^{2+}] $\times$ [SO$_4{}^{2-}$] is equal to (1) 1.1 $\times$ 10^{-10} (2) 1.1 $\times$ 10^{-5} (3) 1.1 $\times$ 10^{-3} (4) 1.1 $\times$ 10^{10}

M-4. According to Reference Table M, which compound is more soluble than BaSO$_4$ at 1 atmosphere and 298 K? (1) AgBr (2) PbCl$_2$ (3) AgI (4) PbCrO$_4$

M-5. According to Reference Table M, which of the following equilibria systems favors the formation of the product or products?
(1) H$_2$(g) + I$_2$(g) $\rightleftarrows$ 2HI(g)
(2) N$_2$(g) + H$_2$(g) $\rightleftarrows$ 2NH$_3$(g)
(3) H$_2$O(l) $\rightleftarrows$ H$^+$(aq) + OH$^-$(aq)
(4) NH$_3$(aq) + H$_2$O(l) $\rightleftarrows$ NH$_4$(aq) + OH$^-$(aq)

M-6. The [OH$^-$] of a solution is 1 $\times$ 10^{-6}. At 1 atmosphere and 298 K, the product of the [H$_3$O$^+$] $\times$ [OH$^-$] is (1) 1 $\times$ 10^{-2} (2) 1 $\times$ 10^{-6} (3) 1 $\times$ 10^{-8} (4) 1 $\times$ 10^{-14}

TABLE N
Standard Electrode Potentials

This table presents a list of reduction reactions and the maximum voltage which can be obtained when the listed half-reaction is coupled with the hydrogen half-cell.

Any reduction reaction will occur in preference to any reduction reaction below it in the table, and will cause the reverse reaction (the oxidation reaction) to occur instead.

Another way to interpret the table is to say that if any two reactions on the list are paired, the one listed higher will go to the right, while the one listed lower will go to the left.

The table also permits calculation of the net voltage of an electro-chemical cell under standard conditions of 25°C (298°K), 1 atm pressure, and 1 molal solutions. This maximum voltage for these conditions is the difference between the two listed potentials. Thus for a cell that has F$_2$ in one half-cell and Cu^{2+} in the other, the net voltage will be the difference between the fluorine potential (+2.87) and the copper potential (+0.34), or 2.53 volts. If the electrode potential of the lower reaction is negative, its sign will change when you find the difference, and it will add to the potential of the higher reaction. For example, if Cu^{2+} is the higher ion, and Al^{3+} is the lower one, the difference is +0.34 − (−1.66) = +0.34 + 1.66 = 2.00 volts.

Typical questions based on this table will be found on pages 123-126.

TABLE O
Vapor Pressure of Water

This information is needed in the laboratory to determine the actual pressure of a gas when collected over water. The vapor pressure of the water is subtracted from the atmospheric pressure to find the vapor pressure of the collected gas. Thus when hydrogen is collected over water, and the atmospheric pressure is 760 torr with a room temperature of 25 °C, we can determine the pressure due to water from the table. If the total pressure of the gas and water vapor equals 760.0 torr, and the vapor pressure of water is 23.8 torr, then the pressure of hydrogen is 760.0 − 23.8 = 736.2 torr. It is this pressure that would then be used to calculate the mass or number of moles of hydrogen in the volume of the collected gas.

This table can also be used to indicate the temperature at which water will boil. Water will boil when its vapor pressure is equal to the atmospheric pressure. Thus if the pressure is 233.7 torr, water will boil at 70°C, the temperature at which it will exert the same pressure.

QUESTIONS

O-1. Water will boil at a temperature of 29°C if the pressure on the surface of the water is   (1) 4.6 mm Hg   (2) 30.0 mm Hg   (3) 92.5 mm Hg   (4) 760 mm Hg

O-2. At what temperature will water boil when its vapor pressure is 55.3 torr?   (1) 0°C   (2) 40°C   (3) 55.3°C   (4) 100°C

O-3. A sample of pure water is boiling at 99°C. The vapor pressure of the water is closest to   (1) 90.0 torr   (2) 363 torr   (3) 526 torr   (4) 760. torr

O-4. When the temperature of a sample of water is changed from 17°C to 20°C, the change in its vapor pressure is   (1) 1.00 torr   (2) 14.5 torr   (3) 3.0 torr   (4) 175 torr

TABLE P
Radii of Atoms

Refer to page 46 for definitions of the type of radii that are presented on this table. The trends on this table show that the radius of atoms decreases from left to right of each period and increases from top to bottom of each group. Many of the values are not present for various atoms, as these elements do not bond in a manner that allows this measurement. Questions that use this table ask you either to recognize the radius of an element simply by reading the table or recognize trends in periods or groups.

Reference Tables for Chemistry

PHYSICAL CONSTANTS AND CONVERSION FACTORS

Name	Symbol	Value(s)	Units
Angstrom unit	Å	1×10^{-10} m	meter
Avogadro number	N_A	6.02×10^{23} per mol	
Charge of electron	e	1.60×10^{-19} C	coulomb
Electron volt	eV	1.60×10^{-19} J	joule
Speed of light	c	3.00×10^{8} m/s	meters/second
Planck's constant	h	6.63×10^{-34} J·s	joule-second
		1.58×10^{-37} kcal·s	kilocalorie-second
Universal gas constant	R	0.0821 L·atm/mol·K	liter-atmosphere/mole-kelvin
		1.98 cal/mol·K	calories/mole-kelvin
		8.31 J/mol·K	joules/mole-kelvin
Atomic mass unit	μ(amu)	1.66×10^{-24} g	gram
Volume standard, liter	L	1×10^{3} cm^3 = 1 dm^3	cubic centimeters, cubic decimeter
Standard pressure, atmosphere	atm	101.3 kPa	kilopascals
		760 mmHg	millimeters of mercury
		760 torr	torr
Heat equivalent, kilocalorie	kcal	4.18×10^{3} J	joules

Physical Constants for H$_2$O

Molal freezing point depression	1.86°C
Molal boiling point elevation	0.52°C
Heat of fusion	79.72 cal/g
Heat of vaporization	539.4 cal/g

STANDARD UNITS

Symbol	Name	Quantity
m	meter	length
kg	kilogram	mass
Pa	pascal	pressure
K	kelvin	thermodynamic temperature
mol	mole	amount of substance
J	joule	energy, work, quantity of heat
s	second	time
C	coulomb	quantity of electricity
V	volt	electric potential, potential difference
L	liter	volume

Selected Prefixes

Factor	Prefix	Symbol
10^6	mega	M
10^3	kilo	k
10^{-1}	deci	d
10^{-2}	centi	c
10^{-3}	milli	m
10^{-6}	micro	μ
10^{-9}	nano	n

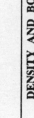

DENSITY AND BOILING POINTS OF SOME COMMON GASES

Name		Density grams/liter at STP*	Boiling Point (at 1 atm) K
Air	—	1.29	—
Ammonia	NH_3	0.771	240
Carbon dioxide	CO_2	1.98	195
Carbon monoxide	CO	1.25	82
Chlorine	Cl_2	3.21	238
Hydrogen	H_2	0.0899	20
Hydrogen chloride	HCl	1.64	188
Hydrogen sulfide	H_2S	1.54	212
Methane	CH_4	0.716	109
Nitrogen	N_2	1.25	77
Nitrogen (II) oxide	NO	1.34	121
Oxygen	O_2	1.43	90
Sulfur dioxide	SO_2	2.92	263

*STP is defined as 273K and 1 atm

Periodic Table of the Elements

This table should be used in the classroom beginning September 1986. The first examination to be based on this revised table is the June 1987 Regents Examination in Chemistry.

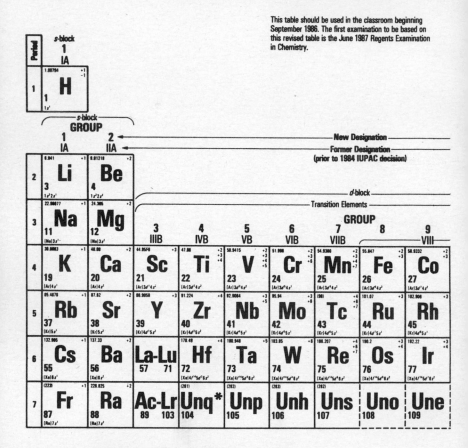

MASS NUMBERS IN PARENTHESES ARE MASS NUMBERS OF THE MOST STABLE OR COMMON ISOTOPE.

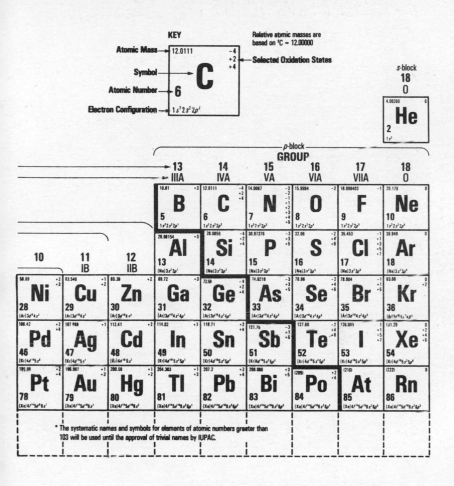

(E)

TABLE OF SOLUBILITIES IN WATER

i — nearly insoluble
ss — slightly soluble
s — soluble
d — decomposes
n — not isolated

	acetate	bromide	carbonate	chloride	chromate	hydroxide	iodide	nitrate	phosphate	sulfate	sulfide
Aluminum	ss	s	n	s	n	i	s	s	i	s	d
Ammonium	s	s	s	s	s	s	s	s	i	s	s
Barium	s	s	i	s	i	s	s	s	i	i	d
Calcium	s	s	i	s	s	ss	s	s	i	ss	d
Copper II	s	s	i	s	i	i	n	s	i	s	i
Iron II	s	s	i	s	n	i	s	s	i	s	i
Iron III	s	s	n	s	i	i	n	s	i	ss	d
Lead	s	ss	i	ss	i	i	ss	s	i	i	i
Magnesium	s	s	i	s	s	i	s	s	i	s	d
Mercury I	ss	ss	i	i	ss	n	i	s	i	ss	i
Mercury II	s	ss	i	s	ss	i	i	s	i	d	i
Potassium	s	s	s	s	s	s	s	s	s	s	s
Silver	ss	i	i	i	ss	n	i	s	i	ss	i
Sodium	s	s	s	s	s	s	s	s	s	s	s
Zinc	s	s	i	s	s	i	s	s	i	s	i

(D)

SOLUBILITY CURVES

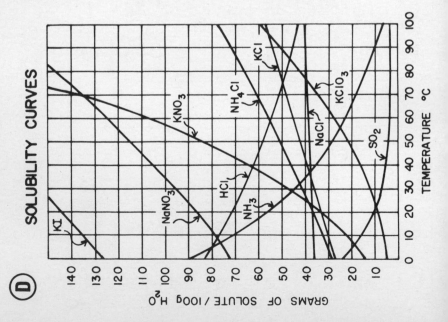

KI, NaNO₃, KNO₃, NH₄Cl, HCl, NH₃, KCl, NaCl, KClO₃, SO₂

GRAMS OF SOLUTE / 100g H₂O

TEMPERATURE °C

SELECTED POLYATOMIC IONS

Hg_2^{2+}	dimercury (I)	CrO_4^{2-}	chromate
NH_4^+	ammonium	$Cr_2O_7^{2-}$	dichromate
$C_2H_3O_2^-$ } CH_3COO^-	acetate	MnO_4^-	permanganate
		MnO_4^{2-}	manganate
CN^-	cyanide	NO_2^-	nitrite
CO_3^{2-}	carbonate	NO_3^-	nitrate
HCO_3^-	hydrogen carbonate	OH^-	hydroxide
		PO_4^{3-}	phosphate
$C_2O_4^{2-}$	oxalate	SCN^-	thiocyanate
ClO^-	hypochlorite	SO_3^{2-}	sulfite
ClO_2^-	chlorite	SO_4^{2-}	sulfate
ClO_3^-	chlorate	HSO_4^-	hydrogen sulfate
ClO_4^-	perchlorate	$S_2O_3^{2-}$	thiosulfate

STANDARD ENERGIES OF FORMATION OF COMPOUNDS AT 1 atm AND 298 K

Compound	Heat (Enthalpy) of Formation* kcal/mol ($\triangle H_f^o$)	Free Energy of Formation* kcal/mol ($\triangle G_f^o$)
Aluminum oxide Al_2O_3(s)	−400.5	−378.2
Ammonia NH_3(g)	−11.0	−3.9
Barium sulfate $BaSO_4$(s)	−352.1	−325.6
Calcium hydroxide $Ca(OH)_2$(s)	−235.7	−214.8
Carbon dioxide CO_2(g)	−94.1	−94.3
Carbon monoxide CO(g)	−26.4	−32.8
Copper (II) sulfate $CuSO_4$(s)	−184.4	−158.2
Ethane C_2H_6(g)	−20.2	−7.9
Ethene (ethylene) C_2H_4(g)	12.5	16.3
Ethyne (acetylene) C_2H_2(g)	54.2	50.0
Hydrogen fluoride HF(g)	−64.8	−65.3
Hydrogen iodide HI(g)	6.3	0.4
Iodine chloride ICl(g)	4.3	−1.3
Lead (II) oxide PbO(s)	−51.5	−45.0
Magnesium oxide MgO(s)	−143.8	−136.1
Nitrogen (II) oxide NO(g)	21.6	20.7
Nitrogen (IV) oxide NO_2(g)	7.9	12.3
Potassium chloride KCl(s)	−104.4	−97.8
Sodium chloride $NaCl$(s)	−98.3	−91.8
Sulfur dioxide SO_2(g)	−70.9	−71.7
Water H_2O(g)	−57.8	−54.6
Water $H_2O(\ell)$	−68.3	−56.7

* Minus sign indicates an exothermic reaction.

Sample equations:

$$2Al(s) + \frac{3}{2}O_2(g) \rightarrow Al_2O_3(s) + 400.5 \text{ kcal}$$

$$2Al(s) + \frac{3}{2}O_2(g) \rightarrow Al_2O_3(s) \quad \triangle H = -400.5 \text{ kcal/mol}$$

SELECTED RADIOISOTOPES

Nuclide	Half-Life	Decay Mode
^{198}Au	2.69 d	β^-
^{14}C	5730 y	β^-
^{60}Co	5.26 y	β^-
^{137}Cs	30.23 y	β^-
^{220}Fr	27.5 s	α
^{3}H	12.26 y	β^-
^{131}I	8.07 d	β^-
^{37}K	1.23 s	β^+
^{42}K	12.4 h	β^-
^{85}Kr	10.76 y	β^-
^{85m}Kr*	4.39 h	γ
^{16}N	7.2 s	β^-
^{32}P	14.3 d	β^-
^{239}Pu	2.44×10^4 y	α
^{226}Ra	1600 y	α
^{222}Rn	3.82 d	α
^{90}Sr	28.1 y	β^-
^{99}Tc	2.13×10^5 y	β^-
^{99m}Tc*	6.01 h	γ
^{232}Th	1.4×10^{10} y	α
^{233}U	1.62×10^5 y	α
^{235}U	7.1×10^8 y	α
^{238}U	4.51×10^9 y	α

y=years; d=days; h=hours; s=seconds
*m = meta stable or excited state of the same nucleus. Gamma decay from such a state is called an isomeric transition (IT).
Nuclear isomers are different energy states of the same nucleus, each having a different measurable lifetime.

I — HEATS OF REACTION AT 1 atm and 298 K

Reaction	ΔH (kcal)
$CH_4(g) + 2O_2(g) \rightarrow CO_2(g) + 2H_2O(\ell)$	-212.8
$C_3H_8(g) + 5O_2(g) \rightarrow 3CO_2(g) + 4H_2O(\ell)$	-530.6
$CH_3OH(\ell) + \frac{3}{2}O_2(g) \rightarrow CO_2(g) + 2H_2O(\ell)$	-173.6
$C_6H_{12}O_6(s) + 6O_2(g) \rightarrow 6CO_2(g) + 6H_2O(\ell)$	-669.9
$CO(g) + \frac{1}{2}O_2(g) \rightarrow CO_2(g)$	-67.7
$C_8H_{18}(\ell) + \frac{25}{2}O_2(g) \rightarrow 8CO_2(g) + 9H_2O(\ell)$	-1302.7
$KNO_3(s) \xrightarrow{H_2O} K^+(aq) + NO_3^-(aq)$	$+8.3$
$NaOH(s) \xrightarrow{H_2O} Na^+(aq) + OH^-(aq)$	-10.6
$NH_4Cl(s) \xrightarrow{H_2O} NH_4^+(aq) + Cl^-(aq)$	$+3.5$
$NH_4NO_3(s) \xrightarrow{H_2O} NH_4^+(aq) + NO_3^-(aq)$	$+6.1$
$NaCl(s) \xrightarrow{H_2O} Na^+(aq) + Cl^-(aq)$	$+0.9$
$KClO_3(s) \xrightarrow{H_2O} K^+(aq) + ClO_3^-(aq)$	$+9.9$
$LiBr(s) \xrightarrow{H_2O} Li^+(aq) + Br^-(aq)$	-11.7
$H^+(aq) + OH^-(aq) \rightarrow H_2O(\ell)$	-13.3

J — SYMBOLS USED IN NUCLEAR CHEMISTRY

alpha particle	^4_2He	α
beta particle (electron)	$^0_{-1}e$	β^-
gamma radiation		γ
neutron	^1_0n	n
proton	^1_1H	p
deuteron	^2_1H	
triton	^3_1H	
positron	$^0_{+1}e$	β^+

IONIZATION ENERGIES AND ELECTRONEGATIVITIES

1								18

| H
313
2.2 | First Ionization Energy (kcal/mol of atoms)
Electronegativity* | He
567 |

| | 2 | 13 | 14 | 15 | 16 | 17 | |

Li 125 1.0	Be 215 1.5	B 191 2.0	C 260 2.6	N 336 3.1	O 314 3.5	F 402 4.0	Ne 497
Na 119 0.9	Mg 176 ·1.2	Al 138 1.5	Si 188 1.9	P 242 2.2	S 239 2.6	Cl 300 3.2	Ar 363
K 100 0.8	Ca 141 1.0	Ga 138 1.6	Ge 182 1.9	As 226 2.0	Se 225 2.5	Br 273 2.9	Kr 323
Rb 96 0.8	Sr 131 1.0	In 133 1.7	Sn 169 1.8	Sb 199 2.1	Te 208 2.3	I 241 2.7	Xe 280
Cs 90 0.7	Ba 120 0.9	Tl 141 1.8	Pb 171 1.8	Bi 168 1.9	Po 194 2.0	At 2.2	Rn 248
Fr 0.7	Ra 122 0.9						

* Arbitrary scale based on fluorine = 4.0

RELATIVE STRENGTHS OF ACIDS IN AQUEOUS SOLUTION AT 1 atm AND 298 K

Conjugate Pairs		K_a
ACID	*BASE*	
$HI = H^+ + I^-$		very large
$HBr = H^+ + Br^-$		very large
$HCl = H^+ + Cl^-$		very large
$HNO_3 = H^+ + NO_3^-$		very large
$H_2SO_4 = H^+ + HSO_4^-$		large
$H_2O + SO_2 = H^+ + HSO_3^-$		1.5×10^{-2}
$HSO_4^- = H^+ + SO_4^{2-}$		1.2×10^{-2}
$H_3PO_4 = H^+ + H_2PO_4^-$		7.5×10^{-3}
$Fe(H_2O)_6^{3+} = H^+ + Fe(H_2O)_5(OH)^{2+}$		8.9×10^{-4}
$HNO_2 = H^+ + NO_2^-$		4.6×10^{-4}
$HF = H^+ + F^-$		3.5×10^{-4}
$Cr(H_2O)_6^{3+} = H^+ + Cr(H_2O)_5(OH)^{2+}$		1.0×10^{-4}
$CH_3COOH = H^+ + CH_3COO^-$		1.8×10^{-5}
$Al(H_2O)_6^{3+} = H^+ + Al(H_2O)_5(OH)^{2+}$		1.1×10^{-5}
$H_2O + CO_2 = H^+ + HCO_3^-$		4.3×10^{-7}
$HSO_3^- = H^+ + SO_3^{2-}$		1.1×10^{-7}
$H_2S = H^+ + HS^-$		9.5×10^{-8}
$H_2PO_4^- = H^+ + HPO_4^{2-}$		6.2×10^{-8}
$NH_4^+ = H^+ + NH_3$		5.7×10^{-10}
$HCO_3^- = H^+ + CO_3^{2-}$		5.6×10^{-11}
$HPO_4^{2-} = H^+ + PO_4^{3-}$		2.2×10^{-13}
$HS^- = H^+ + S^{2-}$		1.3×10^{-14}
$H_2O = H^+ + OH^-$		1.0×10^{-14}
$OH^- = H^+ + O^{2-}$		$< 10^{-36}$
$NH_3 = H^+ + NH_2^-$		very small

Note: $H^+ (aq) = H_3O^+$

Sample equation: $HI + H_2O = H_3O^+ + I^-$

CONSTANTS FOR VARIOUS EQUILIBRIA AT 1 atm AND 298 K

Equation	Constant
$H_2O(\ell) = H^+(aq) + OH^-(aq)$	$K_w = 1.0 \times 10^{-14}$
$H_2O(\ell) + H_2O(\ell) = H_3O^+(aq) + OH^-(aq)$	$K_w = 1.0 \times 10^{-14}$
$CH_3COO^-(aq) + H_2O(\ell) = CH_3COOH(aq) + OH^-(aq)$	$K_b = 5.6 \times 10^{-10}$
$Na^+F^-(aq) + H_2O(\ell) = Na^+(OH)^- + HF(aq)$	$K_b = 1.5 \times 10^{-11}$
$NH_3(aq) + H_2O(\ell) = NH_4^+(aq) + OH^-(aq)$	$K_b = 1.8 \times 10^{-5}$
$CO_3^{2-}(aq) + H_2O(\ell) = HCO_3^-(aq) + OH^-(aq)$	$K_b = 1.8 \times 10^{-4}$
$Ag(NH_3)_2^+(aq) = Ag^+(aq) + 2NH_3(aq)$	$K_{eq} = 8.9 \times 10^{-8}$
$N_2(g) + 3H_2(g) = 2NH_3(g)$	$K_{eq} = 6.7 \times 10^5$
$H_2(g) + I_2(g) = 2HI(g)$	$K_{eq} = 3.5 \times 10^{-1}$

Compound	K_{sp}	Compound	K_{sp}
AgBr	5.0×10^{-13}	Li_2CO_3	2.5×10^{-2}
AgCl	1.8×10^{-10}	$PbCl_2$	1.6×10^{-5}
Ag_2CrO_4	1.1×10^{-12}	$PbCO_3$	7.4×10^{-14}
AgI	8.3×10^{-17}	$PbCrO_4$	2.8×10^{-13}
$BaSO_4$	1.1×10^{-10}	PbI_2	7.1×10^{-9}
$CaSO_4$	9.1×10^{-6}	$ZnCO_3$	1.4×10^{-11}

STANDARD ELECTRODE POTENTIALS
Ionic Concentrations 1 M Water At 298 K, 1 atm

Half-Reaction	E^0 (volts)
$F_2(g) + 2e^- \rightarrow 2F^-$	+2.87
$8H^+ + MnO_4^- + 5e^- \rightarrow Mn^{2+} + 4H_2O$	+1.51
$Au^{3+} + 3e^- \rightarrow Au(s)$	+1.50
$Cl_2(g) + 2e^- \rightarrow 2Cl^-$	+1.36
$14H^+ + Cr_2O_7^{2-} + 6e^- \rightarrow 2Cr^{3+} + 7H_2O$	+1.23
$4H^+ + O_2(g) + 4e^- \rightarrow 2H_2O$	+1.23
$4H^+ + MnO_2(s) + 2e^- \rightarrow Mn^{2+} + 2H_2O$	+1.22
$Br_2(\ell) + 2e^- \rightarrow 2Br^-$	+1.09
$Hg^{2+} + 2e^- \rightarrow Hg(\ell)$	+0.85
$Ag^+ + e^- \rightarrow Ag(s)$	+0.80
$Hg_2^{2+} + 2e^- \rightarrow 2Hg(\ell)$	+0.80
$Fe^{3+} + e^- \rightarrow Fe^{2+}$	+0.77
$I_2(s) + 2e^- \rightarrow 2I^-$	+0.54
$Cu^+ + e^- \rightarrow Cu(s)$	+0.52
$Cu^{2+} + 2e^- \rightarrow Cu(s)$	+0.34
$4H^+ + SO_4^{2-} + 2e^- \rightarrow SO_2(aq) + 2H_2O$	+0.17
$Sn^{4+} + 2e^- \rightarrow Sn^{2+}$	+0.15
$2H^+ + 2e^- \rightarrow H_2(g)$	0.00
$Pb^{2+} + 2e^- \rightarrow Pb(s)$	-0.13
$Sn^{2+} + 2e^- \rightarrow Sn(s)$	-0.14
$Ni^{2+} + 2e^- \rightarrow Ni(s)$	-0.26
$Co^{2+} + 2e^- \rightarrow Co(s)$	-0.28
$Fe^{2+} + 2e^- \rightarrow Fe(s)$	-0.45
$Cr^{3+} + 3e^- \rightarrow Cr(s)$	-0.74
$Zn^{2+} + 2e^- \rightarrow Zn(s)$	-0.76
$2H_2O + 2e^- \rightarrow 2OH^- + H_2(g)$	-0.83
$Mn^{2+} + 2e^- \rightarrow Mn(s)$	-1.19
$Al^{3+} + 3e^- \rightarrow Al(s)$	-1.66
$Mg^{2+} + 2e^- \rightarrow Mg(s)$	-2.37
$Na^+ + e^- \rightarrow Na(s)$	-2.71
$Ca^{2+} + 2e^- \rightarrow Ca(s)$	-2.87
$Sr^{2+} + 2e^- \rightarrow Sr(s)$	-2.89
$Ba^{2+} + 2e^- \rightarrow Ba(s)$	-2.91
$Cs^+ + e^- \rightarrow Cs(s)$	-2.92
$K^+ + e^- \rightarrow K(s)$	-2.93
$Rb^+ + e^- \rightarrow Rb(s)$	-2.98
$Li^+ + e^- \rightarrow Li(s)$	-3.04

VAPOR PRESSURE OF WATER

°C	torr (mmHg)
0	4.6
5	6.5
10	9.2
15	12.8
16	13.6
17	14.5
18	15.5
19	16.5
20	17.5
21	18.7
22	19.8
23	21.1
24	22.4
25	23.8
26	25.2
27	26.7
28	28.3
29	30.0
30	31.8
40	55.3
50	92.5
60	149.4
70	233.7
80	355.1
90	525.8
100	760.0
105	906.1
110	1074.6

RADII OF ATOMS

KEY

Symbol → **F**
Covalent Radius, Å → 0.64
Atomic Radius in Metals, Å → 0.72
Van der Waals Radius, Å → 1.35

A dash (–) indicates data are not available.

Each element lists: Covalent Radius, Å / Atomic Radius in Metals, Å / Van der Waals Radius, Å

Element	Covalent	Metallic	Van der Waals
H	0.37	(–)	1.2
He	(–)	(–)	1.22
Li	1.23	1.52	(–)
Be	0.89	1.13	(–)
B	0.88	0.83	2.08
C	0.77	(–)	1.85
N	0.70	0.55	1.54
O	0.66	0.60	1.40
F	0.64	0.72	1.35
Ne	(–)	(–)	1.60
Na	1.57	1.54	2.31
Mg	1.36	1.60	(–)
Al	1.25	1.43	(–)
Si	1.17	(–)	2.0
P	1.10	1.08	1.90
S	1.04	0.94	1.85
Cl	0.99	(–)	1.81
Ar	1.74	(–)	1.91
K	2.03	2.27	2.31
Ca	1.74	1.97	(–)
Sc	1.44	1.61	(–)
Ti	1.32	1.45	(–)
V	1.22	1.32	(–)
Cr	1.17	1.25	(–)
Mn	1.17	1.24	(–)
Fe	1.17	1.24	(–)
Co	1.16	1.25	(–)
Ni	1.15	1.25	(–)
Cu	1.17	1.28	(–)
Zn	1.25	1.33	(–)
Ga	1.25	1.22	(–)
Ge	1.22	1.23	(–)
As	1.21	1.25	2.0
Se	1.17	(–)	2.0
Br	1.14	(–)	1.95
Kr	1.89	(–)	1.98
Rb	2.16	2.48	2.44
Sr	1.92	2.15	(–)
Y	1.62	1.81	(–)
Zr	1.45	1.60	(–)
Nb	1.34	1.43	(–)
Mo	1.29	1.36	(–)
Tc	(–)	1.36	(–)
Ru	1.24	1.33	(–)
Rh	1.25	1.35	(–)
Pd	1.28	1.38	(–)
Ag	1.34	1.44	(–)
Cd	1.41	1.49	(–)
In	1.50	1.63	(–)
Sn	1.40	1.41	(–)
Sb	1.41	(–)	2.2
Te	1.37	(–)	2.20
I	1.33	(–)	2.15
Xe	2.09	2.18	(–)
Cs	2.35	2.65	2.62
Ba	1.98	2.17	(–)
Hf	1.44	1.56	(–)
Ta	1.34	1.43	(–)
W	1.30	1.37	(–)
Re	1.28	1.37	(–)
Os	1.26	1.34	(–)
Ir	1.26	1.36	(–)
Pt	1.29	1.38	(–)
Au	1.34	1.44	(–)
Hg	1.44	1.60	(–)
Tl	1.55	1.70	(–)
Pb	1.54	1.75	(–)
Bi	1.52	1.55	(–)
Po	1.53	1.67	(–)
At	(–)	(–)	(–)
Rn	2.14	(–)	(–)
Fr	(–)	2.7	(–)
Ra	(–)	2.20	(–)

La–Lu (lanthanide series)

Element	Covalent	Metallic	Van der Waals
La	1.69	1.88	(–)
Ce	1.65	1.83	(–)
Pr	1.65	1.83	(–)
Nd	1.64	1.82	(–)
Pm	(–)	1.81	(–)
Sm	1.66	1.80	(–)
Eu	1.85	2.04	(–)
Gd	1.61	1.80	(–)
Tb	1.59	1.78	(–)
Dy	1.59	1.77	(–)
Ho	1.58	1.77	(–)
Er	1.57	1.76	(–)
Tm	1.56	1.75	(–)
Yb	1.70	1.94	(–)
Lu	1.56	1.73	(–)

Ac–Lr (actinide series)

Element	Covalent	Metallic	Van der Waals
Ac	(–)	1.88	(–)
Th	(–)	1.80	(–)
Pa	(–)	1.61	(–)
U	(–)	1.39	(–)
Np	(–)	1.31	(–)
Pu	(–)	1.51	(–)
Am	(–)	1.84	(–)
Cm	(–)	(–)	(–)
Bk	(–)	(–)	(–)
Cf	(–)	(–)	(–)
Es	(–)	(–)	(–)
Fm	(–)	(–)	(–)
Md	(–)	(–)	(–)
No	(–)	(–)	(–)
Lr	(–)	(–)	(–)

GLOSSARY

absolute zero: The coldest possible temperature, $-273\,°C$ or O K. At this temperature kinetic molecular motions should cease.

accuracy: The nearness of a measurement to the actual or accepted value.

acid: A substance whose water solution contains the hydronium ion (Arrhenius) and/or is a proton donor (Bronsted-Lowry).

acid salt: A salt whose water solution has a pH less than 7. It is derived from a strong acid and a weak base.

activated complex: The temporary unstable union of two reactants.

activation energy: The amount of energy needed to form an activated complex.

addition polymerization: The joining of monomers to form a polymer without the production of other products.

addition reactions: The combination of a substance with an unsaturated hydrocarbon resulting in the formation of only one product.

alcohols: A family of organic compounds the molecules of which consist of a hydrocarbon radical combined with one or more hydroxyl ($-OH$) groups. Their IUPAC name ends in -ol.

aldehydes: A family of organic compounds the molecules of which consist of a hydrocarbon radical combined with a terminal $-CHO$ group. Their IUPAC name ends in -al.

aliphatics: Families of hydrocarbons with open carbon chains.

alkali metal: A member of Col 1(IA) of the Periodic Table. An active metal having an oxidation value of $+1$ in compounds.

alkaline metal: Also called an Alkaline Earth metal. A member of Col 2(IIA) of the Periodic Table having an oxidation value of $+2$ in compounds.

alkanes: The saturated family of hydrocarbons the molecules of which have the general formula C_nH_{2n+2} and contain only single covalent carbon-to-carbon bonds.

alkenes: An unsaturated family of hydrocarbons the molecules of which have the general formula C_nH_{2n} and contain one double covalent carbon-to-carbon bond.

alkyl group: A hydrocarbon radical having the general formula C_nH_{2n+1}

alkynes: An unsaturated family of hydrocarbons the molecules of which have the general formula C_nH_{2n-2}. These compounds contain one triple covalent carbon-to-carbon bond.

alloy: A homogeneous mixture containing two or more metals.

alpha decay: A transmutation in which a helium nucleus is emitted and the resulting daughter nucleus has an atomic number reduced by 2 and an atomic mass reduced by 4.

alpha particle: A helium nucleus.

amine: A type of organic compound the molecules of which consist of a hydrocarbon radical with a functional $-NH_2$ attached.

amphiprotic: A substance that can act either as a proton donor (acid) or a proton acceptor (base).

amphoteric: Property of hydroxides that also act as acids; commonly the hydroxides of aluminum and zinc.

analysis: The decomposition of a compound into simpler substances.

anhydrous: Term applied to a hydrate after the water of hydration has been removed.

anion: A negatively charged ion.

anode: The site of oxidation in an electrochemical cell. It is considered to be negatively charged in an electrochemical cell and positively charged in an electrolytic cell.

aqueous: Term applied to a solution in which water is the solvent. It is indicated by (aq), e.g., NaCl (aq).

aromatics: A family of organic compounds the molecules of which contain one or more benzene rings.

Arrhenius acid: A substance whose water solution contains the hydronium (hydrogen) ion.

Arrhenius base: A substance whose water solution contains the hydroxide ion.

atmosphere (atm): A unit used to describe the pressure of gases. One atm = 760 torr = 760 mm Hg = 14.7 lbs/sq in.

atom: The smallest particle of an element that can enter into a reaction.

atomic mass unit (amu): 1/12 the mass of a carbon-12 atom.

atomic number: The number of protons in the nucleus of an atom.

atomic radius: 1/2 the distance between two adjacent nuclei of atoms of an element in the solid phase.

atomic weight (mass): The weighted average weight (mass) of the isotopes of an element.

Avogadro's hypothesis: All gases, measured at the same temperature and pressure, contain the same number of molecules.

Avogadro's number: The number of particles in a mole, 6.02×10^{23}.

Avogadro's volume: The volume occupied by a mole of a gas at standard temperature and pressure: 22.4 L

base: A substance whose water solution contains hydroxide ions (Arrhenius) and/ or is a proton acceptor (Bronsted-Lowry).

basic salt: A salt whose water solution has a pH greater than 7. It is a salt derived from a strong base and a weak acid.

beta decay: A transmutation in which a beta particle (electron) is emitted and the resulting nucleus has an atomic number increased by 1 and an atomic mass that remains the same.

beta particle: An electron, represented in nuclear equations by $_{-1}^{0}e$.

binary compound: A compound containing two elements.

binding energy: The energy equivalent to the mass defect, represented by E in the equation $E = mc^2$. The amount of energy produced by the conversion of matter into energy in a nuclear reaction.

boiling point: The temperature at which the vapor pressure of a liquid equals the atmospheric pressure.

boiling point elevation: The elevation of the boiling point of a substance due to the addition of solute. One mole of particles elevates the boiling point of water $0.52\,°C$.

bond energy: The amount of energy needed to break a chemical bond.

Boyle's Law: The mathematical expression that represents the inverse relationship between pressure and volume of a gas when the temperature is kept constant: $P_1V_1 = P_2V_2$

breeder reactor: A nuclear reactor that both produces energy and additional nuclear fuel by nuclear transmutations.

bright-line spectrum: A series of spectral lines produced as excited electrons return to lower energy states.

Bronsted-Lowry acid: A proton donor.

Bronsted-Lowry base: A proton acceptor.

calorie: The quantity of heat required to raise the temperature of one gram of water $1\,C°$.

calorimeter: A device used to measure the heat change during a chemical reaction.

carboxyl group: The functional group of organic acid molecules: $-COOH$.

catalyst: A substance that alters the rate of a chemical reaction without itself being permanently changed during the reaction.

cathode: The site of reduction in an electrochemical cell. It is considered to be positively charged in an electrochemical cell and negatively charged in an electrolytic cell.

cation: A positively charged ion.

Celsius scale: A temperature scale with fixed points of $O\,°C$ and $100\,°C$.

chain reaction: A reaction in which the products of each step become reactants in the next step.

Charles's law: The mathematical expression that represents the direct relationship between the volume and temperature of a gas when the temperature is expressed in Kelvin degrees and the pressure is constant: $\dfrac{V_1}{T_1} = \dfrac{V_2}{T_2}$

chemical bond: The force that holds two atoms together. Potential energy is reduced when bonds are formed and increased when bonds are broken.

chemical change: A reaction in which the properties and composition of a substance or substances are altered.

coefficient: The number written in front of a formula in a chemical equation. The coefficients represent both the molecular and mole relationships of the reactants and products.

colligative properties: Properties of solutions that depend on the number of dissolved solute particles.

combination reaction: The union of two or more reactants to form one product.

compound: A substance with a definite composition that can be decomposed into two or more simpler substances.

concentrated: Term applied to a solution that contains a relatively large amount of solute.

condensation: The changing of a vapor or gas into the liquid phase. It is an exothermic reaction in which the potential energy of the substance is reduced while the temperature remains the same.

condensation reaction: A chemical reaction in which water is produced as small molecular units are joined together to form a larger molecule.

conjugate acid-base pairs: A Bronsted-Lowry concept in which two substances differ by a proton (hydrogen ion).

contact process: A commercial process for the production of sulfuric acid.

control rods: The rods in a nuclear reactor that are used to absorb neutrons and control the rate of the reaction. Cadmium and boron are used for this purpose.

coordinate covalent bond: A covalent bond in which one atom donates both of the electrons to the bond pair. It is identical in all respects to a covalent bond. Both the hydronium ion and the ammonium ion contain such a bond.

covalent bond: A bond formed by the sharing of a pair of electrons. A bond formed by two atoms with an electronegativity difference less than 1.7 is considered to be predominately covalent.

covalent radius: The effective distance from the center of the nucleus to the outer valence shell of that atom in a covalent or coordinate bond.

cracking: The breaking of larger petroleum molecules into smaller molecular units.

crystal: A solid substance whose particles have a repeating geometric pattern.

cyclotron: A particle accelerator that accelerates particles by electromagnetic induction.

dating: A method that uses the half-life of radio isotopes to determine the age of a substance or object.

decay: The spontaneous transmutation of a radioactive nucleus.

decomposition: A type of chemical reaction in which a compound is broken apart into simpler substances.

density: The mass of a given volume of a substance. The density of liquids is generally expressed in g/mL; for gases it is expressed in g/L.

deuterium: The isotope of hydrogen that has 1 neutron in the atomic nucleus and therefore an atomic mass of 2.

diatomic gas: A gas consisting of two atoms per molecule: H_2, N_2, O_2, F_2, Cl_2, Br_2, and I_2.

diene: An organic compound whose molecules contain two double covalent bonds.

dihydroxy alcohol: An alcohol whose molecules contain two hydroxy groups per molecule. Antifreeze (ethylene glycol) is such a substance.

dilute: Term applied to a solution that contains a relatively small amount of solute. A process by which the concentration of a solution is reduced.

diluting acids: When diluting acids, the acid is always added to the water.

dipole: A molecule that has an uneven charge distribution. Asymmetrical molecules that contain polar covalent bonds are dipoles.

dissociation: The separation of the ions of an ionic compound, especially during the process of dissolving.

distillate: The product produced by condensation of the vapors produced during distillation.

distillation: The process by which a substance is boiled and the vapors are condensed and recovered.

double bond: The sharing of two pairs of bonding electrons between two atoms.

electrochemical cell: A cell in which the redox reaction is conducted in such a way that the electrons travel through a wire between the substance being oxidized and the substance being reduced.

electrolysis: A chemical reaction that takes place when an electric current is applied to a substance.

electrolyte: A substance whose water solution conducts an electric current.

electron: A fundamental particle of matter having a negative electric charge.

electron-dot symbols: Symbols that contain the symbol of the element and indicate the number of valence electrons.

electronegativity: A measure of the attraction of a nucleus for the electrons in a covalent bond.

electroplating: The process of layering a metal onto a surface in an electrolytic cell.

element: A substance that cannot be decomposed by ordinary chemical means.

empirical formula: A formula showing the simplest ratio of the elements in a chemical compound.

endothermic reaction: A reaction in which the products contain more potential energy than the reactants. ΔH for an endothermic reaction is positive.

end point: That point of a titration when an indicator shows that equivalent amounts of reactants have reacted.

energy: Often defined as the ability to do work. The total amount of energy in a reaction must remain the same. However, it may be changed from one type of energy to another.

enthalpy: A measure of the potential energy of a substance.

entropy: A measure of the amount of randomness of the particles of a substance.

equilibrium: A dynamic chemical condition in which opposing reactions are proceeding at equal rates, producing an apparent constant condition.

equilibrium constant: A mathematical expression that indicates the extent to which a reaction has progressed.

esterification: The reaction between an acid and an alcohol to produce an ester, usually in the presence of a dehydrating agent such as sulfuric acid.

ester: The product, other than water, of the reaction between an acid and an alcohol.

ethers: A family of organic compounds in which hydrocarbon radicals are joined by an oxygen bridge. They are represented by the general formula R-O-R.

evaporation: The process by which molecules in the liquid state escape into the gaseous state.

excited state: The condition that exists when the electron(s) of an atom occupy higher energy levels while lower energy levels are vacant.

exothermic reaction: A chemical reaction in which the products have less potential energy than the reactants. ΔH for an exothermic reaction is negative.

families: The vertical groupings of chemically similar elements in the Periodic Table.

fermentation: The production of ethanol and carbon dioxide by the action of enzymes on an organic compound.

filtration: A method used to separate solids from liquids.

fission: A nuclear reaction in which large nuclei are split into smaller nuclear fragments.

fixed points: Those points on a thermometer that are used to standardize the instrument. Easily reproduced points such as the freezing and boiling points of water are usually used as fixed points.

formula mass: The sum of all of the atomic masses in a formula; primarily used to describe the mass of ionic substances.

fractional distillation: The separation of different liquids in a mixture by using the different boiling points of the components.

free energy: A measure of the tendency of a reaction to proceed spontaneously. It is represented by ΔG in the Gibbs equation: $\Delta G = \Delta H \times (T\Delta S)$.

freezing point: The temperature at which both the solid and liquid phases of a substance can exist in equilibrium.

freezing point depression: The lowering of the normal freezing point of a liquid by the addition of solute. One mole of particles lowers the freezing point of 1L of water by $1.86\,°C$.

functional group: An atom or group of atoms responsible for specific properties and characteristics of organic compounds.

fused: Term used to describe a substance that is normally a solid at room temperature, but has been melted.

fusion: 1. The change of a substance from the solid to the liquid state. 2. A nuclear reaction in which light nuclei combine to form a heavier nucleus.

gamma rays: Nuclear emanations similar to x-rays, but of higher energy content.

gas: A phase of matter without definite volume or shape.

gram: A unit of mass equal to 1/1000 the mass of the standard kilogram.

gram atomic mass: The mass in grams of a mole of a substance; numerically equal to the atomic mass of the substance.

gram formula mass: The mass in grams of the formula mass of a substance. It is used to describe the mass of a mole of ionic substances.

gram molecular mass: The mass in grams of a mole of a substance; numerically the same as the molecular mass of the substance. It is used to describe the mass of a mole of molecular substances.

ground state: The condition of an atom or ion in which the electrons occupy the lowest available energy levels.

group: A vertical set of elements in the Periodic Table. It is also called a family.

Haber Process: A commercial method that fixes nitrogen in the production of ammonia.

half-cell: The oxidation or reduction portion of an electrochemical cell.

half-life: The length of time required for one half of a sample of a radioactive substance to decay.

half-reaction: An equation showing either the oxidation or reduction portion of a redox reaction.

halide: The negative ion of a member of the halogen family.

halogen: A member of Column 17(VIIA) of the Periodic Table.

halogenation: The placement of a halogen atom on a hydrocarbon molecular chain either by substitution or addition.

heat: A form of energy.

heat of combustion: The quantity of heat released by the combustion (burning) of a unit mass of a substance.

heat of condensation: The quantity of heat released during the change of a unit mass of a vapor into the liquid state without a temperature change. It is numerically equal to but of opposite sign to the **heat of vaporization.**

heat of formation: The quantity of heat released or absorbed during the formation of a compound from its elements.

heat of fusion: The quantity of heat absorbed during the change of a unit mass of a solid to a liquid without a temperature change. It is numerically equal to but of opposite sign to the **heat of solidification.**

heat of reaction: The quantity of heat released or absorbed during a chemical reaction. It is a measure of the difference between the potential energy of the reactants and the potential energy of the products.

heat of solidification: The quantity of heat released during the change of a unit mass of a liquid to a solid without a temperature change. It is numerically equal to but of opposite sign to the **heat of fusion.**

heat of vaporization: The quantity of heat absorbed during the change of a unit mass of a liquid to a vapor without a temperature change. It is numerically equal to but of opposite sign to the **heat of condensation.**

heavy water: A molecule of water in which one or both of the hydrogen atoms is deuterium.

heterogeneous: A mixture in which the substances are not uniformly mixed.

homogeneous: A substance in which the particles are uniformly mixed.

homologous series: A family of organic compounds in which the molecules of each member differs from the preceding member by one carbon and two hydrogens ($-CH_2$).

hydrate: The crystalline form of an ionic substance that contains a definite number of water molecules; e.g., $CuSO_4.10H_2O$.

hydration: The addition of water to a compound.

hydride: A binary compound in which hydrogen has an oxidation value of -1.

hydrocarbon: An organic compound whose molecules contain only carbon and hydrogen.

hydrogen bond: The bond between the hydrogen of one molecule and a highly electronegative atom of another molecule.

hydrogen half-cell: The standard for the measurement of half-cell voltages with an arbitrary value of 0.00 V.

hydrolysis: A chemical reaction in which water is a reactant. Often the reaction of a salt and water to produce an acid and a base.

hydronium ion: The combination of a hydrogen ion (proton) and a water molecule to produce H_3O^+. Sometimes referred to as a hydrated proton.

hygroscopic: A substance that absorbs water from the air.

ideal gas: A hypothetical gas that conforms exactly to the gas laws. While no such gas exists, hydrogen and helium gases are the closest to ideal behavior.

immiscible: Term applied to substances that will not mix together to form a solution.

indicators: Substances that undergo color changes and show when a reaction has been completed.

inert gases: Also called noble gases. They are members of Col 18(O) of the Periodic Table and are generally not able to enter into chemical reactions.

inorganic chemistry: The chemistry of compounds other than hydrocarbons and their derivatives.

ion: A particle with an unequal number of positive or negative charges.

ionic bond: A bond in which the force of attraction holding ions together is primarily electrostatic.

ionic radius: The radius of a charged particle. Metallic ions have smaller radii than their atoms, while those of nonmetals have larger radii.

ionization energy: The amount of energy needed to remove the most loosely bound electron from a neutral gaseous atom.

isomers: Compounds that have the same molecular formula, but different structural formulas.

isotopes: Nuclei that have the same number of protons but different numbers of neutrons and hence different atomic masses.

IUPAC: International Union of Pure and Applied Chemistry

IUPAC nomenclature: A system of naming organic compounds as approved by the IUPAC.

joule: A unit of energy in the SI system. One calorie = 4.18 joules.

Kelvin scale: Also called the absolute temperature scale. The zero point is the coldest possible temperature. One Kelvin degree is equivalent to one Celsius degree. A Celsius reading can be converted to Kelvin by adding 273 to the Celsius reading.

kernel: The nucleus and electrons of an atom, except the valence electrons.

ketones: A family of organic compounds whose molecules contain the carbonyl group as the functional group. Propanone (acetone) is the most common member.

kilo-: Prefix meaning 1000.

kinetic energy: Energy of motion.

kinetic theory: A theory that explains the behavior of gases in terms of the motion of their molecules.

linear accelerator: A particle accelerator that accelerates particles by means of electric fields.

liquid: A phase of matter having a definite volume but taking the shape of its container.

liter: The standard unit of volume in the SI system. It is equal to the volume of 1000 milliliters.

litmus: An indicator that is red in acidic and blue in basic solutions.

macromolecules: Molecules formed by covalent network bonding that are large enough to be seen by the eye.

malleable: A property of metals that allows the metals to be hammered or rolled into desired shapes.

mass defect: The amount of matter that was converted into energy as protons and neutrons combined to form nuclei.

mass number: The sum of the protons and neutrons in a nucleus.

melting point: The temperature at which a substance melts and can coexist with the liquid phase of that substance. It is the same as **freezing point,** and involves the addition of potential energy to the substance without a temperature change.

meniscus: The curved surface of a liquid in a container. Instruments are calibrated so that volume readings are taken at the bottom of the meniscus.

metals: Atoms that lose electrons in chemical reactions to become positive ions.

metallic bond: The force that holds metallic atoms together in the solid or liquid phase. It is due to attraction between valence electrons and the positive kernels.

metalloid: Also called a **semi-metal.** Element that has both metallic and nonmetallic characteristics.

miscible: Term applied to substances that can be mixed to form a solution.

mixture: A substance not having definite proportions and containing two or more components that are not chemically combined.

moderator: A substance used to slow down the neutrons produced in a nuclear reactor.

molal boiling point constant: The number of degrees that 1 mole of solute particles will elevate the boiling point of 1,000 g of solvent. The constant for 1L of water is 0.52 °C.

molal freezing point constant: The number of degrees that 1 mole of solute particles will depress the freezing point of 1,000 g of solvent. The constant for 1L of water is 1.86 °C.

molality: The concentration of a solution expressed as the number of moles of solute per 1,000 g of solvent.

molar volume: The volume occupied by 1 mole of a gas. This volume is 22.4 L at STP; it contains 1 mole of molecules.

molarity: The concentration of a solution expressed as the number of moles of solute per liter of solution.

mole: 6.02×10^{23} particles. This number of particles can be obtained by taking the molecular mass of a substance in grams.

molecular formula: A formula that indicates the number of atoms that are present in the smallest particle that has the chemical properties of the substance.

molecular weight (mass): The sum of the atomic weights (masses) of the atoms in a molecular formula.

molecule: The smallest unit of a substance that has the chemical properties of the substance.

monatomic molecule: A molecule that consists of only one atom. The noble (inert) gases exist as monatomic molecules.

monohydroxy alcohol: An alcohol whose molecules contain only one hydroxyl group.

network solid: A solid formed by covalent bonding in which the bonding extends throughout the entire visible sample.

neutralization: A reaction between an Arrhenius acid and an Arrhenius base to produce a salt and water.

neutron: A neutral nuclear particle having a mass of 1 amu.

noble gas: Also called an **inert gas.** A member of Col 18(O) of the Periodic Table. These gases have filled valence electron shells and generally do not enter chemical reactions.

nonelectrolyte: An aqueous solution that does not conduct an electric current.

nonmetals: Elements whose valence electron shells are almost complete.

nonpolar bonds: Covalent bonds in which the two atoms have an equal share of the bonding electrons as measured by their electronegativity values.

nonpolar molecules: Molecules that have a symmetrical shape and a symmetrical charge distribution.

normal boiling point: The boiling point of a liquid at standard pressure.

nuclear fuel: The element used as the source of energy in a nuclear reactor. Often U-235.

nucleons: Particles found in the nucleus. Protons and neutrons are the most commonly identified.

nucleus: The small, dense center of an atom that contains almost all of the mass of the atom in the form of protons and neutrons.

number of orbitals: The number of orbitals at a given principal quantum level is represented by the expression n.

number of sublevels: The number of sublevels at a given principal quantum level is the same as the principal quantum level (n).

octet: A stable configuration of 8 valence electrons.

orbital: The area or space of an atom where an electron of a particular energy content is most likely to be found.

organic acids: Organic compounds the molecules of which contain the carboxyl (– COOH) group as their functional group.

organic chemistry: The chemistry of carbon compounds, particularly hydrocarbons and their derivatives.

ore: A mineral that can be used to produce a metal.

oxidation: The process by which a particle loses an electron or appears to lose an electron as indicated by a gain in oxidation number.

oxidation numbers: Values assigned to particles for the purpose of identifying oxidation and reduction processes.

oxidizing agents: Particles that cause other particles to be oxidized by accepting electrons from them while themselves being reduced.

particle accelerators: Devices that accelerate charged particles by magnetic or electric fields.

period: A horizontal sequence of elements on the Periodic Table that begins with an alkali metal and ends with noble (inert) gas. The first period of the Table begins with hydrogen and ends with helium.

Periodic Law: The properties of the elements are a periodic function of their atomic numbers.

peroxide: A binary compound that contains more oxygen atoms than are normally expected. Oxygen is assigned the oxidation value of -1 in such compounds.

pH: A method of expressing the acidity or basicity of a substance on a scale from 1 to 14. It is the negative of the logarithm of the hydrogen ion concentration.

phenolphthalein: An indicator that is colorless in acidic solutions and pink in basic solutions.

pOH: The negative of the logarithm of the hydroxide ion concentration.

polar bond: A bond in which the electron pair is shared unequally by the two atoms, resulting in a dipole. The element with the higher electronegativity value is assigned the negative portion of the dipole.

polar molecule: A molecule containing polar bonds with an asymmetric shape and therefore an asymmetric charge distribution.

polyatomic ion: Two or more atoms that are chemically combined and possess a net electric charge, also called a **radical.**

polymer: A compound with a high molecular mass that consists of many smaller subunits (monomers) that have been bonded together.

polymerization: The process of forming molecules of high molecular mass by the joining of smaller molecules into a chain.

positron: A fundamental particle with a mass identical to that of an electron, but having a positive charge.

potential energy: Often called stored energy. A particle has potential energy because of its position, phase, or composition.

precipitate: A solid that is formed when two liquids are mixed.

precision: A measurement of the degree of closeness or agreement between two measurements.

primary alcohols: Alcohol molecules in which the hydroxy (OH) group is attached to a primary carbon.

primary carbon: A carbon in a chain of carbons that is directly attached to one other carbon. These carbons are found at the ends of chains or branches.

proton: A particle found in the nucleus having a charge of $+1$ and having a mass of 1 amu.

radiation: Energy emitted from an object.

radical: Also called a **polyatomic ion.** Two or more atoms chemically combined and having a net electric charge.

radioactive dating: A method of determining the age of an object by the use of the half-lives of radioactive elements in the sample.

radioactivity: The spontaneous release of energy by a nucleus.

radioisotope: A radioactive isotope of an element.

reactant: One of the substances consumed in a chemical reaction, a starting substance.

redox: Term used to describe the process in which oxidation and reduction take place.

reducing agent: A particle that causes another particle to be reduced while losing electrons, or being oxidized.

reduction: The process by which a particle gains electrons, as identified by a decrease in oxidation number.

reversible reaction: A reaction in which the products can reform into the reactants.

salt: An ionic substance consisting of a positive metallic ion and a negative ion other than the hydroxide ion.

salt bridge: A passageway for the movement of ions in an electrochemical cell.

saponification: The reaction of a base plus an ester to produce an alcohol and a soap.

saturated hydrocarbon: A hydrocarbon molecule containing only single covalent carbon-to-carbon bonds.

saturated solution: A solution in which as much solute has been dissolved as is possible for the given temperature.

secondary alcohol: An alcohol in which the hydroxy group is attached to a secondary carbon.

secondary carbon: A carbon in an organic compound that is directly attached to two other carbon atoms.

semi-metal: Also called a **metalloid.** Element that has both metallic and nonmetallic characteristics.

significant figures: In a measurement the significant figures represent all of the certain digits plus one that is an estimate.

single bonds: Covalent bonds between atoms in which one pair of electrons is shared between the atoms.

solid: The phase of matter whose particles have a definite crystalline arrangement. Solids have both definite volume and a definite shape.

solubility curve: A curve showing the solubility of a solute as a function of temperature.

solubility product constant: The form of the equilibrium expression that applies to the equilibrium between an ionic solid and its ions. The larger the value, the more soluble the salt.

solute: The dissolved portion of a solution; the substance present in lesser amount.

solution: A homogeneous mixture.

solvent: The part of a solution in which the solute is dissolved; the substance present in the greater amount.

spectrum: The series of lines of radiant energy produced as electrons return from higher to lower energy levels.

spontaneous reaction: A reaction that once begun will continue until one of the reactants has been consumed.

standard conditions: 760 torr and O °C. Referred to as **STP.**

standard electrode potential: The voltage of a half-cell in combination with a standard hydrogen cell.

standard solution: A solution of known concentration.

STP: Standard temperature and pressure.

Stock system: A system of nomenclature in which a Roman numeral is used to show the charge of any metallic ion that can carry different charges.

stoichiometry: The study of the quantitative aspects of equations.

strong acids: Acids that are highly ionized in solution. The degree of ionization is indicated by the magnitude of the ionization constant.

strong bases: Bases that are highly ionized in solution.

sublevels: Divisions of the principal atomic energy levels. The number of possible sublevels is the same as the principal quantum number.

sublimation: A change between the solid and gaseous phases without a noticeable liquid phase.

supersaturated solution: A solution that contains more dissolved solute than would be present in a saturated solution at the same temperature.

symbol: An upper case letter or an upper case letter plus a lower case letter used to represent an atom of an element.

synchrotron: A particle accelerator that accelerates particles by using electromagnets.

temperature: A measure of the average kinetic energy of the particles of a substance.

ternary acid: An acid containing three different elements per molecule.

tertiary alcohol: An alcohol molecule whose hydroxyl group is located on a tertiary carbon.

tertiary carbon: A carbon atom that is directly attached to three carbon atoms.

tincture: A solution in which the solvent is ethanol.

titration: A process in which a solution of known concentration is used to determine the concentration of another solution.

torr: A unit of pressure. Each torr is equivalent to 1 mm Hg. Standard pressure is 760 torr.

tracer: A radioisotope used to follow the path of a chemical reaction.

transition element: An element whose atom has an incomplete d subshell or which gives rise to a cation or cations with incomplete d subshells.

transmutation: The conversion of atoms of one element into a different element.

transuranic element: An element with an atomic number greater than 92.

trihydroxy alcohol: An alcohol molecule with three hydroxy groups, such as 1,2,3, propanetriol (glycerol or glycerine).

triple bond: The sharing of three pairs of electrons between two atoms.

tritium: The isotope of hydrogen whose nuclei contain one proton and two neutrons and have a mass of 3 amu.

unsaturated hydrocarbon: A hydrocarbon molecule that contains at least one double or triple bond.

unsaturated solution: A solution in which more solute can be dissolved at a given temperature.

valence electrons: The s and p electrons at the highest principal quantum level, the outermost electrons of an atom.

van der Waals forces: Weak attractive forces between molecules in the solid and liquid phases. They are the result of temporary dipoles in molecules caused by the random, asymmetric motion of electrons.

van der Waals radius: Half the closest distance between an atom and another atom with which it does not form a bond.

vapor: The gaseous phase of a substance that is normally a solid or liquid at room temperature.

vapor pressure: The pressure exerted by the vapors of a liquid or a solid.

volt: A unit of electrical potential.

water of hydration: Also known as water of crystallization; the number of water molecules chemically attached to a particle of the substance in the solid state.

weak acid: An acid that is only slightly ionized. It will have a small K_a or K_{ion} value.

weak base: A base that is only ionized slightly. It will have a small K_{ion} value.

weak electrolyte: A substance whose water solution is a poor conductor of electricity.

THE COLLEGE BOARD CHEMISTRY
ACHIEVEMENT TEST

The Chemistry Achievement Test is designed to measure your progress in mastering chemical knowledge and your ability to apply and interpret information. The results of your test are scored on a numeric basis with test scores ranging between 200 and 800. Your score can be converted to a percentile rating which shows how you ranked in the total population of students who took this test. Since many colleges use achievement test scores in aiding their selection process, you should investigate the catalogues of the colleges to which you wish to apply in order to determine the required tests. Discuss the matter with your guidance counselor, chemistry teacher, and parents before deciding which tests to take.

The guidance department of your school has a listing of the dates and locations where the achievement tests will be given. The achievement tests are given in English, Social Studies, Math, Biology, Chemistry, Physics, Spanish and French. You may take as many as three of these tests on one day. If you are currently enrolled in a chemistry course, do not take the test before the first week in May, since there will be material on the test which you will probably not have completed in class. You can take the achievement test more than once, and the experience gained from the first time may help improve your grade the next time that you take the exam. If you do take an achievement test more than once, the CEEB will report the average of your previous achievement tests along with the most recent test results.

The material that has been presented in the first sections of this review book covers the majority of material that will be included on the chemistry achievement exam. In this section there is additional material that is not included in the New York State chemistry syllabus, but which may appear on the achievement test. It would be virtually impossible to present all of the material that might be asked on the test, but between the two portions of this book, the vast majority of potential material is covered.

The additional text material is followed by two practice tests which contain questions similar in type to those asked on the actual achievement tests. The test is entirely multiple-choice. There are about 90 questions on the test, and one hour is provided for the exam. Because there is a wide variety in the type of chemistry programs in various schools, the questions are written to be fair to any student, regardless of the type of text and program which he or she may have had. Due to the variety of topics that are covered and the difficulty of some of the questions you may not be able to finish the exam, although you can expect to complete at least 75% of the test questions.

Your objective in taking the Chemistry Achievement Test is to answer the maximum number of questions correctly. Random guessing is penalized, and you should not enter an answer on the answer sheet unless you believe that you can eliminate at least one of the answers as incorrect. Move through the questions rapidly, being sure to not spend too much time on any one question. You may perform scrap work on the test paper. Place this work next to the question that you are answering. When you believe that you know the answer to a question, fill in the answer on the answer sheet. Put an asterisk next to any question in your test booklet that you wish to return to. If you recognize that you have not learned the particular information needed for a question, or cannot remember how to solve a problem, put an "X" through the question and do not return to it unless you have extra time at the end of the exam period. An occasional glance at the clock will serve to remind you of your progress.

The achievement test has questions of varying difficulty. The simplest type of question is simply a "recall" question in which you are asked to remember a specific fact.

Example: Isotopes of a given element have
  (A)   different numbers of protons, but equal neutrons
  (B)   different numbers of neutrons, but equal protons
  (C)   different numbers of neutrons and protons

(D) equal nucleons, but different number of electrons
(E) equal nucleons, and equal numbers of electrons

This question is designed to determine if you know that isotopes of a given element contain equal numbers of protons, but different numbers of neutrons. The test is constructed so that about 30% of the questions fall into this category. Since these are the easiest questions, it is to your advantage to answer as many of them as possible. Begin the exam by rapidly skimming through the test and answering those questions that seem easy to you. Since these information questions can appear in any location, it is important that you read every question at least once, or you might not reach a simple question located near the end of the exam.

Approximately 55% of the test is made up of questions of a more difficult variety. These questions require you to know some factual material and then to apply this knowledge to a situation or solve a mathematical problem.

Example: An element exists in nature composed of two isotopic forms. The mass of one isotope is 32 amu and it comprises 25% of the atoms of this element. The other isotope has a mass of 36 amu and comprises 75% of the atoms of this element. The reported mass of this element would be
(A)   32 amu
(B)   33 amu
(C)   34 amu
(D)   35 amu
(E)   36 amu

In this type of question you are expected to know that the mass of an element is the weighted average of all of the isotopes. You would then be expected to use the information given and calculate the weighted average to be 35 amu.

A third type of question comprises about 15% of the test. In this level of question you are required to interpret given information and integrate information that you already know, and then draw conclusions.

Example: Element A has two valence electrons and a low electronegativity value. Element B has 7 valence electrons and a high electronegativity value. A compound formed between these two elements probably has the formula
(A) A_2B and is a good electrolyte
(B) AB_2 and is a good electrolyte
(C) AB_2 and has colvalent bonding
(D) A_2B and has ionic bonding
(E) AB_2 and has a low melting point

In this question you are expected to know how elements can react by obtaining complete octets of electrons, and then apply the knowledge to predict an ionic bond, and then the properties that accompany such a bond.

PREPARING FOR THE ACHIEVEMENT TEST IN CHEMISTRY

To prepare for this exam, plan your studying for the exam so that you do so over a long time period. If you are currently enrolled in a chemistry class you may have to learn new material that will not be covered in class by the time that you take the exam in May. If you take the exam in June you will probably have completed all of the material. If you have previously finished your chemistry course, allow about a week of review for each of the units in this text. Within the last few days before the achievement exam don't try to learn new material.

Scan through the entire material to remind yourself of those things that you already have learned. It would be helpful to take both the practice Regents exams and the practice college board exams in preparation for the test. The practice college board exams are not actual exams used by the College Entrance Examination Board, but have been designed to present representative material and types of questions.

Whether you are currently enrolled in chemistry or are reviewing, you must commit yourself to a program in order to prepare for the exam. Prepare a written plan of how you will divide your work during the weeks before the exam. You will have to decide what is important to you and eliminate distractions. When you have prepared a plan, stick to it. The results of this test can play an important role in your future. If you are adequately prepared, there is nothing to fear about the test.

BALANCING EQUATIONS

The ability to balance equations is one of the most fundamental skills in chemistry. Many equations can be balanced by inspection. When balancing by inspection, remember that the number of atoms present in an unbalanced equation are the lowest possible values. When you recognize that you have more atoms of an element on one side than on the other, you must raise the number of atoms by using a coefficient. The balancing game is essentially a see-saw affair with numbers of atoms rising until both sides have an equal number of each kind of atom. When balancing equations for multiple-choice tests, remember that one of the answers listed is correct. There is no reason to place any other coefficient in front of the required reagent except for those listed as possible answers.

Not all equations can easily be balanced by the inspection system. When you recognize that the equation is a redox equation follow the procedures listed on page 124 of this book, writing half-reactions, and then finish the balancing by inspection. Because there may be several equations to be balanced on the achievement test, it is an important skill to acquire as it is an easy area in which to score points.

Sample Questions

Directions: Balance the following equations using only integers. Be sure that you reduce them to the lowest integer ratio.

1. $Fe_2O_3 + Na_2CO_3 \longrightarrow NaFeO_2 + CO_2$
2. $Fe_2O_3 + C \longrightarrow Fe + CO$
3. $NO_2 + H_2O \longrightarrow HNO_3 + NO$
4. $P_4O_{10} + H_2O \longrightarrow H_3PO_4$
5. $Na + H_2O \longrightarrow NaOH + H_2$
6. $Al + HCl \longrightarrow AlCl_3 + H_2$
7. $SnO_2 + H_2 \longrightarrow Sn + H_2O$
8. $N_2O_5 \longrightarrow NO_2 + O_2$
9. $CH_4 + S_2 \longrightarrow CS_2 + H_2S$
10. $NH_3 + O_2 \longrightarrow NO + H_2$
11. $Ca(OH)_2 + H_3PO_4 \longrightarrow H_2O + Ca_3(PO_4)_2$
12. $H_2 + NO \longrightarrow H_2O + N_2$
13. $H_2 + Fe_2O_3 \longrightarrow H_2O + Fe_3O_4$
14. $CaC_2 + O_2 \longrightarrow CaCO_3 + CO_2$
15. $Na_2O_2 + H_2O \longrightarrow NaOH + O_2$
16. $Cu + H_2SO_4 \longrightarrow CuSO_4 + H_2O + SO_2$
17. $Al(OH)_3 + H_2SO_4 \longrightarrow Al_2(SO_4)_3 + H_2O$
18. $FeCl_3 + NaOH \longrightarrow Fe(OH)_3 + NaCl$
19. $KOH + Cl_2 \longrightarrow KClO_3 + KCl + H_2O$
20. $Ca_3(PO_4)_2 + H_2SO_4 \longrightarrow CaSO_4 + H_3PO_4$
21. $PbO_2 + HCl \longrightarrow PbCl_2 + Cl_2 + H_2O$
22. $H_2S + O_2 \longrightarrow SO_2 + H_2O$
23. $NaClO_3 \longrightarrow O_2 + NaCl$
24. $Mg(OH)_2 + HCl \longrightarrow H_2O + MgCl_2$
25. $Fe_3O_4 + CO \longrightarrow CO_2 + Fe$
26. $As_2O_3 + I_2 + H_2O \longrightarrow H_3AsO_4 + HI$
27. $N_2H_4 + N_2O_4 \longrightarrow N_2 + H_2O$
28. $Al + I_2 \longrightarrow AlI_3$
29. $C_6H_{12} + O_2 \longrightarrow CO_2 + H_2O$
30. $KO_2 + H_2O + CO_2 \longrightarrow KHCO_3 + O_2$
31. $CH_3OH + O_2 \longrightarrow CO_2 + H_2O$
32. $C_2H_5OH + O_2 \longrightarrow CO_2 + H_2O$
33. $NH_3 + NO \longrightarrow N_2 + H_2O$

EXCESS AND LIMITING REAGENTS

The coefficients in a balanced equation represent the mole ratios by which the elements combine. In the equation

$$2 \text{ Al} + \text{Cr}_2\text{O}_3 \longrightarrow 2 \text{ Cr} + \text{Al}_2\text{O}_3$$

2 moles of aluminum will react with one mole of chromium oxide to produce 2 moles of chromium and one mole of aluminum oxide. If 4 moles of aluminum were reacted it would be necessary to have 2 moles of chromium oxide, and 4 moles of chromium would be produced along with 2 moles of aluminum oxide.

In actual lab or manufacturing practice, the reactants are not mixed in exactly the ratios indicated by the coefficients in the equations. One reactant is added in excess. When the reaction is complete some of this reactant will remain. The reactant that is completely consumed is called the limiting reactant. A typical problem presents given amounts of reactants and asks you to identify both the limiting and excess reagents.

For the reaction shown, suppose that 3 moles of aluminum were reacted with 3 moles of chromium oxide. Identify the limiting and excess reagents. According to the equation the mole ratio between aluminum and chromium oxide is 2:1. Three moles of aluminum will react with 1.5 moles of chromium oxide producing three moles of chromium and 1.5 moles of aluminum oxide. Since all of the aluminum is consumed, aluminum is the limiting reagent. Since only 1.5 moles of the chromium oxide were consumed, with an additional 1.5 moles remaining unreacted, the chromium oxide is the excess reagent.

The amount of product formed when all of the limiting reactant is consumed is termed the theoretical yield. In the example given, the theoretical yield of chromium metal is 3 moles of chromium.

When you are given mole quantities for a reaction, use the following procedure to determine the limiting and excess reagents and the theoretical yield:

1. Calculate the yield of a product, assuming that the first reactant was totally consumed.
2. Calculate the yield of the same product, assuming that the second reactant was totally consumed.

The smaller of these two values represents the limiting reagent and the amount produced represents the theoretical yield. The other reagent is the excess reagent.

Sample Questions

1. Given the reaction:

$$2 \text{ Pb} + \text{O}_2 \longrightarrow 2\text{PbO}$$

If two moles of lead are reacted with 2 moles of oxygen gas, which of the following will be a true statement?
(A) Both of the reactants will be totally consumed.
(B) One mole of lead will remain unreacted.
(C) One mole of lead oxide will be produced.
(D) One mole of oxygen will remain unreacted.
(E) One mole of lead and 0.5 mole of oxygen will remain unreacted.

2. Given the reaction:

$$\text{C}_3\text{H}_8 + 5 \text{ O}_2 \rightarrow 3 \text{ CO}_2 + 4 \text{ H}_2\text{O}$$

Which of the following statements is true if 2 moles of propane are reacted with 10 moles of oxygen gas?
(A) The propane is a limiting reactant.
(B) The propane is an excess reactant.
(C) 4 moles of water are produced.
(D) Both of the reactants are totally consumed.
(E) The oxygen is a limiting reactant.

3. Aluminum oxide is prepared by the following reaction:
$$4 \text{ Al} + 3 \text{ O}_2 \rightarrow 2 \text{ Al}_2\text{O}_3$$
Which of the following statements is true if six moles of aluminum are mixed with three moles of oxygen?
(A) Both of the reactants are totally consumed.
(B) The theoretical yield of aluminum oxide is two moles
(C) One mole of oxygen will remain unreacted.
(D) One mole of aluminum will remain unreacted.
(E) The aluminum is the limiting reactant.

BONDING

The writing of Lewis (electron-dot) structures is a helpful tool in preparing formulas to show the arrangements of atoms within a molecule. It was Lewis who suggested that atoms could share a pair of electrons between two atoms and acquire the stability of noble gas electron configuration. Lewis formulas are constructed by using dots or *x*s to represent the number of valence electrons in an atom.

$$\cdot \text{Li} \qquad +\text{Be}+ \qquad \overset{\times}{\underset{\times \;\; \times}{\text{B}}} \qquad \cdot \overset{..}{\text{C}} \cdot \qquad \cdot \overset{..}{\text{N}} \cdot \qquad \cdot \overset{..}{\underset{.}{\text{O}}}: \qquad \overset{\times\times}{\underset{\times\times}{\times \text{F} \overset{\times}{\times}}} \qquad : \overset{..}{\underset{..}{\text{Ne}}} :$$

Figure 1. Electron-dot diagrams of the second period elements.

Some of the formulas represented in Figure 1 differ slightly from those shown on Page 27, Figure 2-4. These diagrams show the electrons in bonding situations rather than in the ground states shown here. A hydrogen atom can share an electron with another hydrogen atom in a covalent bond, allowing each atom to achieve the electron configuration of the inert gas helium:

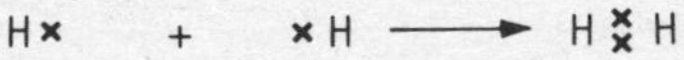

$$\text{H} \times \quad + \quad \times \text{H} \longrightarrow \text{H} \overset{\times}{\underset{\times}{}} \text{H}$$

Most molecules do not acquire the electron configuration of the noble gas helium, but rather that of a noble gas with eight electrons. This tendency to acquire eight valence electrons is referred to as the rule of octets.

1. To draw the structure of molecules, first attempt to join each of the atoms with a single covalent bond. A dashed line can be used to show a pair of electrons joined in a covalent bond.
2. Count the number of valence electrons for all the atoms of the molecule. Remember that each dashed line showing a possible covalent bond represents two electrons.
3. Distribute the unshared electrons so that each atom has a complete octet, or in the case of hydrogen, two electrons.

Structure of HClO

Both hydrogen and chlorine have only one bonding site and are likely to be located at the end of the molecule. Oxygen has two potential sites and is predicted to be the central atom:

$$\text{H}\text{—}\text{O}\text{—}\text{Cl}$$
Number of valence electrons: $1 + 6 + 7 = 14$

Each of the covalent bonds shown represents 2 electrons, therefore 4 electrons have been accounted for; 10 are left to be distributed.

Two pairs of electrons are assigned to oxygen, three to chlorine. Notice that hydrogen has two electrons, the electron structure of helium, and both oxygen and chlorine have stable octets of eight electrons. Distribute these 10 electrons (5 pairs):

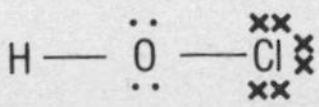

$$\text{H}\text{—} \overset{..}{\underset{..}{\text{O}}} \text{—} \overset{\times\times}{\underset{\times\times}{\text{Cl}}} \overset{\times}{}$$

Structure of Ethyne (C_2H_2)

Sometimes after you have distributed the extra electrons you will notice that you are short of the stable octet configurations:

$$H—C—C—H$$
Number of valence electrons: $1 + 4 + 4 + 1 = 10$

Subtracting for the 6 already used in the three bonds leaves only 4 remaining electrons. When one pair is assigned to each carbon, they are still short two electrons. To overcome this problem you can assign each of those pairs as a covalent bond between the two carbons. Each pair of shared electrons is a covalent bond. This molecule has a three covalent bonds or a triple covalent bond:

$$H—C{\equiv}C—H$$

When two electrons are shared between two atoms, the bond is called a sigma bond. Additional pairs of electrons between adjacent atoms are called pi (π) bonds. The triple bond of the ethyne molecule consists of a sigma bond and two pi bonds. The presence of a double or triple bond is significant because although atoms attached by single bonds are free to rotate (often producing symmetrical nonpolar molecules), atoms bonded by double or triple bonds are not free to rotate.

Structure of Ions

To draw the structural formula of the hydroxide ion, OH^{1-}
   1. Join the two atoms with a single covalent bond:

$$O-H$$

   2. Determine the number of valence electrons, including the effect of the $1-$ charge on the ion:

$$O—H \quad charge$$
Number of valence electrons: $6 + 1 + 1 = 8$

Subtract two for the electrons shown by the dash, and distribute the remaining six (three pairs) around the oxygen.

$$\left[\; :\overset{..}{\underset{..}{O}} — H \; \right]^{1-}$$

Resonance

Although it is possible to produce some possible electron configurations for various substances, the structures do not always agree with observed fact. Consider the proposed structure of sulfur dioxide:

The model suggests that both a single and a double covalent bond exist in the molecule. However, experimental data shows both bond lengths to be the same: longer than a double bond but shorter than a single bond. There is no evidence to show that the bonds are not identical. To explain the behavior of the molecule, two structural formulas are drawn with the understanding that the true structure is somehow intermediate between a single and a double bond. This apparent shifting of bonding and existence of an intermediate bond type is called resonance. Proposed resonance forms may differ by positions of electrons, but not by repositioning of the various atoms. One of the most common molecules to exhibit resonance is the benzene molecule, C_6H_6.

Sample Questions

1. Which of the following represents a possible Lewis structure for a molecule of N_2O_2?

2. Which of the following terms is used to explain the bond length which is intermediate in length between a single and double covalent bond?
   (A) isomerism
   (B) resonance
   (C) sigma bonding
   (D) isotopic
   (E) pi bonding

3. Which of the following represents the bonding between the two atoms in an ethyne molecule?
   (A) 6 shared electrons with one sigma and two pi bonds
   (B) 4 shared electrons with two pi bonds
   (C) 2 shared electrons with one sigma bond
   (D) 4 shared electrons with one sigma and one pi bond
   (E) 6 shared electrons with one sigma and two pi bonds

4. Which of the following would not have a stable octet of electrons?
   (A) Li^{1+}
   (B) Ne
   (C) N^{3-}
   (D) Ca^{2+}
   (E) Cl^{1-}

HEATS OF REACTION

Table G presents values for the heats of formation of various substances. This table can be used to determine the overall heat of reaction. To do this, apply a general rule:

The heat of a reaction = the sum of the heats of formation of the products
— the sum of the heats of formation of the reactants.

Example: What is the heat of the reaction for the following equation?

$$4 NH_3 + 5O_2 \rightarrow 6 H_2O + 4 NO$$

Determine the heat of formation for reactants and products:

$$NH_3 = -46.2 \text{ kJ/mol or } -11.05 \text{ kcal/mol}$$

Note: The heat of formation of a substance in the elemental form is zero.

$$O_2 = 0 \text{kJ/mol or } 0 \text{ kcal/mol}$$
$$H_2O = -241.8 \text{ kJ/mol or } -57.8 \text{ kcal/mol}$$
$$NO = +90.4 \text{ kJ/mol or } +21.6 \text{ kcal/mol}$$

The values given are for one mole of each substance. To determine the total, remember that coefficients represent mole ratios. To determine the totals, multiply each value by the coefficient of that substance.

$$\text{Reactants: } 4 NH_3 + 5 O_2$$

$$4(-46.2 \text{kJ/mol}) + 5(O) = -184.8 \text{ kJ/mol}$$

Products: $6 H_2O + 4 NO$
$$6(-241.8 \text{ kJ/mol}) + 4(90.4 \text{kJ/mol})$$
$$= -1450.8 \text{ kJ/mol} + 361.6 \text{ kJ/mol}$$
$$= -1089.2 \text{ kJ/mol}$$
$$\text{reactants} - \text{products} = \text{heat of reaction}$$
$$-184.8 \text{ kJ/mol} - (-1089.2 \text{ kJ/mol}) = -1274 \text{ kJ/mol}$$

To convert the answer to kcal divide by 4.18 kcal/kJ to get -304.8 kcal.

Calculating Heats of Reaction Using Individual Bond Strengths

Whenever a reaction occurs, the bonds present in the reactants must be broken and reformed into the bonds of the products.

By examining the reaction, these bond changes can be detailed:

$$2 H_2 + O_2 \rightarrow 2 H_2O$$

In this reaction the bonds holding the oxygen and hydrogen molecules must be broken, a process which is endothermic:

$$2 H_2 + \text{energy} \rightarrow 4H$$
$$O_2 + \text{energy} \rightarrow 2O$$

After the bonds of the reactants are broken, the hydrogen to oxygen bonds of the products must be formed, a process which is exothermic:

$$4 H + 2 O \rightarrow 2 H_2O + \text{energy}$$

The bond energies for these bonds are:
H—H 104.2 kcal/mol
O=O 119.0 kcal/mol
H—O 110.9 kcal/mol

There are two moles of H—H to be broken:

2 moles $H_2 \times 104.2$ kcal/mole = +208.4 kcal

There is one mole of $O = O$ to be broken:

$$1 \text{ mole of } O_2 \times 119.0 \text{ kcal/mole} = + 119.0 \text{ kcal}$$
$$\text{Total: } + 327.4 \text{ kcal}$$

When water is formed each mole of water contains two moles of $H - O$ bonds, for a total of 4 moles of $H - O$ bonds:

$$4 \text{ moles of } H - O \times 110.9 \text{ kcal/mole} = -443.6 \text{ kcal}$$

Adding the heat absorbed ($+327.6$ kcal) and the heat released (-444.6 kcal), the net exchange is -116.2 kcal/2 moles of H_2O or 58.1 kcal/mole H_2O.

The entire process can be simplified by simply placing the bond values below the respective formulas and multiplying by the coefficients of each substance.

Problem: What is the heat of formation of HCl?

$$H_2 + Cl_2 \rightarrow 2 \text{ HCl}$$

The respective bond energies are:

H-H 104.3 kcal/mol
Cl-Cl 58.4 kcal/mol
H-Cl 103.1 kcal/mol

The heat of reaction is equal to the sum of the bond energies:

$$H_2 + Cl_2 \rightarrow 2 \text{ HCl}$$

$$\Delta H = +104.3 \text{ kcal} + 58.4 \text{ kcal} + 2(-103.1 \text{ kcal})$$
$$\Delta H = +104.3 \text{ kcal} + 58.4 \text{ kcal} - 206.2 \text{ kcal}$$
$$= +162.7 \text{ kcal} - 206.2 \text{ kcal}$$
$$= -43.5 \text{ kcal} / 2 \text{ mole HCl}$$
$$= -21.8 \text{ kcal/mole HCl}$$

Sample Questions

1. Which of the following best represents the correct method of indicating the calories exchanged when one mole of ethyne (acetylene) reacts according to the following equation:
$$C_2H_2 + 5/2 \ O_2 \longrightarrow 2 \ CO_2 + H_2O$$
H_f^0 in kcal/mole: $C_2H_2 = +54.2$; $CO_2 = -94.1$; $H_2O = -57.8$
   (A) Add 97.6 kcal to the left side of the equation.
   (B) Add 97.6 kcal to the right side of the equation.
   (C) Add 191.8 kcal to the right side of the equation.
   (D) Add 191.8 kcal to the left side of the equation.
   (E) Add 246 kcal to the right side of the equation.

2. What is the ΔH_r for the decomposition of $KClO_3$ according to the following:
$$2 \ KClO_3 \longrightarrow 2KCl + 3 \ O_2$$
H_f^0: $KClO_3 = -93.4$ kcal; $KCl = -104$ kcal
   (A) $+8.6$ kcal
   (B) -8.6 kcal
   (C) $+17.2$ kcal
   (D) -17.2 kcal
   (E) -186.8 kcal

3. Estimate the heat of reaction for the following equation.
$$2 \ H_2S + 3 \ O_2 \longrightarrow 2H_2O + 2 \ SO_2$$
Bond energies: $H - S = -80.9$ kcal/mole
$O = O = -118.9$ kcal/mole

$$H - O = -110.7 \text{ kcal/mole}$$
$$S - O = -118.9 \text{ kcal/mole}$$

(A) $\Delta H = +429.5$ kcal/mole
(B) $\Delta H = -429.5$ kcal/mole
(C) $\Delta H = -918.4$ kcal/mole
(D) $\Delta H = -238.1$ kcal/mole
(E) $\Delta H = +238.1$ kcal/mole

TRIPLE POINT OF WATER

The phase diagram shown on page 7 shows the changes in temperature with the passage of time as heat is being added to a sample of water. Figure 2 is also a phase diagram, but it shows the combined effects of pressure and temperature on the physical state of water. The solid lines divide the diagram into three areas. Any combination of temperature and pressure that produces a plotted point in Section A will result in solid water (ice) being produced. Any combination falling in Section B is a liquid, while Section C represents the gaseous phase.

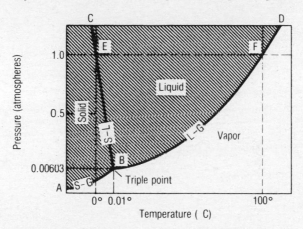

Figure 2. Phase diagram for water (line E–B distorted for emphasis).

The lines themselves represent conditions in which the phases on each side of the line are in equilibrium with each other. Thus the S–L line represents those conditions at which the solid and liquid phases may coexist. For example, when the atmospheric pressure is 1 atm and the temperature is 0°C, both solid and liquid water may exist. This is the condition we recognize as the melting temperature of ice and freezing point of water. The L–G line represents the conditions under which the liquid and gaseous phases may be in equilibrium. The point corresponds to the normal boiling point of water, 100°C. Notice that as the pressure is increased, the boiling point increases, and that reducing pressure reduces the boiling point. The S–G line represents the conditions that allow an equilibrium between the solid and gas phases. Under these conditions ice will pass directly into the gas phase without passing through the liquid phase.

The three lines all meet at a single point, known as the triple point. This point represents the conditions under which all three phases are in equilibrium, 0.00603 atm and 0.01°C.

Inspection of the S–L line for water shows that as pressure increases, the melting point decreases. This behavior is unusual and is related to the density of the liquid and solid phases. Increased pressure favors the formation of the more dense phase (liquid).

LABORATORY SETUPS

Approximately 7% of the chemistry achievement test is devoted to questions relating to the laboratory portion of your chemistry experience. Because laboratory programs vary from school to school, you should not expect to be familiar with every laboratory question on the achievement exam. In this section some typical laboratory setups are presented along with common applications. In addition, tables of tests used to identify common substances are presented.

Preparation of Oxygen, Hydrogen, and Carbon Dioxide

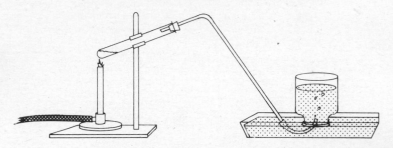

Figure 3. Preparation of oxygen.

Oxygen is typically prepared in the laboratory by heating a mixture of potassium chlorate ($KClO_3$) with a catalyst (MnO_2), as shown in Figure 3. The decomposition equation for the reaction is:

$$2KClO_3(s) \longrightarrow 2\ KCl(s)\ +\ 3\ O_2(g)$$

The oxygen produced by the reaction is first allowed to escape, purging any air that was originally in the test tube. The delivery tube is then placed into inverted collection bottles full of water. The gas displaces the water and pure oxygen is collected in the bottles.

A gas collected in this manner must be only slightly soluble in water. Other gases that are slightly soluble in water, such as carbon dioxide and hydrogen, are also collected by the downward displacement of water, but are generated in a different fashion. A thistle tube is used so that liquid reagents can easily be added.

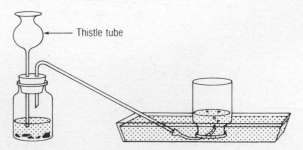

Thistle tube

Figure 4. Preparation of hydrogen and carbon dioxide.

Typical preparation of hydrogen gas:

$$Zn(s)\ +\ HCl(aq)\ \longrightarrow\ ZnCl_2(aq)\ +\ H_2(g)$$

Typical preparation of carbon dioxide:

$$CaCO_3(s) + 2\ HCl(aq) \longrightarrow CaCl_2(aq) + H_2O(l) + CO_2(g)$$

Preparation of Hydrogen Chloride and Chlorine

When a gas is collected that is either soluble in water or reacts with the water it is collected by the displacement of air. Both hydrogen chloride and chlorine are collected in this manner, as shown in Figure 5.

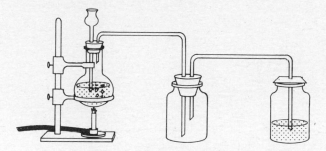

Figure 5. Preparation of hydrogen chloride and chlorine.

Preparation of hydrogen chloride:

$$NaCl + H_2SO_4 \longrightarrow HCl + NaHSO_4$$

Preparation of chlorine gas:

$$MnO_2(s) + 4\ HCl(aq) \longrightarrow MnCl_2(aq) + H_2O(l) + Cl_2(g)$$

Preparation of Ammonia

Ammonia is a gas produced from solid reactants, so a test tube generator is used in a manner similar to the oxygen generation. The ammonia gas is extremely soluble in water and is less dense than air. Thus it is collected by the downward displacement of air, as shown in Figure 6.

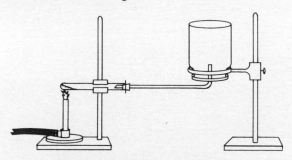

Figure 6. Preparation of ammonia.

Preparation of Bromine and Nitric Acid

Substances such as bromine and nitric acid are active oxidizing agents. It would not be possible to prepare them and have them come into contact with cork or rubber stoppers in a traditional distillation apparatus. Instead a retort is used, so that the nitric acid or bromine only contact glass surfaces.

Preparation of bromine:

$$2\,NaBr + 2\,H_2SO_4 + MnO_2 \longrightarrow Na_2SO_4 + MnSO_4 + 2\,H_2O + Br_2(g)$$

Preparation of nitric acid:

$$NaNO_3 + H_2SO_4 \longrightarrow NaHSO_4 + HNO_3(g)$$

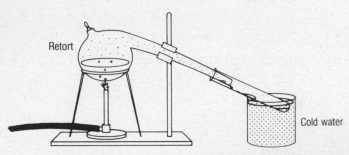

Figure 7. Preparation of bromine and nitric acid.

Distillation

Distillation is a process used to purify and separate mixtures of liquids having different boiling points. The process of distillation can also be used to purify water by separating the pure water from dissolved minerals. Figure 8 shows a typical distillation apparatus. The mixture or impure water is heated in the flask. The substance with the lowest boiling point evaporates first, and the gaseous product enters the condensing tube. The condenser is a tube within a tube. The outer jacket contains running cool water, which lowers the temperature in the inner tube to below the boiling point of the vapor. The vapor from the distilling flask then condenses, passing into a collection container. The material that has undergone evaporation and condensation is called the distillate. When water is distilled, the minerals and other substances with higher boiling points than the water remain behind in the distilling flask.

When liquids with similar boiling points are distilled, they can be separated into groups or fractions of compounds. This process, called fractional distillation, is used to separate crude oil into its useful components (page 153).

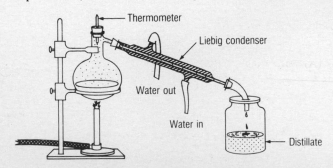

Figure 8. Distillation apparatus.

Sample Questions

1. Gases prepared in the laboratory can be collected either by the displacement of water or air. Which physical property determines which method is selected?
   (A) density
   (B) boiling point
   (C) solubility
   (D) odor
   (C) temperature
2. When a distillation is performed, the volatile product condenses in a
   (A) distillation flask
   (B) buret
   (C) eudiometer
   (D) Liebeg condenser
   (E) Erlenmeyer flask
3. Which of the following would be collected by the downward displacement of air?
   (A) carbon dioxide
   (B) oxygen
   (C) hydrogen chloride
   (D) sulfur dioxide
   (E) ammonia
4. In the laboratory preparation of chlorine, manganese dioxide acts as
   (A) an oxidizing agent
   (B) a reducing agent
   (C) a catalyst
   (D) a Bronsted acid
   (E) a Bronsted base
5. Sulfuric acid is used in the laboratory preparation of other acids because it
   (A) is highly ionized
   (B) is an oxidizing agent
   (C) has a high boiling point
   (D) is inexpensive
   (E) is a catalyst

PRACTICE TEST 1 FOR THE COLLEGE BOARD CHEMISTRY ACHIEVEMENT TEST

SECTION 1

Directions: For each of questions 1–7, select the best answer.

1. Which of the following is formed when any monoprotic acid dissolves in water?
   (A) H_3O^{1+} only
   (B) H_3O and an anion
   (C) H_3O and Cl^{1-}
   (D) H_3O^{1+} and Cl^{1-}
   (E) H_3O^{1+} and an anion
2. In any given family of the periodic table, compared to the member in period 2, the member in period 5 will have
   (A) a larger radius and less metallic properties
   (B) a larger radius and more metallic properties
   (C) a smaller radius and less metallic properties
   (D) a smaller radius and more metallic properties
   (E) an equal radius and identical chemical properties

3. When atoms with electronegativity differences of greater than 1.7 bond, the bond formed is predominately
   (A) nonpolar covalent
   (B) polar covalent
   (C) ionic
   (D) coordinate covalent
   (E) metallic

4. Which of the following is an example of an oxidation reaction?
   (A) $Fe + 2e^- \rightarrow Fe^{2+}$
   (B) $Fe + 2e^- \rightarrow Fe^{2-}$
   (C) $Fe^{2+} + SO_4^{-2} \rightarrow FeSO_4$
   (D) $Fe - 2e^- \rightarrow Fe^{2+}$
   (E) $Fe - 2e^- \rightarrow Fe^{2-}$

5. Which of the following would probably be most soluble in H_2O?
   (A) H_2
   (B) CCl_4
   (C) CsF
   (D) C_8H_{16}
   (E) SiO_2

6. The process of making ammonia from its elements is an example of
   (A) an analysis reaction
   (B) a double replacement reaction
   (C) a decomposition reaction
   (D) an oxidation reduction reaction
   (E) a single replacement reaction

7. When an atom gains an electron, the resulting particle
   (A) has a positive charge
   (B) is an anion
   (C) is repelled by cations
   (D) has its atomic number increased by one
   (E) is an isotope

SECTION 2

Directions: For each of questions 8–17, *one or more* of the answers given is correct. First decide which of the answer(s) is correct. Then select your response:

(A) if 1, 2, and 3 are correct;
(B) if only 1 and 2 are correct;
(C) if only 2 and 3 are correct;
(D) if only 1 is correct;
(E) if only 3 is correct.

DIRECTIONS SUMMARIZED				
A	B	C	D	E
1, 2, & 3	1, 2	2, 3	1	3
	only	only	only	only

8. In a reaction in which heat is produced, the products
   (1) have less potential energy than the reactants
   (2) have a heat of formation with a negative value
   (3) have less entropy than the reactants

9. Which of the following will produce an aqueous solution with a pH greater than 7?
   (1) $NaCl$
   (2) Na_2SO_4
   (3) Na_2CO_3

10. When heat is added to a solid at its melting point
    (1) the temperature increases

(2) the potential energy of the substance increases
(3) the kinetic energy remains the same

11. When a gas is dissolved in water
    (1) the entropy decreases
    (2) the enthalpy decreases
    (3) there is an increase in both entropy and enthalpy

12. When a radioactive nucleus emits a beta negative particle
    (1) the number of neutrons increases
    (2) the number of protons increases
    (3) the mass remains the same

13. In any given family of the periodic table, as you move from top to bottom the
    (1) radius of the atoms increases
    (2) metallic properties increase
    (3) electronegativity decreases

14. As the pressure is increased on a sample of a gas with the temperature remaining constant the
    (1) kinetic energy increases
    (2) concentration of the gas increases
    (3) volume decreases

15. Given the equilibrium system:
$$N_2 + 3H_2 \longleftrightarrow 2NH_3 + heat$$
    Which of the following will cause an increase in the rate of the forward reaction?
    (1) increasing the pressure
    (2) increasing the temperature
    (3) removing some ammonia

16. Each of the halogen atoms possess
    (1) 7 valence electrons
    (2) one partially filled valence orbital
    (3) 5 p electrons at the valence level

17. A reaction which is endothermic and results in a decrease in entropy
    (1) has a negative delta H value
    (2) has a positive delta G value
    (3) has a negative delta S value

SECTION 3

18. Which of the following has the lowest melting point?
    (A) sodium
    (B) oxygen
    (C) carbon
    (D) mercury
    (E) iodine

19. Given a pound of Na_2CO_3 and a pound of K_2CO_3. Compared to the pound of Na_2CO_3, the pound of K_2CO_3 will contain
    (A) more potassium ions and fewer carbonate ions
    (B) more potassium ions and more carbonate ions
    (C) fewer potassium ions and fewer carbonate ions
    (D) fewer potassium ions and more carbonate ions
    (E) more potassium ions, but equal carbonate ions

20. Chemical equilibrium is attained when
    (A) the reactants are totally consumed
    (B) the endothermic reaction is favored
    (C) all of the reactions cease
    (D) the system is closed and at STP
    (E) the free energy is equal to O

21. The number of neutrons present in the nucleus of $_AX^Z$ is equal to
    (A) A
    (B) Z

(C) X
(D) Z – A
(E) X + A

22. In any given family of the periodic table, the element with the smallest atomic radius
    (A) will have the greatest atomic mass
    (B) is located at the top of the family
    (C) is the most metallic
    (D) will have 1 valence electron
    (E) will have the fewest valence electrons

23. Which family of elements would have electrons with a valence configuration of s^2p^4?
    (A) Col 2(IIA)
    (B) Col 14(IVA)
    (C) Col 15(VA)
    (D) Col 17(VIIA)

24. Which of the following would always increase the yield of a product in an equilibrium system?
    (A) raise the temperature
    (B) remove some of the product as it is formed
    (C) lower the pressure
    (D) add a catalyst
    (E) lower the concentration of the reactants

25. Element X forms oxides of the type X_2O. Which of the following would be a correct formula?
    (A) XH_2
    (B) XCl
    (C) XS
    (D) X_2PO_4
    (E) XF_2

26. Which of the following would be the most reactive member of the alkaline family?
    (A) Cs
    (B) Li
    (C) Mg
    (D) Ra
    (E) Fr

27. Which type of bonding orbital would be used by silicon in the compound SiH_4?
    (A) s
    (B) sp
    (C) sp^2
    (D) sp^3
    (E) sp^4

28. Which of the following molecules would most likely have the lowest boiling point?
    (A) fluorine
    (B) chlorine
    (C) bromine
    (D) iodine
    (E) astatine

29. Which of the following will insure that a reaction occurs spontaneously?
    (A) if it proceeds toward minimum enthalpy and minimum entropy
    (B) if it proceeds toward minimum enthalpy and maximum entropy
    (C) if it proceeds toward maximum enthalpy and maximum entropy
    (D) if it proceeds toward maximum enthalpy and minimum entropy
    (E) if it is an exothermic reaction with a negative ΔH value

30. Given the equilibrium system:

$$N_2 + 3H_2 \longleftrightarrow 2NH_3 + heat$$

If the temperature is raised, which of the following would be true?
(A) The value of the equilibrium constant would increase.
(B) The value of the equilibrium constant would decrease.
(C) The value of the equilibrium constant would remain the same.
(D) The exothermic reaction would be favored.

31. The members of the alkali family will readily combine with members of the
(A) noble gases
(B) halogen family
(C) alkaline family
(D) transition series
(E) transuranic elements

SECTION 4

Quantitative Relationships

32. The number of atoms in 44g of carbon dioxide is
(A) $3/44 \times 10^{23}$
(B) 6×10^{23}
(C) 12×10^{23}
(D) 18×10^{23}
(E) 44×10^{23}

33. The ratio of the mass of carbon to hydrogen in the CH_4 molecule is
(A) sometimes 1:4
(B) always 1:4
(C) sometimes 3:1
(D) always 3:1
(E) always 4:3

34. The mass of 11.2 L of oxygen gas at standard conditions would be closest to
(A) 4 g
(B) 8 g
(C) 16 g
(D) 22.4 g
(E) 32 g

35. Which of the following is true if 90 g of water are cooled from 75°C to 25°C?
(A) 4500 calories are absorbed by the water
(B) 4500 calories are released by the water
(C) the potential energy of the water increases
(D) the mass of the water decreases
(E) the water undergoes a phase change

36. 4 liters of a gas have a concentration of 0.5 moles/L. If the pressure is doubled which of the following would be true?
(A) The volume would be 2 liters and the concentration would be 1 mole/L.
(B) The volume would be 2 liters and the concentration would be 0.5 mole/L.
(C) The volume would be 4 liters and the concentration would be 1.0 mole/L.
(D) The volume would be 8 liters and the concentration would be 0.25 mole/L.
(E) The volume would be 8 liters and the concentration would be 0.5 mole/L.

37. The reaction for burning carbon is:
$$C + O_2 \longrightarrow CO_2 + 94.2 \text{ kcal}$$
The number of calories released when 6.0 g of carbon are burned is
(A) $94.2/6.0 \times 10^3$ cal.
(B) 12.0×10^3 cal.
(C) 47.1×10^3 cal.

(D)   94.2 × 10³ cal.
(E)   6(94.2 × 10³) cal

38. Given the reaction:
$$CH_4(g) + 2\ O_2(g) \longrightarrow CO_2(g) + 2H_2O(l) \qquad \Delta H = -212.9\ kcal$$
When one mole of oxygen reacts with methane
(A)   106.5 kcal of heat energy is released
(B)   106.5 kcal of heat energy is absorbed
(C)   212.9 kcal of heat energy is released
(D)   212.9 kcal of heat energy is absorbed
(E)   2(212.9) kcal of heat energy is absorbed

39. Given the equation:
$$2Cu(s) + O_2 \longrightarrow 2CuO + 74.26\ kcal$$
The heat of formation of CuO is equal to
(A)   −37.13 kcal
(B)   +37.13 kcal
(C)   −74.26 kcal
(D)   +74.26 kcal
(E)   −128.5 kcal

40. How many atoms are present in the compound $Al_2(SO_4)_3$?
(A)   3
(B)   9
(C)   10
(D)   14
(E)   17

41. What is the atomic mass of an atom of praseodymium that contains 59 protons, 82 neutrons and 59 electrons?
(A)   59
(B)   82
(C)   118
(D)   141
(E)   200

42. What volume would 1.5 moles of helium occupy at STP?
(A)   5.6 L
(B)   11.2 L
(C)   22.4 L
(D)   33.2 L
(E)   44.8 L

43. A pH of 5, compared to a pH of 8
(A)   contains more OH^{1-} ions
(B)   is more basic
(C)   contains an equal concentration of OH^{1-}
(D)   is less acidic
(E)   contains 1,000 times as many H_3O^{1+} ions

44. If the density of an unknown gas was determined to be 1.54 g/L at STP, the molecular mass of the gas would be
(A)   1.54 amu
(B)   3.08 amu
(C)   34.5 amu
(D)   22.4 amu
(E)   44.8 amu

45. The freezing point depression for water is −1.86°C. What is the freezing point of a solution containing 1.00 mole of ethanol dissolved in 500 mL of water?
(A)   −0.93°C
(B)   +0.93°C
(C)   −1.86°C
(D)   −3.72°C
(E)   +3.72°C

46. If the empirical formula of a substance is CH_2 and its molecular mass is 42 amu, then its molecular formula is
(A) CH_2
(B) C_2H_4

(C) C_3H_6
(D) C_6H_3
(E) C_3H_2

SECTION 5

Directions (questions 47–51): First balance the equations given below using integers only and reduce to lowest integer ratios. Then select the correct coefficient for the substance underlined by selecting from the lettered answers.

Letter	Coefficient
A	1
B	2
C	3
D	4
E	5

47. $\underline{H_2} + Fe_2O_3 \longrightarrow Fe + H_2O$

48. $Al_4C_3 + H_2O \longrightarrow Al(OH)_3 + \underline{CH_4}$

49. $Mn_3Ga_2S_6 \longrightarrow MnS + \underline{Ga_2S} + S_2$

50. $C_8H_8 + O_2 \longrightarrow CO_2 + \underline{H_2O}$

SECTION 6

Questions 52–66: For each of the following questions there is a statement followed by a reason. Select

(A) if both statement and reason are true and the reason explains the statement.
(B) if both statement and reason are true, but the reason does not explain the statement.
(C) if the statement is true, but the reason is false.
(D) if the statement is false, but the reason is true.
(E) if both the statement and the reason are false.

	STATEMENT	REASON
52.	Glacial (conc.) acetic acid is not a good conductor of electricity.	Because it is more highly ionized in dilute solutions.
53.	A 1 molal solution of NaCl depresses the freezing point twice as much as a 1 molal C_2H_5OH solution.	A 1 molal solution of NaCl has twice as many particles as a 1 molal solution of C_2H_5OH.
54.	Sodium metal is stored under water.	Because sodium is a reactive metal.
55.	Sodium carbonate produces a solution with a pH of less than 7.	Because it hydrolyzes to form a strong base and a weak acid.
56.	The reaction between sodium chloride and silver nitrate goes to completion.	Because a precipitate is formed.
57.	Molecular solids generally have high melting points.	Because molecules are held together by ionic bonds
58.	Organic compounds are generally nonelectrolytes.	Because they contain covalent bonds and do not ionize.
59.	Fluorine has only a negative oxidation state.	Because it is the most electronegative element.
60.	Catalysts change the rates of reactions.	Because they change the heats of reaction.

61. Metallic atoms generally react to become negative ions.   Because they generally gain electrons when they react.

62. Many transition elements have more than one oxidation state.   Because they use both s and d electrons in reactions.

63. The atomic radius generally increases from left to right in a given period of the periodic table.   Because the nuclear charge decreases.

64. Some reactions with a negative delta H value are not spontaneous.   Because the T delta S value may be more negative.

65. At equilibrium, the concentration of reactants and products are equal.   Because the forward and reverse reaction are taking place at the same rate.

66. A true solution does not disperse light.   Because the solute particles settle out on standing.

SECTION 7

Base your answers to questions 67 through 71 on the solubility chart showing the grams of solute/100 g of H₂O.

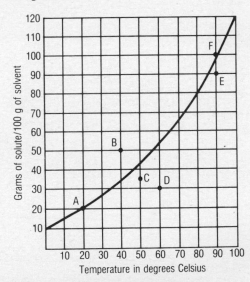

67. How could the solution at point C be made saturated?
    (A) The temperature could be raised 5°C.
    (B) The solution could be cooled 10°C.
    (C) 5 g of solvent could be added.
    (D) 10 g of solute could be added and the temperature raised.
    (E) It could be mixed with the solution described at point A.

68. If a crystal is added to the solution at point B
    (A) The solution will become supersaturated.
    (B) Some solute will precipitate and the solution will become more concentrated.
    (C) The crystal will dissolve and the solution will be supersaturated.
    (D) 50 g of solute will precipitate and the solution will become unsaturated.
    (E) 15 g of solute will precipitate and the solution will become saturated.

69. If the solution at point D is heated to 90°C, how many additional grams of solute must be added to produce a saturated solution?
    (A) 10 g
    (B) 20 g
    (C) 70 g
    (D) 90 g
    (E) 100 g
70. If 50 mL of the solvent in the solution at point A was evaporated
    (A) the solution would be unsaturated
    (B) the solution would be saturated
    (C) approximately 10 g of solute would precipitate
    (D) approximately 20 g of solute would precipitate
    (E) the solution would become more dilute
71. If the solution at point E were allowed to cool to 50°C,
    (A) the solution would become unsaturated
    (B) the solution must become supersaturated
    (C) the addition of 10 g of solute would saturate the solution
    (D) approximately 45 g of solute would precipitate
    (E) 90 g of solute would precipitate
72. An alkali metal is reacted with water and a splint is placed into the resulting gas. Which of the following is correct?
    (A) The gas is oxygen and the splint burns brightly.
    (B) The gas is hydrogen and it supports combustion.
    (C) The gas is hydrogen and it burns.
    (D) The gas is oxygen and it burns.
    (E) The splint is extinguished and gas does not react.
73. Equal volumes of hydrogen and oxygen gases are ignited in an eudiometer. After the reaction, some gas remains.
    (A) The gas is a mixture of hydrogen and oxygen.
    (B) Only oxygen is found in the eudiometer.
    (C) Only hydrogen is found in the eudiometer.
    (D) Hydrogen and water vapor are in the eudiometer.
    (E) Oxygen and water vapor are in the eudiometer.
74. A white crystalline solid is tested and found to be a conductor of electricity both in aqueous solution and when fused, but is not a conductor as a solid. This substance could be
    (A) C_2H_5OH
    (B) KCl
    (C) $K_2Cr_2O_7$
    (D) CH_3COOH
    (E) SiO_2

SECTION 8

75. A sample contains two trapped gases, A and B, which are present in equal concentrations. The gases begin to escape through a tiny opening. After some time the gases are again analyzed and found to contain more of gas A than gas B.
    (A) Gas B must be condensing in the container.
    (B) Gas A must be an inert (noble) gas and does not escape.
    (C) Gas B must be more reactive than gas A.
    (D) Gas A must be lighter than gas B.
    (E) Gas B must be lighter than gas A.
76. A cylinder is massed empty and found to have a mass of 31.23 g. 9.0 mL of a liquid are added and the new mass is determined to be 44.78 g. The density of the liquid is
    (A) 0.66 g/mL
    (B) 1.50 g/mL
    (C) 3.47 g/mL
    (D) 4.98 g/mL
    (E) 13.55 g/mL

77. A flask contains 2.00 grams of methane at STP. When this flask is refilled with an unknown gas, the mass of the gas is found to be 3.00 grams. What is the molecular mass of the unknown gas?
    (A) 3.00 amu
    (B) 6.00 amu
    (C) 16.0 amu
    (D) 24.0 amu
    (E) 32.0 amu

78. Although HCl is a gas it is not collected by the displacement of water because it
    (A) is highly soluble in water
    (B) reacts with water to produce hydrogen gas
    (C) reacts with water to produce chlorine gas
    (D) is more dense than air
    (E) is highly flammable

79. Which of the following is used in the determination of the concentration of an acid by titration?
    (A) retort
    (B) condenser
    (C) crucible
    (D) drying oven
    (E) buret

80. In the laboratory preparation of nitric acid, a retort is used to heat the reactants. Why couldn't a normal distillation flask with a rubber stopper be used?
    (A) Nitric acid is a dehydrating agent.
    (B) Nitric acid is a strong acid.
    (C) The temperature of the reaction would melt the stopper.
    (D) Because the salt produced would corrode the stopper.
    (E) The nitric acid fumes will react with the stopper.

81. A sample is determined to contain a solid and two or more liquids. Which procedures would be used to separate these components?
    (A) filtration and distillation
    (B) titration and crystallization
    (C) crystallization followed by filtration
    (D) fractional distillation followed by crystallization
    (E) crystallization followed by titration

82. Which of the following procedures should be used to show that a solution is basic?
    (A) Add phenolphthalein; if the solution is basic it will turn colorless.
    (B) Place a strip of blue litmus into the solution; if it remains blue, the solution is basic.
    (C) Place a strip of blue litmus into the solution; if it turns red, the solution is basic.
    (D) Add colorless phenolphthalein; if it turns pink, the solution is basic.
    (E) Add red litmus; if it remains red, the solution is basic.

83. A mixture of carbon dioxide, water vapor, and oxygen is cooled until all three of the substances condense. What is the correct order in which they will condense?
    (A) water vapor, carbon dioxide, oxygen
    (B) water vapor, oxygen, carbon dioxide
    (C) carbon dioxide, water vapor, oxygen
    (D) carbon dioxide, oxygen, water vapor
    (E) oxygen, carbon dioxide, water vapor

84. When substances are heated to high temperatures they emit colors useful in their identification. An instrument used in this type of analysis is the
    (A) colorimeter
    (B) Geiger counter
    (C) calorimeter
    (D) spintharoscope
    (E) spectroscope

85. A student adds zinc to HCl in the laboratory setup shown, but fails to collect any hydrogen. Which of the following might explain the failure?
    (A) Hydrogen is soluble in water.
    (B) Zinc is not an active metal and will not react.
    (C) Considerable heat must be added to achieve results.
    (D) The thistle tube is above the acid level.
    (E) The student may have forgotten the MnO_2 catalyst.

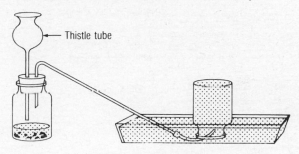

Thistle tube

86. A gas was determined to be lighter than air, soluble in water. When litmus was placed into its aqueous solution it turned blue. The gas may have been
    (A) oxygen
    (B) methane
    (C) hydrogen
    (D) hydrogen chloride
    (E) ammonia
87. When a substance is distilled, the product collected by condensation is called the
    (A) distillate
    (B) precipitate
    (C) solvent
    (D) solute
    (E) reagent
88. In a laboratory notebook which of the following should be included?
    (A) A description of the physical changes that took place during an experiment.
    (B) A description of the chemical changes that took place during an experiment.
    (C) A description of the physical and chemical changes that took place during an experiment.
    (D) A description of only those observations that seemed important at the time.
    (E) A description that includes only data read from instruments.

PRACTICE TEST 2 FOR THE COLLEGE BOARD CHEMISTRY ACHIEVEMENT TEST

SECTION 1

1. With which of the following elements will hydrogen form an ionic bond?
    (A) sulfur
    (B) oxygen
    (C) magnesium
    (D) carbon
    (E) nitrogen

2. When the halogen family is considered, from fluorine to iodine, which of the following is true?
    (A) The atomic radius increases and metallic properties increase
    (B) The atomic radius increases and metallic properties decrease
    (C) The atomic radius increases and the electronegativity increases
    (D) The atomic radius decreases and the metallic properties increase
    (E) The atomic radius decreases and the metallic properties decrease
3. An aqueous solution of HNO_3
    (A) contains more nitrate ions than hydrogen ions
    (B) does not contain any hydroxide ions
    (C) contains an equal number of hydrogen and hydroxide ions
    (D) must be more acidic than a solution of HNO_2
    (E) contains more hydrogen than hydroxide ions
4. If a neutron is absorbed by an atom
    (A) its atomic number increases by 1
    (B) it will then emit a beta negative particle
    (C) its mass will increase by 1
    (D) it will become a radioisotope
    (E) it will undergo fission
5. The alkane, alkene, alkyne and benzene families are similar in that they each
    (A) contain both single and double covalent bonds
    (B) are homologous families with $-CH_2$ as the incremental change
    (C) have the same general formula
    (D) produce ions in aqueous solution
    (E) undergo addition reactions
6. The dispersion of light by a colloid is called the
    (A) Tyndal effect
    (B) Haber effect
    (C) excited state
    (D) moderating effect
    (E) van der Waals effect
7. Which of the following is an amphoteric substance?
    (A) $C_6H_{12}O_6$
    (B) HCl
    (C) $NaCl$
    (D) CH_3COOH
    (E) $Zn(OH)_2$
8. The isotope of hydrogen called tritium contains
    (A) three protons
    (B) one proton and two neutrons
    (C) one proton and three neutrons
    (D) two protons and two neutrons
    (E) two protons and three neutrons

SECTION 2

Directions: For each of the following questions, *one or more* of the answers given is correct. First decide which of the answer(s) is correct. Then select your response:

(A) if 1, 2, and 3 are correct;
(B) if only 1 and 2 are correct;
(C) if only 2 and 3 are correct;
(D) if only 1 is correct;
(E) if only 3 is correct.

DIRECTIONS SUMMARIZED				
A	B	C	D	E
1, 2, & 3	1, 2	2, 3	1	3
	only	only	only	only

9. In moving from left to right in any given period of the periodic table,
   (1) electronegativity decreases
   (2) metallic characteristics decrease
   (3) the radius decreases
10. Which of the following aqueous solutions contains hydronium ions?
    (1) NaOH(aq)
    (2) HCl(aq)
    (3) H_2SO_4(aq)
11. In the formula $Al_2(SO_4)_3$ there are
    (1) 4 ions
    (2) 3 sulfate radicals
    (3) 16 atoms
12. On the periodic table
    (1) the alkali and alkaline families are adjacent
    (2) the halogen and noble (inert) gas families are adjacent
    (3) the alkali and halogen families are adjacent
13. Which of the following contains ions?
    (1) HCl(g)
    (2) HCl(l)
    (3) HCl(aq)
14. Which of the following can conduct an electric current?
    (1) NaCl(s)
    (2) NaCl(l)
    (3) NaCl(aq)
15. In the compounds NH_3, N_2O_4, and NO, nitrogen exhibits oxidation states of
    (1) -3
    (2) $+2$
    (3) $+4$
16. According to the kinetic-molecular theory, the kinetic energy of a substance
    (1) increases during fusion
    (2) decreases during condensation
    (3) increases with increasing temperature
17. Which of the following formulas represents a hydride?
    (1) MgH_2
    (2) LiH
    (3) NH_3
18. During the process of nuclear fusion
    (1) lighter nuclei combine to form heavier nuclei
    (2) energy is absorbed
    (3) each nucleon gains mass
19. Hydrocarbons
    (1) all contain only single bonds
    (2) contain only hydrogen and carbon
    (3) are all combustible

SECTION 3

20. Copper metal is deposited on the negative electrode in a solution of copper chloride. Which best explains this behavior?
    (A) The copper ions are positively charged.
    (B) The copper ions have been oxidized.
    (C) The copper ions were repelled by the chloride ions.
    (D) The copper ions donated electrons to the electrode.
    (E) Ionic substances are electrolytes in aqueous solutions.
21. In period 2 of the periodic table, the most metallic element
    (A) is gaseous at room temperature
    (B) has the greatest number of valence electrons
    (C) has the highest ionization energy
    (D) has the smallest nuclear charge
    (E) has the highest positive oxidation state

22. Hydrogen gas is produced when
    (A)   an acid neutralizes a base
    (B)   copper reacts with concentrated nitric acid
    (C)   water molecules combine with the H^{1+} ion
    (D)   HCl gas is bubbled through water
    (E)   zinc reacts with dilute HCl
23. Potassium exhibits only a +1 oxidation state in compounds because
    (A)   it is an alpha emitter
    (B)   it is a beta negative emitter
    (C)   it loses one valence electron
    (D)   it gains one valence electron
    (E)   it is a beta positive emitter
24. Which of the following can be used to illustrate the Law of Multiple Proportions?
    (A) NH_3 and NH_4^{1+}
    (B) $FeCl_2$ and Fe_2O_3
    (C) N_2O and NO
    (D) HCl and H_2SO_4
    (E) O_2 and O_3
25. Which family of elements would have electrons with a valence configuration of s^2p^4?
    (A) 2(IIA)
    (B) 14(IVA)
    (C) 15(VA)
    (D) 16(VIA)
    (E) 17(VIIA)
26. Element X forms oxides of the type X_2O_3. Which of the following would be a correct formula?
    (A) XCl_3
    (B) XH_2
    (C) XS
    (D) X_2PO_4
    (E) XF_2
27. Which of the following would produce a water solution with a pH less than 7?
    (A) Na_2CO_3
    (B) $NaOH$
    (C) $NaCl$
    (D) NH_4Cl
    (E) NH_4OH
28. Which of the following types of bonds is responsible for the attraction of molecules in the liquid and solid phases?
    (A)   nonpolar covalent
    (B)   polar covalent
    (C)   ionic
    (D)   hydrogen bonding
    (E)   van der Waals forces
29. Which of the following contains both ionic and covalent bonds?
    (A) NH_4Cl
    (B) H_2O
    (C) CH_4
    (D) CH_3OH
    (E) $NaCl$
30. One mole of water
    (A)   occupies 22.4 L at STP
    (B)   has a mass of 6.02×10^{23} g
    (C)   contains 3 moles of atoms
    (D)   contains 6.02×10^{-23} molecules
    (E)   has a mass of 22.5 g
31. Which of the following would probably be the best electrolyte?
    (A)   solid NaCl
    (B)   an aqueous solution of C_2H_5OH

(C) an aqueous solution of HCl
(D) a tincture of iodine
(E) liquid bromine

32. In the experiment in which Rutherford bombarded gold foil with alpha particles, he showed that
(A) most of the matter was concentrated in the center
(B) alpha particles were really helium nuclei
(C) electrons were negatively charged
(D) gold was a dense element
(E) Tompson's "cannonball" model of the atom was correct

33. At higher altitudes, the atmospheric pressure
(A) decreases and boiling points decrease
(B) decreases and boiling points increase
(C) increases and boiling points increase
(D) increases and boiling points decrease
(E) decreases and boiling points remain the same

34. Which period of the periodic table contains the most electronegative element?
(A) 1
(B) 2
(C) 3
(D) 4
(E) 5

35. Which of the following elements would have the same valence electron arrangement as iodine?
(A) fluorine
(B) xenon
(C) tellurium
(D) indium
(E) cesium

36. Which of the following would most likely contain only one type of molecule?
(A) a bag of sugar
(B) a box of cake mix
(C) a bag of potato chips
(D) a pound of bacon
(E) a quart of milk

37. When a crystal is added to a solution and additional crystals immediately form
(A) the original solution was unsaturated
(B) the original solution was a colloidal dispersion
(C) the original solution was saturated
(D) the original solution was at the triple point
(E) the original solution was supersaturated

38. What is the name of a salt produced by the reaction of nitrous acid and a base?
(A) a nitrate
(B) a nitrite
(C) a pernitrate
(D) a hyponitrate
(E) a hyponitrite

39. Which of the following is an empirical formula?
(A) N_2O_4
(B) H_2O_2
(C) C_6H_6
(D) C_6H_5Cl
(E) $C_6H_{12}O_6$

40. The percentage of oxygen in CH_3COOH is
(A) 26.7%
(B) 53%
(C) 33%
(D) 25%
(E) 50%

41. A compound is found to contain 36.7% potassium, 33.3% chlorine and 30.0% oxygen. The empirical formula of the compound is
    (A) $KClO$
    (B) $KClO_2$
    (C) $KClO_3$
    (D) $KClO_4$
    (E) K_2ClO_3

42. Which of the following is **not** a possible molecular mass for a compound with the formula XY_2 if X has isotopes with masses of 11, 12, and 13 and Y has isotopes with masses of 16, 17, and 18?
    (A) 48
    (B) 40
    (C) 46
    (D) 43
    (E) 47

43. The pH of a solution has been decreased from 5 to 2. The acidity of the solution has
    (A) increased by a factor of 3
    (B) decreased by a factor of 3
    (C) increased by a factor of 1,000
    (D) decreased by a factor of 1,000
    (E) increased by a factor of 30

44. How many moles of acid are required to neutralize 250. mL of 4.00 M NaOH?
    (A) 0.250
    (B) 0.500
    (C) 1.00
    (D) 2.00
    (E) 4.00

45. The number of ions produced when 1 mole of $AlCl_3$ dissolves in water is
    (A) 1
    (B) 4
    (C) 6.02×10^{23}
    (D) 12.04×10^{23}
    (E) 24.08×10^{23}

46. Given equal volumes of methane gas and oxygen gas at the same conditions. The ratio of the atoms in the methane to the oxygen will be
    (A) 1:1
    (B) 2:1
    (C) 1:2
    (D) 5:2
    (E) 2:5

47. The mass of 33.6 L of oxygen at STP is approximately
    (A) 8.0 g
    (B) 16.0 g
    (C) 32.0 g
    (D) 48.0 g
    (E) 64.0 g

48. If a gas has a density of 1.0 g/L, its molecular mass would be
    (A) 1.0 amu
    (B) 5.6 amu
    (C) 11.2 amu
    (D) 22.4 amu
    (E) 44.8 amu

49. A compound was found to have an empirical formula of CH_2. Which of the following is not a possible molecular mass of the compound?
    (A) 70 amu
    (B) 21 amu
    (C) 28 amu
    (D) 42 amu
    (E) 56 amu

50. The number of atoms represented by 3 $BaCl_2 \cdot 2H_2O$ is
    (A) 8
    (B) 9
    (C) 24
    (D) 27
    (E) 45
51. 22.4 L of nitrogen gas at STP contains the same number of atoms as
    (A) 11.2 L of CO
    (B) 22.4 L of helium at STP
    (C) 22.4 L of iron at STP
    (D) 22.4 L of CO
    (E) 33.6 L of CO_2

SECTION 4

Directions: First balance the equations given below using integers only and reduce to lowest integer ratios. Then select the correct coefficient for the substance underlined by selecting from the lettered answers:

Letter	Coefficient
A	1
B	2
C	3
D	4
E	5

52. $Cu + HNO_3 \longrightarrow Cu(NO_3)_2 + \underline{H_2O} + NO$
53. $NH_3 + \underline{O_2} \longrightarrow NO + H_2O$
54. $H_2S + \underline{SbCl_3} \longrightarrow Sb_2S_3 + HCl$
55. $KOH + \underline{Cl_2} \longrightarrow KClO_3 + KCl + H_2O$
56. $\underline{Ca_3(PO_4)_2} + H_2SO_4 \longrightarrow CaSO_4 + H_3PO_4$

SECTION 5

For each of the following questions there is a statement followed by a reason. Select:

(A) if both statement and reason are true and the reason explains the statement
(B) if both statement and reason are true, but the reason does not explain the statement
(C) if the statement is true, but the reason is false
(D) if the statement is false, but the reason is true
(E) if both the statement and reason are false

STATEMENT	REASON
57. A true solution disperses light.	Because solutions are heterogeneous.
58. A crystal added to a supersaturated solution causes precipitation of solute.	Because the crystal provides a nucleation site.
59. The kernel of a chlorine atom has a net charge of +17.	Because chlorine has 7 valence electrons.
60. Carbon-12 and carbon-14 are isotopes.	Because each atom contains 6 protons.
61. After two half-life periods, all the atoms of a radioactive element will decay.	Because during a half life, half of the given atoms decay.
62. Carbon tetrachloride molecules are nonpolar.	Because the bonds between carbon atoms and chlorine atoms are nonpolar.

63. Aqueous solutions of ionic compounds are nonelectrolytes.   Because ionic solids dissociate into molecules.
64. Xenon has a higher BP than argon.   Because van der Waals forces are directly related to the number of electrons.
65. Metals are generally good conductors of electricity.   Metals lose electrons in chemical reactions to become positive ions.
66. Fluorine is the most reactive nonmetal.   Because it forms a diatomic molecule.
67. NH_4NO_2(aq) is a good electrolyte.   Because it contains covalent bonding.

SECTION 6

68. Which of the following combinations is not possible?
    (A) A solution which is both saturated and concentrated.
    (B) A solution which is both saturated and dilute.
    (C) A solution which is supersaturated and concentrated.
    (D) A solution which is unsaturated and concentrated.
    (E) A solution which is concentrated and dilute.
69. Given the equation:
$$FeCl_3 + 3\ NaOH \longrightarrow Fe(OH)_3 + 3\ NaCl$$
    How many moles of iron III hydroxide will be produced if 40.0 grams of sodium hydroxide are reacted with excess iron III chloride?
    (A) 0.25
    (B) 0.33
    (C) 0.50
    (D) 1.00
    (E) 3.00
70. Given the reaction:
$$PbO_2 + 4HCl \longrightarrow PbCl_2 + Cl_2 + 2H_2O$$
    How many moles of chlorine gas will be produced if 2.0 moles of hydrogen chloride are reacted with 2.0 moles of lead II oxide?
    (A) 0.5
    (B) 1.0
    (C) 2.0
    (D) 3.0
    (E) 4.0
71. Identify the conjugate acid-base pair in the following equation:
$$NaBr + H_3PO_4 \longrightarrow HBr + NaH_2PO_4$$
    (A) $NaBr + H_3PO_4$
    (B) $NaBr + HBr$
    (C) $NaBr + NaH_2PO_4$
    (D) $HBr + NaH_2PO_4$
    (E) $H_3PO_4 + HBr$
72. A gas is found to be extremely soluble in water. When litmus paper is placed in the aqueous solution of this gas it turns red. The gas is probably
    (A) CO_2
    (B) O_2
    (C) NH_3
    (D) N_2
    (E) HCl
73. 30.0 mL of a 2.0 M HCl solution are required to neutralize 20.0 mL of a NaOH solution. The concentration of the NaOH solution is
    (A) 0.5 M
    (B) 1.0 M
    (C) 1.5 M
    (D) 2.0 M
    (E) 3.0 M

74. Which of the following would be used in a laboratory procedure to determine the percentage of water in a crystal?
    (A) buret
    (B) calorimeter
    (C) graduated cylinder
    (D) crucible
    (E) pipet

75. The constant dry mass of a crucible is determined to be 31.04 g. A crystal is added and the total mass is found to be 38.76 g. After heating to a constant mass the crucible and contents have a mass of 37.60 g. What is the percentage of water in the crystals?
    (A) 1.16%
    (B) 7.72%
    (C) 15.0%
    (D) 37.6%
    (E) 85.0%

76. What is the pressure due to methane if 4 moles of methane (CH_4) are mixed with 2 moles of oxygen in a container and the total pressure is found to be 720 torr?
    (A) 60 torr
    (B) 120 torr
    (C) 240 torr
    (D) 480 torr
    (E) 640 torr

77. What is the correct symbol of "X" in the following equation?
$$_{94}Pu^{239} + {_0}n^1 \longrightarrow {_{38}}Sr^{90} + X + 3{_0}n^1$$
    (A) $_{58}Ce^{147}$
    (B) $_{56}Ba^{147}$
    (C) $_{56}Ba^{148}$
    (D) $_{56}Ba^{149}$
    (E) $_{56}U^{149}$

78. When chlorine is added to a hydrocarbon a reaction occurs. Blue litmus is placed into the product and it turns red. Which of the following is probably true?
    (A) C_2H_4 was a reactant and HCl was one of the products.
    (B) C_2H_4 was a reactant and C_3H_5Cl was a product.
    (C) C_2H_4 was a reactant and $C_2H_4Cl_2$ was the only product.
    (D) C_2H_6 was a reactant and $C_2H_4Cl_2$ was the only product.
    (E) C_2H_6 was a reactant and HCl and C_2H_5Cl were products.

79. What are the products of the reaction between potassium hydroxide and a fat?
    (A) a monohydroxy alcohol and soap
    (B) a dihydroxy alcohol and salts of fatty acids
    (C) a trihydroxy alcohol and fatty acids
    (D) a trihydroxy alcohol and salts of fatty acids
    (E) an alcohol, an acid, and water

80. Identify the reducing agent in the following equation:
$$As_2O_3 + I_2 + H_2O \longrightarrow H_3AsO_4 + HI$$
    (A) As^{3+}
    (B) O^{2-}
    (C) I^0
    (D) H^{1+}
    (E) O^{1-}

81. Given the following heats of formation:
$$NH_3(g): -11.2 \text{ kcal}$$
$$NO(g): +21.8 \text{ kcal}$$
$$H_2O(g): -58.4 \text{ kcal}$$
Which of the following would be a correct equation?
    (A) $4NH_3(g) + 6NO(g) \longrightarrow 5N_2(g) + 6H_2O(g) + 264.4 \text{ kcal}$
    (B) $4NH_3(g) + 6NO(g) + 264.4 \text{ kcal} \longrightarrow 5N_2(g) + 6H_2O(g)$

(C) $4NH_3(g) + 6NO(g) + 88.6$ kcal $\longrightarrow 5N_2(g) + 6H_2O(g)$
(D) $4NH_3(g) + 6NO(g) \longrightarrow 5N_2(g) + 6H_2O(g) + 88.6$ kcal
(E) $4NH_3(g) + 6NO(g) \longrightarrow 5N_2(g) + 6H_2O(g) + 47.8$ kcal

82. Which of the following would not be appropriate units to express the concentration of a solution?
(A)   g solute/cm³ solvent
(B)   % of solute present
(C)   moles of solute/Liter of solution
(D)   moles of solute/1,000 g of solvent
(E)   g solute/cm solvent

83. Which of the following is true if the K_{eq} for an equilibrium system is equal to 4.5×10^{16}?
(A)   The products are favored.
(B)   The reaction is rapid and the products are favored.
(C)   The reactants and products are present in equal amounts at equilibrium.
(D)   The reactants are favored.
(E)   The reaction is rapid and the reactants are favored.

84. Which of the following best explains why carbon dioxide is a nonpolar molecule while carbon monoxide is polar?
(A)   Carbon dioxide has nonpolar bonds, while carbon monoxide has polar bonds.
(B)   Carbon dioxide has polar bonds, while carbon monoxide has nonpolar bonds.
(C)   Both molecules have nonpolar bonds, but carbon dioxide is an asymmetric molecule while carbon monoxide is symmetrical.
(D)   Both molecules have polar bonds, but carbon dioxide is a symmetrical molecule while carbon monoxide is asymmetrical.
(E)   Carbon dioxide has nonpolar bonds and is symmetrical, while carbon monoxide has polar bonds and is asymmetrical.

85. Which of the following hydroxides is the least soluble?
(A) $Cd(OH)_2$ $K_{sp} = 2 \times 10^{-14}$
(B) $Cu(OH)_2$ $K_{sp} = 2 \times 10^{-19}$
(C) $Fe(OH)_3$ $K_{sp} = 5 \times 10^{-38}$
(D) $Pb(OH)_2$ $K_{sp} = 4 \times 10^{-15}$
(E) $Ca(OH)_2$ $K_{sp} = 1.3 \times 10^{-6}$

86. Which is a redox reaction?
(A) $Ba^{2+} + SO_4^{2-} \longrightarrow BaSO_4$
(B) $H^{1+} + OH^{1-} \longrightarrow H_2O$
(C) $Sn^0 + Sn^{4+} \longrightarrow 2Sn^{2+}$
(D) $H^{1+} + NH_3 \longrightarrow NH_4^{1+}$
(E) $AgNO_3(aq) + NaCl(aq) \longrightarrow AgCl(s) + NaNO_3(aq)$

87. Which of the following is the correct equilibrium constant for the following system:

$$2Al(OH)_3 + 3H_2SO_4 \longrightarrow Al_2(SO_4)_3 + 6H_2O$$

(A) $K_{eq} = \dfrac{[Al_2(SO_4)_3] + [6H_2O]}{[2Al(OH)_3] + [3H_2SO_4]}$

(B) $K_{eq} = \dfrac{[Al_2(SO_4)_3] + [H_2O]^6}{[Al(OH)_3]^2 + [H_2SO_4]^3}$

(C) $K_{eq} = \dfrac{[Al_2(SO_4)_3] \, [H_2O]^6}{[Al(OH)_3]^2 \, [H_2SO_4]^3}$

(D) $K_{eq} = \dfrac{[Al(OH)_3]^2 \, [H_2SO_4]^3}{[Al_2(SO_4)_3] \, [H_2O]^6}$

(E) $K_{eq} = \dfrac{[Al(OH)_3]^2 + [H_2SO_4]^3}{[Al_2(SO_4)_3] + [H_2O]^6}$

88. What is the theoretical yield of iron metal when 8 moles of iron III oxide are reacted with 8 moles of carbon monoxide according to the following reaction?

$$Fe_3O_4 + 4\,CO \longrightarrow 4\,CO_2 + 3\,Fe$$

   (A) 2 moles
   (B) 3 moles
   (C) 4 moles
   (D) 6 moles
   (E) 8 moles

INDEX

Absolute (Kelvin) scale, 4
Absolute zero, 11–12
Acetic acid, 137
Acetone, 128, 138
Acetylene, 128
Acetylene series, *see* Alkynes
Acid base chart, 205
Acids, defined, 100–102; strength of, 106, 107–108; organic, 137; dilution of, 172–173
Actinoid series, 46
Activated complex, 80, 82
Activation energy, 3, 79, 80, 82; in organic compounds, 126
Addition polymerization, 142
Addition reactions, 139–140
Alcohols, 135–137
Aldehydes, 137, 138
Alkali metals, 51–52
Alkaline earth metals, 51–52
Alkanes, 129
Alkenes, 129
Alkynes, 130
Alloying, 150
Alpha decay, 29
Alpha particles, 150
Amines, 137
Amino acids, 137
Ammonia gas, preparation of, 231
Amphoteric (amphiprotic) substances, 102, 190–191
Angstrom unit, 48
Anode, defined, 122
Applied research, 145
Arrhenius theory, 101
Atomic (nuclear) energy, 2, 156–160
Atomic mass (atomic weight), 20, 156
Atomic mass unit (amu), 20
Atomic number, 19
Atomic radius, 46
Atoms, structure and properties of, 19–30
Avogadro's hypothesis (law), 15, 60
Avogadro's number, 16, 20, 59
Balance, using a, 168, 170
Balancing, chemical equations, 124–125, 222–223
Bases, 101–102; strength of, 106, 108

Battery, defined, 151; dry cell, 151–152; lead storage, 151; NiCad (nickel-cadmium), 151–152
Benzene, 132–133, 227
Beta decay, 29
Binding energy, 156–157
Bohr model, 21
Boiling point, 16–17; of solutions, 74
Bonds, 32–39, 224–226; triple, 52; in organic compounds, 126–127; double and triple, 127, 128
Boyle's law, 9–10
Breeder reactor, 162–163
Bromine, preparation of, 231–232
Bronsted-Lowry theory, 101–102
Butane, 129
Calorie, defined, 4
Calorimeter, 5, 179
Carbon, bonding of, 126–127; *also see* Organic chemistry
Carbon dioxide, preparation of, 230
Catalysts, 80, 82, 88, 146
Cathode, defined, 122
Cathodic protection, of metals, 150
Cells, *see* Chemical cells
Celsius scale, 4
Chains, in organic compounds, 132
Charles's law, 11–12
Chemical bonds, 32–39
Chemical cells, 118, 150; electric potential of, 120–121
Chemical change, and energy 3; *also see* Reactions
Chemical energy, 2; and electrical energy, 119
Chemical equations, *see* Equations
Chemical equilibrium, 86–96, 145
Chemical formulas, *see* Formulas
Chemical mathematics, 59–78
Chemical reactions, 79–98
Chemistry, defined, 18
Chlorine gas, preparation of, 231
Coefficients, 44, 223
Colligative properties, 74
Combined gas laws, 77
Compounds defined, 1; naming of, 42, 129; organic, 126–142
Concentration, 72; and equilibrium, 87, 145; and reaction rates, 82, 145

254

Regents

Examinations

REVIEWING FOR THE CHEMISTRY REGENTS EXAM

The following topics represent an analysis of several past Regents exams and are the 78 concepts that are asked most often. A page reference is given after each concept so that you can easily review any topic.

1. Recognition and properties of elements, compounds, and mixtures (1)
2. Ability to calculate calories. (4)
3. Understand and apply Avogadro's Hypothesis. (15)
4. Definition and examples of sublimation. (18)
5. Interpret phase change diagram & related energy changes. (6)
6. Relation between vapor pressure of a liquid and its boiling point. (16)
7. Kelvin and Celsius temperature scales, conversions, and fixed points. (3)
8. Solving of Boyle's Law problems. (9)
9. Solving Charles's law problems. (11)
10. Relation of number of protons, neutrons, and electrons in atoms and ions. (19)
11. Definition and recognition of isotopes. (19)
12. Electron dot symbols. (27)
13. Numbers of electrons, and their configurations in atoms and ions. (25)
14. Relation of principal quantum number (n), number of sublevels, and number of electrons. (23)
15. Ground and excited state atoms, meaning of spectral lines. (21)
16. Ionization energy, trends on periodic table. (27, 47)
17. Balancing and using mole ratios in equations. (43, 67)
18. Identifying bond types by using electronegativity values. (33)
19. Properties and characteristics of covalent bonding. (34)
20. Definition and examples of coordinate covalent bonding. (35)
21. Van der Waals forces. (39)
22. Properties and characteristics of ionic bonding. (33)
23. Formula writing, including the Stock system. (41)
24. Nomenclature. (42)
25. Name alkali, alkaline, halogen, and noble gas families; identify members. (51–53)
26. Identify transition elements and know properties. (57)
27. Properties of families (groups) on the periodic table. (51)
28. Properties of periods of the periodic table. (55)
29. Atom and ion size; electron configuration of each. (46–48)
30. Solving percent composition problems. (62)
31. Calculate empirical formulas and relation to true formula. (64)
32. Use of table of solubilities. (187)
33. Colligative properties, number of particles from a given formula. (74)
34. Using equations to determine relations between moles, grams, volume of a gas, and number of particles. (67)
35. Relation between density and volume of a gas at STP. (75)
36. Interpreting potential energy changes in a chemical reaction. (80)
37. Use of table G to predict stability of a compound. (188)

CHEMISTRY

June 20, 1989

Part I

Answer all 56 questions in this part.   [65]

Directions (I-56): For *each* statement or question, select the word or expression that, of those given, best completes the statement or answers the question.

1. Which process occurs when dry ice, $CO_2(s)$, is changed into $CO_2(g)$?
   (1) crystallization
   (2) condensation
   (3) sublimation
   (4) solidification

2. Which of the following substances can *not* be decomposed by chemical change?
   (1) sulfuric acid
   (2) ammonia
   (3) water
   (4) argon

3. Which formula represents a binary compound?
   (1) NH_4NO_3
   (2) CH_4
   (3) CH_3COCH_3
   (4) $CaCO_3$

4. One reason that a real gas deviates from an ideal gas is that the molecules of the real gas have
   (1) a straight-line motion
   (2) no net loss of energy on collision
   (3) a negligible volume
   (4) forces of attraction for each other

5. The heat of fusion of a substance is the energy measured during a
   (1) phase change
   (2) temperature change
   (3) chemical change
   (4) pressure change

6. Given an atom with the electron configuration $1s^2 2s^2 2p^3$, how many orbitals are completely filled?
   (1) 1
   (2) 2
   (3) 3
   (4) 4

7. What is the mass number of an atom which contains 21 electrons, 21 protons, and 24 neutrons?
   (1) 21
   (2) 42
   (3) 45
   (4) 66

8. Which principal energy level has a maximum of three sublevels?
   (1) 1
   (2) 2
   (3) 3
   (4) 4

9. In the equation $^{232}_{90}Th \rightarrow\ ^{228}_{88}Ra + X$, which particle is represented by the letter X?
   (1) an alpha particle
   (2) a beta particle
   (3) a positron
   (4) a deuteron

10. What is the total number of valence electrons in an atom with the electron configuration $1s^2 2s^2 2p^6 3s^2 3p^3$?
    (1) 6
    (2) 2
    (3) 3
    (4) 5

11. Which particle is given off when $^{32}_{15}P$ undergoes a transmutation reaction?
    (1) an alpha particle
    (2) a beta particle
    (3) a neutron
    (4) a positron

12. When the equation
    __Al(s) + __O_2(g) → __Al_2O_3(s) is correctly balanced using the smallest whole numbers, the coefficient of Al(s) is
    (1) 1   (3) 3
    (2) 2   (4) 4

13. Which electron dot formula represents a nonpolar molecule?

    (1) H:Ċ:Ċl: with H above and H below the C
    (3) H:Ċ:H with H above and H below the C

    (2) H:N̈: with H above and H below the N
    (4) H:Ö: with H below

14. When a calcium atom loses its valence electrons, the ion formed has an electron configuration which is the same as an atom of
    (1) Cl   (3) K
    (2) Ar   (4) Sc

15. In which of the following liquids are hydrogen bonds between molecules the strongest?
    (1) HI(ℓ)   (3) HCl(ℓ)
    (2) HBr(ℓ)   (4) HF(ℓ)

16. Which is the correct formula for titanium (III) oxide?
    (1) Ti_2O_3 (3) Ti_3O_2
    (2) TiO   (4) Ti_2O_4

17. Which compound in the solid state has a high melting point and conducts electricity when it is liquefied?
    (1) carbon dioxide   (3) hydrogen chloride
    (2) silicon dioxide   (4) potassium chloride

18. Which element at STP exists as monatomic molecules?
    (1) N   (3) Cl
    (2) O   (4) Ne

19. Element X forms the compounds XCl_3 and X_2O_3. In the Periodic Table, element X would most likely be found in Group
    (1) 1 (IA)   (3) 13 (IIIA)
    (2) 2 (IIA)   (4) 14 (IVA)

20. In which of the following periods of the Periodic Table are transition elements found?
    (1) 1   (3) 3
    (2) 2   (4) 4

21. Which element is a liquid at room temperature?
    (1) K   (3) Hg
    (2) I_2 (4) Mg

22. When a sodium atom becomes an ion, the size of the atom
    (1) decreases by gaining an electron
    (2) decreases by losing an electron
    (3) increases by gaining an electron
    (4) increases by losing an electron

23. As the elements of Period 2 are considered in succession from left to right, there is a general decrease in
    (1) ionization energy
    (2) electronegativity
    (3) metallic character
    (4) nonmetallic character

24. Given the reaction:
$$(NH_4)_2CO_3 \rightarrow 2NH_3 + CO_2 + H_2O$$
What is the minimum amount of ammonium carbonate that reacts to produce 1.0 mole of ammonia?
(1) 0.25 mole   (3) 17 moles
(2) 0.50 mole   (4) 34 moles

25. The approximate percent by mass of potassium in $KHCO_3$ is
(1) 19%   (3) 39%
(2) 24%   (4) 61%

26. Which quantity of salt will form a saturated solution in 100 grams of water at 45 °C?
(1) 30 g of KCl   (3) 60 g of KNO_3
(2) 35 g of NH_4Cl (4) 110 g of $NaNO_3$

27. How many moles of water are contained in 0.250 mole of $CuSO_4 \bullet 5H_2O$?
(1) 1.25   (3) 40.0
(2) 4.50   (4) 62.5

28. How many grams of ammonium chloride (gram formula mass = 53.5 g) are contained in 0.500 L of a 2.00 M solution?
(1) 10.0 g   (3) 53.5 g
(2) 26.5 g   (4) 107 g

29. Given the balanced equation:
$$NaOH + HCl \rightarrow NaCl + H_2O$$
What is the total number of grams of H_2O produced when 116 grams of the product, NaCl, is formed?
(1) 9.0 g   (3) 36 g
(2) 18 g   (4) 54 g

30. In a chemical reaction, the difference between the potential energy of the products and the potential energy of the reactants is the
(1) heat of reaction   (3) free energy
(2) heat of fusion   (4) activation energy

31. The diagram below shows a bottle containing $NH_3(g)$ dissolved in water. How can the equilibrium $NH_3(g) \rightleftarrows NH_3(aq)$ be reached?

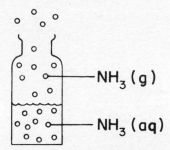

(1) Add more water   (3) Cool the contents.
(2) Add more $NH_3(g)$.   (4) Stopper the bottle.

32. In order for a chemical reaction to occur, there must *always* be
(1) an effective collision between reacting particles
(2) a bond that breaks in a reactant particle
(3) reacting particles with a high charge
(4) reacting particles with a high kinetic energy

33. According to Reference Table *I*, the dissolving of which salt is accompanied by the release of energy?
    (1) LiBr
    (2) NH_4Cl
    (3) NaCl
    (4) KNO_3

34. Which factors must be equal in a reversible chemical reaction at equilibrium?
    (1) the concentrations of the reactants and products
    (2) the potential energies of the reactants and products
    (3) the activation energies of the forward and reverse reactions
    (4) the rates of reaction of the forward and reverse reactions

35. Which O.1 M solution has the highest concentration of H_3O^+ ions?
    (1) CH_3COOH
    (2) NaCl
    (3) KBr
    (4) $Ba(OH)_2$

36. When equal volumes of 0.5 M HCl and 0.5 M NaOH are mixed, the pH of the resulting solution is
    (1) 1
    (2) 2
    (3) 7
    (4) 4

37. Which of the following is the best conductor of electricity?
    (1) NaCl(s)
    (2) NaCl(aq)
    (3) $C_6H_{12}O_6(s)$
    (4) $C_6H_{12}O_6(aq)$

38. When an Arrhenius acid is dissolved in water, it produces
    (1) H^+ as the only positive ion in solution
    (2) NH_4^+ as the only positive ion in solution
    (3) OH^- as the only negative ion in solution
    (4) HCO_3^- as the only negative ion in solution

39. Given the reaction:
$$HCl(aq) + H_2O(\ell) \rightarrow X(aq) + Y(aq)$$
    Which pair does $X(aq) + Y(aq)$ represent?
    (1) $H_3O^+ + Cl^-$
    (2) $H_2Cl^+ + OH^-$
    (3) $HClO + H_2$
    (4) $H^+ + H_2OCl^-$

40. Which compound reacts with an acid to form a salt and water?
    (1) CH_3Cl
    (2) CH_3COOH
    (3) KCl
    (4) KOH

41. According to Reference Table *L*, which species is amphoteric (amphiprotic)?
    (1) HS^-
    (2) HCl
    (3) NH_4^+
    (4) HBr

42. In which compound does chlorine have the highest oxidation number?
    (1) KClO
    (2) $KClO_2$
    (3) $KClO_3$
    (4) $KClO_4$

43. All redox reactions involve
    (1) the gain of electrons, only
    (2) the loss of electrons, only
    (3) both the gain and the loss of electrons
    (4) neither the gain nor the loss of electrons

44. Which is the oxidizing agent in the reaction $2Fe^{2+} + Cl_2 \rightarrow 2Fe^{3+} + 2Cl^-$?
    (1) Fe^{2+}
    (2) Cl_2
    (3) Fe^{3+}
    (4) Cl^-

45. In the reaction $4Zn + 10HNO_3 \rightarrow 4Zn(NO_3)_2 + NH_4NO_3 + 3H_2O$, the zinc is
    (1) reduced and the oxidation number changes from 0 to +2
    (2) oxidized and the oxidation number changes from 0 to +2
    (3) reduced and the oxidation number changes from +2 to 0
    (4) oxidized and the oxidation number changes from +2 to 0

46. Which ion can be both an oxidizing agent and a reducing agent?
    (1) Sn^{2+}
    (2) Cu^{2+}
    (3) Al^{3+}
    (4) Fe^{3+}

47. The diagram below represents an electrochemical cell.

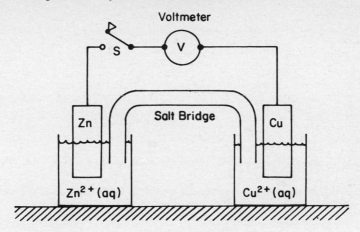

When switch S is closed, which particles undergo reduction?
(1) Zn^{2+} ions
(2) Zn atoms
(3) Cu^{2+} ions
(4) Cu atoms

48. All organic compounds must contain the element
(1) hydrogen
(2) nitrogen
(3) carbon
(4) oxygen

49. Which structural formula represents a compound that is an isomer of

$$
\begin{array}{c}
H H H Br \\
| | | | \\
H-C-C-C-C-H? \\
| | | | \\
H H H Br
\end{array}
$$

(1)
$$
\begin{array}{c}
Br H H H H \\
| | | | | \\
H-C-C-C-C-C-H \\
| | | | | \\
Br H H H H
\end{array}
$$

(3)
$$
\begin{array}{c}
Br Br Br \\
| | | \\
H-C-C-C-H \\
| | | \\
H | H \\
 H-C-H \\
 | \\
 H
\end{array}
$$

(2)
$$
\begin{array}{c}
H Br H H \\
| | | | \\
H-C-C-C-C-Br \\
| | | | \\
H H H H
\end{array}
$$

(4)
$$
\begin{array}{c}
H \\
| \\
Br-C-Br \\
| \\
H-C-H \\
| \\
H-C-H \\
| \\
H-C-H \\
| \\
H
\end{array}
$$

50. Which hydrocarbon is a member of the series with the general formula C_nH_{2n-2}?
    (1) ethyne
    (2) ethene
    (3) butane
    (4) benzene

51. Which structural formula represents an aromatic hydrocarbon?

52. Which is the structural formula of methane?

Note that questions 53 through 56 have only three choices.

53. A 100.-milliliter sample of helium gas is placed in a sealed container of fixed volume. As the temperature of the confined gas increases from 10.°C to 30.°C, the internal pressure
    (1) decreases
    (2) increases
    (3) remains the same

54. As NaCl(s) dissolves according to the equation NaCl(s) → Na⁺(aq) + Cl⁻(aq), the entropy of the system
    (1) decreases
    (2) increases
    (3) remains the same

55. As the number of neutrons in the nucleus of an atom increases, the nuclear charge of the atom
    (1) decreases
    (2) increases
    (3) remains the same

56. As the elements in Group 2 (IIA) of the Periodic Table are considered from top to bottom, the chemical reactivity of each succeeding element generally
    (1) decreases
    (2) increases
    (3) remains the same

Part II

This part consists of twelve groups, each containing five questions. Each group tests a major area of the course. Choose seven of these twelve groups. Be sure that you answer all five questions in each group chosen.   [35]

Group 1 – Matter and Energy

If you choose this group, be sure to answer questions 57–61.

57. When a quantity of electricity is converted to heat, the heat energy produced is measured in
    (1) volts   (3) calories
    (2) amperes   (4) degrees

58. The boiling point of water at standard pressure is
    (1) 0.000 K   (3) 273 K
    (2) 100. K   (4) 373 K

59. A 0.500-mole sample of a gas has a volume of 11.2 liters at 273 K. What is the pressure of the gas?
    (1) 11.2 torr   (3) 380. torr
    (2) 273 torr   (4) 760. torr

60. Which temperature represents absolute zero?
    (1) 0 K   (3) 273 K
    (2) 0 °C   (4) 273 °C

61. Which sample of water has the greatest vapor pressure?
    (1) 100 mL at 20 °C   (3) 20 mL at 30 °C
    (2) 200 mL at 25 °C   (4) 40 mL at 35 °C

Group 2 – Atomic Structure

If you choose this group, be sure to answer questions 62–66.

62. Which element has no known stable isotope?
    (1) carbon   (3) polonium
    (2) potassium   (4) phosphorus

63. Which is the electron dot symbol of an atom of boron in the ground state?

    (1) $\cdot\dot{B}:$ (3) $\cdot\dot{B}:$

    (2) $B\cdot$ (4) $\dot{B}:$

64. Which is an electron configuration of a fluorine atom in the excited state?
    (1) $1s^2 2s^2 2p^4$ (3) $1s^2 2s^2 2p^4 3s^1$
    (2) $1s^2 2s^2 2p^5$ (4) $1s^2 2s^2 2p^5 3s^1$

65. The maximum number of electrons that a single orbital of the $3d$ sublevel may contain is
    (1) 5   (3) 3
    (2) 2   (4) 4

66. Which nuclide contains the greatest number of neutrons?
    (1) ^{37}Cl (3) ^{40}Ar
    (2) ^{39}K (4) ^{41}Ca

Group 3 — Bonding

If you choose this group, be sure to answer questions 67-71.

67. When a salt dissolves in water, the water molecules are attracted by dissolved salt particles. This attraction is called
    (1) atom-atom
    (2) molecule-molecule
    (3) ion-ion
    (4) molecule-ion

68. Which atom has the *least* attraction for the electrons in a bond between that atom and an atom of hydrogen?
    (1) carbon   (3) oxygen
    (2) nitrogen   (4) fluorine

69. Which element consists of positive ions immersed in a "sea" of mobile electrons?
    (1) sulfur   (3) calcium
    (2) nitrogen   (4) chlorine

70. Which of the following liquids has the weakest van der Waal's forces of attraction between its molecules?
    (1) $Xe(\ell)$ (3) $Ne(\ell)$
    (2) $Kr(\ell)$ (4) $He(\ell)$

71. Which molecule is nonpolar and contains a nonpolar covalent bond?
    (1) CCl_4 (3) HF
    (2) F_2 (4) HCl

Group 4 — Periodic Table

If you choose this group, be sure to answer questions 72-76.

72. The highest ionization energies in any period are found in Group
    (1) 1 (IA)   (3) 17 (VIIA)
    (2) 2 (IIA)   (4) 18 (O)

73. The alkaline earth metals are found in Group
    (1) 1 (IA)   (3) 11 (IB)
    (2) 2 (IIA)   (4) 12 (IIB)

74. Which sequence of atomic numbers represents elements which have similar chemical properties?
    (1) 19, 23, 30, 36   (3) 3, 12, 21, 40
    (2) 9, 16, 33, 50   (4) 4, 20, 38, 88

75. Which salt solution is most likely to be colored?
    (1) $KClO_3(aq)$ (3) $K_2CrO_4(aq)$
    (2) $KNO_3(aq)$ (4) $K_2SO_4(aq)$

76. Which of the following Group 17 (VIIA) elements has the highest melting point?
    (1) fluorine   (3) bromine
    (2) chlorine   (4) iodine

Group 5 — Mathematics of Chemistry

If you choose this group, be sure to answer questions 77-81.

77. Which gas would diffuse most rapidly under the same conditions of temperature and pressure?
    (1) gas A, molecular mass = 4
    (2) gas B, molecular mass = 16
    (3) gas C, molecular mass = 36
    (4) gas D, molecular mass = 49

78. When 20 grams of water is cooled from 20 °C to 10 °C, the number of calories of heat released is
    (1) 10   (3) 30
    (2) 20   (4) 200

79. What is the empirical formula of a compound whose composition by mass is 40.% sulfur and 60.% oxygen?
    (1) SO_2 (3) S_2O_3
    (2) SO_3 (4) S_2O_7

80. Which ratio of solute-to-solvent could be used to prepare a solution with the highest boiling point?
    (1) 1 g of NaCl dissolved per 100 g of water
    (2) 1 g of NaCl dissolved per 1000 g of water
    (3) 1 g of $C_{12}H_{22}O_{11}$ dissolved per 100 g of water
    (4) 1 g of $C_{12}H_{22}O_{11}$ dissolved per 1000 g of water

81. What is the mass of 3.0×10^{23} atoms of neon?
    (1) 1.0 g   (3) 10. g
    (2) 0.50 g   (4) 20. g

Group 6 — Kinetics and Equilibrium

If you choose this group, be sure to answer questions 82–86.

82. One mole of each of the salts below is added to a liter of water. Which salt will produce the highest concentration of carbonate ions ($CO_3{}^{2-}$)?
    (1) $MgCO_3$, $K_{sp} = 1.2 \times 10^{-5}$
    (2) $CaCO_3$, $K_{sp} = 5.0 \times 10^{-9}$
    (3) $BaCO_3$, $K_{sp} = 2.6 \times 10^{-9}$
    (4) $ZnCO_3$, $K_{sp} = 1.4 \times 10^{-11}$

83. Which is the expression for the free energy change of a chemical reaction?
    (1) $\triangle H = \triangle G - T\triangle S$
    (2) $\triangle G = \triangle S - T\triangle H$
    (3) $\triangle G = \triangle H - T\triangle S$
    (4) $\triangle S = \triangle G - T\triangle H$

84. What is the heat of formation of $H_2O(\ell)$, in kilocalories per mole, at 1 atmosphere and 298 K?
    (1) -79.7 (3) -56.7
    (2) -68.3 (4) -54.6

85. Based on Reference Table M, which of the following is the *least* soluble compound?
    (1) AgBr   (3) Ag_2CrO_4
    (2) AgCl   (4) AgI

86. Above 0 °C, ice changes spontaneously to water according to the following equation:
    $$H_2O(s) + heat \rightarrow H_2O(\ell).$$
    The changes in $H_2O(s)$ involve
    (1) an absorption of heat and a decrease in entropy.
    (2) a release of heat and a decrease in entropy
    (3) an absorption of heat and an increase in entropy
    (4) a release of heat and an increase in entropy

Group 7 — Acids and Bases

If you choose this group, be sure to answer questions 87–91.

87. What is the hydroxide ion concentration of a solution that has a hydronium ion concentration of 1×10^{-9} mole per liter at 298 K?
    (1) 1×10^{-5} mole per liter
    (2) 1×10^{-7} mole per liter
    (3) 1×10^{-9} mole per liter
    (4) 1×10^{-14} mole per liter

88. In the reaction
    $$HSO_4{}^- + H_2O \rightleftarrows H_3O^+ + SO_4{}^{2-},$$
    an acid-base conjugate pair is
    (1) $HSO_4{}^-$ and $SO_4{}^{2-}$
    (2) $HSO_4{}^-$ and H_2O
    (3) $SO_4{}^{2-}$ and H_3O^+
    (4) $SO_4{}^{2-}$ and H_2O

89. Which type of reaction is represented by the following equation?

$$Al_2S_3 + 6H_2O \rightarrow 2Al(OH)_3 + 3H_2S$$

    (1) neutralization
    (2) dehydration
    (3) electrolysis
    (4) hydrolysis

90. If 50. milliliters of 0.50 M HCl is used to completely neutralize 25 milliliters of KOH solution, what is the molarity of the base?

    (1) 1.0 M
    (2) 0.25 M
    (3) 0.50 M
    (4) 2.5 M

91. At 298 K, which metal will release $H_2(g)$ when reacted with HCl(aq)?

    (1) Au(s)
    (2) Zn(s)
    (3) Hg(ℓ)
    (4) Ag(s)

Group 8 — Redox and Electrochemistry

If you choose this group, be sure to answer questions 92–96.

92. Based on Reference Table N, which half-cell has a greater reduction potential than the standard hydrogen half-cell?

    (1) $Na^+ + e^- \rightarrow Na(s)$
    (2) $Ni^{2+} + 2e^- \rightarrow Ni(s)$
    (3) $Pb^{2+} + 2e^- \rightarrow Pb(s)$
    (4) $Sn^{4+} + 2e^- \rightarrow Sn^{2+}$

Base your answers to questions 93 and 94 on the following reaction.

$$Mg(s) + 2Ag^+(aq) \rightarrow Mg^{2+}(aq) + 2Ag(s)$$

93. Which species undergoes a loss of electrons?

    (1) Mg(s)
    (2) $Ag^+(aq)$
    (3) $Mg^{2+}(aq)$
    (4) Ag(s)

94. What is the cell voltage (E^0) for the overall reaction?

    (1) +1.57 V
    (2) +2.37 V
    (3) +3.17 V
    (4) +3.97 V

95. Given the reaction:

$$2H_2O + electricity \rightarrow 2H_2 + O_2$$

In which type of cell would this reaction most likely occur?

    (1) a chemical cell, because it is exothermic
    (2) an electrolytic cell, because it is exothermic
    (3) a chemical cell, because it is endothermic
    (4) an electrolytic cell, because it is endothermic

96. Which reaction will take place spontaneously?

    (1) $Cu + 2H^+ \rightarrow Cu^{2+} + H_2$
    (2) $2Au + 6H^+ \rightarrow 2Au^{3+} + 3H_2$
    (3) $Pb + 2H^+ + Pb^{2+} + H_2$
    (4) $2Ag + 2H^+ \rightarrow 2Ag^+ + H_2$

Group 9 — Organic Chemistry

If you choose this group, be sure to answer questions 97–101.

97. Which structural formula represents a dihydroxy alcohol?

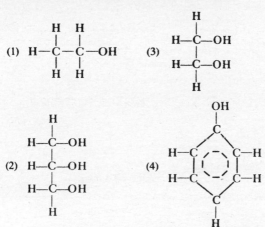

98. In the alkane series, each molecule contains
    (1) only one double bond
    (2) two double bonds
    (3) one triple bond
    (4) all single bonds

99. The process of opening double bonds and joining monomer molecules to form polyvinyl chloride is called
    (1) addition polymerization
    (2) condensation polymerization
    (3) dehydration polymerization
    (4) neutralization polymerization

100. Which hydrocarbon will undergo a substitution reaction with chlorine?
    (1) methane   (3) propene
    (2) ethyne   (4) butene

101. Which class of compounds has the general formula $R_1 - O_1 - R_2$?
    (1) esters   (3) ethers
    (2) alcohols   (4) aldehydes

Group 10 — Applications of Chemical Principles

If you choose this group, be sure to answer questions 102–106.

102. When a battery is in use, stored chemical energy is first changed to
    (1) electrical energy   (3) light energy
    (2) heat energy   (4) mechanical energy

103. The reaction $CuO + CO \rightarrow CO_2 + Cu$ is an example of
    (1) reduction, only
    (2) oxidation, only
    (3) both oxidation and reduction
    (4) neither oxidation nor reduction

104. Which group of metals is normally obtained by the electrolysis of their fused salts?
    (1) Group 17 (VIIA)   (3) Group 7 (VIIB)
    (2) Group 2 (IIA)   (4) Group 4 (IVB)

105. Which type of reaction is the Haber process, $N_2(g) + 3H_2(g) \rightarrow 2NH_3(g)$ + heat?
    (1) exothermic, with an increase in entropy
    (2) exothermic, with a decrease in entropy
    (3) endothermic, with an increase in entropy
    (4) endothermic, with a decrease in entropy

106. Kerosene is a mixture of compounds called
    (1) esters   (3) aldehydes
    (2) alcohols   (4) hydrocarbons

Group 11 — Nuclear Chemistry

If you choose this group, be sure to answer questions 107–111.

107. Given the equation: $^{14}_{7}N + ^{4}_{2}He \rightarrow X + ^{17}_{8}O$
    When the equation is correctly balanced, the particle represented by the X will be
    (1) $^{0}_{-1}e$ (3) $^{1}_{1}H$
    (2) $^{1}_{0}n$ (4) $^{2}_{1}H$

108. Which substance may serve as both a moderator and coolant in some nuclear reactors?
    (1) carbon dioxide   (3) graphite
    (2) boron   (4) heavy water

109. Iodine-131 is used for diagnosing thyroid disorders because it is absorbed by the thyroid gland and
    (1) has a very short half-life
    (2) has a very long half-life
    (3) emits alpha radiation
    (4) emits gamma radiation

110. Which particle can *not* be accelerated by the electric or the magnetic field in a particle accelerator?
    (1) electron   (3) helium nucleus
    (2) neutron   (4) hydrogen nucleus

111. A radioactive-dating procedure to determine the age of a mineral compares the mineral's remaining amounts of isotope ^{238}U and isotope
    (1) ^{206}Pb (3) ^{214}Pb
    (2) ^{206}Bi (4) ^{214}Bi

Group 12 — Laboratory Activities

If you choose this group, be sure to answer questions 112–116.

112. A student investigated samples of four different substances in the solid state. The table is a record of the behaviors observed (marked with an X) when each solid was tested.

Behavior Tested	Sample I	Sample II	Sample III	Sample IV
High Melting Point	X		X	
Low Melting Point		X		X
Soluble in Water	X			X
Insoluble in Water		X	X	
Decomposed Under High Heat		X		
Stable Under High Heat	X		X	X
Electrolyte	X			X
Nonelectrolyte		X	X	

Based on the tabulated results, which of the solids investigated had the characteristics most closely associated with those of an organic compound?
    (1) Sample I   (3) Sample III
    (2) Sample II   (4) Sample IV

113. The graph below represents four solubility curves. Which curve best represents the solubility of a gas in water?

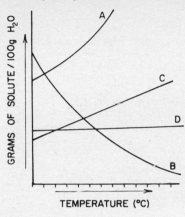

(1) *A*   (3) *C*
(2) *B*   (4) *D*

114. Which diagram represents a graduated cylinder?

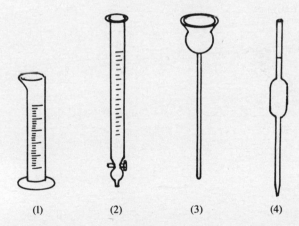

(1)   (2)   (3)   (4)

115. Which procedure represents the safest technique to use for diluting a concentrated acid?
    (1) Add the acid to the water quickly.
    (2) Add the water to the acid quickly.
    (3) Add the acid slowly to the water with steady stirring.
    (4) Add the water slowly to the acid with steady stirring.

116. Which measurement contains three significant figures?
    (1) 0.05 g   (3) 0.056 g
    (2) 0.050 g   (4) 0.0563 g

CHEMISTRY

June 21, 1990

Part I

Answer all 56 questions in this part.   [65]

Directions (1–56): For *each* statement or question, select the word or expression that, of those given, best completes the statement or answers the question.

1. A 300.-milliliter container that is filled with 100. milliliters of oxygen and 200. milliliters of hydrogen has a total pressure of 750. millimeters of mercury. What is the partial pressure of the oxygen?
   (1) 100. mmHg   (3) 250. mmHg
   (2) 200. mmHg   (4) 500. mmHg

2. When a sample of a gas is heated at constant pressure, the average kinetic energy of its molecules
   (1) decreases, and the volume of the gas increases
   (2) decreases, and the volume of the gas decreases
   (3) increases, and the volume of the gas increases
   (4) increases, and the volume of the gas decreases

3. Which equation represents sublimation?
   (1) $NH_3(g) \rightarrow NH_3(\ell)$ (3) $HCl(g) \rightarrow HCl(aq)$
   (2) $H_2O(\ell) \rightarrow H_2O(g)$ (4) $CO_2(s) \rightarrow CO_2(g)$

4. An example of a heterogeneous mixture is
   (1) soil   (3) carbon monoxide
   (2) sugar   (4) carbon dioxide

5. Which is the orbital notation for the electrons in the third principal energy level of an argon atom in the ground state?

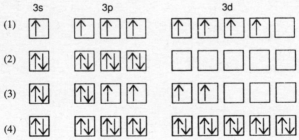

6. Given the reaction: $^{234}_{91}Pa \rightarrow X + ^{0}_{-1}e$
   When the equation is correctly balanced, the nucleus represented by X is

   (1) $^{234}_{92}U$ (3) $^{230}_{90}Th$

   (2) $^{235}_{92}U$ (4) $^{232}_{90}Th$

7. In which sublevel would an electron have the highest energy?
   (1) $4s$ (3) $4d$
   (2) $4p$ (4) $4f$

8. An atom that has an electron configuration of $1s^22s^22p^63s^23p^63d^54s^2$ is classified as
   (1) an alkali metal   (3) a transition element
   (2) an alkaline earth metal   (4) a noble gas element

9. What is the first ionization energy of an element that has the electron configuration $1s^22s^22p^6$?
   (1) 119 kcal/mol   (3) 363 kcal/mol
   (2) 239 kcal/mol   (4) 497 kcal/mol

10. The atoms in a sample of an element must contain nuclei with the same number of
    (1) electrons
    (2) protons
    (3) neutrons
    (4) nucleons

11. Given the unbalanced equation:

    __Al$_2$(SO$_4$)$_3$ + __Ca(OH)$_2$ → __Al(OH)$_3$ + __CaSO$_4$

    When the equation is completely balanced using the smallest whole-number coefficients, the sum of the coefficients is
    (1) 5
    (2) 9
    (3) 3
    (4) 4

12. Which is the formula for magnesium sulfide?
    (1) MgS
    (2) MgSO$_3$
    (3) MnS
    (4) MnSO$_3$

13. Which formula represents a polar molecule?
    (1) CH$_4$
    (2) Cl$_2$
    (3) NH$_3$
    (4) N$_2$

14. Which is an empirical formula?
    (1) C$_2$H$_2$
    (2) H$_2$O
    (3) H$_2$O$_2$
    (4) C$_6$H$_{12}$O$_6$

15. Atoms of which of the following elements have the strongest attraction for electrons?
    (1) aluminum
    (2) chlorine
    (3) silicon
    (4) sodium

16. Van der Waals forces of attraction between molecules always decrease with
    (1) increasing molecular size and increasing distance between the molecules
    (2) increasing molecular size and decreasing distance between the molecules
    (3) decreasing molecular size and increasing distance between the molecules
    (4) decreasing molecular size and decreasing distance between the molecules

17. Which group of elements in the Periodic Table contains a semimetal (metalloid)?
    (1) 1 (IA)
    (2) 7 (VIIB)
    (3) 13 (IIIA)
    (4) 18 (0)

18. Which element in Period 4 of the Periodic Table exhibits the most nonmetallic properties?
    (1) Ca
    (2) Cr
    (3) Ga
    (4) Br

19. Which of the following gases is monatomic at STP?
    (1) hydrogen
    (2) chlorine
    (3) oxygen
    (4) helium

20. Which electron configurations represent the first two elements in Group 17 (VIIA) of the Periodic Table?
    (1) $1s^2 2s^1$ and $1s^2 2s^2$
    (2) $1s^2 2s^2$ and $1s^2 2s^2 2p^1$
    (3) $1s^2 2s^2 2p^5$ and [Ne]$3s^2 3p^5$
    (4) $1s^2 2s^2 2p^6$ and [Ne]$3s^2 3p^5$

21. Which element within any given period of the Periodic Table would always have the *lowest* first ionization energy?
    (1) an alkali metal
    (2) an alkaline earth metal
    (3) a halogen
    (4) a noble gas

22. Which of the following aqueous solutions is blue?
    (1) Na$_2$SO$_4$(aq)
    (2) K$_2$SO$_4$(aq)
    (3) MgSO$_4$(aq)
    (4) CuSO$_4$(aq)

23. A compound has an empirical formula of CH$_2$ and a molecular mass of 56. What is its molecular formula?
    (1) CH$_2$
    (2) C$_2$H$_4$
    (3) C$_3$H$_6$
    (4) C$_4$H$_8$

24. According to Reference Table D, approximately how many grams of $KClO_3$ are needed to saturate 100 grams of H_2O at 40°C?
    (1) 6
    (2) 16
    (3) 38
    (4) 47

25. Given the reaction: $H_2(g) + Cl_2(g) \rightarrow 2HCl(g)$
    What is the total volume of H_2 gas consumed when 22.4 liters of Cl_2 gas completely reacts?
    (1) 11.2 L
    (2) 22.4 L
    (3) 44.8 L
    (4) 89.6 L

26. Which represents the greatest mass of chlorine?
    (1) 1 mole of chlorine
    (2) 1 atom of chlorine
    (3) 1 gram of chlorine
    (4) 1 molecule of chlorine

27. Which gas sample contains a total of 3.0×10^{23} molecules?
    (1) 71 g of Cl_2
    (2) 2.0 g of H_2
    (3) 14 g of N_2
    (4) 38 g of F_2

28. What is the percent by mass of hydrogen in CH_3COOH (formula mass = 60.)?
    (1) 1.7%
    (2) 5.0%
    (3) 6.7%
    (4) 7.1%

29. A flask at 25°C is partially filled with water and stoppered. After a period of time the water level remained constant. Which relationship best explains this observation?
    (1) The rate of condensation exceeds the rate of evaporation.
    (2) The rates of condensation and evaporation are both zero.
    (3) The rate of evaporation exceeds the rate of condensation.
    (4) The rate of evaporation equals the rate of condensation.

30. Which change represents an increase of entropy?
    (1) $I_2(s) \rightarrow I_2(g)$
    (2) $I_2(g) \rightarrow I_2(\ell)$
    (3) $H_2O(g) \rightarrow H_2O(\ell)$
    (4) $H_2O(\ell) \rightarrow H_2O(s)$

31. Which is the correction equilibrium constant expression for the reaction below?

    $N_2(g) + 3H_2(g) \rightleftarrows 2NH_3(g)$

    (1) $K_{eq} = \dfrac{[NH_3]^2}{[N_2][H_2]^3}$

    (2) $K_{eq} = \dfrac{[N_2][H_2]^3}{[NH_3]^2}$

    (3) $K_{eq} = \dfrac{[2NH_3]}{[2N][3H_2]}$

    (4) $K_{eq} = \dfrac{[2N][3H_2]}{[NH_3]^2}$

32. Given the reaction: $A + B \rightarrow C + D$

    The reaction will most likely occur at the greatest rate if A and B represent
    (1) nonpolar molecular compounds in the solid phase
    (2) ionic compounds in the solid phase
    (3) solutions of nonpolar molecular compounds
    (4) solutions of ionic compounds

33. The ionization constants (K_a's) of four acids are shown below. Which K_a represents the *weakest* of these acids?
    (1) $K_a = 1.0 \times 10^{-5}$
    (3) $K_a = 1.0 \times 10^{-4}$
    (3) $K_a = 7.1 \times 10^{-3}$
    (4) $K_a = 1.7 \times 10^{-2}$

34. The potential energy diagram shown below represents the reaction
    $R + S$ + energy → T.

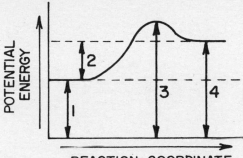

REACTION COORDINATE

Which numbered interval represents the potential energy of the product T?
(1) 1   (3) 3
(2) 2   (4) 4

35. According to Reference Table L, which ion can act as a Brönsted acid?
    (1) a sulfate ion   (3) a sulfide ion
    (2) a hydrogen sulfate ion   (4) a sulfite ion

36. Hydrogen gas is produced when dilute hydrochloric acid is added to
    (1) copper   (3) gold
    (2) silver   (4) magnesium

37. Which of the following 0.1 M solutions is the best conductor of electricity?
    (1) $H_2S(aq)$ (3) $C_6H_{12}O_6(aq)$
    (2) $HCl(aq)$ (4) $C_{12}H_{22}O_{11}(aq)$

38. How many milliliters of a 4.0-molar solution of HCl are needed to completely neutralize 60. milliliters of a 3.2-molar solution of NaOH?
    (1) 24 mL   (3) 60. mL
    (2) 48 mL   (4) 75 mL

39. Which equation illustrates H_2O acting as a Brönsted-Lowry base?
    (1) $H^+(aq) + H_2O → H_3O^+(aq)$
    (2) $CH_3COO^-(aq) + H_2O → CH_3COOH(aq) + OH^-(aq)$
    (3) $2Na + 2H_2O → 2NaOH(aq) + H_2$
    (4) $C + H_2O → CO + H_2$

40. The OH^- ion concentration is greater than the H_3O^+ ion concentration in a water solution of
    (1) CH_3OH (3) HCl
    (2) $Ba(OH)_2$ (4) H_2SO_4

41. For a redox reaction to occur, there must be a transfer of
    (1) protons   (3) electrons
    (2) neutrons   (4) ions

42. In which substance is the oxidation number of nitrogen zero?
    (1) N_2 (3) NO_2
    (2) NH_3 (4) N_2O

43. In the reaction $2Al + 3Ni(NO_3)_2 → 2Al(NO_3)_3 + 3Ni$, the aluminum is
    (1) reduced and its oxidation number increases
    (2) reduced and its oxidation number decreases
    (3) oxidized and its oxidation number increases
    (4) oxidized and its oxidation number decreases

44. In the reaction $Mg + Cl_2 \rightarrow MgCl_2$, the correct half-reaction for the oxidation that occurs is
   (1) $Mg + 2e^- \rightarrow Mg^{2+}$
   (2) $Cl_2 + 2e^- \rightarrow 2Cl^-$
   (3) $Mg \rightarrow Mg^{2+} + 2e^-$
   (4) $Cl_2 \rightarrow 2Cl^- + 2e^-$

45. In the reaction $Zn(s) + Cu^{2+}(aq) \rightarrow Zn^{2+}(aq) + Cu(s)$, the reducing agent is
   (1) $Zn(s)$ (3) $Cu^{2+}(aq)$
   (2) $Cu(s)$ (4) $Zn^{2+}(aq)$

46. A chemical cell is made up of two half-cells connected by a salt bridge and an external conductor. What is the function of the salt bridge?
   (1) to permit the migration of ions
   (2) to prevent the migration of ions
   (3) to permit the mixing of solutions
   (4) to prevent the flow of electrons

47. Which compound is a member of the hydrocarbon series with the general formula C_nH_{2n-6}?
   (1) C_3H_8 (3) C_5H_8
   (2) C_4H_8 (4) C_7H_8

48. Which of the following compounds has the highest normal boiling point?
   (1) C_2H_6 (3) C_4H_{10}
   (2) C_3H_8 (4) C_5H_{12}

49. The type of reaction represented by the reaction $C_2H_4 + H_2 \rightarrow C_2H_6$ is called
   (1) substitution   (3) addition
   (2) polymerization   (4) esterification

50. What is the formula of pentene?
   (1) C_4H_8 (3) C_5H_{10}
   (2) C_4H_{10} (4) C_5H_{12}

51. The four single bonds of a carbon atom are spatially directed toward the corners of a regular
   (1) triangle   (3) square
   (2) rectangle   (4) tetrahedron

Note that questions 52 through 56 have only three choices.

52. As the number of carbon atoms in a hydrocarbon molecule increases, the number of possible isomers generally
   (1) decreases   (3) remains the same
   (2) increases

53. As water in a sealed container is cooled from 20°C to 10°C, its vapor pressure
   (1) decreases   (3) remains the same
   (2) increases

54. As the atoms of the elements in Group 16 (VIA) are considered in order from top to bottom, their electronegativities
   (1) decrease   (3) remain the same
   (2) increase

55. Given the reaction at equilibrium:

   $CO(g) + \frac{1}{2}O_2(g) \rightleftarrows CO_2(g) + 67.7$ kcal

   As the temperature increases, the rate of the forward reaction
   (1) decreases   (3) remains the same
   (2) increases

56. As an electron in an atom moves from the ground state to an excited state, the potential energy of the electron
   (1) decreases   (3) remains the same
   (2) increases

Part II

This part consists of twelve groups, each containing five questions. Each group tests a major area of the course. Choose seven of these twelve groups. Be sure that you answer all five questions in each group chosen.   [35]

Group 1 – Matter and Energy

If you choose this group, be sure to answer questions 57–61.

57. The temperature of a sample of a substance changes from $10.°C$ to $20.°C$. How many Kelvin degrees does the temperature change?
    (1) 10.   (3) 283
    (2) 20.   (4) 293

58. The diagram below represents a gas confined in a cylinder fitted with a movable piston.

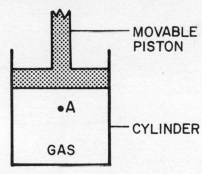

    As the piston moves toward point A at constant temperature, which relationship involving pressure (P) and volume (V) is correct?
    (1) $P + V = k$ (3) $P \div V = k$
    (2) $P - V = k$ (4) $P \times V = k$

59. Water will boil at a temperature of $40°C$ when the pressure on its surface is
    (1) 14.5 torr   (3) 55.3 torr
    (2) 17.0 torr   (4) 760. torr

60. Which change of phase is exothermic?
    (1) $H_2O(s) \rightarrow H_2O(g)$ (3) $H_2S(g) \rightarrow H_2S(\ell)$
    (2) $CO_2(s) \rightarrow CO_2(\ell)$ (4) $NH_3(\ell) \rightarrow NH_3(g)$

61. How many kilocalories are equivalent to 10 calories?
    (1) 0.001 kcal   (3) 1000 kcal
    (2) 0.01 kcal   (4) 10,000 kcal

Group 2 – Atomic Structure

If you choose this group, be sure to answer questions 62–66.

62. Which of the following particles has the *least* mass?
    (1) an electron   (3) a deuteron
    (2) a proton   (4) a neutron

63. The nucleus of an atom of $^{127}_{53}I$ contains
    (1) 53 neutrons and 127 protons   (3) 53 protons and 74 neutrons
    (2) 53 protons and 127 neutrons   (4) 53 protons and 74 electrons

64. Which is the atomic number of an atom with six valence electrons?
    (1) 6   (3) 10
    (2) 8   (4) 12

65. In an electric field, which emanation is deflected toward the negative electrode?
    (1) beta particle
    (2) alpha particle
    (3) x rays
    (4) gamma rays

66. What is the maximum number of electrons in an energy level with a principal quantum number of 3?
    (1) 6
    (2) 9
    (3) 3
    (4) 18

Group 3 – Bonding

If you choose this group, be sure to answer questions 67–71.

67. The attraction between water molecules and an Na^+ ion or a Cl^- ion occurs because water molecules are
    (1) linear
    (2) symmetrical
    (3) polar
    (4) nonpolar

68. Which compound contains both covalent bonds and ionic bonds?
    (1) NaCl(s)
    (2) HCl(g)
    (3) $NaNO_3$(s)
    (4) N_2O_5(g)

69. What is the name for the sodium salt of the acid $HClO_2$?
    (1) sodium chlorite
    (2) sodium chloride
    (3) sodium chlorate
    (4) sodium perchlorate

70. Which of the following liquids is the best conductor of electricity?
    (1) $CCl_4(\ell)$
    (2) $H_2O(\ell)$
    (3) $CH_3OH(\ell)$
    (4) NaOH(aq)

71. Which formula represents a molecular solid?
    (1) NaCl(s)
    (2) $C_6H_{12}O_6$(s)
    (3) Cu(s)
    (4) KF(s)

Group 4 – Periodic Table

If you choose this group, be sure to answer questions 72–76.

72. Which groups contain metals that are so active chemically that they occur naturally only in compounds?
    (1) 1 (IA) and 2 (IIA)
    (2) 2 (IIA) and 12 (IIB)
    (3) 1 (IA) and 11 (IB)
    (4) 11 (IB) and 12 (IIB)

73. Which group contains elements in the solid, liquid, and gaseous phase at room temperature?
    (1) 17 (VIIA)
    (2) 2 (IIA)
    (3) 18 (0)
    (4) 4 (IVB)

74. Of all the elements, the one with the highest electronegativity is found in Period
    (1) 1
    (2) 2
    (3) 3
    (4) 4

75. An ion of which element is smaller than its atom?
    (1) F
    (2) O
    (3) Cl
    (4) Na

76. Which of the Group 15 (VA) elements can lose an electron most readily?
    (1) N
    (2) P
    (3) Sb
    (4) Bi

Group 5 – Mathematics of Chemistry

If you choose this group, be sure to answer questions 77–81.

77. How many calories of heat energy are absorbed in raising the temperature of 10. grams of water from 5.0°C to 20.°C?
    (1) 2.5×10^2
    (2) 2.0×10^2
    (3) 1.5×10^2
    (4) 5.0×10^1

78. At STP, which of the following gases has the higest rate of diffusion?
    (1) He
    (2) Ne
    (3) Ar
    (4) Kr

79. Compared to the normal freezing point and boiling point of water, a 1-molal solution of sugar in water will have a
    (1) higher freezing point and a lower boiling point
    (2) higher freezing point and a higher boiling point
    (3) lower freezing point and a lower boiling point
    (4) lower freezing point and a higher boiling point

80. A compound consists of 46.7% nitrogen and 53.3% oxygen by mass. What is its empirical formula?
    (1) NO
    (2) NO_2
    (3) N_2O
    (4) N_2O_3

81. Given the reaction: $4Al + 3O_2 \rightarrow 2Al_2O_3$

    How many moles of Al_2O_3 will be formed when 27 grams of Al reacts completely with O_2?
    (1) 1.0
    (2) 2.0
    (3) 0.50
    (4) 4.0

Group 6 – Kinetics and Equilibrium

If you choose this group, be sure to answer questions 82–86.

82. Which change would most likely increase the rate of a chemical reaction?
    (1) decreasing a reactant's concentration
    (2) decreasing a reactant's surface area
    (3) cooling the reaction mixture
    (4) adding a catalyst to the reaction mixture

83. A solution in which equilibrium exists between undissolved and dissolved solute is always
    (1) saturated
    (2) unsaturated
    (3) dilute
    (4) concentrated

84. Which compound has the *smallest* K_{sp} at 298 K?
    (1) AgCl
    (2) AgI
    (3) $PbCl_2$
    (4) PbI_2

85. Given the system at equilibrium:

    $AgCl(s) \rightleftarrows Ag^+(aq) + Cl^-(aq)$

    When 0.1 M HCl is added to the system, the equilibrium will shift to the
    (1) right and the concentration of $Ag^+(aq)$ will decrease
    (2) right and the concentration of $Ag^+(aq)$ will increase
    (3) left and the concentration of $Ag^+(aq)$ will decrease
    (4) left and the concentration of $Ag^+(aq)$ will increase

86. When a reaction has a negative ΔG, it must be
    (1) exothermic
    (2) endothermic
    (3) spontaneous
    (4) nonspontaneous

Group 7 – Acids and Bases

If you choose this group, be sure to answer questions 87–91.

87. What is the H^+ ion concentration of an aqueous solution that has a pH of 11?
    (1) 1.0×10^{-11} mol/L
    (2) 1.0×10^{-3} mol/L
    (3) 3.0×10^{-1} mol/L
    (4) 11×10^{-1} mol/L

88. According to Reference Table *L*, which species is amphiprotic?
    (1) NH_4^+
    (2) NH_2^-
    (3) HS^-
    (4) S^{2-}

89. An indicator was used to test a water solution with a pH of 12. Which indicator color would be observed?
    (1) colorless with litmus
    (2) red with litmus
    (3) colorless with phenolphthalein
    (4) pink with phenolphthalein

90. Which of the following Brönsted acids has the strongest conjugate base?
    (1) HF
    (2) HCl
    (3) HBr
    (4) HI

91. Which equation represents a neutralization reaction?
    (1) $H^+(aq) + OH^-(aq) \rightarrow H_2O(\ell)$
    (2) $Ag^+(aq) + I^-(aq) \rightarrow AgI(s)$
    (3) $Zn(s) + 2HCl(aq) \rightarrow ZnCl_2(aq) + H_2(g)$
    (4) $NaCl(aq) + AgNO_3(aq) \rightarrow NaNO_3(aq) + AgCl(s)$

Group 8 – Redox and Electrochemistry

If you choose this group, be sure to answer questions 92–96.

92. According to Reference Table N, which will reduce Mg^{2+} to $Mg(s)$?
    (1) Fe(s)
    (2) Ba(s)
    (3) Pb(s)
    (4) Ag(s)

93. Based on Reference Table N, which of the following ions is most easily oxidized?
    (1) F^-
    (2) Cl^-
    (3) Br^-
    (4) I^-

94. Which overall reaction in a chemical cell has the highest net potential (E^0)?
    (1) $Zn(s) + 2H^+ \rightarrow Zn^{2+} + H_2(g)$
    (2) $Ni(s) + 2H^+ \rightarrow Ni^{2+} + H_2(g)$
    (3) $Mg(s) + 2H^+ \rightarrow Mg^{2+} + H_2(g)$
    (4) $Sn(s) + 2H^+ \rightarrow Sn^{2+} + H_2(g)$

95. When the redox equation

    $$\_Cr^{3+}(aq) + 3Mn(s) \rightarrow \_Mn^{2+}(aq) + \_Cr(s)$$

    is completely balanced, the coefficient of $Cr^{3+}(aq)$ will be
    (1) 1
    (2) 2
    (3) 3
    (4) 4

96. Given the reaction:

    $$Zn(s) + Cu^{2+}(aq) \rightleftarrows Zn^{2+}(aq) + Cu(s)$$

    When the chemical cell reaction reaches equilibrium, the measured voltage will be
    (1) 0.00 V
    (2) 0.34 V
    (3) 0.76 V
    (4) 1.10 V

Group 9 – Organic Chemistry

If you choose this group, be sure to answer questions 97–101.

97. Which pair of compounds are isomers?
    (1) C_6H_6 and C_6H_{12}
    (2) C_2H_4 and C_2H_6
    (3) CH_3CH_2OH and CH_3COOH
    (4) CH_3CH_2OH and CH_3OCH_3

98. Alkanes *differ* from alkenes in that alkanes
    (1) are hydrocarbons
    (2) are saturated compounds
    (3) have the general formula C_nH_{2n}
    (4) undergo addition reactions

99. In which type of reaction are long-chain molecules formed from smaller molecules?
    (1) substitution
    (2) saponification
    (3) fermentation
    (4) polymerization

100. What is the total number of hydroxyl groups contained in one molecule of 1,2-ethanediol?
    (1) 1
    (2) 2
    (3) 3
    (4) 4

101. Primary alcohols can be dehydrated to produce
    (1) ethers
    (2) organic acids
    (3) esters
    (4) aldehydes

Group 10 – Applications of Chemical Principles

If you choose this group, be sure to answer questions 102–106.

102. Which element is commercially obtained by the electrolysis of its fused salt?
    (1) silver
    (2) copper
    (3) helium
    (4) sodium

103. Natural gas is composed mostly of
    (1) butane
    (2) gasoline
    (3) methane
    (4) propane

104. The Haber process is used in the commercial preparation of
    (1) hydrochloric acid
    (2) sulfuric acid
    (3) ammonia
    (4) sulfur

105. The extent to which the metals zinc and aluminum corrode is limited because they
    (1) are semimetals
    (2) are amphoteric
    (3) form self-protective coatings by neutralization
    (4) form self-protective coatings by oxidation

106. Which is the negative electrode of a nickel oxide-cadmium battery?
    (1) Ni
    (2) Cd
    (3) $Ni(OH)_2$
    (4) $Cd(OH)_2$

Group 11 – Nuclear Chemistry

If you choose this group, be sure to answer questions 107–111.

107. In the reaction $^{27}_{13}Al + {}^{4}_{2}He \rightarrow X + {}^{1}_{0}n$, the isotope represented by X is
    (1) $^{29}_{12}Mg$
    (2) $^{28}_{13}Al$
    (3) $^{27}_{14}Si$
    (4) $^{30}_{15}P$

108. Diagnostic injections of radioisotopes used in medicine normally have
    (1) short half-lives and are quickly eliminated from the body
    (2) short half-lives and are slowly eliminated from the body
    (3) long half-lives and are quickly eliminated from the body
    (4) long half-lives and are slowly eliminated from the body

109. Which radioactive isotope is often used as a tracer to study organic reaction mechanisms?
    (1) carbon-12
    (2) carbon-14
    (3) uranium-235
    (4) uranium-238

110. The fission process in a reactor can be regulated by adjusting the number of neutrons available. This is done by the use of
    (1) moderators
    (2) control rods
    (3) coolants
    (4) shielding

111. Particle accelerators can be used to increase the kinetic energy of
    (1) deuterium
    (2) neutrons
    (3) protons
    (4) tritium

Group 12 – Laboratory Activities

If you choose this group, be sure to answer questions 112–116.

112. The graph below represents the relationship between the vapor pressure and temperature of four liquids.

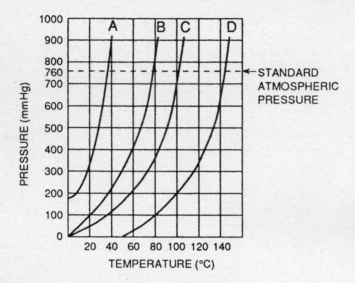

Which liquid has a normal boiling point of 79°C?
(1) A   (3) C
(2) B   (4) D

113. Which represents an Erlenmeyer flask?

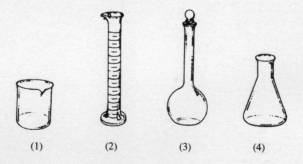

(1)   (2)   (3)   (4)

114. A student obtained the following data while cooling a substance. The substance was originally in the liquid phase at a temperature below its boiling point.

Time (minutes)	0.5	1.0	1.5	2.0	2.5	3.0	3.5	4.0	4.5	5.0	5.5	6.0
Temperature (°C)	70.	63	57	54	53	53	53	53	53	52	51	48

What is the freezing point of the substance?
(1) 70.°C   (3) 53°C
(2) 59°C   (4) 48°C

115. In a laboratory exercise to determine the density of a substance, a student found the mass of the substance to be 6.00 grams and the volume to be 2.0 milliliters. Expressed to the correct number of significant figures, the density of the substance is
(1) 3.000 g/mL   (3) 3.0 g/mL
(2) 3.00 g/mL   (4) 3 g/mL

116. A 1.20-gram sample of a hydrated salt is heated to a constant mass of 0.80 gram. What was the percent by mass of water contained in the original sample?
(1) 20.   (3) 50.
(2) 33   (4) 67

CHEMISTRY

June 20, 1991

Part I

Answer all 56 questions in this part. [65]

Directions (1–56): For *each* statement or question, select the word or expression that, of those given, best completes the statement or answers the question.

1. In a sample of pure copper, all atoms have atomic numbers which are
   (1) the same and the atoms have the same number of electrons
   (2) the same but the atoms have a different number of electrons
   (3) different but the atoms have the same number of electrons
   (4) different and the atoms have a different number of electrons

2. When the pressure exerted on a confined gas at constant temperature is doubled, the volume of the gas is
   (1) halved   (3) tripled
   (2) doubled   (4) quartered

3. At STP, which gas has properties most similar to those of an ideal gas?
   (1) NH_3 (3) O_2
   (2) CO_2 (4) H_2

4. A sealed flask contains a mixture of 1.0 mole of $N_2(g)$ and 2.0 moles of $O_2(g)$ at 25°C. If the total pressure of this gas mixture is 6.0 atmospheres, what is the partial pressure of the $N_2(g)$?
   (1) 6.0 atm   (3) 3.0 atm
   (2) 2.0 atm   (4) 9.0 atm

5. When an exothermic reaction occurs in a water solution, the temperature of the solution
   (1) increases because energy is given off by the reaction
   (2) increases because energy is absorbed by the reaction
   (3) decreases because energy is given off by the reaction
   (4) decreases because energy is absorbed by the reaction

6. The total number of electrons in a neutral atom of every element is always equal to the atom's
   (1) mass number
   (2) number of neutrons
   (3) number of protons
   (4) number of nucleons

7. The mass of an electron is approximately equal to $\frac{1}{1836}$ of the mass of
   (1) a positron   (3) an alpha particle
   (2) a proton   (4) a beta particle

8. Which electron configuration represents an atom in an excited state?
   (1) $1s^2 2s^2 2p^4$ (3) $1s^2 2s^2 2p^5 3s^1$
   (2) $1s^2 2s^2 2p^5$ (4) $1s^2 2s^2 2p^6 3s^1$

9. Gamma rays are emanations that have
   (1) mass but no charge
   (2) charge but no mass
   (3) neither mass nor charge
   (4) both mass and charge

10. The diagram shows the characteristic spectral line patterns of four elements. Also shown are spectral lines produced by an unknown substance. Which pair of elements is present in the unknown?

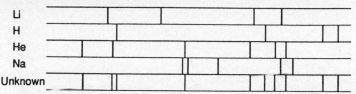

Li
H
He
Na
Unknown

   (1) lithium and sodium
   (2) sodium and hydrogen
   (3) lithium and helium
   (4) helium and hydrogen

11. The electron configuration of an atom in the ground state is $1s^2 2s^2 2p^2$. The total number of occupied principal energy levels in this atom is
   (1) 1   (3) 3
   (2) 2   (4) 4

12. Which sublevel is being filled with electrons in elements with atomic numbers 21 through 29?
   (1) $3s$ (3) $3d$
   (2) $4p$ (4) $4d$

13. Which kind of energy is stored in a chemical bond?
   (1) potential energy   (3) activation energy
   (2) kinetic energy   (4) ionization energy

14. Which type of bond is found in a molecule of methane?
   (1) a covalent bond   (3) an ionic bond
   (2) a hydrogen bond   (4) a metallic bond

15. Which electron dot formula represents a polar molecule?

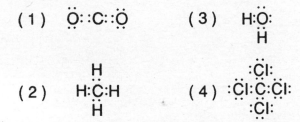

16. The correct formula for calcium phosphate is
   (1) $CaPO_4$ (3) Ca_3P_2
   (2) $Ca_2(PO_4)_3$ (4) $Ca_3(PO_4)_2$

17. The van der Waals forces of attraction between molecules always become stronger as molecular size
   (1) increases, and the distance between the molecules increases
   (2) increases, and the distance between the molecules decreases
   (3) decreases, and the distance between the molecules increases
   (4) decreases, and the distance between the molecules decreases

18. Given the unbalanced equation:

$$Ca(OH)_2 + (NH_4)_2SO_4 \rightarrow CaSO_4 + NH_3 + H_2O$$

What is the sum of the coefficients when the equation is completely balanced using the smallest whole-number coefficients?
   (1) 5   (3) 9
   (2) 7   (4) 11

19. Which group in the Periodic Table contains elements that are all gases at STP?
   (1) 11 (IB)   (3) 12 (IIB)
   (2) 17 (VIIA)   (4) 18 (0)

20. Which period of the Periodic Table contains more metallic elements than non-metallic elements?
   (1) Period 1   (3) Period 3
   (2) Period 2   (4) Period 4

21. Bromine has chemical properties most similar to
   (1) fluorine   (3) krypton
   (2) potassium   (4) mercury

22. Which element in Period 5 of the Periodic Table is a transition element?
   (1) Sr   (3) Ag
   (2) Sb   (4) Xe

23. Which first ionization energy is the most probable for a very reactive metal?
   (1) 90 kcal/mol   (3) 402 kcal/mol
   (2) 260 kcal/mol   (4) 567 kcal/mol

24. The properties of elements are periodic functions of their
   (1) mass numbers   (3) atomic radii
   (2) atomic masses   (4) atomic numbers

25. Which group contains elements in three phases of matter at STP?
   (1) noble gases
   (2) transition elements
   (3) alkaline earth metals
   (4) halogens

26. According to Reference Table E, which of the following compounds will form a saturated solution that is the most dilute?
   (1) ammonium chloride
   (2) calcium carbonate
   (3) potassium iodide
   (4) sodium nitrate

27. Given the reaction:

$$2C_2H_6(g) + 7O_2(g) \rightarrow 4CO_2(g) + 6H_2O(g)$$

What is the total number of liters of $CO_2(g)$ produced by the complete combustion of 1 liter of $C_2H_6(g)$?
   (1) 1 L   (3) 0.5 L
   (2) 2 L   (4) 4 L

28. When 20. milliliters of 1.0 M HCl is diluted to a total volume of 60. milliliters, the concentration of the resulting solution is
   (1) 1.0 M   (3) 0.33 M
   (2) 0.50 M   (4) 0.25 M

29. What is the total mass in grams of 0.75 mole of SO_2?
   (1) 16 g   (3) 32 g
   (2) 24 g   (4) 48 g

30. A solution containing 60. grams of $NaNO_3$ completely dissolved in 50. grams of water at 50.°C is classified as being
   (1) saturated
   (2) supersaturated
   (3) dilute and unsaturated
   (4) dilute and saturated

31. Assume that the potential energy of the products in a chemical reaction is 60 kilocalories. This reaction would be exothermic if the potential energy of the reactants were
    (1) 50 kcal
    (2) 20 kcal
    (3) 30 kcal
    (4) 80 kcal

32. Which species can act as a Brönsted-Lowry acid?
    (1) SO_2
    (2) CO_2
    (3) NH_4^+
    (4) PO_4^{3-}

33. If a catalyst is added to a system at equilibrium and the temperature and pressure remain constant, there will be no effect on the
    (1) rate of the forward reaction
    (2) rate of the reverse reaction
    (3) activation energy of the reaction
    (4) heat of reaction

34. A 1-cubic-centimeter cube of sodium reacts more rapidly in water at 25°C than does a 1-cubic-centimeter cube of calcium at 25°C. This difference in rate of reaction is most closely associated with the different
    (1) surface area of the metal cubes
    (2) nature of the metals
    (3) density of the metals
    (4) concentration of the metals

35. Given the reaction at equilibrium:

    $$X_2(g) + 2Y_2(g) \rightleftarrows 2XY_2(g) + 80 \text{ kcal}$$

    The equilibrium point will shift to the right if the pressure is
    (1) increased and the temperature is increased
    (2) increased and the temperature is decreased
    (3) decreased and the temperature is increased
    (4) decreased and the temperature is decreased

36. Given the reaction at equilibrium:

    $$A(g) \rightleftarrows B(g) + C(\ell)$$

    Which equilibrium constant indicates an equilibrium mixture with the smallest concentration of $B(g)$?
    (1) $K_{eq} = 1.0 \times 10^{-10}$
    (2) $K_{eq} = 1.0 \times 10^0$
    (3) $K_{eq} = 1.0 \times 10^1$
    (4) $K_{eq} = 1.0 \times 10^{10}$

37. An acid has an ionization constant (K_a) of 1.0×10^{-8}. This value indicates that the acid is
    (1) weak
    (2) strong
    (3) extremely soluble
    (4) slightly soluble

38. When NaOH(aq) reacts completely with HCl(aq) and the resulting solution is evaporated to dryness, the solid remaining is
    (1) an ester
    (2) an alcohol
    (3) a salt
    (4) a metal

39. In the reaction

    $$NH_3(g) + H_2O(\ell) \rightarrow NH_4^+(aq) + OH^-(aq),$$

    the $NH_3(g)$ acts as
    (1) a Brönsted acid, only
    (2) a Brönsted base, only
    (3) both a Brönsted acid and a Brönsted base
    (4) neither a Brönsted acid nor a Brönsted base

40. Which equation represents a neutralization reaction?
    (1) $Ca(OH)_2 \rightarrow Ca^{2+} + 2OH^-$
    (2) $CaCl_2 \rightarrow Ca^{2+} + 2Cl^-$
    (3) $H^+ + OH^- \rightarrow HOH$
    (4) $H^+ + F^- \rightarrow HF$

41. Which compound is a strong electrolyte?
    (1) $C_6H_{12}O_6$ (3) HNO_2
    (2) CH_3OH (4) H_2SO_4

42. In the redox reaction

$$C(s) + H_2O(g) \rightarrow CO(g) + H_2(g),$$

there is competititon between C atoms and H atoms for
    (1) protons   (3) electrons
    (2) neutrons   (4) positrons

43. In which species does hydrogen have an oxidation number of -1?
    (1) H_2O (3) NaH
    (2) H_2 (4) NaOH

44. In the reaction $Pb + 2Ag^+ \rightarrow Pb^{2+} + 2Ag$, the oxidizing agent is
    (1) Ag^+ (3) Pb
    (2) Ag   (4) Pb^{2+}

45. In the reaction $2Mg + O_2 \rightarrow 2MgO$, the magnesium is the
    (1) oxidizing agent and is reduced
    (2) oxidizing agent and is oxidized
    (3) reducing agent and is reduced
    (4) reducing agent and is oxidized

46. According to Reference Table N, which is the strongest reducing agent?
    (1) Li(s)   (3) $F_2(g)$
    (2) Na(s)   (4) $Br_2(\ell)$

47. Given the reaction:

$$\_\_Cr + \_\_Fe^{2+} \rightarrow \_\_Cr^{3+} + \_\_Fe$$

When the reaction is completely balanced using the smallest whole-number coefficients, the sum of the coefficients is
    (1) 10   (3) 3
    (2) 6   (4) 4

48. For simplicity, the structure of benzene is often represented as

(1)   (3)

(2)   (4)

49. Which is the general formula for the alkane series of hydrocarbons?
    (1) C_nH_{2n+2} (3) C_nH_{2n-2}
    (2) C_nH_{2n} (4) C_nH_{2n-6}

50. Which is an accurate description of the two compounds shown below?

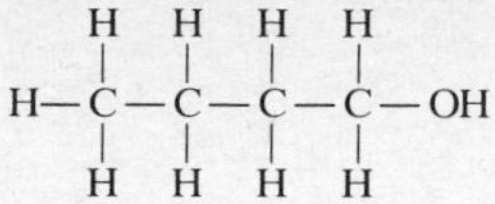

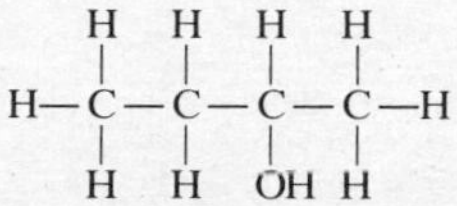

```
      H   H   H   H
      |   |   |   |
  H — C — C — C — C — OH
      |   |   |   |
      H   H   H   H


      H   H   H   H
      |   |   |   |
  H — C — C — C — C —H
      |   |   |   |
      H   H   OH  H
```

(1) They are isotopes of butanol.
(2) They are isomers of butanol.
(3) They are alkanes.
(4) They are alkenes.

51. Which is a product of the hydrolysis of an animal fat by a strong base?
   (1) water   (3) soap
   (2) gasoline   (4) toluene

52. Which is a saturated hydrocarbon?
   (1) ethene   (3) propene
   (2) ethyne   (4) propane

Note that questions 53 through 56 have only three choices.

53. As an acid solution is added to a basic solution, the pH of the basic solution
   (1) decreases
   (2) increases
   (3) remains the same

54. Given the equation: $I + I \rightarrow I_2$
   As the atoms of the iodine react to form molecules of iodine, the stability of the iodine
   (1) decreases
   (2) increases
   (3) remains the same

55. As heat is added to a liquid that is boiling at constant pressure, the temperature of the liquid
   (1) decreases
   (2) increases
   (3) remains the same

56. As the number of moles per liter of a reactant in a chemical reaction increases, the number of collisions between the reacting particles
   (1) decreases
   (2) increases
   (3) remains the same

Part II

This part consists of twelve groups, each containing five questions. Each group tests a major area of the course. Choose seven of these twelve groups. Be sure that you answer all five questions in each group chosen. [35]

Group 1 — Matter and Energy

If you choose this group, be sure to answer questions 57–61.

57. The table below shows the changes in the volume of a gas as the pressure changes at constant temperature.

P (atm)	V (mL)
0.5	1000
1.0	500
2.0	250

Which equation best expresses the relationship between pressure and volume for the gas?

(1) $\dfrac{P}{V} = 500$ atm · mL

(2) $PV = 500$ atm · mL

(3) $\dfrac{V}{P} = 500$ atm · mL

(4) $PV = \dfrac{1}{500}$ atm · mL

58. According to Reference Table I, the dissolving of $NH_4Cl(s)$ in water is
    (1) exothermic and the heat of reaction is negative
    (2) exothermic and the heat of reaction is positive
    (3) endothermic and the heat of reaction is negative
    (4) endothermic and the heat of reaction is positive

59. Which pair are classified as chemical substances?
    (1) mixtures and solutions
    (2) compounds and solutions
    (3) elements and mixtures
    (4) compounds and elements

60. The graph below represents the uniform cooling of a substance, starting with the substance as a gas above its boiling point.

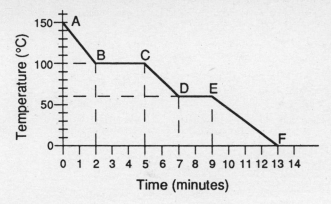

How much time passes between the first appearance of the liquid phase of the substance and the presence of the substance completely in its solid phase?
(1) 5 minutes   (3) 7 minutes
(2) 2 minutes   (4) 4 minutes

61. Which potential energy diagram represents an exothermic reaction?

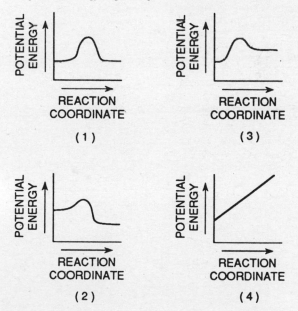

Group 2 — Atomic Structure

If you choose this group, be sure to answer questions 62–66.

62. Compared to an atom of calcium-40, an atom of potassium-39 contains fewer
    (1) protons
    (2) neutrons
    (3) occupied sublevels
    (4) occupied principal energy levels

63. An experiment using alpha particles to bombard a thin sheet of gold foil indicated that most of the volume of the atoms in the foil is taken up by
    (1) electrons   (3) neutrons
    (2) protons   (4) empty space

64. An atom contains a total of 25 electrons. When the atom is in the ground state, how many different principal energy levels will contain electrons?
    (1) 1   (3) 3
    (2) 2   (4) 4

65. Energy is released when an electron changes from a sublevel of
    (1) $1s$ to $2p$ (3) $3s$ to $2s$
    (2) $2s$ to $3s$ (4) $3p$ to $5s$

66. If 3.0 grams of ^{90}Sr in a rock sample remained in 1989, approximately how many grams of ^{90}Sr were present in the original rock sample in 1933?
    (1) 9.0 g   (3) 3.0 g
    (2) 6.0 g   (4) 12. g

Group 3 — Bonding

If you choose this group, be sure to answer questions 67–71.

67. Which is an empirical formula?
    (1) H_2O_2 (3) C_2H_2
    (2) H_2O (4) C_3H_6

68. In which compound does the bond between the atoms have the *least* ionic character?
    (1) HF   (3) HBr
    (2) HCl   (4) HI

69. Hydrogen bonds are formed between molecules when hydrogen is covalently bonded to an element that has a
    (1) small atomic radius and low electronegativity
    (2) large atomic radius and low electronegativity
    (3) small atomic radius and high electronegativity
    (4) large atomic radius and high electronegativity

70. The kind of attractions that result in the dissolving of sodium chloride in water are
    (1) ion-ion   (3) atom-atom
    (2) molecule-ion   (4) molecule-atom

71. What kind of bond is formed in the reaction shown below?

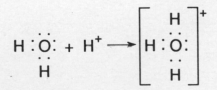

    (1) metallic bond
    (2) hydrogen bond
    (3) network bond
    (4) coordinate covalent bond

Group 4 — Periodic Table

If you choose this group, be sure to answer questions 72-76.

72. Element X is in Group 2 (IIA) and element Y is in Group 17 (VIIA). A compound formed between these two elements is most likely to have the formula
    (1) X_2Y (3) X_2Y_7
    (2) XY_2 (4) X_7Y_2

73. An ion of which element is larger than its atom?
    (1) Al   (3) Ca
    (2) Br   (4) Sr

74. Which element in Period 3 has the largest covalent atomic radius?
    (1) Cl   (3) Na
    (2) Al   (4) P

75. Which element in Group 15 (VA) has the most metallic character?
    (1) N   (3) As
    (2) P   (4) Bi

76. Which noble gas would most likely form a compound with fluorine?
    (1) He   (3) Ar
    (2) Ne   (4) Kr

Group 5 — Mathematics of Chemistry

If you choose this group, be sure to answer questions 77-81.

77. A compound contains 16% carbon and 84% sulfur by mass. What is the empirical formula of this compound?
    (1) CS_2 (3) CS
    (2) C_2S_2 (4) C_2S

78. Given the reaction:

$$2Al + 3H_2SO_4 \rightarrow 3H_2 + Al_2(SO_4)_3$$

The total number of moles of H_2SO_4 needed to react completely with 5.0 moles of Al is
    (1) 2.5 moles   (3) 7.5 moles
    (2) 5.0 moles   (4) 9.0 moles

79. The percent, by mass, of water in $BaCl_2 \cdot 2H_2O$ (formula mass = 243) is equal to
    (1) $\frac{18}{243} \times 100$ (3) $\frac{243}{18} \times 100$
    (2) $\frac{36}{243} \times 100$ (4) $\frac{243}{36} \times 100$

80. What is the maximum number of grams of water at 10.°C that can be heated to 30.°C by the addition of 40.0 calories of heat?
    (1) 1.0 g   (3) 20. g
    (2) 2.0 g   (4) 30. g

81. Which solution containing 1 mole of solute dissolved in 1000 grams of water has the lowest freezing point?
    (1) KOH(aq)   (3) C_2H_5OH(aq)
    (2) $C_2H_{12}O_6$(aq)   (4) $C_{12}H_{22}O_{11}$(aq)

Group 6 — Kinetics and Equilibrium

If you choose this group, be sure to answer questions 82–86.

82. What is the free energy change for a system at equilibrium?
    (1) one
    (2) greater than one
    (3) zero
    (4) less than zero

83. Which is the correct equilibrium expression for the reaction

    $4NH_3(g) + 5O_2(g) \rightleftarrows 4NO(g) + 6H_2O(g)$?

    (1) $K_{eq} = \dfrac{[NO]^4 [H_2O]^6}{[NH_3]^4 [O_2]^5}$

    (2) $K_{eq} = \dfrac{[NO]^4 + [H_2O]^6}{[NH_3]^4 + [O_2]^5}$

    (3) $K_{eq} = \dfrac{[4NO] [6H_2O]}{[4NH_3] [5O_2]}$

    (4) $K_{eq} = \dfrac{[4NO] + [6H_2O]}{[4NH_3] + [5O_2]}$

84. When $AgNO_3(aq)$ is mixed with $NaCl(aq)$, a reaction occurs which tends to go to completion because
    (1) a gas is formed
    (2) water is formed
    (3) a weak acid is formed
    (4) a precipitate is formed

85. Given the reaction at equilibrium:

    $2CO(g) + O_2(g) \rightleftarrows 2CO_2(g)$

    Which statement regarding this reaction is always true?
    (1) The rates of the forward and reverse reactions are equal.
    (2) The reaction occurs in an open system.
    (3) The masses of the reactants and the products are equal.
    (4) The concentrations of the reactants and the products are equal.

86. According to Reference Table G, $ICl(g)$ is formed from its elements in a reaction that is
    (1) exothermic and spontaneous
    (2) exothermic and not spontaneous
    (3) endothermic and spontaneous
    (4) endothermic and not spontaneous

Group 7 — Acids and Bases

If you choose this group, be sure to answer questions 87–91.

87. What are the relative ion concentrations in an acid solution?
    (1) more H^+ ions than OH^- ions
    (2) fewer H^+ ions than OH^- ions
    (3) an equal number of H^+ ions and OH^- ions
    (4) H^+ ions but no OH^- ions

88. According to Reference Table L, which molecule is amphiprotic?
    (1) HCl
    (2) H_2SO_4
    (3) NH_3
    (4) H_2S

89. An aqueous solution with a pH of 4 would have a hydroxide ion concentration of
    (1) 1×10^{-4} mol/L
    (2) 1×10^{-7} mol/L
    (3) 1×10^{-10} mol/L
    (4) 1×10^{-14} mol/L

90. What is the molarity of an NaOH solution if 20. milliliters of 2.0 M HCl is required to exactly neutralize 10. milliliters of the NaOH solution?
    (1) 1.0 M
    (2) 2.0 M
    (3) 0.50 M
    (4) 4.0 M

91. According to Reference Table N, which metal will react with 0.1 M HCl?
    (1) Au(s)
    (2) Ag(s)
    (3) $Hg(\ell)$
    (4) Mg(s)

Group 8 — Redox and Electrochemistry

If you choose this group, be sure to answer questions 92–96.

92. When equilibrium is attained in a chemical cell, the cell voltage is
    (1) between 0 and -1
    (2) 0
    (3) between 0 and $+1$
    (4) greater than $+1$

93. Given the reaction:

$$Al(s) + 3Ag^+ \rightarrow Al^{3+} + 3Ag(s)$$

    Based on Reference Table N, what is the potential (E^0) for the overall reaction?
    (1) $+.74$ V   (3) $+2.46$ V
    (2) $+1.66$ V   (4) $+4.06$ V

94. According to Reference Table N, which atom-ion pair will react spontaneously?
    (1) $Ag + Au^{3+}$ (3) $Ni + Al^{3+}$
    (2) $Pb + Co^{2+}$ (4) $Zn + Ca^{2+}$

Base your answers to questions 95 and 96 on the diagram below of an electrolytic cell in which the electrodes are tin and copper.

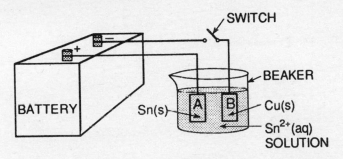

95. When the switch is closed, what will happen to the two electrodes?
    (1) B will dissolve and A will become coated with tin.
    (2) A will dissolve and B will become coated with tin.
    (3) B will dissolve and A will become coated with copper.
    (4) A will dissolve and B will become coated with copper.

96. In this electrolytic cell, electrode A is designated as the
    (1) anode and is positive
    (2) anode and is negative
    (3) cathode and is positive
    (4) cathode and is negative

Group 9 — Organic Chemistry

If you choose this group, be sure to answer questions 97–101.

97. Which structural formula represents a monohydroxy alcohol?

(1) H—C—C—C—H

(2) H—C—C—C—H

(3) H—C—C—C—H

(4) H—C—C—O—C—H

98. Which is *not* a naturally occurring polymer?
    (1) starch
    (2) cellulose
    (3) protein
    (4) nylon

99. When C_2H_4 molecules polymerize, the name of the polymer formed is
    (1) polymethylene
    (2) polyethylene
    (3) polypropylene
    (4) polybutylene

100. In the molecule represented by the formula

$$R-\overset{\displaystyle H}{\underset{\displaystyle H}{\vphantom{|}C}}-OH,$$

R could be
    (1) CH
    (2) CH_2
    (3) CH_3
    (4) CH_4

101. The equation $CH_3OH + CH_3OH \rightarrow CH_3OCH_3 + H_2O$ illustrates the
    (1) oxidation of alcohols to form a ketone
    (2) oxidation of alcohols to form an acid
    (3) dehydration of alcohols to form a polymer
    (4) dehydration of alcohols to form an ether

Group 10 — Applications of Chemical Principles

If you choose this group, be sure to answer questions 102–106.

102. The process of separating petroleum into components based on differences in their boiling points is called
    (1) cracking
    (2) hydrogenation
    (3) destructive distillation
    (4) fractional distillation

103. Given the nickel oxide–cadmium reaction:

$$2NiOOH + Cd + 2H_2O \rightarrow 2Ni(OH)_2 + Cd(OH)_2$$

During discharge, the Cd electrode
    (1) is oxidized
    (2) is reduced
    (3) gains electrons
    (4) gains mass

104. Natural gas is composed mostly of
    (1) butane
    (2) octane
    (3) methane
    (4) propane

105. In a reaction that has achieved equilibrium, the point of equilibrium is least likely to be shifted when
    (1) the temperature is increased
    (2) a catalyst is added
    (3) products are partially removed
    (4) reactants are added

106. The redox reaction in a battery during discharge can best be described as
    (1) nonspontaneous and occurring in a chemical cell
    (2) spontaneous and occurring in a chemical cell
    (3) nonspontaneous and occurring in an electrolytic cell
    (4) spontaneous and occurring in an electrolytic cell

Group 11 — Nuclear Chemistry

If you choose this group, be sure to answer questions 107–111.

107. Radioisotopes used in medical diagnosis should have
    (1) short half-lives and be quickly eliminated from the body
    (2) short half-lives and be slowly eliminated from the body
    (3) long half-lives and be quickly eliminated from the body
    (4) long half-lives and be slowly eliminated from the body

108. Particle accelerators are primarily used to
    (1) detect radioactive particles
    (2) identify radioactive particles
    (3) increase a particle's kinetic energy
    (4) increase a particle's potential energy

109. Compared to a nuclear reaction, a chemical reaction differs in that the energy produced by a chemical reaction results primarily from
    (1) a conversion of some of the reactant's mass
    (2) a loss of potential energy by the reactants
    (3) the fusion of two nuclei
    (4) the fission of a nucleus

110. Which pair of isotopes can serve as fissionable nuclear fuels?
    (1) U-235 and Pb-208
    (2) U-235 and Pu-239
    (3) Pb-208 and Pu-239
    (4) Pb-206 and U-235

111. The nuclear reaction $_2^4He + _{13}^{27}Al \rightarrow _{15}^{30}P + _0^1n$ is an example of
    (1) nuclear fusion
    (2) nuclear fission
    (3) natural transmutation
    (4) artificial transmutation

Group 12 — Laboratory Activities

If you choose this group, be sure to answer questions 112–116.

112. Which volume measurement is expressed in four significant figures?
    (1) 5.50 mL   (3) 5,500 mL
    (2) 550. mL   (4) 5,500. mL

113. A student in a laboratory determined the boiling point of a substance to be 71.8°C. The accepted value for the boiling point of this substance is 70.2°C. What is the percent error of the student's measurement?
    (1) 1.60%   (3) 2.23%
    (2) 2.28%   (4) 160.%

114. The table below was compiled from experimental laboratory data.

INDICATOR	CHANGE	pH RANGE AT WHICH CHANGE OCCURS
Bromthymol Blue	yellow → blue	6.2 – 7.6
Thymol Blue	red → yellow	1.2 – 2.8
Methyl Orange	red → yellow	3.1 – 4.4

At what pH would all three indicators appear as yellow?
(1) 1.9　　　　　　　　　　　　(3) 4.7
(2) 2.9　　　　　　　　　　　　(4) 8.7

　Base your answers to questions 115 and 116 on the graph below which shows the equilibrium vapor pressure curves of liquids A, B, C, and D.

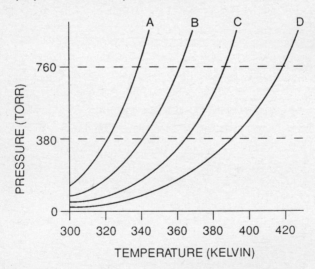

115. Which liquid has the strongest intermolecular forces of attraction at 320 K?
(1) A　　　　　　　　　　　　(3) C
(2) B　　　　　　　　　　　　(4) D

116. Which liquid has the lowest normal boiling point?
(1) A　　　　　　　　　　　　(3) C
(2) B　　　　　　　　　　　　(4) D

CHEMISTRY

June 23, 1992

PART I

Answer all 56 questions in this part. [65]

Directions (1–56): For *each* statement or question, select the word or expression that, of those given, best completes the statement or answers the question.

1. Which substance can be decomposed by a chemical change?
   (1) beryllium   (3) methanol
   (2) boron   (4) magnesium

2. The particles in a crystalline solid are arranged
   (1) randomly and far apart
   (2) randomly and close together
   (3) regularly and far apart
   (4) regularly and close together

3. The strongest intermolecular forces of attraction exist in a liquid whose heat of vaporization is
   (1) 100 cal/g   (3) 300 cal/g
   (2) 200 cal/g   (4) 400 cal/g

4. If the pressure on the surface of water in the liquid state is 355.1 torr, the water will boil at
   (1) 0°C   (3) 80°C
   (2) 40°C   (4) 100°C

5. When a substance was dissolved in water, the temperature of the water increased. This process is described as
   (1) endothermic, with the release of energy
   (2) endothermic, with the absorption of energy
   (3) exothermic, with the release of energy
   (4) exothermic, with the absorption of energy

6. Compared to the entire atom, the nucleus of the atom is
   (1) smaller and contains most of the atom's mass
   (2) smaller and contains little of the atom's mass
   (3) larger and contains most of the atom's mass
   (4) larger and contains little of the atom's mass

7. All isotopes of a given element must have the same
   (1) atomic mass
   (2) atomic number
   (3) mass number
   (4) number of neutrons

8. In the equation $^{234}_{90}Th \rightarrow\ ^{234}_{91}Pa + X$, which particle is represented by X?

   (1) $^{0}_{-1}e$ (3) $^{1}_{1}H$

   (2) $^{4}_{2}He$ (4) $^{0}_{+1}e$

9. Four valence electrons of an atom in the ground state would occupy the
   (1) s sublevel, only
   (2) p sublevel, only
   (3) s and p sublevels, only
   (4) s, p, and d sublevels

10. Which particle has a mass of approximately one atomic mass unit and a unit positive charge?
    (1) a neutron   (3) a beta particle
    (2) a proton   (4) an alpha particle

11. An atom of carbon-14 contains
    (1) 8 protons, 6 neutrons, and 6 electrons
    (2) 6 protons, 6 neutrons, and 8 electrons
    (3) 6 protons, 8 neutrons, and 8 electrons
    (4) 6 protons, 8 neutrons, and 6 electrons

12. In an atom that has an electron configuration of $1s^2 2s^2 2p^3$, what is the total number of electrons in its sublevel of highest energy?
    (1) 1
    (2) 2
    (3) 3
    (4) 4

13. The correct electron dot formula for hydrogen chloride is
    (1) H : Cl
    (2) : Ḧ : Cl
    (3) H : C̈l :
    (4) : H : C̈l :

14. What is the total mass of oxygen in 1.00 mole of $Al_2(CrO_4)_3$?
    (1) 192 g
    (2) 112 g
    (3) 64.0 g
    (4) 48.0 g

15. Which molecule is nonpolar and has a symmetrical shape?
    (1) HCl
    (2) CH_4
    (3) H_2O
    (4) NH_3

16. What is the correct formula for ammonium carbonate?
    (1) $NH_4(CO_3)_2$
    (2) NH_4CO_3
    (3) $(NH_4)_2(CO_3)_2$
    (4) $(NH_4)_2CO_3$

17. What type of bonding is present within a network solid?
    (1) hydrogen
    (2) covalent
    (3) ionic
    (4) metallic

18. The table below lists four different chemical bonds and the amount of energy released when 1 mole of each of the bonds is formed.

Bond	Energy Released in Formation (kcal/mole)
H–F	135
H–Cl	103
H–Br	87
H–I	71

Which bond is the most stable?
    (1) H–F
    (2) H–Cl
    (3) H–Br
    (4) H–I

19. Which element is in Group 2 (IIA) and Period 7 of the Periodic Table?
    (1) magnesium
    (2) manganese
    (3) radium
    (4) radon

20. Which ion has the largest radius?
    (1) I^-
    (2) Cl^-
    (3) Br^-
    (4) F^-

21. An atom in the ground state contains 8 valence electrons. This atom is classified as a
    (1) metal
    (2) semimetal
    (3) noble gas
    (4) halogen

22. Nonmetals in the solid state are poor conductors of heat and tend to
    (1) be brittle
    (2) be malleable
    (3) have a shiny luster
    (4) have good electrical conductivity

23. Which group contains elements composed of diatomic molecules at STP?
    (1) 11 (IB)   (3) 7 (VIIB)
    (2) 2 (IIA)   (4) 17 (VIIA)

24. Which metal atoms can form ionic bonds by losing electrons from both the outer-most and next to outermost principal energy levels?
    (1) Fe   (3) Mg
    (2) Pb   (4) Ca

25. Which species contains the greatest percent by mass of hydrogen?
    (1) OH^- (3) H_3O^+
    (2) H_2O (4) H_2O_2

26. Given the reaction:

$$CH_4(g) + 2O_2(g) \rightarrow CO_2(g) + 2H_2O(g)$$

How many moles of oxygen are needed for the complete combustion of 3.0 moles of $CH_4(g)$?
    (1) 6.0 moles   (3) 3.0 moles
    (2) 2.0 moles   (4) 4.0 moles

27. How many moles of $N_2(g)$ molecules would contain exactly 4.0 moles of nitrogen atoms?
    (1) 1.0   (3) 3.0
    (2) 2.0   (4) 4.0

28. What mass contains 6.0×10^{23} atoms?
    (1) 6.0 g of carbon   (3) 3.0 g of helium
    (2) 16 g of sulfur   (4) 28 g of silicon

29. Which is a homogeneous mixture?
    (1) $I_2(s)$ (3) $HCl(g)$
    (2) $I_2(\ell)$ (4) $HCl(aq)$

30. When a catalyst is added to a chemical reaction, there is a change in the
    (1) heat of reaction
    (2) rate of reaction
    (3) potential energy of the reactants
    (4) potential energy of the products

31. A piece of Mg(s) ribbon is held in a bunsen burner flame and begins to burn according to the equation $2Mg(s) + O_2(g) \rightarrow 2MgO(s)$. The reaction begins because the reactants
    (1) are activated by heat from the bunsen burner flame
    (2) are activated by heat from the burning magnesium
    (3) underwent an increase in entropy
    (4) underwent a decrease in entropy

32. Raising the temperature speeds up the rate of a chemical reaction by increasing
    (1) the effectiveness of the collisions, only
    (2) the frequency of the collisions, only
    (3) both the effectiveness and the frequency of the collisions
    (4) neither the effectiveness nor the frequency of the collisions

33. Which tendencies favor a spontaneous reaction?
    (1) decreasing enthalpy and decreasing entropy
    (2) decreasing enthalpy and increasing entropy
    (3) increasing enthalpy and decreasing entropy
    (4) increasing enthalpy and increasing entropy

34. Which formula represents a salt?
    (1) KOH   (3) CH_3OH
    (2) KCl   (4) CH_3COOH

35. What is the H_3O^+ ion concentration of a solution whose OH^- ion concentration is 1×10^{-3} M?
    (1) 1×10^{-4} M
    (2) 1×10^{-7} M
    (3) 1×10^{-11} M
    (4) 1×10^{-14} M

36. Which of the following acids is the weakest?
    (1) H_2S
    (2) HF
    (3) H_3PO_4
    (4) HNO_2

37. Given the reaction at equilibrium:

    $$NH_4^+ + OH^- \rightleftarrows H_2O + NH_3$$

    Which species is the Brönsted-Lowry acid in the forward reaction?
    (1) NH_3
    (2) H_2O
    (3) OH^-
    (4) NH_4^+

38. To neutralize 1 mole of sulfuric acid, 2 moles of sodium hydroxide are required. How many liters of 1 M NaOH are needed to exactly neutralize 1 liter of 1 M H_2SO_4?
    (1) 1
    (2) 2
    (3) 0.5
    (4) 4

39. What is the conjugate base of NH_3?
    (1) NH_4^+
    (2) NH_2^-
    (3) NO_3^-
    (4) NO_2^-

40. An aqueous solution of an ionic compound turns red litmus blue, conducts electricity, and reacts with an acid to form a salt and water. This compound could be
    (1) HCl
    (2) NaI
    (3) KNO_3
    (4) LiOH

41. Oxygen will have a positive oxidation number when combined with
    (1) fluorine
    (2) chlorine
    (3) bromine
    (4) iodine

42. In the reaction $2Al(s) + 3Cu^{2+}(aq) \rightarrow 2Al^{3+}(aq) + 3Cu(s)$, the Al(s)
    (1) gains protons
    (2) loses protons
    (3) gains electrons
    (4) loses electrons

43. The purpose of a salt bridge in an electrochemical cell is to
    (1) allow for the flow of molecules between the solutions
    (2) allow for the flow of ions between the solutions
    (3) prevent the flow of molecules between the solutions
    (4) prevent the flow of ions between the solutions

44. In the reaction $Pb + 2Ag^+ \rightarrow Pb^2 + 2Ag$, the Ag^+ is
    (1) reduced, and the oxidation number changes from +1 to 0
    (2) reduced, and the oxidation number changes from +2 to 0
    (3) oxidized, and the oxidation number changes from 0 to +1
    (4) oxidized, and the oxidation number changes from +1 to 0

45. Which half-reaction correctly represents oxidation?
    (1) $Mg + 2e^- \rightarrow Mg^{2+}$
    (2) $Mg^{2+} + 2e^- \rightarrow Mg$
    (3) $Mg^{2+} \rightarrow Mg + 2e^-$
    (4) $Mg \rightarrow Mg^{2+} + 2e^-$

46. When the equation $\_Pb^{2+} + \_Au^{3+} \rightarrow \_Pb^{4+} + \_Au$ is correctly balanced using the smallest whole-number coefficients, the coefficient of the Pb^{2+} will be
    (1) 1
    (2) 2
    (3) 3
    (4) 4

47. Which alcohol reacts with C_2H_5COOH to produce the ester $C_2H_5COOC_2H_5$?
    (1) CH_3OH
    (2) C_2H_5OH
    (3) C_3H_7OH
    (4) C_4H_9OH

48. A compound with the molecular formula C_7H_8 could be a member of the hydro-carbon series which has the general formula
    (1) C_nH_{2n}
    (2) C_nH_{2n-2}
    (3) C_nH_{2n-6}
    (4) C_nH_{2n+2}

49. Given the equation:

    $C_6H_{12}O_6 \xrightarrow{\text{zymase}} 2C_2H_5OH + 2CO_2$

    The reaction represented by this equation is called
    (1) esterification
    (2) saponification
    (3) fermentation
    (4) polymerization

50. Which structural formula represents an isomer of

$$
\begin{array}{ccc}
H & H & H \\
| & | & | \\
H-C-C-C=O? \\
| & | \\
H & H
\end{array}
$$

(1)
$$
\begin{array}{ccc}
H & H & H \\
| & | & | \\
H-C-C-O-C-H \\
| & | & | \\
H & H & H
\end{array}
$$

(2)
$$
\begin{array}{ccc}
H & O & H \\
| & \| & | \\
H-C-C-C-H \\
| & & | \\
H & & H
\end{array}
$$

(3)
$$
\begin{array}{ccc}
H & H & H \\
| & | & | \\
H-C-C-C-OH \\
| & | & | \\
H & H & H
\end{array}
$$

(4)
$$
\begin{array}{ccc}
H & H & O \\
| & | & \diagup\!\!\diagdown \\
H-C-C-C \\
| & | & \diagdown \\
H & H & OH
\end{array}
$$

51. Which compound can undergo an addition reaction?
    (1) CH_4
    (2) C_2H_4
    (3) C_3H_8
    (4) C_4H_{10}

Note that questions 52 through 56 have only three choices.

52. A closed system is shown in the diagram below.

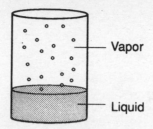

The rate of vapor formation at equilibrium is
(1) less than the rate of liquid formation
(2) greater than the rate of liquid formation
(3) equal to the rate of liquid formation

53. If the pressure on a given mass of gas in a closed system is increased and the temperature remains constant, the volume of the gas will
(1) decrease
(2) increase
(3) remain the same

54. Given the reaction at equilibrium:

$$N_2(g) + O_2(g) = 2NO(g)$$

If the temperature remains constant and the pressure increases, the number of moles of $NO(g)$ will
(1) decrease
(2) increase
(3) remain the same

55. As a chemical bond forms between two hydrogen atoms, the potential energy of the atoms
(1) decreases
(2) increases
(3) remains the same

56. As the elements in Period 3 of the Periodic Table are considered in order of increasing atomic number, the ability of each successive element to act as a reducing agent
(1) decreases
(2) increases
(3) remains the same

PART II

This part consists of twelve groups, each containing five questions. Each group tests a major area of the course. Choose seven of these twelve groups. Be sure that you answer all five questions in each group chosen. [35]

Group 1—Matter and Energy

If you choose this group, be sure to answer questions 57–61.

57. Compared to the average kinetic energy of 1 mole of water at 0°C, the average kinetic energy of 1 mole of water at 298 K is
(1) the same, and the number of molecules is the same
(2) the same, but the number of molecules is greater
(3) greater, and the number of molecules is greater
(4) greater, but the number of molecules is the same

58. Which formula represents a binary compound?
    (1) Ne
    (2) Br_2
    (3) C_3H_8
    (4) H_2SO_4

59. At standard pressure, which element at 25°C could undergo a change of phase when the temperature is decreased?
    (1) aluminum
    (2) chlorine
    (3) silicon
    (4) sulfur

60. Which change results in a release of energy?
    (1) the melting of $H_2O(s)$
    (2) the boiling of $H_2O(\ell)$
    (3) the evaporation of $H_2O(\ell)$
    (4) the condensation of $H_2O(g)$

61. A cylinder is filled with 2.00 moles of nitrogen, 3.00 moles of argon, and 5.00 moles of helium. If the gas mixture is at STP, what is the partial pressure of the argon?
    (1) 152 torr
    (2) 228 torr
    (3) 380. torr
    (4) 760. torr

Group 2—Atomic Structure

If you choose this group, be sure to answer questions 62–66.

62. The total number of orbitals in a *d* sublevel is
    (1) 1
    (2) 5
    (3) 3
    (4) 7

63. Compared to ^{37}K, the isotope ^{42}K has a
    (1) shorter half-life and the same decay mode
    (2) shorter half-life and a different decay mode
    (3) longer half-life and the same decay mode
    (4) longer half-life and a different decay mode

64. A sample of ^{131}I decays to 1.0 gram in 40. days. What was the mass of the original sample?
    (1) 8.0 g
    (2) 16 g
    (3) 32 g
    (4) 4.0 g

65. What is the total number of occupied sublevels in an atom of chlorine in the ground state?
    (1) 1
    (2) 5
    (3) 3
    (4) 9

66. The characteristic bright-line spectrum of sodium is produced when its electrons
    (1) return to lower energy levels
    (2) jump to higher energy levels
    (3) are lost by the neutral atoms
    (4) are gained by the neutral atoms

Group 3—Bonding

If you choose this group, be sure to answer questions 67–71.

67. A substance that has a melting point of 1074 K conducts electricity when dissolved in water, but does *not* conduct electricity in the solid phase. The substance is most likely
    (1) an ionic solid
    (2) a network solid
    (3) a metallic solid
    (4) a molecular solid

68. Which quantity is represented by the symbol Ne?
    (1) 1 gram of neon
    (2) 1 liter of neon
    (3) 1 mole of neon
    (4) 1 atomic mass unit of neon

69. The diagram below represents a water molecule.

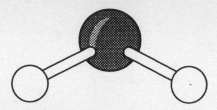

This molecule is best described as
(1) polar with polar covalent bonds
(2) polar with nonpolar covalent bonds
(3) nonpolar with polar covalent bonds
(4) nonpolar with nonpolar covalent bonds

70. The diagrams below represent an ionic crystal being dissolved in water.

According to the diagrams, the dissolving process takes place by
(1) hydrogen bond formation
(2) network bond formation
(3) van der Waals attractions
(4) molecule-ion attractions

71. When the equation
$$\_Al_2(SO_4)_3 + \_ZnCl_2 \rightarrow \_AlCl_3 + \_ZnSO_4$$
is correctly balanced using the smallest whole-number coefficients, the sum of the coefficients is
(1) 9   (3) 5
(2) 8   (4) 4

Group 4—Periodic Table

If you choose this group, be sure to answer questions 72–76.

72. Which aqueous salt solution has a color?
(1) $BaSO_4(aq)$ (3) $SrSO_4(aq)$
(2) $CuSO_4(aq)$ (4) $MgSO_4(aq)$

73. Which category is composed of elements that have both positive and negative oxidation states?
(1) the alkali metals
(2) the transition metals
(3) the halogens
(4) the alkaline earths

74. As the atoms of the elements from atomic number 3 to atomic number 9 are considered in sequence from left to right on the Periodic Table, the covalent atomic radius of each successive atom is
(1) smaller, and the nuclear charge is less
(2) smaller, and the nuclear charge is greater
(3) larger, and the nuclear charge is less
(4) larger, and the nuclear charge is greater

75. Which element is so active chemically that it occurs naturally only in compounds?
    (1) potassium
    (2) silver
    (3) copper
    (4) sulfur

76. Which element is a solid at room temperature and standard pressure?
    (1) bromine
    (2) iodine
    (3) mercury
    (4) neon

Group 5—Mathematics of Chemistry

If you choose this group, be sure to answer questions 77–81.

77. The temperature of 100 grams of water changes from 16°C to 20°C. What is the total number of calories of heat energy absorbed by the water?
    (1) 25
    (2) 40
    (3) 100
    (4) 400

78. When ethylene glycol (an antifreeze) is added to water, the boiling point of the water
    (1) decreases, and the freezing point decreases
    (2) decreases, and the freezing point increases
    (3) increases, and the freezing point decreases
    (4) increases, and the freezing point increases

79. A sample of a compound contains 24 grams of carbon and 64 grams of oxygen. What is the empirical formula of this compound?
    (1) CO
    (2) CO_2
    (3) C_2O_2
    (4) C_2O_4

80. Which gas has approximately the same density as C_2H_6 at STP?
    (1) NO
    (2) NH_3
    (3) H_2S
    (4) SO_2

81. At a temperature of 273 K, a 400.-milliliter gas sample has a pressure of 760. millimeters of mercury. If the pressure is changed to 380. millimeters of mercury, at which temperature will this gas sample have a volume of 551 milliliters?
    (1) 100 K
    (2) 188 K
    (3) 273 K
    (4) 546 K

Group 6—Kinetics and Equilibrium

If you choose this group, be sure to answer questions 82–86.

82. According to Reference Table E, which salt would have the smallest K_{sp} value?
    (1) $AlBr_3$
    (2) $PbBr_2$
    (3) $NaBr$
    (4) $AgBr$

83. Given the solution at equilibrium:

$$CaF_2(s) \rightleftarrows Ca^{2+}(aq) + 2F^-(aq)$$

What is the solubility product expression (K_{sp})?
    (1) $K_{sp} = [Ca^{2+}][F^-]$
    (2) $K_{sp} = [Ca^{2+}][2F^-]$
    (3) $K_{sp} = [Ca^{2+}][F^-]^2$
    (4) $K_{sp} = [Ca^{2+}]^2[F^-]$.

84. Based on Reference Table G, which compound will form spontaneously from its elements?
    (1) carbon dioxide (g)
    (2) nitrogen (II) oxide (g)
    (3) ethene (g)
    (4) ethyne (g)

85. Given the reaction:

$$2Na(s) + 2H_2O(\ell) \rightarrow 2Na^+(aq) + 2OH^-(aq) + H_2(g)$$

This reaction goes to completion because one of the products formed is
    (1) an insoluble base
    (2) a soluble base
    (3) a precipitate
    (4) a gas

86. Given the reaction at equilibrium:

$$PbCl_2(s) \rightleftarrows Pb^{2+}(aq) + 2Cl^-(aq)$$

When KCl(s) is added to the system, the equilibrium shifts to the
(1) right, and the concentration of Pb^{2+}(aq) ions decreases
(2) right, and the concentration of Pb^{2+}(aq) ions increases
(3) left, and the concentration of Pb^{2+}(aq) ions decreases
(4) left, and the concentration of Pb^{2+}(aq) ions increases

Group 7—Acids and Bases
If you choose this group, be sure to answer questions 87–91.

87. Given the reaction:

$$HF(aq) \rightleftarrows H^+(aq) + F^-(aq)$$

Which expression represents the equilibrium constant (K_a) for the acid HF?

(1) $K_a = \dfrac{[H^+][F^-]}{[HF]}$

(3) $K_a = \dfrac{[HF]}{[H^+][F^-]}$

(2) $K_a = [H^+][F^-]$

(4) $K_a = 2[HF]$

88. According to Reference Table L, which substance is amphoteric (amphiprotic)?
(1) HNO_3
(2) NO_2^-
(3) HCO_3^-
(4) HF

89. Which substance can act as an Arrhenius acid in aqueous solution?
(1) NaI
(2) HI
(3) LiH
(4) NH_3

90. Which of the following metals will react most readily with HCl(aq) to release hydrogen gas?
(1) aluminum
(2) copper
(3) silver
(4) gold

91. The diagram below illustrates an apparatus used to test the conductivity of various solutions.

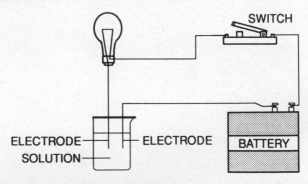

When the switch is closed, which of the following 1-molar solutions would cause the bulb to glow most brightly?
(1) ammonia
(2) acetic acid
(3) carbonic acid
(4) sulfuric acid

Group 8—Redox and Electrochemistry

If you choose this group, be sure to answer questions 92–96.

92. Given the reaction:

$$Zn(s) + Br_2(aq) \rightarrow Zn^{2+}(aq) + 2Br^-(aq)$$

What is the net cell potential (E^0) for the overall reaction?
(1) +0.76 V   (3) +1.85 V
(2) −1.09 V   (4) 0.00 V

93. Which half-cell reaction serves as the arbitrary standard used to determine the standard electrode potentials?
(1) $Na^+ + e^- \rightarrow Na(s)$
(2) $Ag^+ + e^- \rightarrow Ag(s)$
(3) $F_2(g) + 2e^- \rightarrow 2F^-$
(4) $2H^+ + 2e^- \rightarrow H_2(g)$

94. According to Reference Table N, which element will react spontaneously with Al^{3+} at 298 K?
(1) Cu   (3) Li
(2) Au   (4) Ni

Base your answers to questions 95 and 96 on the diagram below which represents the electroplating of a metal fork with Ag(s).

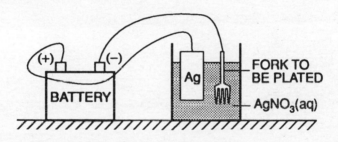

95. Which part of the electroplating system is provided by the fork?
(1) the anode, which is the negative electrode
(2) the cathode, which is the negative electrode
(3) the anode, which is the positive electrode
(4) the cathode, which is the positive electrode

96. Which equation represents the half-reaction that takes place at the fork?
(1) $Ag^+ + NO_3^- \rightarrow AgNO_3$
(2) $AgNO_3 \rightarrow Ag^+ + NO_3^-$
(3) $Ag^+ + e^- \rightarrow Ag(s)$
(4) $Ag(s) \rightarrow Ag^+ + e^-$

Group 9—Organic Chemistry

If you choose this group, be sure to answer questions 97–101.

97. Which type of reaction is used in the production of nylon?
(1) substitution   (3) esterification
(2) saponification   (4) polymerization

98. Which of the following hydrocarbons has the highest normal boiling point?
(1) butene   (3) pentene
(2) ethene   (4) propene

99. Which is the structural formula for 2-propanol?

(1)
$$H—\underset{\underset{H}{|}}{\overset{\overset{H}{|}}{C}}—\underset{\underset{H}{|}}{\overset{\overset{H}{|}}{C}}—\underset{\underset{H}{|}}{\overset{\overset{H}{|}}{C}}—OH$$

(2)
$$H—\underset{\underset{H}{|}}{\overset{\overset{H}{|}}{C}}—\underset{\underset{OH}{|}}{\overset{\overset{H}{|}}{C}}—\underset{\underset{H}{|}}{\overset{\overset{H}{|}}{C}}—H$$

(3)
$$H—\underset{\underset{H}{|}}{\overset{\overset{H}{|}}{C}}—\underset{\underset{H}{|}}{\overset{\overset{H}{|}}{C}}—\underset{\underset{H}{|}}{\overset{\overset{H}{|}}{C}}—\underset{\underset{H}{|}}{\overset{\overset{H}{|}}{C}}—OH$$

(4)
$$H—\underset{\underset{H}{|}}{\overset{\overset{H}{|}}{C}}—\underset{\underset{H}{|}}{\overset{\overset{H}{|}}{C}}—\underset{\underset{OH}{|}}{\overset{\overset{H}{|}}{C}}—\underset{\underset{H}{|}}{\overset{\overset{H}{|}}{C}}—H$$

100. Which is the general formula for organic acids?

(1) $R—C{\overset{O}{\diagdown H}}$

(2) $R—C{\overset{O}{\diagdown OH}}$

(3) ${\overset{R_1}{\underset{R_2}{\diagup}}}C=O$

(4) $R_1—O—R_2$

101. Which is the structural formula for diethyl ether?

(1)
```
        H   H       H   H
        |   |       |   |
   H — C — C — O — C — C — H
        |   |       |   |
        H   H       H   H
```

(2)
```
        H   H       H   H
        |   |       |   |
   H — C — C — C — C — C — H
        |   |   ‖   |   |
        H   H   O   H   H
```

(3)
```
        H           H
        |           |
   H — C — O — C — H
        |           |
        H           H
```

(4)
```
        H           H
        |           |
   H — C — C — C — H
        |   ‖   |
        H   O   H
```

Group 10—Applications of Chemical Principles

If you choose this group, be sure to answer questions 102–106.

102. What is produced when sulfur is burned during the first step of the contact process?
   (1) sulfuric acid   (3) sulfur trioxide
   (2) sulfur dioxide   (4) pyrosulfuric acid

103. A common gaseous fuel that is often found with petroleum is
   (1) carbon monoxide   (3) methane
   (2) carbon dioxide   (4) ethene

104. Which method is commonly used to separate the components of petroleum into simpler substances by using their differences in boiling points?
   (1) fractional crystallization
   (2) fractional distillation
   (3) esterification
   (4) saponification

105. Given the reaction in a lead storage battery:

$$Pb + PbO_2 + 2H_2SO_4 \rightarrow 2PbSO_4 + 2H_2O$$

When the battery is being discharged, which change in the oxidation state of lead occurs?
(1) Pb is oxidized to Pb^{2+}.
(2) Pb is oxidized to Pb^{4+}.
(3) Pb^{2+} is reduced to Pb.
(4) Pb^{4+} is reduced to Pb.

106. Which metal oxide is most easily reduced by carbon?
(1) aluminum   (3) magnesium
(2) iron   (4) sodium

Group 11—Nuclear Chemistry
If you choose this group, be sure to answer questions 107–111.

107. Which isotopic ratio needs to be determined when the age of ancient wooden objects is investigated?
(1) uranium-235 to uranium-238
(2) hydrogen-2 to hydrogen-3
(3) nitrogen-16 to nitrogen-14
(4) carbon-14 to carbon-12

108. Given the reaction: $^9_4Be + {}^1_1H \rightarrow {}^4_2He + X$

Which species is represented by X?

(1) ^8_3Li (3) ^8_5B

(2) ^6_3Li (4) $^{10}_5B$

109. A particle accelerator has no effect on the velocity of
(1) an alpha particle   (3) a neutron
(2) a beta particle   (4) a proton

110. In a fusion reaction, a major problem related to causing the nuclei to fuse into a single nucleus is the
(1) small mass of the nuclei
(2) large mass of the nuclei
(3) attractions of the nuclei
(4) repulsions of the nuclei

111. A radioisotope is called a tracer when it is used to
(1) kill bacteria in food
(2) kill cancerous tissue
(3) determine the age of animal skeletal remains
(4) determine the way in which a chemical reaction occurs

Group 12—Laboratory Activities
If you choose this group, be sure to answer questions 112–116.

112. Which measurement contains a total of three significant figures?
(1) 0.012 g   (3) 1,205 g
(2) 0.125 g   (4) 12,050 g

113. The diagram below shows a section of a 100-milliliter graduated cylinder.

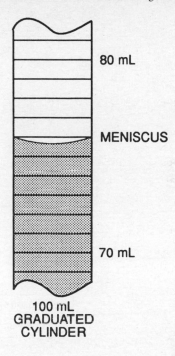

80 mL

MENISCUS

70 mL

100 mL
GRADUATED
CYLINDER

When the meniscus is read to the correct number of significant figures, the volume of water in the cylinder would be recorded as

(1) 75.7 mL   (3) 84.3 mL
(2) 75.70 mL   (4) 84.30 mL

114. A student collected the data shown below to determine experimentally the density of distilled water.

Mass of graduated cylinder + distilled
    H_2O sample .... 163 g
Mass of empty graduated cylinder ... 141 g
Mass of distilled H_2O sample ....   g
Volume of distilled H_2O sample ..... 25.3 mL

Based on the experimental data collected, what is the density of the distilled water?

(1) 1.0 g/mL   (3) 0.87 g/mL
(2) 0.253 g/mL   (4) 1.15 g/mL

115. A laboratory experiment was performed to determine the percent by mass of water in a hydrate. The accepted value is 36.0% water. Which observed value has an error of 5.00%?
    (1) 31.0% water
    (2) 36.0% water
    (3) 37.8% water
    (4) 41.0% water

116. Which is the safest technique for diluting concentrated sulfuric acid?
    (1) Add the water to the acid quickly.
    (2) Add the water to the acid and shake rapidly.
    (3) Add water to the acid while stirring steadily.
    (4) Add acid to the water while stirring steadily.

CHEMISTRY

June 23, 1993

PART I

Answer all 56 questions in this part. [65]

Directions (1–56): For *each* statement or question, select the word or expression that, of those given, best completes the statement or answers the question.

1. If two systems at different temperatures have contact with each other, heat will flow from the system at
   (1) 20.°C to a system at 303 K
   (2) 30.°C to a system at 313 K
   (3) 40.°C to a system at 293 K
   (4) 50.°C to a system at 333 K

2. The graph below represents the uniform heating of a solid, starting below its melting point.

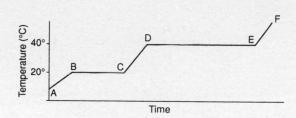

   Which portion of the graph shows the solid and liquid phases of the substance existing in equilibrium?
   (1) *AB*
   (2) *BC*
   (3) *CD*
   (4) *DE*

3. What occurs when the temperature of 10.0 grams of water is changed from 15.5°C to 14.5°C?
   (1) The water absorbs 10.0 calories.
   (2) The water releases 10.0 calories.
   (3) The water absorbs 155 calories.
   (4) The water releases 145 calories.

4. Under the same conditions of temperature and pressure, a liquid differs from a gas because the particles of the liquid
   (1) are in constant straight-line motion
   (2) take the shape of the container they occupy
   (3) have no regular arrangement
   (4) have stronger forces of attraction between them

5. Compared to the mass of an SO_2 molecule, the mass of an O_2 molecule is
   (1) one-fourth as great
   (2) one-half as great
   (3) the same
   (4) twice as great

6. Under which conditions does a real gas behave most nearly like an ideal gas?
   (1) high pressure and low temperature
   (2) high pressure and high temperature
   (3) low pressure and low temperature
   (4) low pressure and high temperature

7. Which statement best describes an electron?
   (1) It has a smaller mass than a proton and a negative charge.
   (2) It has a smaller mass than a proton and a positive charge.
   (3) It has a greater mass than a proton and a negative charge.
   (4) It has a greater mass than a proton and a positive charge.

8. Which principal energy level has no *f* sublevel?
   (1) 5
   (2) 6
   (3) 3
   (4) 4

9. What is the mass number of an atom which contains 28 protons, 28 electrons, and 34 neutrons?
   (1) 28   (3) 62
   (2) 56   (4) 90

10. In an experiment, alpha particles were used to bombard gold foil. As a result of this experiment, the conclusion was made that the nucleus of an atom is
   (1) smaller than the atom and positively charged
   (2) smaller than the atom and negatively charged
   (3) larger than the atom and positively charged
   (4) larger than the atom and negatively charged

11. Given the reaction: $^{131}_{53}I \rightarrow \, ^{131}_{54}Xe + X$

   Which particle is represented by X?
   (1) alpha   (3) neutron
   (2) beta   (4) proton

12. Which orbital notation represents an atom in the ground state with 6 valence electrons?

   (1)

   (2)

   (3)

   (4)

13. A white crystalline salt conducts electricity when it is melted and when it is dissolved in water. Which type of bond does this salt contain?
   (1) ionic   (3) covalent
   (2) metallic   (4) network

14. Which diagram best represents the structure of a water molecule?

   (1) O⟨ H H   (2) H⟨ O O   (3) O—H—O   (4) H—H—O

15. What is the total number of moles of oxygen atoms present in 1 mole of $Mg(ClO_3)_2$?
   (1) 5   (3) 3
   (2) 2   (4) 6

16. Which bond has the greatest ionic character?
   (1) H —— Cl   (3) H —— O
   (2) H —— F   (4) H —— N

17. Which type of bonding accounts for the unusually high boiling point of water?
    (1) ionic bonding
    (2) covalent bonding
    (3) hydrogen bonding
    (4) network bonding

18. Which is the correct formula for carbon (II) oxide?
    (1) CO
    (2) CO_2
    (3) C_2O
    (4) C_2O_3

19. Based on Reference Table G, which of the following compounds is *least* stable?
    (1) $CO(g)$
    (2) $CO_2(g)$
    (3) $HF(g)$
    (4) $HI(g)$

20. Which electronegativity is possible for an alkali metal?
    (1) 1.0
    (2) 2.0
    (3) 3.0
    (4) 4.0

21. When metals form ions, they tend to do so by
    (1) losing electrons and forming positive ions
    (2) losing electrons and forming negative ions
    (3) gaining electrons and forming positive ions
    (4) gaining electrons and forming negative ions

22. Boron and arsenic are similar in that they both
    (1) have the same ionization energy
    (2) have the same covalent radius
    (3) are in the same family of elements
    (4) are metalloids (semimetals)

23. Group 18 (0) elements Kr and Xe have selected oxidation states of other than zero. These oxidation states are an indication that these elements have
    (1) no chemical reactivity
    (2) some chemical reactivity
    (3) stable nuclei
    (4) unstable nuclei

24. The color of Na_2CrO_4 is due to the presence of
    (1) a noble gas
    (2) a halogen
    (3) a transition element
    (4) an alkali metal

25. Given the reaction:

$$Ca + 2H_2O \rightarrow Ca(OH)_2 + H_2$$

What is the total number of moles of Ca needed to react completely with 4.0 moles of H_2O?
    (1) 1.0
    (2) 2.0
    (3) 0.50
    (4) 4.0

26. The percent by mass of Ca in $CaCl_2$ is equal to

    (1) $\frac{40}{111} \times 100$
    (2) $\frac{111}{40} \times 100$
    (3) $\frac{3}{1} \times 100$
    (4) $\frac{1}{3} \times 100$

27. What is the total mass of 3.01×10^{23} atoms of helium gas?
    (1) 8.00 g
    (2) 2.00 g
    (3) 3.50 g
    (4) 4.00 g

28. Given the reaction:

$$2C_2H_6(g) + 7O_2(g) \rightarrow 4CO_2(g) \times 6H_2O(g)$$

What is the total number of liters of carbon dioxide formed by the complete combustion of 28.0 liters of $C_2H_6(g)$?
    (1) 14.0 L
    (2) 28.0 L
    (3) 56.0 L
    (4) 112 L

29. When sodium chloride is dissolved in water, the resulting solution is classified as a
    (1) heterogeneous compound
    (2) homogeneous compound
    (3) heterogeneous mixture
    (4) homogeneous mixture

30. According to Reference Table *D*, a temperature change from 60°C to 90°C has the *least* effect on the solubility of
    (1) SO_2
    (2) NH_3
    (3) KCl
    (4) $KClO_3$

31. Which series of physical changes represents an entropy increase during each change?
    (1) gas → liquid → solid
    (2) liquid → gas → solid
    (3) solid → gas → solid
    (4) solid → liquid → gas

32. Given the reaction at equilibrium:

$$2H_2(g) + O_2(g) \leftrightarrows 2H_2O(g) + heat$$

Which concentration changes occur when the temperature of the system is increased?
    (1) The $[H_2]$ decreases and the $[O_2]$ decreases.
    (2) The $[H_2]$ decreases and the $[O_2]$ increases.
    (3) The $[H_2]$ increases and the $[O_2]$ decreases.
    (4) The $[H_2]$ increases and the $[O_2]$ increases.

33. The change of reactants into products will always be spontaneous if the products, compared to the reactants, have
    (1) lower enthalpy and lower entropy
    (2) lower enthalpy and higher entropy
    (3) higher enthalpy and lower entropy
    (4) higher enthalpy and higher entropy

Base your answers to questions 34 and 35 on the potential energy diagram of a chemical reaction shown below.

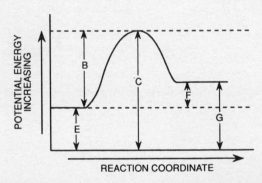

34. Which interval represents the heat of reaction ($\triangle H$)?
    (1) *E*
    (2) *F*
    (3) *C*
    (4) *G*

35. Interval *B* represents the
    (1) potential energy of the products
    (2) potential energy of the reactants
    (3) activation energy
    (4) activated complex

36. Based on Reference Table *L*, which solution best conducts electricity?
    (1) 0.1 M HCl
    (2) 0.1 M CH_3COOH
    (3) 0.1 M H_2S
    (4) 0.1 M H_3PO_4

37. Based on Reference Table *E*, a 1-gram quantity of which salt, when placed in 250 milliliters of water and stirred, will produce a solution with the greatest electrical conductivity?
    (1) AgI
    (2) AgCl
    (3) $AgNO_3$
    (4) Ag_2CO_3

38. According to the Brönsted-Lowry theory, an acid is
    (1) a proton donor, only
    (2) a proton acceptor, only
    (3) a proton donor and a proton acceptor
    (4) neither a proton donor nor a proton acceptor

39. Which salt is formed when hydrochloric acid is neutralized by a potassium hydroxide solution?
    (1) potassium chloride   (3) potassium chlorite
    (2) potassium chlorate   (4) potassium perchlorate

40. Given the equation:

$$H_2O + HF \rightleftharpoons H_3O^+ + F^-$$

    Which pair represents Brönsted-Lowry acids?
    (1) HF and F^- (3) H_2O and F^-
    (2) HF and H_3O^+ (4) H_2O and H_3O^+

41. What is the pH of a solution that has an OH^- ion concentration of 1×10^{-5} mole per liter ($K_w = 1 \times 10^{-14}$)?
    (1) 1   (3) 7
    (2) 5   (4) 9

42. Which half-reaction correctly represents reduction?
    (1) $Fe^{2+} + 2e^- \rightarrow Fe$ (3) $Fe + 2e^- \rightarrow Fe^{2+}$
    (2) $Fe^{2+} + e^- \rightarrow Fe^{3+}$ (4) $Fe + e^- \rightarrow Fe^{3+}$

43. In which compound does hydrogen have an oxidation number of -1?
    (1) NH_3 (3) HCl
    (2) KH (4) H_2O

44. In the reaction $2H_2(g) + O_2(g) \rightarrow 2H_2O(g)$, the oxidizing agent is
    (1) H_2 (3) H^+
    (2) O_2 (4) O^{2-}

45. Which reaction occurs when a strip of magnesium metal is placed in a solution of $CuCl_2$?
    (1) The chloride ion is oxidized.   (3) The magnesium metal is oxidized.
    (2) The chloride ion is reduced.   (4) The magnesium metal is reduced.

46. Given the reaction:

$$Zn(s) + Cu^{2+}(aq) \rightarrow Zn^{2+}(aq) + Cu(s)$$

    Which particles must be transferred from one reactant to the other reactant?
    (1) ions   (3) protons
    (2) neutrons   (4) electrons

47. Which redox equation is correctly balanced?
    (1) $Cr^{3+} + Mg \rightarrow Cr + Mg^{2+}$ (3) $Sn^{4+} + H_2 \rightarrow Sn + 2H^+$
    (2) $Al^{3+} + K \rightarrow Al + K^+$ (4) $Br_2 + Hg \rightarrow Hg^{2+} + 2Br^-$

48. Organic chemistry is the chemistry of compounds containing the element
    (1) carbon   (3) nitrogen
    (2) hydrogen   (4) oxygen

49. The isomers CH_3OCH_3 and CH_3CH_2OH differ in
    (1) molecular formula   (3) number of atoms
    (2) molecular structure   (4) formula mass

50. Given the molecule:

```
        H
        |
   H — C — H
        |
        H
```

    Replacing a hydrogen atom on this molecule with the functional group ——OH will change the original properties of the molecule to those of an
    (1) ester   (3) acid
    (2) ether   (4) alcohol

51. Which structural formula represents a member of the series of hydrocarbons having the general formula C_nH_{2n-2}?

(1)
$$H-\underset{\underset{H}{|}}{\overset{\overset{H}{|}}{C}}-\underset{\underset{H}{|}}{\overset{\overset{H}{|}}{C}}-H$$

(2)
$$\underset{H}{\overset{H}{\diagdown}}C=C\underset{\diagdown H}{\overset{\diagup H}{}}$$

(3) $H-C\equiv C-H$

(4)
$$H-\underset{\underset{H}{|}}{\overset{\overset{H}{|}}{C}}-\underset{\underset{H}{|}}{\overset{\overset{H}{|}}{C}}=C\underset{\diagdown H}{\overset{\diagup H}{}}$$

52. What is the total number of valence electrons in a carbon atom in the ground state?
   (1) 6
   (2) 2
   (3) 12
   (4) 4

Note that questions 53 through 56 have only three choices.

53. As the elements of Group 17 (VIIA) are considered in order of increasing atomic number, the nonmetallic character of each successive element
   (1) decreases
   (2) increases
   (3) remains the same

54. As the atoms of the metals of Group 1 (IA) in the ground state are considered in order from top to bottom, the number of occupied principal energy levels
   (1) decreases
   (2) increases
   (3) remains the same

55. As the mass number of the isotopes of hydrogen increases, the number of protons
   (1) decreases
   (2) increases
   (3) remains the same

56. As $Cu(NO_3)_2$ is dissolved in pure water, the pH of the resulting solution
   (1) decreases
   (2) increases
   (3) remains the same

PART II

This part consists of twelve groups, each containing five questions. Each group tests a major area of the course. Choose seven of these twelve groups. Be sure that you answer all five questions in each group chosen. [35]

Group 1—Matter and Energy

If you choose this group, be sure to answer questions 57–61.

57. Which phase change represents sublimation?
   (1) solid → gas
   (2) solid → liquid
   (3) gas → solid
   (4) gas → liquid

58. Which property of a sample of mercury is different at 320 K than at 300 K?
   (1) atomic mass
   (2) atomic radius
   (3) vapor pressure
   (4) melting point

59. Which statement describes a chemical property of the element iodine?
    (1) Its crystals are a metallic gray.
    (2) It dissolves in alcohol.
    (3) It forms a violet-colored gas.
    (4) It reacts with hydrogen to form a gas.

60. The characteristic which distinguishes a true solid from other phases of matter at STP is that in a true solid, the particles are
    (1) vibrating and changing their relative positions
    (2) vibrating without changing their relative positions
    (3) motionless but changing their relative positions
    (4) motionless without changing their relative positions

61. The volume of a given mass of an ideal gas at constant pressure is
    (1) directly proportional to the Kelvin temperature
    (2) directly proportional to the Celsius temperature
    (3) inversely proportional to the Kelvin temperature
    (4) inversely proportional to the Celsius temperature

Group 2—Atomic Structure

If you choose this group, be sure to answer questions 62–66.

62. Neutral atoms of ^{35}Cl and ^{37}Cl differ with respect to their number of
    (1) electrons   (3) neutrons
    (2) protons   (4) positrons

63. What is the total number of electrons present in an atom of $^{59}_{27}Co$?
    (1) 27   (3) 59
    (2) 32   (4) 86

64. Which of the following atoms has the greatest nuclear charge?
    (1) Al   (3) Si
    (2) Ar   (4) Na

65. An element has an atomic number of 18. What is the principal quantum number (n) of its outermost electrons?
    (1) 1   (3) 3
    (2) 2   (4) 4

66. What is the total mass of ^{222}Rn remaining in an original 160-milligram sample of ^{222}Rn after 19.1 days?
    (1) 2.5 mg   (3) 10. mg
    (2) 5.0 mg   (4) 20. mg

Group 3—Bonding

If you choose this group, be sure to answer questions 67–71.

67. In a nonpolar covalent bond, electrons are
    (1) located in a mobile "sea" shared by many ions
    (2) transferred from one atom to another
    (3) shared equally by two atoms
    (4) shared unequally by two atoms

68. Which compound has the same empirical and molecular formula?
    (1) acetylene   (3) ethane
    (2) ethene   (4) methane

69. When the equation
    $\_C_8H_{16} + \_O_2 \rightarrow \_CO_2 + \_H_2O$ is correctly balanced using the smallest whole number coefficients, the coefficient of O_2 is
    (1) 1   (3) 12
    (2) 8   (4) 16

70. Which species can form a coordinate covalent bond with an H^+ ion?
    (1) H·   (3) H^+
    (2) H:$^-$ (4) H : H

71. In which chemical system are molecule-ion attractions present?
    (1) KCl(g)   (3) KCl(s)
    (2) KCl(ℓ)   (4) KCl(aq)

Group 4—Periodic Table

If you choose this group, be sure to answer questions 72–76.

72. Which atom has a radius larger than the radius of its ion?
    (1) Cl   (3) S
    (2) Ca   (4) Se

73. The chemical properties of the elements are periodic functions of their atomic
    (1) masses   (3) numbers
    (2) weights   (4) radii

74. Which of the following substances is the best conductor of electricity?
    (1) NaCl(s)   (3) $H_2O(\ell)$
    (2) Cu(s)   (4) $Br_2(\ell)$

75. Which halogen is a solid at STP?
    (1) fluorine   (3) bromine
    (2) chlorine   (4) iodine

76. Atoms of nonmetals generally react with atoms of metals by
    (1) gaining electrons to form ionic compounds
    (2) gaining electrons to form covalent compounds
    (3) sharing electrons to form ionic compounds
    (4) sharing electrons to form covalent compounds

Group 5—Mathematics of Chemistry

If you choose this group, be sure to answer questions 77–81.

77. What is the empirical formula of a compound composed of 2.8% by mass of boron and 97% by mass of iodine?
    (1) BI_2 (3) BI_3
    (2) B_2I (4) B_3I

78. A gas has a volume of 2 liters at 323 K and 3 atmospheres. When its temperature is changed to 273 K and the pressure is changed to 1 atmosphere, the new volume of the gas would be equal to

    (1) $2\,L \times \dfrac{273\,K}{323\,K} \times \dfrac{1\,atm}{3\,atm}$ (3) $2\,L \times \dfrac{273\,K}{323\,K} \times \dfrac{3\,atm}{1\,atm}$

    (2) $2\,L \times \dfrac{323\,K}{273\,K} \times \dfrac{1\,atm}{3\,atm}$ (4) $2\,L \times \dfrac{323\,K}{273\,K} \times \dfrac{3\,atm}{1\,atm}$

79. Which gas could have a density of 2.05 grams per liter at STP?
    (1) N_2O_3 (3) HF
    (2) NO_2 (4) HBr

80. What is the total number of calories of heat energy absorbed when 10.0 grams of water is vaporized at its normal boiling point?
    (1) 7.97   (3) 5390
    (2) 53.9   (4) 7970

81. How many moles of a nonvolatile, nonelectrolyte solute are required to lower the freezing point of 1,000 grams of water by 5.58 C°?
    (1) 1   (3) 3
    (2) 2   (4) 4

Group 6—Kinetics and Equilibrium

If you choose this group, be sure to answer questions 82–86.

82. Based on Reference Table G, which compound forms spontaneously even though the ΔH for its formation is positive?
    (1) $C_2H_4(g)$ (3) ICl(g)
    (2) $C_2H_2(g)$ (4) HI(g)

83. Given the reaction at equilibrium:
$$AgCl(s) \rightleftarrows Ag^+(aq) + Cl^-(aq)$$
The addition of Cl^- ions will cause the concentration of Ag^+ (aq) to
    (1) decrease as the amount of AgCl(s) decreases
    (2) decrease as the amount of AgCl(s) increases
    (3) increase as the amount of AgCl(s) decreases
    (4) increase as the amount of AgCl(s) increases

84. The expression $\triangle H - T\triangle S$ is equal to the change in
    (1) binding energy   (3) free energy
    (2) ionization energy   (4) activation energy

85. At room temperature, which reaction would be expected to have the fastest reaction rate?
    (1) $Pb^{2+}(aq) + S^{2-}(aq) \rightarrow PbS(s)$
    (2) $2H_2(g) + O_2(g) \rightarrow 2H_2O(\ell)$
    (3) $N_2(g) + 2O_2(g) \rightarrow 2NO_2(g)$
    (4) $2KClO_3(s) \rightarrow 2KCl(s) + 3O_2(g)$

86. Which statement is true for a saturated solution?
    (1) It must be a concentrated solution.
    (2) It must be a dilute solution.
    (3) Neither dissolving nor crystallizing is occurring.
    (4) The rate of dissolving equals the rate of crystallizing.

Group 7—Acids and Bases

If you choose this group, be sure to answer questions 87–91.

87. When an Arrhenius base is placed in H_2O, the only negative ion present in the solution is
    (1) OH^- (3) H^-
    (2) H_3O^- (4) O^2

88. Which solution will change red litmus to blue?
    (1) HCl(aq)   (3) $CH_3OH(aq)$
    (2) NaCl(aq)   (4) NaOH(aq)

89. A chloride ion, $[: \ddot{C}l :]^-$, acts as a Brönsted base when it combines with
    (1) an OH^- ion   (3) an H^- ion
    (2) a K^+ ion   (4) an H^+ ion

90. Which equation illustrates amphoterism?
    (1) $NaCl \rightarrow Na^+ + Cl^-$
    (2) $NaOH \rightarrow Na^+ + OH^-$
    (3) $H_2O + H_2O \rightarrow H_3O^+ + OH^-$
    (4) $HCl + H_2O \rightarrow H_3O^+ + Cl^-$

91. In a titration, the endpoint of a neutralization reaction was reached when 37.6 milliliters of an HCl solution was added to 17.3 milliliters of a 0.250 M NaOH solution. What was the molarity of the HCl solution?
    (1) 0.115 M   (3) 0.250 M
    (2) 0.203 M   (4) 0.543 M

Group 8—Redox and Electrochemistry

If you choose this group, be sure to answer questions 92–96.

Base your answers to questions 92 and 93 on the diagram below which represents an electrochemical cell.

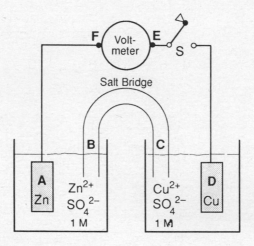

92. Which statement correctly describes the direction of flow for the ions in this cell when the switch is closed?
    (1) Ions move through the salt bridge from B to C, only.
    (2) Ions move through the salt bridge from C to B, only.
    (3) Ions move through the salt bridge in both directions.
    (4) Ions do not move through the salt bridge in either direction.

93. When the switch is closed, which group of letters correctly represents the direction of electron flow?
    (1) $A \rightarrow B \rightarrow C \rightarrow D$ (3) $D \rightarrow C \rightarrow B \rightarrow A$
    (2) $A \rightarrow F \rightarrow E \rightarrow D$ (4) $D \rightarrow E \rightarrow F \rightarrow A$

94. Based on Reference Table N, which metal will react with H^+ ions to produce $H_2(g)$?
    (1) Au   (3) Cu
    (2) Ag   (4) Mg

95. What is the standard electrode potential (E^0) assigned to the half-reaction $Cu^{2+} + 2e^- \rightarrow Cu(s)$ when compared to the standard hydrogen half-reaction?
    (1) $+0.34$ V   (3) $+0.52$ V
    (2) -0.34 V   (4) -0.52 V

96. Which species acts as the anode when the reaction $Zn(s) + Pb^{2+}(aq) \rightarrow Zn^{2+}(aq) + Pb(s)$ occurs in an electrochemical cell?
    (1) $Zn(s)$ (3) $Pb^{2+}(aq)$
    (2) $Zn^{2+}(aq)$ (4) $Pb(s)$

Group 9—Organic Chemistry

If you choose this group, be sure to answer questions 97–101.

97. The products of condensation polymerization are a polymer and
    (1) carbon dioxide   (3) ethanol
    (2) water   (4) glycerol

98. Given the equation:

$$C_6H_{12}O_6 \rightarrow 2C_2H_5OH + 2CO_2$$

The chemical process illustrated by this equation is
(1) fermentation   (3) esterification
(2) saponification   (4) polymerization

99. Which two compounds are monohydroxy alcohols?
(1) ethylene glycol and ethanol   (3) methanol and ethanol
(2) ethylene glycol and glycerol   (4) methanol and glycerol

100. Which type of compound is represented by the structural formula shown below?

```
    H  H     H  H
    |  |     |  |
H — C — C — O — C — C — H
    |  |     |  |
    H  H     H  H
```

(1) a ketone   (3) an ester
(2) an aldehyde   (4) an ether

101. Which is the structural formula for 2-chlorobutane?

```
          H  H  H  Cl
          |  |  |  |
(1)  H — C — C — C — C — H
          |  |  |  |
          H  H  H  Cl
```

```
          H  H  H  Cl
          |  |  |  |
(2)  H — C — C — C — C — H
          |  |  |  |
          H  H  H  H
```

```
          H  Cl H  H
          |  |  |  |
(3)  H — C — C — C — C — H
          |  |  |  |
          H  H  H  H
```

```
          H  H  Cl H
          |  |  |  |
(4)  H — C — C — C — C — H
          |  |  |  |
          H  H  Cl H
```

Group 10—Applications of Chemical Principles

If you choose this group, be sure to answer questions 102–106.

102. Given the lead-acid battery reaction:

$$Pb + PbO_2 + 2H_2SO_4 \underset{\text{charge}}{\overset{\text{discharge}}{\rightleftharpoons}} 2PbSO_4 + 2H_2O$$

When the reaction produces electricity, which element changes oxidation states?
(1) Pb   (3) H
(2) O   (4) S

103. During fractional distillation of petroleum, which of the following fractions has the *lowest* boiling point?
(1) C_8H_{18} (3) $C_{15}H_{32}$
(2) $C_{12}H_{26}$ (4) $C_{18}H_{38}$

104. What is the original source of many textiles and most plastics?
(1) coal   (3) petroleum
(2) wood   (4) mineral ores

105. Given a reaction that occurs in the contact process:

$$2SO_2(g) + O_2(g) \rightleftarrows 2SO_3(g) + heat$$

Adding a catalyst to this system causes the
(1) activation energy to decrease
(2) activation energy to increase
(3) heat of reaction to decrease
(4) heat of reaction to increase

106. Given the reaction:

$$2Al + Cr_2O_3 \rightarrow Al_2O_3 + 2Cr$$

When this reaction is used to produce chromium, the aluminum is acting as
(1) a catalyst
(2) an alloy
(3) an oxidizing agent
(4) a reducing agent

Group 11—Nuclear Chemistry

If you choose this group, be sure to answer questions 107–111.

107. The diagram below shows a nuclear reaction in which a neutron is captured by a heavy nucleus.

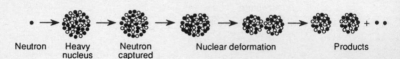

| Neutron | Heavy nucleus | Neutron captured in nucleus | Nuclear deformation | Products |

Which type of reaction is illustrated by the diagram?
(1) an endothermic fission reaction
(2) an exothermic fission reaction
(3) an endothermic fusion reaction
(4) an exothermic fusion reaction

108. Heavy water and graphite are two examples of materials that can be used in a nuclear reactor to slow down neutrons. These materials are called
(1) fuels
(2) shields
(3) coolants
(4) moderators

109. Which particle can *not* be accelerated in a magnetic field?
(1) alpha particle
(2) beta particle
(3) neutron
(4) proton

110. Which radioisotope is used to diagnose thyroid disorders?
(1) cobalt-60
(2) iodine-131
(3) technetium-99
(4) uranium-238

111. Given the transmutation:

$$^1_0n + ^{235}_{92}U \rightarrow ^{141}_{56}Ba + X + 3^1_0n$$

The element X has an atomic number of
(1) 36
(2) 89
(3) 92
(4) 93

Group 12—Laboratory Activities

If you choose this group, be sure to answer questions 112–116.

112. Which diagram represents a test tube holder (clamp)?

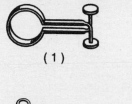

(1)

(3)

(2)

(4)

113. In a laboratory exercise to determine the volume of a mole of gas at STP, a student determines the volume to be 2.25 liters greater than the accepted value of 22.4 liters. The percent error in the student's value is
    (1) 2.25%
    (2) 10.0%
    (3) 20.2%
    (4) 24.7%

114. To determine the density of an irregularly shaped object, a student immersed the object in 21.2 milliliters of H_2O in a graduated cylinder, causing the level of the H_2O to rise to 27.8 milliliters. If the object had a mass of 22.4 grams, what was the density of the object?
    (1) 27.8 g/mL
    (2) 6.6 g/mL
    (3) 3.0 g/mL
    (4) 3.4 g/mL

115. A material will be used to fill an empty beaker to level A, as shown in the diagram below.

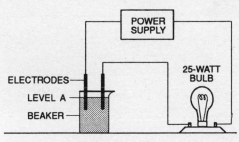

Which material, when used to fill the beaker to level A, would cause the bulb to glow brightly?
    (1) $C_6H_{12}O_6(s)$
    (2) $C_6H_{12}O_6(aq)$
    (3) $KCl(s)$
    (4) $KCl(aq)$

116. A solid is dissolved in a beaker of water. Which observation suggests that the process is endothermic?
    (1) The solution gives off a gas.
    (2) The solution changes color.
    (3) The temperature of the solution decreases.
    (4) The temperature of the solution increases.

CHEMISTRY

June 22, 1994

PART I

Answer all 56 questions in this part. [65]

Directions (1–56): For *each* statement or question, select the word or expression that, of those given, best completes the statement or answers the question.

1. The amount of energy needed to change a given mass of ice to water at constant temperature is called the heat of
   (1) condensation
   (2) crystallization
   (3) fusion
   (4) formation

2. Which equation represents the phase change called sublimation?
   (1) $CO_2(s) \rightarrow CO_2(g)$
   (2) $H_2O(s) \rightarrow H_2O(\ell)$
   (3) $H_2O(\ell) \rightarrow H_2O(g)$
   (4) $NaCl(\ell) \rightarrow NaCl(s)$

3. Which substance can *not* be decomposed into simpler substances?
   (1) ammonia
   (2) aluminum
   (3) methane
   (4) methanol

4. In which sample are the particles arranged in a regular geometric pattern?
   (1) $HCl(\ell)$
   (2) $NaCl(aq)$
   (3) $N_2(g)$
   (4) $I_2(s)$

5. How many calories are equivalent to 35 kilocalories?
   (1) 0.035 calorie
   (2) 0.35 calorie
   (3) 3,500 calories
   (4) 35,000 calories

6. How does the ground state electron configuration of the hydrogen atom differ from that of a ground state helium atom?
   (1) Hydrogen has one electron in a higher energy level.
   (2) Hydrogen has two electrons in a lower energy level.
   (3) Hydrogen contains a half-filled orbital.
   (4) Hydrogen contains a completely filled orbital.

7. Which type of radiation would be attracted to the positive electrode in an electric field?
   (1) $_{-1}^{0}e$
   (2) $_{1}^{1}H$
   (3) $_{2}^{3}He$
   (4) $_{0}^{1}n$

8. Which electron configuration represents an atom in an excited state?
   (1) $1s^2 2s^2$
   (2) $1s^2 2s^2 3s^1$
   (3) $1s^2 2s^2 2p^6$
   (4) $1s^2 2s^2 2p^6 3s^1$

9. Which electron transition represents the release of energy?
   (1) $1s$ to $3p$
   (2) $2s$ to $2p$
   (3) $3p$ to $1s$
   (4) $2p$ to $3s$

10. The atomic number of any atom is equal to the number of
    (1) neutrons in the atom, only
    (2) protons in the atom, only
    (3) neutrons plus protons in the atom
    (4) protons plus electrons in the atom

11. The mass of an electron is approximately $\frac{1}{1836}$ times the mass of
    (1) $_{1}^{1}H$
    (2) $_{1}^{2}H$
    (3) $_{1}^{3}H$
    (4) $_{2}^{4}He$

12. Which nuclear reaction is classified as alpha decay?

(1) $^{14}_{6}C \rightarrow {}^{14}_{7}N + {}^{0}_{-1}e$

(3) $^{226}_{88}Ra \rightarrow {}^{222}_{86}Rn + {}^{4}_{2}He$

(2) $^{42}_{19}K \rightarrow {}^{42}_{20}Ca + {}^{0}_{-1}e$

(4) $^{3}_{1}H \rightarrow {}^{0}_{-1}e + {}^{3}_{2}He$

13. Which diagram correctly shows the relationship between electronegativity and atomic number for the elements of Period 3?

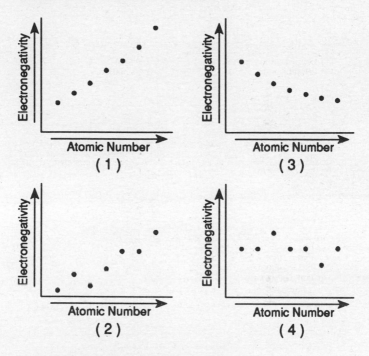

14. Which statement is true concerning the reaction $N(g) + N(g) \rightarrow N_2(g) + $ energy?
    (1) A bond is broken and energy is absorbed.
    (2) A bond is broken and energy is released.
    (3) A bond is formed and energy is absorbed.
    (4) A bond is formed and energy is released.

15. Hydrogen bonding is strongest between molecules of
    (1) H_2S (3) H_2Se
    (2) H_2O (4) H_2Te

16. A chemical formula is an expression used to represent
    (1) mixtures, only   (3) compounds, only
    (2) elements, only   (4) compounds and elements

17. When calcium chloride is dissolved in water, to which énd of the adjacent water molecules will a calcium ion be attracted?
    (1) the oxygen end, which is the negative pole
    (2) the oxygen end, which is the positive pole
    (3) the hydrogen end, which is the negative pole
    (4) the hydrogen end, which is the positive pole

18. How do the chemical properties of the Na atom and the Na$^+$ ion compare?
    (1) They are the same because each has the same atomic number.
    (2) They are the same because each has the same electron configuration.
    (3) They are different because each has a different atomic number.
    (4) They are different because each has a different electron configuration.

19. Which element in Group 16 (VIA) has *no* stable isotopes?
    (1) sulfur   (3) tellurium
    (2) selenium   (4) polonium

20. Which element is a member of the halogen family?
    (1) K   (3) I
    (2) B   (4) S

21. Most nonmetals have the properties of
    (1) high ionization energy and poor electrical conductivity
    (2) high ionization energy and good electrical conductivity
    (3) low ionization energy and poor electrical conductivity
    (4) low ionization energy and good electrical conductivity

22. The metalloids that are included in Group 15 (VA) are antimony (Sb) and
    (1) N   (3) As
    (2) P   (4) Bi

23. Which of the following atoms has the largest atomic radius?
    (1) Na   (3) Mg
    (2) K   (4) Ca

24. In which group does each element have a total of four electrons in the outermost principal energy level?
    (1) 1 (IA)   (3) 16 (VIA)
    (2) 18 (0)   (4) 14 (IVA)

25. Which properties are characteristic of the Group 1 (IA) metals?
    (1) high reactivity and the formation of stable compounds
    (2) high reactivity and the formation of unstable compounds
    (3) low reactivity and the formation of stable compounds
    (4) low reactivity and the formation of unstable compounds

26. Which quantity is equivalent to 39 grams of LiF?
    (1) 1.0 mole   (3) 0.50 mole
    (2) 2.0 moles   (4) 1.5 moles

27. Which quantity represents 0.500 mole at STP?
    (1) 22.4 liters of nitrogen   (3) 32.0 grams of oxygen
    (2) 11.2 liters of oxygen   (4) 28.0 grams of nitrogen

28. When 0.50 liter of a 12 M solution is diluted to 1.0 liter, the molarity of the new solution is
    (1) 6.0 M   (3) 12 M
    (2) 2.4 M   (4) 24 M

29. What is the percent by mass of oxygen in Fe_2O_3 (formula mass = 160)?
    (1) 16%   (3) 56%
    (2) 30.%   (4) 70.%

30. Given the equation:

$$6CO_2(g) + 6H_2O(\ell) \rightarrow C_6H_{12}O_6(s) + 6O_2(g)$$

What is the *minimum* number of liters of $CO_2(g)$, measured at STP, needed to produce 32.0 grams of oxygen?
    (1) 264 L   (3) 32.0 L
    (2) 192 L   (4) 22.4 L

31. Given the reaction:

$$Mg(s) + 2HCl(aq) \rightarrow MgCl_2(aq) + H_2(g)$$

The reaction occurs more rapidly when a 10-gram sample of Mg is powdered, rather than in one piece, because powdered Mg has
(1) less surface area
(2) more surface area
(3) a lower potential energy
(4) a higher potential energy

32. According to Reference Table I, in which reaction do the products have a higher energy content than the reactants?
(1) $CH_4(g) + 2O_2(g) \rightarrow CO_2(g) + 2H_2O(\ell)$

(2) $CH_3OH(\ell) + \frac{3}{2}O_2(g) \rightarrow CO_2(g) + 2H_2O(\ell)$

(3) $NH_4Cl(s) \xrightarrow{H_2O} NH_4^+(aq) + Cl^-(aq)$

(4) $NaOH(s) \xrightarrow{H_2O} Na^+(aq) + OH^-(aq)$

33. Which equation correctly represents the free energy change in a chemical reaction?
(1) $\Delta G = \Delta H + T\Delta S$
(2) $\Delta G = \Delta H - T\Delta S$
(3) $\Delta G = \Delta T - \Delta H\Delta S$
(4) $\Delta G = \Delta S - T\Delta H$

34. Adding a catalyst to a chemical reaction will
(1) lower the activation energy needed
(2) lower the potential energy of the reactants
(3) increase the activation energy needed
(4) increase the potential energy of the reactants

35. Under which conditions are gases most soluble in water?
(1) high pressure and high temperature
(2) high pressure and low temperature
(3) low pressure and high temperature
(4) low pressure and low temperature

36. A solution of a base differs from a solution of an acid in that the solution of a base
(1) is able to conduct electricity
(2) is able to cause an indicator color change
(3) has a greater $[H_3O^+]$
(4) has a greater $[OH^-]$

37. Given the reaction:

$$HCl(g) + H_2O(\ell) \rightarrow H_3O^+(aq) + Cl^-(aq)$$

Which reactant acted as a Brönsted-Lowry acid?
(1) $HCl(g)$, because it reacted with chloride ions
(2) $H_2O(\ell)$, because it produced hydronium ions
(3) $HCl(g)$, because it donated protons
(4) $H_2O(\ell)$, because it accepted protons

38. Which of the following aqueous solutions is the *poorest* conductor of electricity? [Refer to Reference Table L]
(1) 0.1 M H_2S
(2) 0.1 M HF
(3) 0.1 M HNO_2
(4) 0.1 M HNO_3

39. According to the Arrhenius theory, the acidic property of an aqueous solution is due to an excess of
(1) H_2
(2) H^+
(3) H_2O
(4) OH^-

40. Which pH value indicates the most basic solution?
(1) 7
(2) 8
(3) 3
(4) 11

41. A 3.0-milliliter sample of HNO_3 solution is exactly neutralized by 6.0 milliliters of 0.50 M KOH. What is the molarity of the HNO_3 sample?
    (1) 1.0 M
    (2) 0.50 M
    (3) 3.0 M
    (4) 1.5 M

42. As 100 milliliters of 0.10 molar KOH is added to 100 milliliters of 0.10 molar HCl at 298 K, the pH of the resulting solution will
    (1) decrease to 3
    (2) decrease to 14
    (3) increase to 7
    (4) increase to 13

43. What is the oxidation number of oxygen in HSO_4^-?
    (1) +1
    (2) −2
    (3) +6
    (4) −4

44. Which half-reaction correctly represents a reduction reaction?
    (1) $Sn^0 + 2e^- \rightarrow Sn^{2+}$
    (2) $Na^0 + e^- \rightarrow Na^+$
    (3) $Li^0 + e^- \rightarrow Li^+$
    (4) $Br_2^0 + 2e^- \rightarrow 2Br^-$

45. Given the reaction:
$$2Na + 2H_2O \rightarrow 2Na^+ + 2OH^- + H_2$$
Which substance is oxidized?
    (1) H_2
    (2) H^+
    (3) Na
    (4) Na^+

46. Which change occurs when an Sn^{2+} ion is oxidized?
    (1) Two electrons are lost.
    (2) Two electrons are gained.
    (3) Two protons are lost.
    (4) Two protons are gained.

47. Based on Reference Table N, which of the following elements is the strongest reducing agent?
    (1) Fe
    (2) Sr
    (3) Cu
    (4) Cr

48. An electrochemical cell that generates electricity contains half-cells that produce
    (1) oxidation half-reactions, only
    (2) reduction half-reactions, only
    (3) spontaneous redox reactions
    (4) nonspontaneous redox reactions

49. Which structural formula represents a molecule of butane?

(1)

$$H-\overset{\overset{\displaystyle H}{|}}{C}=\overset{\overset{\displaystyle H}{|}}{C}-\overset{\overset{\displaystyle H}{|}}{C}=\overset{\overset{\displaystyle H}{|}}{C}-H$$

(2)

$$H-\overset{\overset{\displaystyle H}{|}}{\underset{\underset{\displaystyle H}{|}}{C}}-\overset{\overset{\displaystyle H}{|}}{C}=\overset{\overset{\displaystyle H}{|}}{C}-\overset{\overset{\displaystyle H}{|}}{\underset{\underset{\displaystyle H}{|}}{C}}-H$$

(3)

$$H-\overset{\overset{\displaystyle H}{|}}{\underset{\underset{\displaystyle H}{|}}{C}}-\overset{\overset{\displaystyle H}{|}}{\underset{\underset{\displaystyle H}{|}}{C}}-\overset{\overset{\displaystyle H}{|}}{\underset{\underset{\displaystyle H}{|}}{C}}-\overset{\overset{\displaystyle H}{|}}{\underset{\underset{\displaystyle H}{|}}{C}}-H$$

(4)

$$H-C\equiv C-\overset{\overset{\displaystyle H}{|}}{\underset{\underset{\displaystyle H}{|}}{C}}-\overset{\overset{\displaystyle H}{|}}{\underset{\underset{\displaystyle H}{|}}{C}}-H$$

50. If a hydrocarbon molecule contains a triple bond, its IUPAC name ends in
   (1) "ane"   (3) "one"
   (2) "ene"   (4) "yne"

51. Which compound is an organic acid?
   (1) CH_3OH (3) CH_3COOH
   (2) CH_3OCH_3 (4) CH_3COOCH_3

52. Which structural formula represents the product formed from the reaction of Cl_2 and C_2H_4?

(1)

$$H-\underset{\underset{Cl}{|}}{\overset{\overset{H}{|}}{C}}-\underset{\underset{Cl}{|}}{\overset{\overset{H}{|}}{C}}-H$$

(2)

$$H-\overset{\overset{Cl}{|}}{C}=\overset{\overset{Cl}{|}}{C}-H$$

(3) $H-C\equiv C-Cl$

(4)

$$H-\underset{\underset{H}{|}}{\overset{\overset{H}{|}}{C}}-\underset{\underset{H}{|}}{\overset{\overset{H}{|}}{C}}-Cl$$

53. Which homologous series contains the compound toluene?
    (1) alkene   (3) alkyne
    (2) benzene   (4) alkane

Note that questions 54 through 56 have only three choices.

54. As the elements in Group 17 (VIIA) are considered in order from top to bottom, the strength of the van der Waals forces between the atoms of each successive element is
    (1) less
    (2) greater
    (3) the same

55. As the number of effective collisions between the reactant particles in a chemical reaction decreases, the rate of the reaction
    (1) decreases
    (2) increases
    (3) remains the same

56. A sealed container of nitrogen gas contains 6×10^{23} molecules at STP. As the temperature increases, the mass of the nitrogen will
    (1) decrease
    (2) increase
    (3) remain the same

PART II

This part consists of twelve groups, each containing five questions. Each group tests a major area of the course. Choose seven of these twelve groups. Be sure that you answer all five questions in each group chosen. [35]

Group I — Matter and Energy

If you choose this group, be sure to answer questions 57–61.

57. Which pair must represent atoms of the same element?

    (1) $^{14}_{6}X$ and $^{14}_{7}X$

    (3) $^{2}_{1}X$ and $^{4}_{2}X$

    (2) $^{12}_{6}X$ and $^{13}_{6}X$

    (4) $^{13}_{6}X$ and $^{14}_{7}X$

58. Which graph best represents a change of phase from a gas to a solid?

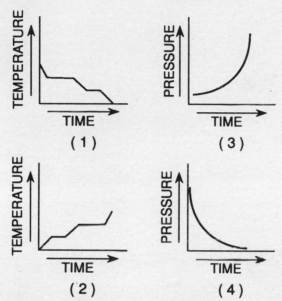

59. At 1 atmosphere and 20°C, all samples of $H_2O(\ell)$ must have the same
    (1) mass   (3) volume
    (2) density   (4) weight

60. The total quantity of molecules contained in 5.6 liters of a gas at STP is
    (1) 1.0 mole   (3) 0.50 mole
    (2) 0.75 mole   (4) 0.25 mole

61. A sample of gas has a volume of 2.0 liters at a pressure of 1.0 atmosphere. When the volume increases to 4.0 liters, at a constant temperature, the pressure will be
    (1) 1.0 atm   (3) 0.50 atm
    (2) 2.0 atm   (4) 0.25 atm

Group 2 — Atomic Structure

If you choose this group, be sure to answer questions 62–66.

62. Which radioactive sample would contain the greatest remaining mass of the radioactive isotope after 10 years?
    (1) 2.0 grams of ^{198}Au (3) 4.0 grams of ^{32}P
    (2) 2.0 grams of ^{42}K (4) 4.0 grams of ^{60}Co

63. Neutral atoms of the same element can differ in their number of
    (1) neutrons   (3) protons
    (2) positrons   (4) electrons

64. In which reaction is the first ionization energy greatest?
    (1) $Na + energy \rightarrow Na^+ + e^-$ (3) $Mg + energy \rightarrow Mg^+ + e^-$
    (2) $K + energy \rightarrow K^+ + e^-$ (4) $Al + energy \rightarrow Al^+ + e^-$

65. If 75.0% of the isotopes of an element have a mass of 35.0 amu and 25.0% of the isotopes have a mass of 37.0 amu, what is the atomic mass of the element?
    (1) 35.0 amu   (3) 36.0 amu
    (2) 35.5 amu   (4) 37.0 amu

66. What is the maximum number of electrons that may be present in the fourth principal energy level of an atom?
    (1) 8   (3) 18
    (2) 2   (4) 32

Group 3 — Bonding

If you choose this group, be sure to answer questions 67–71.

67. Which compound contains ionic bonds?
    (1) N_2O (3) CO
    (2) Na_2O (4) CO_2

68. What is the total number of moles of atoms in one mole of $(NH_4)_2SO_4$?
    (1) 10   (3) 14
    (2) 11   (4) 15

69. A substance was found to be a soft, nonconducting solid at room temperature. The substance is most likely
    (1) a molecular solid   (3) a metallic solid
    (2) a network solid   (4) an ionic solid

70. Two atoms with an electronegativity difference of 0.4 form a bond that is
    (1) ionic, because electrons are shared
    (2) ionic, because electrons are transferred
    (3) covalent, because electrons are shared
    (4) covalent, because electrons are transferred

71. Which species contains a coordinate covalent bond?

Group 4 — Periodic Table

If you choose this group, be sure to answer questions 72–76.

72. As the elements Li to F in Period 2 of the Periodic Table are considered in succession, how do the relative electronegativity and the covalent radius of each successive element compare?
    (1) The relative electronegativity decreases, and the covalent radius decreases.
    (2) The relative electronegativity decreases, and the covalent radius increases.
    (3) The relative electronegativity increases, and the covalent radius decreases.
    (4) The relative electronegativity increases, and the covalent radius increases.

73. A characteristic of most nonmetallic solids is that they are
    (1) brittle
    (2) ductile
    (3) malleable
    (4) conductors of electricity

74. In which category of elements in the Periodic Table do all of the atoms have valence electrons in the second principal energy level?
    (1) Group 2 (IIA)
    (2) Period 2
    (3) the alkaline earth family
    (4) the alkali metals family

75. Which element can form a chloride with a general formula of MCl_2 or MCl_3?
    (1) Fe
    (2) Al
    (3) Mg
    (4) Zn

76. Which ion has the same electron configuration as an H^- ion?
    (1) Cl^-
    (2) F^-
    (3) K^+
    (4) Li^+

Group 5 — Mathematics of Chemistry

If you choose this group, be sure to answer questions 77–81.

77. What is the molecular formula of a compound with the empirical formula P_2O_5 and a gram-molecular mass of 284 grams?
    (1) P_2O_5
    (2) P_5O_2
    (3) $P_{10}O_4$
    (4) P_4O_{10}

78. How many molecules are in 0.25 mole of CO?
    (1) 1.5×10^{23}
    (2) 6.0×10^{23}
    (3) 3.0×10^{23}
    (4) 9.0×10^{23}

79. If the pressure and Kelvin temperature of 2.00 moles of an ideal gas at STP are doubled, the resulting volume will be
    (1) 5.60 L
    (2) 11.2 L
    (3) 22.4 L
    (4) 44.8 L

80. The freezing point of a 1.00-molal solution of $C_2H_4(OH)_2$ is closest to
    (1) $+1.86°C$
    (2) $-1.86°C$
    (3) $-3.72°C$
    (4) $+3.72°C$

81. The molarity (M) of a solution is equal to the
    (1) $\dfrac{\text{number of grams of solute}}{\text{liter of solvent}}$
    (2) $\dfrac{\text{number of grams of solute}}{\text{liter of solution}}$
    (3) $\dfrac{\text{number of moles of solute}}{\text{liter of solvent}}$
    (4) $\dfrac{\text{number of moles of solute}}{\text{liter of solution}}$

Group 6 — Kinetics and Equilibrium

If you choose this group, be sure to answer questions 82–86.

82. Given the reaction at equilibrium:

$$Mg(OH)_2(s) \rightleftarrows Mg^{2+}(aq) + 2OH^-(aq)$$

The solubility product constant for this reaction is correctly written as
(1) $K_{sp} = [Mg^{2+}][2OH^-]$
(3) $K_{sp} = [Mg^{2+}][OH^-]^2$
(2) $K_{sp} = [Mg^{2+}] + [2OH^-]$
(4) $K_{sp} = [Mg^{2+}] + [OH^-]^2$

83. Based on Reference Table D, which salt solution could contain 42 grams of solute per 100 grams of water at 40°C?
(1) a saturated solution of $KClO_3$
(3) an unsaturated solution of NaCl
(2) a saturated solution of KCl
(4) an unsaturated solution of NH_4Cl

84. The value of the equilibrium constant of a chemical reaction will change when there is an increase in the
(1) temperature
(3) concentration of the reactants
(2) pressure
(4) concentration of the products

85. Given a saturated solution of silver chloride at constant temperature:

$$AgCl(s) \rightleftarrows Ag^+(aq) + Cl^-(aq)$$

As NaCl(s) is dissolved in the solution, the concentration of the Ag^+ ions in the solution
(1) decreases, and the concentration of Cl^- ions increases
(2) decreases, and the concentration of Cl^- ions remains the same
(3) increases, and the concentration of Cl^- ions increases
(4) increases, and the concentration of Cl^- ions remains the same

86. In which reaction will the point of equilibrium shift to the left when the pressure on the system is increased?
(1) $C(s) + O_2(g) \rightleftarrows CO_2(g)$
(3) $2Mg(s) + O_2(g) \rightleftarrows 2MgO(s)$
(2) $CaCO_3(s) \rightleftarrows CaO(s) + CO_2(g)$
(4) $2H_2(g) + O_2(g) \rightleftarrows 2H_2O(g)$

Group 7 — Acids and Bases

If you choose this group, be sure to answer questions 87–91.

87. If an aqueous solution turns blue litmus red, which relationship exists between the hydronium ion and hydroxide ion concentrations?
(1) $[H_3O^+] > [OH^-]$
(3) $[H_3O^+] = [OH^-] = 10^{-7}$
(2) $[H_3O^+] < [OH^-]$
(4) $[H_3O^+] = [OH^-] = 10^{-14}$

88. Which metal will react with hydrochloric acid and produce $H_2(g)$?
(1) Au
(3) Mg
(2) Cu
(4) Hg

89. The concentration of hydrogen ions in a solution is 1.0×10^{-5} M at 298 K. What is the concentration of hydroxide ions in the same solution?
(1) 1.0×10^{-14} M
(3) 1.0×10^{-7} M
(2) 1.0×10^{-9} M
(4) 1.0×10^{-5} M

90. Given the reactions X and Y below:

$$X: H_2O + NH_3 \rightarrow NH_4^+ + OH^-$$
$$Y: H_2O + HSO_4^- \rightarrow H_3O^+ + SO_4^{2-}$$

Which statement describes the behavior of the H_2O in these reactions?
(1) Water acts as an acid in both reactions.
(2) Water acts as a base in both reactions.
(3) Water acts as an acid in reaction X and as a base in reaction Y.
(4) Water acts as a base in reaction X and as an acid in reaction Y.

91. In the reaction

$$H_2PO_4^- + H_2O \rightleftharpoons H_3PO_4 + OH^-$$

which pair represents an acid and its conjugate base?
(1) H_2O and H_2PO_4 (3) H_3PO_4 and OH^-
(2) H_2O and H_3PO_4 (4) H_3PO_4 and $H_2PO_4^-$

Group 8 — Redox and Electrochemistry

If you choose this group, be sure to answer questions 92–96.

92. Based on Reference Table N, which half-cell has a lower reduction potential than the standard hydrogen half-cell?
(1) $CU^{2+} + 2e^- \rightarrow Cu(s)$ (3) $I_2(s) + 2e^- \rightarrow 2I^-$
(2) $Fe^{2+} + 2e^- \rightarrow Fe(s)$ (4) $Cl_2(g) + 2e^- \rightarrow 2Cl^-$

93. Which equation represents a redox reaction?
(1) $2Na^+ + S^{2-} \rightarrow Na_2S$
(2) $H^+ + C_2H_3O_2^- \rightarrow HC_2H_3O_2$
(3) $NH_3 + H^+ + Cl^- \rightarrow NH_4^+ + Cl^-$
(4) $Cu + 2Ag^+ + 2NO_3^- \rightarrow 2Ag + Cu^{2+} + 2NO_3^-$

94. Which half-reaction shows both the conservation of mass and the conservation of charge?
(1) $Cl_2 + 2e^- \rightarrow 2Cl^-$ (3) $2Br^- + 2e^- \rightarrow Br_2$
(2) $Cl_2 \rightarrow Cl^- + 2e^-$ (4) $Br^- \rightarrow Br_2 + 2e^-$

95. In an electrolytic cell, to which electrode will a positive ion migrate and undergo reduction?
(1) the anode, which is negatively charged
(2) the anode, which is positively charged
(3) the cathode, which is negatively charged
(4) the cathode, which is positively charged

96. Given the equation:

$$\_\_KMnO_4 + \_\_HCl \rightarrow \_\_KCl + \_\_MnCl_2 + \_\_Cl_2 + \_\_H_2O$$

What is the coefficient of H_2O when the equation is correctly balanced?
(1) 8   (3) 16
(2) 2   (4) 4

Group 9 — Organic Chemistry

If you choose this group, be sure to answer questions 97–101.

97. Which is a product of a condensation reaction?
(1) O_2 (3) H_2
(2) CO_2 (4) H_2O

98. A molecule of ethane and a molecule of ethene both have the same
(1) empirical formula   (3) number of carbon atoms
(2) molecular formula   (4) number of hydrogen atoms

99. Which is an example of a monohydroxyl alcohol?
(1) methanal   (3) glycol
(2) methanol   (4) glycerol

100. Which property is generally characteristic of an organic compound?
(1) low melting point   (3) soluble in polar solvents
(2) high melting point   (4) insoluble in nonpolar solvents

101. Which is the structural formula of an aldehyde?

(1)
```
     H
     |
H —  C — OH
     |
     H
```

(2)
```
        O
       ⫽
H — C
       \
        H
```

(3)
```
        O
       ⫽
H — C
       \
        OH
```

(4)
```
     H          H
     |          |
H —  C —  O  —  C — H
     |          |
     H          H
```

Group 10 — Applications of Chemical Principles

If you choose this group, be sure to answer questions 102–106.

102. Given the reaction for the nickel-cadmium battery:

$$2NiOOH + Cd + 2H_2O \rightarrow 2Ni(OH)_2 + Cd(OH)_2$$

Which species is oxidized during the discharge of the battery?
(1) Ni^{3+} (3) Cd
(2) Ni^{2+} (4) Cd^{2+}

103. Petroleum is a natural source of
(1) alcohols   (3) esters
(2) hydrocarbons   (4) ketones

104. Which acid is formed during the contact process?
(1) HNO_2 (3) H_2SO_4
(2) HNO_3 (4) H_2S

105. Group 1 and Group 2 metals are obtained commercially from their fused compounds by
(1) reduction with CO   (3) reduction with Al
(2) reduction by heat   (4) electrolytic reduction

106. Which balanced equation represents a cracking reaction?
(1) $C_4H_{10} \rightarrow C_2H_6 + C_2H_4$ (3) $C_4H_{10} + Br_2 \rightarrow C_4H_9Br + HBr$
(2) $C_4H_8 + 6O_2 \rightarrow 4CO_2 + 4H_2O$ (4) $C_4H_8 + Br_2 \rightarrow C_4H_8Br_2$

Group II — Nuclear Chemistry

If you choose this group, be sure to answer questions 107–111.

107. Bombarding a nucleus with high-energy particles that change it from one element into another is called
    (1) a half-reaction
    (2) a breeder reaction
    (3) artificial transmutation
    (4) natural transmutation

108. Given the nuclear reaction:

$$^{14}_{7}N + ^{4}_{2}He \rightarrow ^{1}_{1}H + X$$

Which isotope is represented by the X when the equation is correctly balanced?
    (1) $^{17}_{8}O$
    (2) $^{18}_{8}O$
    (3) $^{17}_{9}F$
    (4) $^{18}_{9}F$

109. Which conditions are required to form $^{4}_{2}He$ during the fusion reaction in the Sun?
    (1) high temperature and low pressure
    (2) high temperature and high pressure
    (3) low temperature and low pressure
    (4) low temperature and high pressure

110. The temperature levels in a nuclear reactor are maintained primarily by the use of
    (1) shielding
    (2) coolants
    (3) moderators
    (4) control rods

111. In an experiment, radioactive Pb *(NO₃)₂ [*indicates radioactive Pb^{2+} ions] was added to the following equilibrium system:

$$PbCl_2(s) \rightleftarrows Pb^{2+}(aq) + 2Cl^-(aq)$$

When equilibrium was reestablished, some of the $PbCl_2(s)$ was recovered from the system and dried. Testing showed the $PbCl_2(s)$ was radioactive. Which statement is best supported by this result?
    (1) At equilibrium, the rates of chemical change are equal.
    (2) At equilibrium, the rates of chemical change are unequal.
    (3) The process of dynamic equilibrium is demonstrated.
    (4) The process of dynamic equilibrium is not demonstrated.

Group 12 — Laboratory Activities

If you choose this group, be sure to answer questions 112–116.

112. Which diagram represents an Erlenmeyer flask?

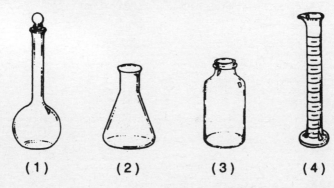

(1)   **(2)**   **(3)**   **(4)**

113. Salt *A* and salt *B* were dissolved separately in 100-milliliter beakers of water. The water temperatures were measured and recorded as shown in the table below.

	Salt A	Salt B
Initial water temperature:	25.1°C	25.1°C
Final water temperature:	30.2°C	20.0°C

Which statement is a correct interpretation of these data?
(1) The dissolving of only salt *A* was endothermic.
(2) The dissolving of only salt *B* was exothermic.
(3) The dissolving of both salt *A* and salt *B* was endothermic.
(4) The dissolving of salt *A* was exothermic and the dissolving of salt *B* was endothermic.

114. Which measurement has the greatest number of significant figures?
(1) 6.060 mg   (3) 606 mg
(2) 60.6 mg   (4) 60600 mg

115. The graph below was constructed by a student to show the relationship between temperature and time as heat was uniformly added to a solid below its melting point.

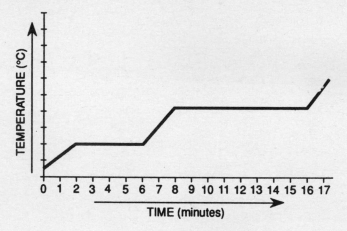

What is the total length of time that the solid phase was in equilibrium with the liquid phase?
(1) 6 min   (3) 8 min
(2) 10 min   (4) 4 min

116. The following data were collected at the endpoint of a titration performed to find the molarity of an HCl solution.

Volume of acid (HCl) used = 14.4 mL
Volume of base (NaOH) used = 22.4 mL
Molarity of standard base (NaOH) = 0.20 M

What is the molarity of the acid solution?
(1) 1.6 M   (3) 0.31 M
(2) 0.64 M   (4) 0.13 M